MICHEL-JEAN SEDAINE
(1719–1797)

Michel-Jean Sedaine (1719–1797)

Theatre, Opera and Art

DAVID CHARLTON
and MARK LEDBURY

Routledge
Taylor & Francis Group
LONDON AND NEW YORK

First published 2000 by Ashgate Publishing

Reissued 2018 by Routledge
2 Park Square, Milton Park, Abingdon, Oxon OX14 4RN
52 Vanderbilt Avenue, New York, NY 10017

Routledge is an imprint of the Taylor & Francis Group, an informa business

Publisher's Note
The publisher has gone to great lengths to ensure the quality of this reprint but points out that some imperfections in the original copies may be apparent.

A Library of Congress record exists under LC control number:

ISBN 13: 978-0-367-13479-2 (hbk)
ISBN 13: 978-0-367-13480-8 (pbk)
ISBN 13: 978-0-429-02673-7 (ebk)

Contents

List of Illustrations

Acknowledgements

The editors would like to thank all who made possible the Sedaine bicentennial conference in London, 1997, and who have helped to make the present book. The conference enjoyed the financial support of the British Council (Brussels), the *Music & Letters* Trust, Cambridge University Press, the History Research Centre of the University of Portsmouth and the Department of Music, Royal Holloway, University of London. Its success and conviviality would not have been possible without essential practical help by Helen Burke Ledbury, Hannah Godfrey-Mahapatra and Patricia Scholfield.

The fortunes of this project would have been very different without the enthusiasm of Rachel Lynch at Ashgate Publishing, and her colleagues. In the various stages of book preparation we have, moreover, profited from the expertise, patience and goodwill of all the contributors. Further help or advice of various kinds has generously been given by Mlle Monique Abud, Ms Annette Beckmann, Dr Annegret Fauser, Ms Barbara Lasic, Professor Neil McWilliam, Dr Sophia Rosenfeld and Dr Nicole Wild. Mr Robert Wells was responsible for creating the music examples. Ms Jan Hart has played an extensive and invaluable role in both formatting and editing the book's contents. Thanks are due to all those librarians and picture librarians who co-operated in the gathering of visual and bibliographical materials for the volume. Ongoing financial support has been forthcoming from our respective institutions, the Department of Music, Royal Holloway, University of London, and the Department of Art History and Archeology, University of Manchester. The Humanities Research Board of The British Academy is also thanked for its provision of a Research Leave award to David Charlton.

DC, ML

Notes on Contributors

David Charlton is Reader in Music at Royal Holloway, University of London. Among his recent publications are the collection *French Opera 1730–1830: Meaning and Media* (Ashgate, 2000) and an account of nineteenth-century French works in *The Oxford Illustrated History of Opera* (1994). He is currently editing the *Cambridge Companion to Grand Opera* and, with Nicole Wild, the *Répertoire musical du Théâtre national de l'Opéra-Comique, 1762–1971*.

Manuel Couvreur is *chercheur qualifié* with the FNRS, and teaches at the Université Libre de Bruxelles in literature and in art history. His numerous publications include the book *Jean-Baptiste Lully* (1992) and various contributions to *Etudes sur le XVIIIe siècle*, for which he has guest-edited three issues. He is director of the research team working on the Théâtre de la Monnaie and edited *Le Théâtre de la Monnaie au XVIIIe siècle* (1996) and *La Monnaie wagnérienne* (1998).

John Dunkley is Reader in French at the University of Aberdeen. His interests include French social history, education and the theatre. He has published *Gambling in France, 1685–1792* (1985) and editions of eighteenth-century plays: Crébillon, *Electre* (1980), Regnard, *Le Joueur* (1986), Sedaine, *Le Philosophe sans le savoir* (1993), Destouches, *L'Irrésolu* (1995) and Boindin, *Quatre Comédies, 1701–1707* (1997). He co-edited *Culture and Revolution* (1990) and *Voices in the Air: French dramatists and the resources of language* (1992).

Mark Ledbury is Lecturer in Art History at the University of Manchester. His research focuses on relationships between the visual arts and theatre in eighteenth-century France, and his thesis on Greuze and Sedaine is to be published as *Fusing Genre. The Artistic Experiments of Greuze and Sedaine* by the Voltaire Foundation. He currently has articles in press on David and his pupils, and is researching a new book on melodrama and visual representation in France, 1780–1820.

Raphaëlle Legrand is *maître de conférences* at the Université François-Rabelais, Tours. She has made a particular study of the operas of Rameau, especially *Dardanus* (the subject of her doctoral dissertation) and also works on Lully. Her writing on opéra-comique includes 'La scène et le public de l'Opéra-Comique de 1762 à 1789' for *L'Opéra-comique en France au XVIIIe siècle* (1992) and her *Forms and Figures in Baroque Music*, with two compact discs, was translated and published in 1998 by Harmonia Mundi.

Michel Noiray is *chercheur* at the Institut de Recherche sur le Patrimoine Musical en France (Centre national de la recherche scientifique / Bibliothèque nationale de France). His publications have specialised in studies of Gluck, of *opéra-comique* and Italian opera, more recently those by Mozart, with guides to *Così fan tutte* (1990) and *Don Giovanni* (1996) for *L'Avant-Scène Opéra*. His edited translation of Charles Burney's *The Present State of Music* was issued in 1992 and he is currently writing a handbook of musical terminology.

Sophia Rosenfeld is Assistant Professor of History at the University of Virginia, Charlottesville. She is the author of articles on the deaf and the legal system, censorship, and language theory in eighteenth-century France. Her forthcoming book is entitled *A Revolution in Language: the Problem of Signs in late Eighteenth-Century France*.

Martine de Rougemont is Professor at the Institut des Etudes Théâtrales at the Université de Paris III. She specialises in eighteenth-century French theatre, and her book *La Vie théâtrale en France au XVIIIe siècle* (1988) is well known to all scholars in the field. She is also the author of *Paradrames* (1998) and of many articles and essays on French theatre. She has edited a diverse array of texts relating to theatre, including Restif de La Bretonne's *Le Mimographe*.

Patrick Taïeb is *maître de conférences* at the Université de Rouen, whose doctoral dissertation concerned the *opéra-comique* and its overtures, 1781–1801. He has published articles on Henri-Montan Berton and, with Raphaëlle Legrand, 'L'Opéra-Comique sous le Consulat et l'Empire' in *Le Théâtre lyrique en France au XIXe siècle* (1995).

Abbreviations

(a) Bibliographical abbreviations

Charlton, *Grétry*	David Charlton, *Grétry and the Growth of Opéra-comique* (Cambridge: Cambridge University Press, 1986)
Collé, *Journal et mémoires*	Charles Collé, *Journal et mémoires sur les hommes de lettres, les ouvrages dramatiques et les événements les plus mémorables du règne de Louis XV (1748–1772)* ed. Honoré Bonhomme (3 vols, Paris: Didot, 1868, repr. Geneva, 1967)
Correspondance littéraire	*Correspondance littéraire, philosophique et critique par Grimm, Diderot, Raynal, Meister, etc.*, ed. Maurice Tourneux (16 vols, Paris: Garnier frères, 1877–82)
Grétry, *Mémoires*	André-Ernest-Modeste Grétry, *Mémoires, ou Essais sur la musique* (3 vols, Paris: Imprimerie de la République, An V [1796–7]; repr. New York, 1971)
Ledbury, 'Greuze and Sedaine'	Greuze, Sedaine and Hybrid Genre in Late Eighteenth-Century France', D.Phil. dissertation, University of Sussex, 1996
Mémoires secrets	[Louis Petit de Bachaumont et al.], *Mémoires secrets pour servir à l'histoire de la République des lettres en France, depuis 1762 jusqu'à nos jours* (36 vols, London: John Adamson, 1777–89)

Sedaine, 'Quelques réflexions'	Michel-Jean Sedaine, 'Quelques réflexions inédits de Sedaine sur l'opéra-comique' in René Charles Guilbert de Pixérécourt, *Théâtre choisi* (4 vols, Paris and Nancy: Chez l'auteur, 1841–3), IV, pp. 501–16
Rayner, 'Sedaine's Dramatic Work'	'The Social and Literary Aspects of Sedaine's Dramatic Work', M.A. dissertation, Westfield College, University of London, 1960

(b) Library abbreviations

FRANCE:

BNF	Bibliothèque Nationale de France
F-B	Besançon, Bibliothèque Municipale
F-CH	Chantilly, Musée Condé
F-Pa	Paris, Bibliothèque de l'Arsenal
F-Pcarn	Paris, Musée Carnavalet
F-Pcf	Paris, Comédie-Française
F-Phvp	Paris, Bibliothèque Historique de la Ville de Paris
F-Pm	Paris, Bibliothèque Mazarine
F-Pn	Paris, Bibliothèque Nationale
F-Pn (Est)	Paris, Bibliothèque Nationale, Département des Estampes
F-Pn (Mus)	Paris, Bibliothèque Nationale, Département de la Musique
F-Po	Paris, Bibliothèque-Musée de l'Opéra
F-Psc	Paris, Société des Auteurs, Compositeurs et Editeurs de Musique
F-Psg	Paris, Bibliothèque Sainte-Geneviève

GREAT BRITAIN:

GB-Lbl	London, British Library
GB-Lpro	London, Public Record Office
GB-Lu	London, University Senate House Library
GB-Lv	London, Victoria and Albert Museum

UNITED STATES OF AMERICA:

US-NYpm	New York, Pierpont Morgan Library

Introduction

Researching Sedaine

Mark Ledbury, David Charlton

This book arises from a conference organised to commemorate the bicentenary of Sedaine's death in 1797, an occasion which might otherwise have passed unnoticed. Sedaine's is still not a familiar name, even in the circles of *dix-huitièmistes*. However, the nine chapters in Parts I–III of this book all point to the interest Sedaine's life and work is now provoking in many scholarly disciplines. It is regrettable that, as the writer of some of the most important *livrets* for *opéra-comique*, and the most innovative drama, in later eighteenth-century France, he should have taken so long to become an object of serious study among musicologists, literary scholars and historians.

If Sedaine speaks today to literary history, theatre history and opera studies, it is because he possessed a multivalent vision, one which accounts for both his past neglect and his present rediscovery. Like many others, he believed that the established, 'official' genres needed to be reformed; unlike many, he made it his business to transform the actual language and operation of the theatre arts he practised. Until later eighteenth-century opera and drama in France become better understood, Sedaine's immense importance for the development of Romantic opera and theatre risks remaining generally concealed; to reveal something of this importance is one main reason for publishing the present volume.

Another aim has been to gather in one place both research tools and research texts designed to facilitate future work: for example a general bibliography of Sedaine editions, manuscripts and research literature as well as the edited texts of seventeen of his prefaces. The chapters in this book cover a range of disciplines, and contribute to the third aim of this work, which is the encouragement of further interdisciplinary thinking as such. Sedaine's work was, like that of many French writers, influenced by English trends and traditions: a fourth aim of our volume is to bring together French and English research, experience and systems of analysis, hopefully to the mutual benefit of those working in each language and tradition.

One inherent difficulty lies in explaining Sedaine's achievement in tidy phrases. Another such difficulty relates to our misunderstanding of the oxymoronically labelled '*opéra-comique*', which merely means opera with spoken dialogue. Yet another originates in tracking Sedaine's work and influence across different disciplines, not forgetting his poetry. Nevertheless we might say that his business in these domains was 'fusing the arts', which was the title of the original 1997 bicentennial conference.

Some past critical neglect can better be understood in the light of the particular history of Sedaine scholarship, which tells us much about the nature of academic enquiry more generally. When George Sand asked herself why she could not study Sedaine, she came to a simple conclusion:

> Pourquoi ne me fut-il possible d'étudier Sedaine? Est-ce parce que je ne sais pas étudier? Ou parce que Sedaine n'est pas à étudier? ... Je crois que Sedaine ne l'est guère.[1]

For her, Sedaine was an exceptional (and, by implication, marginal) individual; her view encapsulated a persistent nineteenth-century belief, which took root even from the first obituary notices, and stressed the exceptional early life and virtuous personality of Sedaine, together with his innate gifts, rather than analysing the particular qualities of his dramatic experiments.[2] It was this focus on the 'natural' and particular virtues of the man which helped to fuel the revival, in the nineteenth century, of interest in Sedaine and his work. Here was a charming oddity – a naive mason poet, self-taught, supposedly following and giving no example – inimitable, in George Sand's words. The revival of interest in him formed part of that cosy mythology of virtuous *ancien régime* living that was so vital to late nineteenth-century conservative nostalgia. Certainly the biographies of Sedaine which have come down to us are deeply influenced by it, and have consequently been more of a hindrance than an aid to scholarly understanding of Sedaine's life and work.[3] It was no coincidence that Gautier and others associated Sedaine with Greuze, who was of course being rediscovered and recreated in much the same way by the

---

[1] George Sand, 'Avant-Propos', *Le Mariage de Victorine* (Paris: Blanchard, 1851), p. 7.

[2] Evidence of the nineteenth-century construction of Sedaine can be found in *opéra-comique* itself. Sedaine was the hero of *Poëte et maçon, comédie vaudeville en un acte*, written by de Leuven, Roche and Antonin (Paris: Barba, 1833), first performed at the Théâtre du Palais-Royal on 3 August 1833, in which Sedaine's popular origins and protective nature are stressed, as the virtuous man of the people shields various artisans from unpleasant employers. The most important obituary notices are: Constance-Marie Pipelet, *Eloge historique de M. J. Sedaine ... Lu par l'auteur à la 54e séance publique du lycée des arts, le 30 Messidor an V* (Paris: Desenne, 1797); Angélique de Vandeul, 'Notice historique sur Sedaine' in *Correspondance littéraire*, XVI (1797), pp. 234–46; anon. (Jean-Nicolas Dufort de Cheverny), 'Notice sur la vie de Sedaine', Blois, Bibliothèque Municipale, Ms. 98–9, published in Mark Ledbury, 'Greuze, Sedaine and Hybrid Genre in Late Eighteenth-Century France', D.Phil. dissertation, U. of Sussex, 1996, hereafter 'Greuze and Sedaine'.

[3] Emile Guieysse-Frère, *Michel Sedaine. Ses protecteurs et ses amis* (Paris: Flammarion, 1907); Renée de Mont-Louis, *Sedaine, sa vie, anecdotes* (Limoges: Ardant, 1879 etc.).

Goncourt brothers.[4] At least George Sand and the Romantic generation recognised Sedaine's dramatic talent. One striking reference in Delacroix's journal makes this very clear:

> 24 avril [1846]. – J'ai vu hier soir le *Déserteur* de Sedaine: voici un genre qui semble bien près de la perfection de l'art dramatique, si ce n'est pas la perfection même.[5]

This was, of course, partly because the innovations, preoccupations and experiments of Sedaine's work so clearly prefigured those of the early nineteenth-century Romantic generation, and to some extent it is still true that where Sedaine has been accorded importance, it is as a precursor of later and seemingly more important work, whether this be the Romantic *drame*, grand opera or the melodrama.[6]

However, the tone for much of the serious critical commentary on Sedaine in the later nineteenth and early twentieth centuries was set by Sand's famous correspondent Gustave Flaubert.[7] His contempt for Sedaine was fuelled by a passionate concern for the precise and correct use of language, and his scorn for Sedaine's incorrections soon became an orthodoxy among scholars (with the notable exception of Félix Gaiffe).[8] Brunetière, for example, could write: 'Jamais homme n'eut moins que lui cette faculté du véritable écrivain, qui est comme de changer ce qu'il touche en universel.'[9]

When Ladislas Günther wrote the first major thesis in French on Sedaine in 1907, its review by one of the giants of the French university world, Daniel Mornet (who, with Gustave Lanson, was to a great degree responsible for the re-creation of the literary and intellectual canon of eighteenth-century literary study in early twentieth-century France), contained a damning verdict on the object of Günther's thesis. Mornet expressed the view that Sedaine did not repay study, and

---

[4] For Théophile Gautier's comments, see *Le Moniteur universel*, 9 March 1863. For the Goncourts' views on Greuze, see Edmond and Jules de Goncourt, *Greuze* (Paris: Dentu, 1863).

[5] Eugène Delacroix, *Journal*, ed. André Joubin (3 vols, Paris: Plon, 1932), III, p. 441. This revival at the Opéra-Comique lasted from 1843 to 1849, and from 1853 to 1857.

[6] For Sedaine as a precursor of the melodrama, see especially the comments of Guilbert de Pixérécourt in 'Dernières réflexions de l'auteur sur le mélodrame' in *Théâtre choisi* (4 vols, Paris and Nancy: Chez l'auteur, 1841–3), IV, pp. 493–500.

[7] See Gustave Flaubert, *Correspondance* (Paris: Club de L'Honnête Homme, 1975), XV, pp. 442–4.

[8] Félix Gaiffe, *Le Drame en France au XVIIIe siècle* (Paris: Armand Colin, 1910).

[9] Ferdinand Brunetière, *Les Epoques du théâtre français (1636–1850)* (Paris: Hachette, 1909), p. 301.

that he would never be a major figure.[10] The neglect of, even scorn for, Sedaine in early twentieth-century literary criticism in this respect merely echoed the commentaries of the more conservative eighteenth-century journals, which seized on the lack of beauty and correctness in Sedaine's writing style. Commentators on French drama, then and now, have cherished the poetic beauty of the language of its major canonical figures, and the experiments of an author who was prepared at all times to sacrifice a notion of poetic beauty to the imperatives of naturalistic dialogue, stage effect and collaborative musical innovation was bound to fall foul of what Voltaire called 'la police de Parnasse'.[11]

Although he was perceived by his contemporaries from the earliest stages of his career as a talented creator of stage effects,[12] his place in the canon of French dramatic literature has been only a minor one. By many scholars of spoken drama he is still seen as an imitator – a more or less successful, but more or less slavish follower of Diderot, a mere *metteur en scène* of the dramatic ideas of the *philosophe*. This view has prevailed through much scholarship, down to one recent edition of *Le Philosophe sans le savoir*.[13] It is a view which Gaiffe saw as incomplete many years ago, but which only the work of Pierre Frantz appears bold enough to recognise as profoundly false: recent work has attempted to show that *Le Philosophe sans le savoir* was not an imitation but a collaboration, and one which is significant not so much for Sedaine's application of Diderot's theory as for Diderot's conscious borrowing of the special individual talent of Sedaine for his own ideological and aesthetic purposes.[14] Sedaine's writing was highly diverse, as George Sand recognised long ago, and no reader who seriously engages with, say, *Le Philosophe sans le savoir*, *La Gageure imprévue* or *Félix ou l'Enfant trouvé* can sustain the view that Sedaine was a derivative or univocal talent.

This persistent reputation as a naive and clumsy, technically deficient writer has begun to be seriously reexamined in the light of the new understanding of Sedaine's intentions and priorities that research into *opéra-comique* has brought.[15] Even at the beginning of the century, some scholars began to diverge from the

---

[10] Daniel Mornet, review of Ladislas Günther, *L'Œuvre dramatique de Sedaine* (Paris: Larose, 1908) in *Revue de l'histoire littéraire française* (1909), pp. 827–9.

[11] See for example Julien Geoffroy, *Cours de littérature dramatique* (2nd ed., 6 vols, Paris: Blanchard, 1825), I, p. 307.

[12] See for example Grimm's judgements of Sedaine in the *Correspondance littéraire*, III (August 1761), pp. 457–8.

[13] Günther, *Sedaine*, p. 258: 'Les théories de Diderot sont donc pour Sedaine une espèce de catéchisme qu'il cherche à appliquer à sa pièce.' See also Robert Garapon, 'Introduction' to Sedaine, *Le Philosophe sans le savoir* (Paris: Société des Textes Français Modernes, 1990), p. xxvi and passim.

[14] Ledbury, 'Greuze and Sedaine', pp. 100–34.

[15] Dufort's obituary notice makes it clear that Sedaine's grammatical errors were often deliberate and part of a dramatic strategy. See Ledbury, 'Greuze and Sedaine', pp. 358–69.

prevailing view and found renewed interest in Sedaine's work: many of these scholars, interestingly, were not French, and their work to some extent filled gaps left by neglect in the French academic establishment.[16] It was a real pleasure to have among us at the conference one of the most important and unsung of an earlier generation of Sedaine scholars, Margaret Rayner, whose dissertation of 1960 remains an important work.[17] Spurred by the work of Rayner and others, more recent generations of scholars have sought to investigate Sedaine and his work in new ways, and to reestablish his importance, to the extent that, in a recent literary encyclopedia, Pierre Frantz has written that: 'L'influence de Sedaine dans l'histoire du théâtre français a été au moins aussi grande que celle de Diderot.'[18]

It is worth dwelling for a moment on the reasons for this change in critical fortune. First, the *opéra-comique* as a genre and an institution has come under renewed critical attention in recent years from musicologists, literary historians and cultural historians. Much of this renewed interest has been stimulated by the research into what has become known as popular culture.[19] The *opéra-comique*, from its origins in fair theatre through its transformation into semi-official genre and its influence over the development of dramatic discourse, is being reappraised in the context of the creation of a sophisticated public sphere in eighteenth-century France.[20]

The *opéra-comique* as a genre has also become the object of serious musicological study, and it is from musicology that much of the current revival of interest in Sedaine has taken its lead. Building on work done in the earlier part of this century, recent studies have brought to light the innovative complexity of later eighteenth-century *opéra-comique,* and much recent writing has been devoted to all aspects of the genre in France.[21] From Louise Parkinson Arnoldson on, the

---

16 In addition to Günther, see especially Martin Gisi, *Sedaine, sein Leben und seine Werke* (Berlin: Weidmann, 1883); Louise Parkinson Arnoldson, *Sedaine et les musiciens de son temps* (Paris: L'Entente Linotypiste, 1934).

17 Margaret Rayner, 'The Social and Literary Aspects of Sedaine's Dramatic Work', M.A. dissertation, Westfield College, U. of London, 1960, hereafter 'Sedaine's Dramatic Work'.

18 Pierre Frantz, 'Sedaine' in Jean-Pierre de Beaumarchais, Daniel Couty, Alain Rey (eds), *Dictionnaire des littératures de langue française* (3 vols, Paris: Bordas, 1987), III, pp. 2316–18 [2318].

19 For an overview of the growth of the study of popular culture, see Peter Burke, *Popular Culture in Early Modern Europe* (rev. ed., Aldershot: Ashgate Publishing, 1996), pp. 1–64.

20 For a history of *opéra-comique* which places it in a directly political context, see Robert M. Isherwood, *Farce and Fantasy. Popular Entertainment in Eighteenth-Century Paris* (Oxford: Oxford University Press, 1986).

21 Some of the most important early work on *opéra-comique* was: Georges Cucuel, *Les Créateurs de l'opéra-comique français* (Paris: Félix Alcan, 1914); Arthur Pougin, *Monsigny et son*

important relationships between Sedaine and three musicians, Philidor, Monsigny, and Grétry, have given him prominence, and the contributions from musicologists in this collection reflect the continuing central role of music historians in the reappraisal of Sedaine's *œuvre*.

Sedaine's own role in the development of *opéra-comique* was at least recognised by Cucuel, Pougin and early pioneers of *opéra-comique* research, but it is only in recent years that he has begun to feature prominently in the history of spoken drama. This is partly because in recent years there have been significant changes in the way in which French drama is studied and appreciated. Martine de Rougemont's *La Vie théâtrale en France au XVIIIème siècle* shifted the emphasis in study from text to dramatic apparatus, audience, stage and genre.[22] John Lough, Henri Lagrave and others have also contributed to this major shift, which has allowed Sedaine's own important place as a radical innovator to be restored.[23] The research set out in the present collection, dealing with many aspects of Sedaine's stagecraft, will make a further contribution to this realignment.

The chapters which follow also bear witness to the increasing interest in Sedaine as an interdisciplinary figure. Rather than being a recapitulation of the nineteenth-century view of Sedaine as the naive mason poet, they represent a recognition that Sedaine's work and career brought him into contact not only with other writers but with a whole series of figures in other fields. Art historians are increasingly turning their attention to Sedaine's role in the early life and career of Jacques-Louis David.[24] Some interest is being shown in his role at the Académie Royale d'Architecture.[25] He was, as was recognised by Henri Stein, 'mêlé à toute la vie intellectuelle de son temps',[26] and his role in certain key developments in

---

temps (Paris: Fischbacher, 1908). Modern studies include: Corinne Pré, 'Le Livret d'opéra-comique en France de 1741 à 1789', thèse de Doctorat ès Lettres, U. de Paris III, 1982; David Charlton, *Grétry and the Growth of Opéra-comique* (Cambridge: Cambridge University Press, 1986), hereafter Charlton, *Grétry*; Philippe Vendrix (ed.), *L'Opéra-comique en France au XVIIIe Siècle* (Liège: Mardaga, 1992).

22 Martine de Rougemont, *La Vie théâtrale en France au XVIIIe siècle* (Geneva and Paris: Champion, 1988).

23 See especially Henri Lagrave, *Le Théâtre et le public à Paris de 1715 à 1750* (Paris: Plon, 1972); John Lough, *Paris Theatre Audiences of the Seventeenth and Eighteenth Centuries* (Oxford: Oxford University Press, 1957); Jacqueline de Jomaron (ed.), *Le Théâtre en France* (2nd ed., Paris: Armand Colin, 1992); Pierre Peyronnet, *La Mise en scène au XVIIIe siècle* (Paris: Nizet, 1974).

24 Thomas Crow, *Emulation. Making Artists for Revolutionary France* (New Haven and London: Yale University Press, 1995), pp. 5–30; Ledbury, 'Greuze and Sedaine', pp. 279–322.

25 See for example the excellent thorough study by Wolfgang Scholler, *Die Académie Royale d'Architecture. Anatomie einer Institution* (Köln and Weimar: Böhlau, 1993); Jacques Guillerme, 'Über einige Wandlungen des Wahren in der Architektur', *Daidalos. Berlin Architectural Journal*, VIII (1983), pp. 38–47.

26 Henri Stein, *Augustin Pajou* (Paris: Librairie Centrale des Beaux-Arts, 1912), p. 58.

stage design, painting and architecture will be an important part of the rehabilitation of Sedaine as a significant figure in eighteenth-century French cultural history.

There remains also the important question of how Sedaine can be mapped onto our understanding of the political culture of *ancien-régime* France. Both Emile Maude and, more recently, Karin Pendle have termed Sedaine's work Revolutionary.[27] However, the question regarding the extent to which he was engaged or otherwise in a pre-Revolutionary or bourgeois struggle, a point which has caused controversy in the interpretation of *Le Philosophe sans le savoir* and other plays, is being superseded by more subtle and less teleological questions.[28] In this new climate, more attention is given to Sedaine's concepts of patriotism, virtue and citizenship in spoken and sung dramas, and his experiments in putting controversial and topical themes centre-stage in periods of political tension, whether these be the aftermath of the Seven Years' War, the Maupeou revolution or the French Revolution itself.[29] Historians are beginning to look at the *drame* afresh to see that the epithet *bourgeois* is not merely misleading but limiting, and are turning to wider questions of theatrical representation (of women, of dissenting religion, of conflict, etc.) to determine the political and public import of drama in

---

[27] Emile Maude, 'Les Deux Sedaine', *Le Censeur* (2 Feb. 1907), pp. 152–5 [153]; Karin Pendle, 'L'Opéra-comique à Paris de 1762 à 1789' in Vendrix (ed.), *L'Opéra-comique en France*, pp. 79–117 [104].

[28] On the 'bourgeois or not' debate, see especially Elisabeth Guibert-Sledziewski, 'Le Spectacle bourgeois des antagonismes des classes: *Le Philosophe sans le savoir* de Sedaine', *Dix-huitième siècle*, VII (1975), pp. 259–74; Haydn Mason, '*Le Philosophe sans le savoir* de Sedaine: an aristocratic *drame bourgeois*?', *French Studies*, XXX (1976), pp. 405–18.

[29] Sedaine himself has left ample evidence of his interest in political issues, but to generalise about his political views is still difficult. *Guillaume Tell* (composed under exceptional political circumstances) is the best evidence of direct Revolutionary sympathies, but it must be remembered that, in their way, *Le Philosophe sans le savoir*, *Maillard ou Paris sauvé*, *Raimond V* and *Félix ou l'Enfant trouvé* also engaged directly with issues which were, in the terms of the *ancien régime*, explicitly political (commerce, the duel, patriotism, virtue, court corruption, etc.). Sedaine was accused fairly frequently of anti-court or even Revolutionary sentiment, and has left some telling remarks about political life both in his correspondence and more specifically in his prefaces. However, to decide whether Sedaine was Revolutionary or not should not be the main question: what is more important is the fact that Sedaine felt that drama could and should be political in a wider sense, dealing directly with moral issues: in this way, to examine *Maillard* in the context of the *parlements* crisis, for example, might give us a more nuanced view of Sedaine's 'politics'. On Sedaine and the Revolution, see Auguste Rey, *Notes sur mon village. La Vieillesse de Sedaine* (Paris: Champion, 1906); Stanislas Rzewuski, 'Sedaine et la Révolution', *Le Gaulois*, 16 January 1907; Emile Maude, 'Les deux Sedaine'; for Sedaine's own political comments, see for example his letter of 4 February 1793 to the Comédie-Française in F-Pcf, *dossier Sedaine*, on the subject of the meanings of *Le Philosophe sans le savoir*.

general and Sedaine's drama in particular in a century in which theatricality was one of the pillars of public and political life.

But in this area, as in many others, much needs to be done in the domain of Sedaine research. Perhaps the most telling sign of his neglect is that there is still no scholarly biography of Michel-Jean Sedaine. Only the work of Auguste Rey has helped map some of Sedaine's late life.[30] There still remain large gaps in our knowledge, which only the discovery of more reliable biographical and other documentation will allow us to fill. Mark Ledbury has endeavoured in 'A Sedaine Bibliography' (Chapter 11) to point out the locations of such material as may be needed for the beginnings of such a study.

Research into Sedaine's creative work, although more advanced and copious than biographical studies, is still in fact in its infancy. Much of Sedaine's known output still remains in manuscript form – most notably *Raimond V* among his spoken dramas and the two *opéras-comiques Robin et Marion* and *Pagamin de Monègue* still await publication. Recently, Sedaine's last major drama, a substantial, five-act comedy, *Hinkelmann ou les journalistes*, written as a commission for Catherine II of Russia and long thought lost, has been located: consequently it too deserves publication.[31] Apart from *Le Philosophe sans le savoir*, which is now acknowledged as a key drama of the late eighteenth century, almost all Sedaine's dramas would benefit from more active and detailed scholarly attention. However, it is also likely that future discoveries will oblige us to revise our views on when Sedaine's career started and ended. We may have to envisage the possibility that he contributed anonymously to fair or private theatres early in his career, before he began to work officially for Monnet. There is also evidence that he collaborated on dramas by others later in life than has previously been realised.[32]

However, perhaps the single most beneficial step in the restoring of Sedaine to a place of prominence would be the professional revival of performances of Sedaine's plays and of those *opéras-comiques* for which he wrote *livrets*. It was constantly said of Sedaine's plays that their full merit could only be appreciated in performance; and until serious revivals are accorded to his works, we must all depend on the very partial evidence of the texts. It is to be hoped that the recent revival in interest in early opera and period performance might embolden

---

[30] Auguste Rey, *Notes sur mon village. La Vieillesse de Sedaine*; idem, 'Le Mariage de Sedaine', *Revue de l'histoire de Versailles et de Seine-et-Oise*, XI (1910), pp. 5–15.

[31] F-Pa, Rondel Ms 727: for details of its discovery, see Ledbury, 'Greuze and Sedaine', Appx 1.

[32] See the draft letters of 1 Vendémiaire, An IV in the dossier *Sedaine* in F-Pcf, in which Sedaine makes it clear that he is the joint author of *L'espièglerie de garnison*, which is known under the title *Les Espiègleries de garnison* as the work of Favières. See also the drafts of *L'espièglerie* in F-Pan, AJ 13/1102.

musicians and opera companies.[33] When Vadé and Dauvergne's *Les Troqueurs* was recorded in 1994 it was warmly received,[34] and this repertoire holds more than historical interest for contemporary audiences.

Sedaine's spoken drama has fared even worse. Directors and actors have inherited a view of the *drame* as wordy and impossible to perform, and this seems to prevent an appreciation of Sedaine's gifts for theatre spectacle, and his modernity. There have, however, been some revivals of his work and *La Gageure imprévue* enjoyed a certain success in 1998 in Paris. It is hoped that *Le Philosophe sans le savoir*, along with Sedaine's other spoken and musical dramas, might also be imaginatively staged for the twenty-first century by theatre and opera groups increasingly aware of the buried treasures of their repertoire.

The chapters in this book will, we hope, forever dispel the notion that Sedaine is not worth studying, and will contribute to a modern, and long overdue, critical reassessment.

---

33 *Le Déserteur* was staged at the Théâtre Impériale de Compiègne in October 1993, directed by Pierre Jourdan, conducted by Michel Swierczewski. Sound and video recordings were made.

34 Capella Coloniensis, conducted by William Christie (Harmonia Mundi HMC 901454).

PART I

Genre and Representation

Chapter 1

Sedaine and the Question of Genre

Mark Ledbury

It has long been asserted that the concept of genre was central to the way in which the arts were understood in *ancien-régime* France: one of the fissures that divide early modern artistic practice from modern practice is seen to be the abandonment of those rigid systems of genre which formed the dominant discourse in the production and reception of all art.[1] More recent research has stressed that generic structures, like other aesthetic discourses, are connected in complex ways to wider social structures. It is certainly true that the need to classify and construct orders was an essential aspect not just of the rationale of academies, but of the politics of the court society which spawned them, and indeed of everyday life.[2] Félibien's famous pronouncement concerning the hierarchy of genres did more than establish an upward progression of types of painting. It also made clear the philosophical, religious and social bases for this hierarchy, as it classed painters according to the complex and finely graded

---

1 On the importance of the concept of genre in painting and drama in early modern and Revolutionary Europe, see especially Rensselaer Lee, *Ut Pictura Poesis: The Humanistic Theory of Painting* (New York: Norton, 1967); Jean Locquin, *La Peinture d'histoire en France de 1747 à 1785* (Paris: Laurens, 1912); Udolpho van de Sandt, '"Grandissima opera del pittore sara l'istoria". Notes sur la hiérarchie des genres sous la révolution', *La Revue de l'art*, LXXXIII (1989), pp. 71–9; Jacques Scherer, *La Dramaturgie classique en France* (Paris: Nizet, 1950); Jacques Chouillet, *L'Esthétique des lumières* (Paris: Presses Universitaires de France, 1974); idem, *La Formation des idées esthétiques de Diderot* (Paris: Armand Colin, 1973); Annie Becq, *La Genèse de l'esthétique française moderne* (Paris: Albin Michel, 1994); Marian Hobson, *The Object of Art* (Cambridge: Cambridge University Press, 1982); idem, 'Genres and Limits: Fielding, Sterne, Diderot', *Rivista di letterature moderne e comparate*, XLIII (1990), pp. 109–28. For methodological reflection on the nature of genre, see Jean-Marie Schaeffer, *Qu'est ce qu'un genre littéraire?* (Paris: Editions du Seuil, 1989).

2 On the connections between court society and the academies see, for example, Peter Burke, *The Fabrication of Louis XIV* (New Haven and London: Yale University Press, 1992); for other famous classifying and hierarchising systems of painting in French theory see, for example, Roger de Piles,. *Cours de peinture par principes*, ed. Jacques Thuillier (Paris: Gallimard, 1989); Charles Batteux, *Les Beaux-arts réduits à un même principe* (Paris: Durand, 1746). Many of the theorists are well anthologised and annotated in Baldine Saint-Girons, *Dictionnaire des sources esthétiques du XVIIIe siècle* (Paris: Philippe Sers, 1990).

systems by which rank was understood at court.[3] In literature and drama too, as Bray and others have shown, the progressive emphasis on generic rules as a structure for the production and reception of creative writing was associated with the hegemony of academic thinking.[4]

If hierarchical structures of thought and behaviour were central to the mind-set of the court society and left their mark on its artistic products, the same might also be said of what has come to be known as the 'Enlightenment project'. For many different and often opposite reasons, the *encyclopédistes* and other *philosophes* from Buffon to Diderot all argued for the importance of genre and generic categorisation as a key to organising and understanding the complexity of nature and culture.

However, as I have argued in other work, discourse on genre mutated in the course of the eighteenth century from a discourse of hierarchy to a discourse of opposition.[5] Theorists such as Roger De Piles, the abbé Du Bos, Claude-Henri Watelet and Voltaire started to recast the taxonomy of hierarchies of genre in terms of an overarching oppositional structure which, of course, associated the notion of genre with that of gender.[6] The opposition of genres was the structure around which debate was facilitated, and in aesthetic disputes such as La Font's attack on the Académie Royale de Peinture et de Sculpture in the 1740s, or the long-running Italian/French opera dispute (including the *querelle des bouffons*), or many other eighteenth-century aesthetic disputes, the language of opposition is clear. La Font's critical terminology was specifically derived from gender opposition, as he railed against Boucher's feminised mythologies and demanded a male and noble style.[7]

This shift is related to the re-formation of the political sphere in the course of the eighteenth century, one in which finely divided hierarchies and shades of nobility which dominated the systems of patronage and clientage in the court society themselves become increasingly recast as oppositions, whether in models of government, reason, science or art. Such oppositional

---

3 André Félibien, *Conférences de l'Académie Royale de Peinture et de Sculpture pendant l'année 1667* (Paris, 1699), 'Préface'.

4 See Réné Bray, *La Formation de la doctrine classique en France* (Paris: Garnier, 1966), pp. 303–6; Jacques Truchet, *La Tragédie classique en France* (Paris: Presses Universitaires de France, 1950).

5 Ledbury, 'Greuze and Sedaine', pp. 13–44.

6 On the gendering of the Enlightenment see, for example, Dorinda Outram, *The Enlightenment* (London: Macmillan, 1995), pp. 80–95. Work in other fields, mainly by feminist historians, has made explicit the relation of dramatic genre to gender. See, for example, Linda Bember, *Comic Women, Tragic Men. A Study of Gender and Genre in Shakespeare* (Stanford: Stanford University Press, 1982).

7 See La Font de Saint-Yenne, *Réflexions sur la peinture* (The Hague: Neaulme, 1747).

thinking was integral to the ideologies of the French Revolution when a succession of oppositions became central to Revolutionary rhetoric.[8]

One brief but central example of this movement from hierarchy to opposition is the treatment of genre in the *Encyclopédie*. Voltaire's article on literary genre begins by asserting the multiplicity of different genres, but later states:

> Chaque genre a des nuances différentes; on peut au fond les réduire à deux, le simple et le relevé. Ces deux genres qui embrassent tant d'autres ont des beautés nécessaires qui leur sont également communes.[9]

This tendency to convert a hierarchised taxonomy into an opposition between two separate, even opposed, genres is also evident in Watelet's adjacent article on genre in painting, in which he states: 'Le mot *genre* ... sert à distinguer de la classe des peintres d'histoire, ceux qui, bornés à certains objets, se font une étude particulière de les peindre.'[10] Watelet thus explicitly narrows Félibien's hierarchy into an opposition between history painting and all the rest, now simply defined (by default) as 'non-history'.

Diderot is often credited with a revolution in thinking on genre in painting and drama. However, he too succumbs to the same kind of thinking. At points in the *Entretiens sur le Fils naturel* he, or rather his idealistic partner in dialogue, Dorval, seems to be saying that the opposition that exists between tragedy and comedy might be nuanced by his new genre, the *genre sérieux*.[11] One year later, however, Diderot reverted to an oppositional understanding of genre in *De la poésie dramatique*, where his new genres are subsumed into subsections of the most opposed categories of drama.

> La comédie gaie, qui a pour objet le ridicule et le vice, la comédie sérieuse, qui a pour objet la vertu et les devoirs de l'homme. La tragédie, qui aurait pour objet nos malheurs domestiques; la tragédie,

---

8 On shifts in the political culture of the *ancien régime*, see Keith Michael Baker (ed.), *The Political Culture of the Old Régime* (Oxford: Clarendon Press, 1988); Dale Van Kley, *The Damiens Affair and the Unraveling of the Ancien Régime 1750–1770* (Princeton: Princeton University Press, 1984); Peter Jones, *Reform and Revolution in France. The Politics of Transition 1774–1791* (Cambridge: Cambridge University Press, 1995).

9 Denis Diderot and Jean Le Rond d'Alembert (eds), *Encyclopédie ou dictionnaire raisonné des sciences, des arts et des métiers* (Paris, 1751–65), VII (1757), article 'Genre de style (Littérature)', pp. 594–5.

10 Ibid., 'Genre (Peinture)', p. 597.

11 See Diderot, *Entretiens sur le Fils naturel* in Alain Ménil (ed.), *Diderot et le théâtre. Le Drame* (Paris: Pocket, 1995), p. 113.

> qui a pour objet les catastrophes publiques et les malheurs des grands.[12]

In painting too, his interventions are often seen as nuancing the division established by De Piles, Du Bos and Watelet; however, in the *Essais sur la peinture*, his most involved intervention on genre, Diderot's quarrel is not with the fundamental oppositional structure of genre, but with what should be included within this opposition:

> Il me semble que la division de la peinture en peinture de genre et peinture d'histoire est sensée, mais je voudrais qu'on eût un peu plus consulté la nature dans cette division.[13]

He goes on to try to recategorise the painters of domestic life as part of the history category. However at no time does he question the need for a fundamental division. If I stress Diderot's conformism rather than his undoubted originality here, it is to demonstrate how even the most brilliant thinkers involved with the *Encyclopédie*, as well as more conservative strains of Enlightenment thought represented by Watelet, tend to assume a 'natural' oppositional order of genre.

Two important aspects of the theoretical reworking of hierarchy as opposition were the difficulty in reconciling and compromising between the opposing poles, and the horror and fascination provoked by the possible products of such a collapse. In the articles referred to above by Watelet and Voltaire there are stark warnings about the danger of overstepping borders and seeking to escape from oppositional structures. Watelet felt that the attempt to cross boundaries between the high and the low would lead to the production of monsters. Even Diderot, who had theorised an intermediate genre, saw some mixtures and hybrids as dangerous and impossible.

> Les peintres et les poètes ont le droit de tout oser; mais ce droit ne s'étend pas jusqu'à la licence de fondre des espèces dans un même individu. ... Vous voyez que la tragi-comédie ne peut être qu'un mauvais genre, parce qu'on y confond deux genres éloignés et séparés par une barrière naturelle.[14]

It is against this background that some of Sedaine's struggles and innovations in many areas emerge as more widely significant. The history of his practice and much other practice in all the arts in the eighteenth century is in some senses the history of the creative interrogation of systems of genre; although it

---

12 Diderot, *De la poésie dramatique* in Ménil (ed.), *Diderot et le théâtre*, p. 163.

13 Diderot, *Essais sur la peinture*, ed. Gita May (Paris: Hermann, 1985), p. 65.

14 Diderot, *Entretiens sur le Fils naturel*, p. 114.

is possible to see the eighteenth century as a conservative one, resistant to innovation and 'playing by the rules', we must also recognise that, often in marginal or undervalued spaces (such as types of lyric theatre) this same eighteenth century saw the gradual erosion of the strict separation and opposition of genres.[15] Such processes and tensions can be seen in perhaps uniquely sharp focus in the work of Sedaine, who was throughout his life actively involved with generic experiment and challenge, from his early poetry right through to the end of his life. This chapter will draw not only on his dramatic ideas and experiments but also his early interventions in poetry and his relatively unknown contribution to debates in architecture and the visual arts, to explore his engagement with the fraught but crucial question of genre.

In broad terms, one might say that Sedaine's thinking on genre evolved from a dependence on the structures and modes of thinking on genre mapped out by Boileau and seventeenth-century theorists, through subsequent engagement with Enlightenment models of genre to a finally more radical and less comfortable interrogation of genre which was to have a profound impact on his own career, and which I believe constitutes one reason for his enduring importance as a writer and man of the theatre.

The lower, comic and marginal genres of poetry and drama became the focus of Sedaine's attention from the time of his first poetry, which is, incidentally, critically underexplored.[16] It cannot be stressed enough that Sedaine was not a naive or uneducated talent but a fiercely autodidactic one; his poetry, with its mixture of translations and renditions of ancient poetry, its songs and dramatico-musical *essais*, is clear evidence of a sophisticated, literary intelligence learning from a wide variety of sources. The urbane ironic 'faux-naif' style which Charlton has analysed as an important part of the rhetoric of his dramatic prefaces is also powerfully present in his early verse collections.[17] His early poetic interventions on genre are also laced with this irony, as Sedaine engages with the didactic texts by Boileau and Horace which provide him with points of departure.

One of the longest and most significant of these early poems on genre was the *Satyre contre le goût des ouvrages poissards*. This curious poem aimed criticism at the works of the dramatist Jean-Joseph Vadé (1720–57), who was Sedaine's friend and one of the promotors of his early career.[18] In this work,

---

15 See Hobson, 'Genres and Limits', pp. 109–11.

16 What commentary there is tends to be split between dismissive surveys, for example in Emile Faguet, *Histoire de la poésie française de la renaissance au romantisme*, IX, *Les Poètes secondaires du XVIIIe siècle* (Paris: Boivin, 1935), pp. 28–34, and philological work, for example Theodore Kant, *Die Sprache in Sedaines 'Recueil de poésies'* (Hamburg: Lütcke & Wolff, 1901).

17 See Chapter 9 of the present work.

18 On Vadé, see Alexander Parks Moore, *The 'Genre Poissard' and the French Stage of the Eighteenth Century* (New York: Columbia University Institute of French Studies,

Sedaine rather ironically set himself up as a new Boileau ('Prête-moi s'il se peut, contre un nouvel affront/Les traits dont tu flétris le burlesque Scarron')[19] and goes on to denounce the vogue for *poissard* plays. After describing a time when

> Aux plus exactes moeurs ta muse fut fidelle,
> Jamais un mot hardi dans tes tableaux divers
> Ne souilla tes sujets aussi purs que tes vers

he regrets that

> Cet heureux temps n'est plus; les marchés et les halles
> Infectent les esprits des jargons les plus sales:
> C'est un marais bourbeux que ce sacré vallon
> La fange y cache aux yeux les trésors d'Apollon.[20]

This alignment of the city, corruption and bad writing, and the horror of mixture evident here, seemed to imply that Sedaine argued as a purist, an upholder of the traditions of rules and the strict separation of high and low genres, who objected to fair cultures permeating wider artistic realms. However, in the articulation of what seem like fairly orthodox, even clichéd views of the infection of drama by street slang, there is in Sedaine's own poetic tone some lingering metaphorical enjoyment of the combination of the mud and slime of *les halles* with the sacred ground of the muses, which is at least a renegotiation of the boundaries of criticism.

Sedaine's longest and most ambitious single poem, *Le Vaudeville*, a history and defence of *opéra-comique*, also stressed the problematic evolution and categorisation of low or popular genres:

> Il est un genre au dessous du Burlesque
> Phoebus honteux ne peut le nommer presque

1935). Vadé is himself an important and neglected writer. In the third edition of the *Recueil de poésies* (London [Paris]: Chez l'auteur etc., 1780), p. 81, Sedaine wrote of the circumstances of writing and publishing this work: 'Je n'ai fait imprimer cette satyre qu'après la mort de Vadé. Je ne l'avois fait voir qu'à lui, alors il me pria de la donner au public, ce que je crus ne devoir pas faire.' This hints that Sedaine perhaps believed that, as a piece of mock-didactic writing, his *satyre* might be misunderstood if published, and that he saw it rather as a kind of ironic experiment for a more private circle. For evidence of Sedaine's involvement in the Vadé circle, see Jean-Nicolas Dufort de Cheverny, 'Notice sur la vie de Sedaine' in Ledbury, 'Greuze and Sedaine', p. 360: 'Sedaine ... lié avec le chansonnier Vadé et une société de jeunes gens aimables faisoit des pièces ...'.

[19] Sedaine, *Satyre contre le goût des ouvrages poissards* in *Recueil de poésies* (2 vols in 1, Paris: Duchesne, 1760), II, p. 72.

[20] Ibid., p. 73.

Enfant du peuple, et du peuple chéri
Il prit naissance au pied du pilori.[21]

At the end of the second *chant*, he warns against *amphigouri*, playing on the fact that this was both a poetic term for a deliberate nonsense and a familiar one for unintentionally confused, unconnected writing.[22]

Là, pour donner des plus burlesques loix
De Melpomène il contrefait la voix
La croassant ses phrases imbéciles,
Il confond tout, les genres et les styles.
[...]
Défiez vous, auteurs de chansonnettes
De son jargon, de ses graves sornettes.[23]

Sedaine's work seemed thus to reinforce prevalent discourse on genre, taking its cue from the seventeenth century and following taste in his aversion to mixture of genres and crossing of boundaries. This may be the autodidact's attempt to show himself to be well versed in the rules of genre decorum, but even in his most Boileau-esque passages, Sedaine's didacticism is suffused with a deep irony and mock-seriousness, as if he wished subtly to acknowledge his own partiality to those registers and vocabularies which were prohibited or shunned.

Consequently, there are hints even within these didactic works of his experiments to come: he places heavy emphasis on the possibilities of the lower genre in *Le Vaudeville*, rejects *parades*, and combines eulogy of Favart as reformer with evident belief in the possibilities of *opéra-comique* which he praises as a newly legitimate genre.[24] For Sedaine, the experiments of Favart had shown that *opéra-comique* could relinquish its dependency on parody of classical models and become an independently creative genre. It is in this context that we must understand his later, very contentious claim that comedy is more relevant to the spirit of his century than tragedy.[25] In this attack on the relevance and importance of tragedy, the seeds of Sedaine's later and more challenging work are sown. For he seems to argue that comedy is not an amusing but always inferior genre, but rather a more appropriate, more culturally and socially alert mode than its superior, tragedy, and that

---

21 Sedaine, *Le Vaudeville* in *Recueil de poésies* (1760), I, p. 179.

22 One of the most famous French *amphigouris* is contained in Rabelais's *Pantagruel*, chapters 11–13. Dramatic *amphigouris* were written by Paul Scarron (with whose work Sedaine was very familiar) and Charles Collé.

23 Ibid., p. 172.

24 Ibid., p. 193: 'ainsi ce siècle a fixé les destins / d'un joli genre ignoré des latins'.

25 Ibid., pp. 210–11.

furthermore the creation and development of new genres was not a dangerous transgression but a necessary artistic process.

Sedaine's poetry is also a useful indicator of the sources of his later dramatic work. Clearly, he was as a young poet interested in the fable and the *conte*, and his *Pièces fugitives* (1752) and later *Recueil de poésies* contain a variety of work in both poetic genres.[26] These poems are the first indications of his debt to the work of Jean de La Fontaine. La Fontaine would be a fertile source for Sedaine throughout his dramatic career, and it is worth stressing that Sedaine built his often quite complex dramas on the foundations of these slight tales, themselves mixtures of less regarded genres. This is significant in the context of the genre debate, as it shows how the well-read Sedaine actively chose to use the slight, sometimes crude genre of *conte* as inspiration, signalling, as Vadé had done before him, a belief in the potential of less elevated subject matter.[27]

This impulse to explore and expand the lower genre would find its outlet in Sedaine's first forays into dramatic writing for the public, in the enterprise of Jean Monnet. I do not believe Sedaine's famous narrative of reluctant submission to the advances of a persuasive Monnet in 1756.[28] It is clear from Dufort's obituary notice that Sedaine's fondness for fair theatre was nourished by contact with Vadé and others and that he was particularly keen to write for music theatre from the beginnings of his literary career.[29] The *Impromptu de Thalie* included in the *Pièces fugitives* and the pastoral *Anacréon* were written between 1751 and 1752. In the alternative version of the 'Quelques réflexions' cited by Arthur Pougin, the date of the approach by Monnet is 1751.[30] However, the date of Sedaine's first known production for Monnet, 1756, was also the date of the publication of Pierre Patu's translations of English short comic plays and ballad opera, *Choix de petites pièces du théâtre anglais*, which provided him with material out of which his subsequent works evolved. As Margaret Rayner pointed out, Sedaine's contact with Patu's volumes was deep and important.[31] These volumes contained much more than the material which he would adapt in *Le Diable à quatre* and in *Le Roi et le fermier*. In volume

---

26 See *Pièces fugitives*, pp. 81–97, and *Recueil de poésies* (1760), I, pp. 102–33; II, pp. 17–36.

27 See Clarence Brenner, 'Dramatizations of French Short Stories in the Eighteenth Century' (University of California Publications in Modern Philology, XXXIII) (Berkeley: University of California Press, 1947), pp. 1–31. For a consideration of borrowings from La Fontaine, see also David Charlton, 'Continuing Polarities', in *French Opera, 1730–1830: Meaning and Media* (Aldershot: Ashgate, 2000).

28 Sedaine, 'Quelques réflexions', pp. 501–2.

29 Dufort de Cheverny, 'Notice sur la vie de Sedaine', in Ledbury, 'Greuze and Sedaine', p. 360.

30 Arthur Pougin, *Monsigny et son temps* (Paris: Fischbacher, 1908), pp. 48–50.

31 Rayner, 'Sedaine's Dramatic Work', pp. 49ff.

two he would have found the important translation of Gay's *The Beggar's Opera*, and Swift's review of the 'Newgate pastoral' in the *Gazeteer*, in which issues of genre were explored in detail. He would also have read the translation of Gay's extraordinary 1715 *The What D'ye Call It*, whose accompanying preface, with its myriad ironic references to genre, would have provided a bold and ironic counterpoint to any study of Boileau. The dynamic of Gay's work and much alternative, parodic theatre in Britain had revolved around the denial of genre expectations, and here Sedaine found this kind of experiment theorised in a jocular but complex way. Ballad opera as it developed after 1728 was a self-conscious, parodic amalgam of traditions and genres, and John Gay's work was an example of how a hybrid form could be made the vehicle of a complex and successful drama.[32] From the beginning of his career as a dramatist Sedaine wished to exploit the inevitably hybrid nature of unofficial theatre to create aesthetically coherent, attractive (and later, moral) works. In the British ballad opera model, and more specifically in the work of Gay, Sedaine found evidence of how mixed, non-traditional and previously scorned traditions could be put to stylish and socially satirical use. As the preface to *The What D'ye Call It* claimed, 'The whole art of the *Tragi-Comi-Pastoral Farce* lies in interweaving the several kinds of the drama with each other, so that they cannot be distinguished or separated.'[33] There are some precise resonances in Sedaine's later work of his reading of *The What D'ye Call It*. Firstly, Gay's jocular preface to the work discusses the register of characters' language, and contains a fairly uncommon citation of part of a line from Horace, *tragicus plerumque dolet sermone pedestri*, which Sedaine was to include on the title page of his prose tragedy, *Maillard ou Paris sauvé*.[34] More

[32] Of course, Gay himself seems to have been aware of French vaudeville traditions as well and it is likely that some of his experiments with song as ironic and parodic meta-narrative might themselves be derived from, or in some way indebted to, French fair theatre. On the musical and dramatic parody in *The Beggar's Opera* see the classic studies: Bertrand Bronson, 'The Beggar's Opera' in *Studies in the Comic* (Berkeley: University of California Press, 1941), pp. 197–231, which focuses on the parodic elements and the relationship of the work to operatic traditions; Adriaan Ernst Hugo Swaen, 'The Airs and Tunes of John Gay's *Beggar's Opera*', *Anglia*, XLIII (1919), pp. 152–90. See also Peter Lewis, *The Beggar's Opera* (London: Macmillan, 1976). Edmond M. Gagey, *Ballad Opera* (New York: Blum, 1937), p. 31, reminds us that Gay was in Paris in 1717 and 1719 and heard the audiences singing there (whether serious or comic opera); also 'numerous companies of French players' appeared at the Little Haymarket Theatre London, 1720–28 (ibid.), whose repertory is listed in Allardyce Nicoll, *A History of the Early Eighteenth-Century Drama* (Cambridge: Cambridge University Press, 1929).

[33] See John Gay, *The What D'ye Call It* in *Dramatic Works*, ed. John Fuller (3 vols, Oxford: Clarendon Press, 1983), II, p. 174. Also Gagey, *Ballad Opera*, pp. 53–65.

[34] See John Gay, *The What D'ye Call It*, p. 175. The citation is from Horace, *The Art of Poetry*, line 95, and is translated as '[Telephus and Peleus] often express their grief in prosaic language' in Theodor Siegfried Dorsch (ed. and trans.), *Classical Literary Criticism* (London: Penguin Classics, 1967), p. 82.

importantly, the mixture of cynical and pastoral characters, the theme of desertion and the device of the pardon, as well as tragi-comic imprisonment scenes, seem to have had a profound influence on Sedaine's most daring mixed work, *Le Déserteur*.

Of course, it was not merely Sedaine, but the whole enterprise of Parisian *opéra-comique* that increased in ambition in the 1750s and early 1760s. The elevation of the low, theorised ironically in Gay, started to become practical reality in Jean Monnet's ambitious second period in charge of the Opéra-Comique.[35] His innovations in costume, stage design and choreography raised the fair theatres into an increasingly successful and therefore problematic rival to the main stages in France.[36] The ambition of the whole Monnet enterprise contributed to a mixing of genre on the institutional level. *Les Troqueurs*, Vadé and Dauvergne's important 1753 *opéra-comique*, was seen by Monnet as a cheeky refutation of the premisses of the *querelle des bouffons*,[37] and therefore could be seen as an attempt to collapse another well-known and particularly virulent genre opposition, that between Italian (comic) and French (serious) opera.[38] We must also see the 'takeover' of the Opéra-Comique by the Comédie-Italienne in 1762 in these terms. This was what is known in business as a reverse takeover, involving the actors of the Opéra-Comique backing into the official institution. Sedaine's autobiographical narrative of the phenomenal success of *On ne s'avise jamais de tout* [39] makes the claim that he and his work were partly responsible for the fusion of the two theatres. Sedaine's analysis may seem rather far-fetched and self-aggrandising. Essentially, however, his point is not far from the truth: that the merger resulted from the tensions between the popularity of fair theatre and the impossibility of its achievements being matched by the king's official players, the Comédie-Italienne.[40]

It would seem, therefore, that Sedaine's ambitious and experimental work in *opéra-comique* owes much to this early engagement with British

---

35 For a history of the vicissitudes of Monnet's enterprises in Paris, Lyon and London, see Arthur Heulhard, *Jean Monnet. Vie et aventures d'un entrepreneur de spectacles au XVIIIe siècle* (Paris, 1884).

36 See Peter Davies, 'Heir to Anacreon: Charles-Simon Favart in the Theatrical Life of Eighteenth-Century France', Ph.D. dissertation, Yale U., 1968.

37 See Jean Monnet, *Supplément au roman comique, ou mémoires pour servir à la vie de Jean Monnet* (London: n. p., 1773), pp. 43–6. Dauvergne was an established composer of works in the high French style, who here turned to emulate the new Italianate style.

38 Elisabeth Cook, 'Querelle des Bouffons' in Stanley Sadie (ed.), *The New Grove Dictionary of Opera* (4 vols, London: Macmillan, 1992), III, pp. 1198–200; William Weber, '*La Musique Ancienne* in the Waning of the Ancien Régime', *Journal of Modern History*, LVI (March 1984), pp. 58–88.

39 Sedaine, 'Quelques réflexions', pp. 506–7.

40 See pp. 220–21, below; also Robert M. Isherwood, *Farce and Fantasy. Popular Entertainment in Eighteenth-Century Paris* (Oxford: Oxford University Press, 1986).

ballad opera traditions. However, Sedaine's successful *opéras-comiques* of the late 1750s and early 1760s made a crucial generic step forward: they sharply reduced, and soon eliminated, the parodic use of popular melodies acting as ironic meta-narratives (vaudevilles), in favour of new, sophisticated music for each production, the score serving a variety of dramatic purposes. He managed to mix this rather varied, modern and in the end still elitist mode with an intense and sincere interest in the rhythm of popular speech and activity. Without wishing to fall back on the naive myth of Sedaine the mason poet, we can be clear that Sedaine was interested in capturing and harnessing the idioms of the unsophisticated and in using them not just to challenge traditional poetics but to exploit the rich rhythms of ordinary speech by lifting it out of grotesque caricature into more dignified, though still comic, dialogue. His longstanding and close friend Dufort insists on this in his obituary notice, stressing how Sedaine borrowed much from conversations overheard in Paris streets, and citing Sedaine's maxim that: 'On produit le vrai comique, en saississant ses effets; en étudiant les hommes qui ne s'étudient pas.'[41] In the way that Gay had created characters whose material poverty was starkly opposed by their sharp wits and even sharper language, Sedaine, too, crafted interesting characters who seem to us inseparable from their humble environments, and whose utterances (spoken and sung) command critical respect.

In a very important sense, then, Sedaine's experiments were both aesthetically and socially inspired. The dual inspirations of an encounter with a sophisticated mixed and satirical tradition, and his interest in elevating people and material considered beneath aesthetic value, can be seen as pushing Sedaine to seek in genres regarded as inferior, limited and vulgar the material for serious and innovative drama. This initiative started him on a collision course with aesthetic purists from early in his career. Although the *Année littéraire* had reviewed the first edition of Sedaine's poetry rather favourably in 1754, when Sedaine was a novelty mason poet, its 1760 review of the *Recueil de poésies*, published after its author had given up 'le ciseau et le marteau', is much more contemptuous, especially on the subject matter of Sedaine's work. His *Epître à mon habit*, for example, is regarded as 'bas' and aesthetically beyond the pale: 'Il est facheux que le sujet soit bas; ces sortes de cadres sont proscrits des atteliers de nos poètes modernes.'[42] This would be a recurring theme of criticism as Sedaine's career progressed and as his work became more ambitious. The prefaces to his *opéras-comiques* through the 1750s and 1760s

[41] Dufort de Cheverny, 'Notice sur la vie de Sedaine', in Ledbury, 'Greuze and Sedaine', p. 359; idem, *Mémoires du comte Dufort de Cheverny*, ed. Robert de Crèvecœur (4th ed., 2 vols, Paris: Plon, 1909), I, p. 235.

[42] For the first review, see *Année littéraire* (1754), VI, pp. 183–92; for this comment, see *Année littéraire* (1760), IV, p. 340.

are testament to this ambition, and a clear indication of this desire to both explore and elevate popular music drama.

If we examine any of the early, 'slighter' *opéras-comiques*, we cannot fail to notice Sedaine's enjoyment of genre mixture and of the elevation of the socially and aesthetically low. In *On ne s'avise jamais de tout*, for example, we find Sedaine mixing not only generic codes but patterns of speech. His hero Dorval, capable of a register of sincerity in the opening ariette, is a master of vocal as well as visual disguise, running through a repertoire of exaggerations, stutters and circumlocutions in his efforts to outwit Tue and Margarita and make contact with Lise.[43] Sedaine's interest in mixing different registers of language also emerges in scenes between Tue and Margarita.[44] The characterisation is also mixed. The guardian, Tue, has a name and a character out of the best fair traditions, but a profession (medicine) out of traditional Molièresque comedy. He has traces of the *commedia dell'arte* Cassandre figure in his violent desires and his wish to imprison Lise and kill Dorval, but is also a hapless burlesque fool and a self-inflated bourgeois *à la* Molière. Dorval, too, has the guile and the desire of the heroes of traditional fair theatre but is also allowed emotional soliloquies befitting the helpless heroes of *comédie larmoyante*. The plot mixes elements straight out of popular theatre (old man tries to marry young woman and is outwitted by the pair of young lovers) with a story of sentimental young love familiar from 'higher' comedy. Further, its scenes of tenderness follow seamlessly on from those of pure, physical farce.[45] Seventeen musical numbers of great functional variety reinterpret the Italian *intermezzi* and widen its range of musical expression. Yet, as so often with Sedaine, all is rooted in La Fontaine.

As Sedaine's work became more complex, his advocacy of the comic against the tragic, and of the rhythms of ordinary speech against more explicitly poetic registers, became more pronounced. In the preface to *Le Jardinier et son seigneur* he justified his use of the 'style bas et peu élevé' by rephrasing Madame Simon's dialogue in pedantic alexandrines, and thereby pointed to what he saw as the limitations of the 'marche constamment pesante de notre grand Vers Alexandrin'[46] and the superiority for his musical and poetic purposes of the rhythms of ordinary speech. By this time, his advocacy of the potential of critically disparaged comic genres was striking a chord with many others, including Grimm, who wrote that: 'J'avoue naturellement que je

---

[43] *On ne s'avise jamais de tout*, sc. VI, VIII.

[44] Ibid., sc. V.

[45] Ibid., sc. XI–XII for example.

[46] Sedaine, *Le Jardinier et son seigneur* (Paris: Hérissant, 1761), 'Avertissement', p. 5.

préfère sa petite comédie du *Jardinier et son seigneur* à beaucoup de nos tragédies modernes qui ont eu du succès à la comédie Française.'[47]

In addition to exploring the generic possibilities of comic opera, *Le Jardinier et son seigneur*, through its use of what I would call 'ironic pastoral' to expose affectation and corruption in court circles, was the first of Sedaine's works to explore in any explicit way the possibilities of social commentary open to *opéra-comique*, for which Rousseau's *Le Devin du village* had provided some kind of blueprint. By adroitly mixing pathos, irony and pastoral, and by the introduction of the characters of the actresses, who did not feature in the original *conte*, Sedaine tentatively suggested how this genre could be lent additional moral purpose. This ironic pastoral was partially the result of experiment in mixture within his own parameters. He combined and ironised the legacies of Le Sage, Favart and Vadé, and as he made elevating claims for his genre so he also became increasingly adept at mixing the serious with the comic, the urban with the pastoral. In other words, Sedaine's *opéra-comique* was a self-conscious hybrid of types of an already hybrid musico-dramatic genre, a mixture of mixtures, a cross-breed of the genre's traditional forms.

The preface to *Le Roi et le fermier* reconfirmed Sedaine's ambition within music drama.[48] He was to re-emphasise this in his later reminiscences:

> En 1762, j'ai effectué ce que j'avais cru impossible, d'élever le ton de ce genre, et de mettre même un roi sur la scène dans un ouvrage en trois actes qui occupât la scène aussi longtemps qu'une pièce à cinq actes au théâtre français.[49]

Here Sedaine makes clear comparison between his work and the five-act plays of spoken theatre, and his reference to setting the king on stage indicates that he was already starting to think of his work as an alternative to tragedy, and even one of equivalent worth. The work contains no comic characters at all and does not end with a wedding or even a pairing-off. As Michel Noiray discusses in Chapter 5 below, it is about the responsibilities of different estates in society, and it echoes, not just by implication, the acute criticism of princely courts found in Dodsley's original.

By the merger of the Comédie-Italienne and the Opéra-Comique in 1762, Sedaine and the playwrights, musicians, dancers and entrepreneurs of *opéra-comique* had established that a genre mixing spoken dialogue with an original musical score was capable, in their hands, of engaging with anything between farce and a serious moral tale. However, though it might have drawn audiences

---

47 *Correspondance littéraire*, IV (1 Aug. 1761) , p. 457.

48 See p. 243 for the full text of this preface.

49 Sedaine, 'Quelques réflexions', p. 507.

away from the Comédie-Française, Sedaine's work did not at this point challenge the powerful fundamental opposition of genre in any direct way. This was mainly because drama involving music had always been regarded as an anomaly within the classical rules of genre. However, the discussions that took place in 1763 between Sedaine, Diderot and Grimm and the subsequent evolution of *Le Philosophe sans le savoir* marked a new step in Sedaine's ambition.[50] *Le Philosophe* is clearly an engaged, partisan drama which saw Sedaine deploy his skills at stagecraft to make a direct intervention in a dramatic dispute which allied questions of genre with wider philosophical and political disputes. It is not, however, a slavishly Diderotian drama, and what *Le Philosophe* represents is nothing less than the *opéra-comique* coming to the rescue of the Diderotian vision of ideal drama, as Sedaine exploited all the resources of choreography, dialogue and spectacle learned through *opéra-comique* to intervene to make serious comedy a stage reality, rather than a utopian fantasy. Diderot, who in public tried to use Sedaine's success as proof of the innate correctness of his personal model, in private recognised this, and understood what Sedaine had achieved: 'les terreurs de la tragédie produites avec les moyens de l'opéra-comique'.[51]

With *Le Philosophe sans le savoir* Sedaine thus continued a process already begun, which would show how the less privileged terms of the genre opposition could successfully aspire to seriousness and equivalence. His work therefore contributed to the process through which comedy's potential for social and moral seriousness could be realised. He had not, however, fundamentally challenged the privileged term of the genre opposition that ruled drama: tragedy. He retained the generic term *comédie* for *Le Philosophe sans le savoir*, even avoiding the more controversial term *drame*. However, the logic of his experimentation, and the confidence which the success of *Le Philosophe sans le savoir* gave him, would lead him to test oppositions of genre further, and would result in his losing the support of the philosophical faction and incurring the wrath of authorities, actors, censors and critics.

The period between 1765 and 1771 was one of intense creativity and experimentation for Sedaine, a period in which he wrote his daring opera *Aline, reine de Golconde*,[52] his delicate, imaginative comedy *La Gageure imprévue*,[53] and perhaps his most extraordinary work to that date, the *drame mêlé de chants Le Déserteur*, which, though first performed in 1769, had been written in 1765

---

50 For a discussion of these events, see Ledbury, 'Greuze and Sedaine', pp. 107–17.

51 Diderot–Sophie Volland, 20 December 1765, in Diderot, *Lettres à Sophie Volland*, ed. André Babelon (3 vols, Paris: Gallimard, [1930]), II, p. 108.

52 On *Aline*, see Manuel Couvreur, Chapter 4 in this volume.

53 On *La Gageure imprévue*, see the critical edition by Robert Niklaus (Exeter: U. of Exeter, 1973); as e-text: http://www.exeter.ac.uk/french/textes/gageure/frameset.htm

or 1766.[54] *Le Philosophe* had been a calculated, subtly negotiated integration of *opéra-comique* techniques and new ideas in spoken drama. *Le Déserteur* on the other hand gloried in the self-conscious mixing of the tragic and comic that all Enlightenment theory so rejected.[55] Nowhere was this better exemplified than in the prison-based juxtaposition of Montauciel's drunken interventions with the unfolding near-tragedy of Alexis and Louise.[56] As the most obvious example of transgression, this was the one most commented upon by contemporary critics.

Sedaine had once again used his preface to point to the new effects that this innovative music drama was achieving and had rather provocatively stressed the ancient roots of his work in Greek theatrical practice.[57] The critical response which Sedaine reports in his later 'Quelques réflexions' was strong and emotional, as the sentiment of pathetic terror spread like contagion through an audience.[58] Less charitable commentators, at the time and since, stressed instead the affront caused by the confusion of genres, techniques and registers in the work. Not everyone went as far as Geoffroy's early nineteenth-century judgement that Sedaine's work was 'un mélange monstrueux du comique le plus triviale et du tragique le plus outré'[59] but the gist of much commentary was that the play transgressed rules of genre and taste.[60] One anonymous pamphlet linked Sedaine's dramaturgy with the author's experience in building construction:

> Qu'il est aisé d'amonuler ainsi incident sur incident, pour donner à cet amas informe le nom de drame! C'est appeler un château un assemblage de petites maisonnettes de brique, de pierre, de bois et

---

54 This is the conclusion one must draw from Sedaine's discussion in 'Quelques réflexions', p. 512. On *Le Déserteur,* see especially Rayner, 'Sedaine's Dramatic Work'; Daniel Heartz, 'The Beginnings of the Operatic Romance. Rousseau, Sedaine and Monsigny', *Eighteenth-Century Studies*, XV (1982), pp. 149–78; Pougin, *Monsigny et son temps*, esp. pp. 129–37. For musical commentary, see Raphaëlle Legrand, Chapter 6 in this volume.

55 On the history of tragi-comedy as a genre, see Martin Herrick, *Tragicomedy. Its Origin and Development in Italy, France and England* (Urbana: University of Illinois Press, 1962).

56 Sedaine, *Le Déserteur* (Paris: Hérissant, 1770), Act II, sc. V–VI.

57 See pp. 254–5 below.

58 Sedaine, 'Quelques réflexions', pp. 512–13. For statistics on the work's enormous popularity in France, see Charlton, *Grétry*. The work became for a time the most popular stage work, in any genre, seen in Germany.

59 Julien-Louis Geoffroy, *Cours de littérature dramatique* (6 vols, Paris: Blanchard, 1825), I, p. 307.

60 See for example *Mémoires secrets*, IV (16 April 1769), pp. 257–8; *Année littéraire* (1770), VIII, pp. 3–18.

> d'argille, plantées au hasard l'une après de l'autre. Quel édifice, quel architecture![61]

However, whether the metaphor was biological (Sedaine's text as monster) or architectural, as here, the point was the same: his work was an affront that was dangerous precisely because of its popularity and emotional effect, and a sure portent of the collapse of taste, decency and standards. *Le Déserteur*'s mixture of terror, pathos and outrageous comedy was particularly bold at a time when the new forms of drama were being attacked by parodists, journalists, actors and even at court.[62] Even Sedaine's use of the term *drame* to describe *Le Déserteur* might be described as provocative, since the term had become associated with politically suspect, aesthetically mould-breaking work.

It was clear that in attempting to juxtapose the comic and the tragic quite so self-consciously and evidently, Sedaine had raised the stakes of his experimentation, and crossed a major barrier. One might speculate again that English models provided him with some inspiration. Later reports would associate Sedaine's discovery of Shakespeare with the translations published in 1772–82 by Letourneur.[63] However, Sedaine's involvement with the Monnet circle, and his interest in the British stage, had already led him to an engagement with Shakespeare which manifested itself in 1764 in the reference to *The Merry Wives of Windsor* concluding the preface to *L'Anneau perdu et retrouvé*.[64] It is likely that, as the profile of the British dramatist was raised in France in the 1760s, Sedaine's interest intensified. Shakespeare's startling juxtapositions of tragic and comic scenes would have provided Sedaine with a bold example of the dramatic possibilities of generic mixture. He would have been familiar with many examples of tragicomedy, which was not a new or unknown genre in France.

The final assault on this generic structure, and the one which had the greatest impact on Sedaine's career, was the prose tragedy *Maillard ou Paris sauvé*, which he started writing probably as early as 1769, and which was complete and presented to the Comédie-Française in 1771. In this work,

---

61 Anon., *Remerci[e]ment du public à la préface du Déserteur, représenté pour la première fois le 6 mars 1769* (n.p., n.d.), p. 14.

62 See Félix Gaiffe, *Le Drame en France au XVIIIe siècle* (Paris: Armand Colin, 1910), 'Le milieu, les résistances'. I examined this particular moment in 'The Threat of Mixed Genre', a paper presented to the annual conference of the British Society for Eighteenth-Century Studies, January 1994.

63 See for example, Louis Moland writing in the Introduction to *Théâtre de Sedaine* (Paris: Garnier frères, n.d.[1919?]): 'Lorsque la traduction de Letourneur vint à paraître, il n'eut rien de plus pressé que de la lire ou plutôt la dévorer. Il en étoit dans l'extase, dans le ravissement. Il parloit de Shakespeare à tout ce qu'il rencontrait.'

64 See this volume, p. 249; La Place's *Le Théâtre anglois* (1745–9) contained a version of *The Merry Wives of Windsor*.

Sedaine finally attempted to engage overtly with the high genre, the privileged term in the dramatic opposition, the noblest aspiration of all playwrights and the critical yardstick of dramatic seriousness. It has to be remembered that when Sedaine started to write the tragedy he was at the height of his public fame and ambition. However, after what can only be called the ordeal of *Maillard* he was never again to write a spoken drama specifically for the Comédie-Française,[65] and the bitter taste it left in his mouth would linger in his words and works for the rest of his career.

The reasons for this radical change in fortune are many, but any explanation ought first to try to answer the perplexing question of why Sedaine should have wanted to write a tragedy in the first place. After all, until this point Sedaine had been trying to explore the potential of the non-tragic and show that the low genres had serious dramatic and moral potential.

The motives for Sedaine's decision to tackle tragedy head-on were part personal, part aesthetic. First, Sedaine was desperate to be officially accepted as a writer, and had ambitions to become a member of the Académie Française.[66] This ambition might seem surprising, but it is clear that for the autodidact Sedaine, who had always challenged the hegemony of poetic and aesthetic rules, and had in the late 1760s seen his work represented on all the main stages of Paris, to become one of the *quarante* would be a sign of ultimate approbation, as well as an ironic victory for reformers and innovators. Sedaine was aware that to attain such status, however, he would have to essay a more serious and elevated subject. Tragedy, the privileged repository of France's great writing, was therefore a natural aspiration. But Sedaine had another point to prove. He was evidently attempting to modernise and even to revolutionise the tragic genre. Sedaine's innovatory zeal meant that his models of tragedy would not be the traditional ones. He intended to revive old debates and provoke new ones both by his choice of subject matter (an inglorious moment from a problematic period in French history, which featured a divided

---

[65] Although *Raimond V* was performed in the place of *Maillard* on 22 September 1789, it was not written for production in France, being a commission for Catherine II of Russia.

[66] Sedaine was finally made a member of the Académie Française in 1786, in the wake of *Richard Cœur-de-Lion,* but not without controversy. It is clear from a letter written to Marmontel on 5 October 1785, and published by Hippolyte Rigault in *Conversations littéraires et morales* (Paris: Charpentier, 1859), p. 224, that Sedaine asked twelve times to be considered before he was accepted, and this letter is clear proof of his long-standing academic ambition.

country and a king in powerless captivity)[67] and by his choice of prose as a vehicle.[68]

These choices were to lead directly to the collision of Sedaine's ambitious innovations with the final immovable object of generic structure, as a range of influential authorities restated the need for tragedy to be preserved from the kind of experiment that Sedaine had made his *modus operandi* in previous work. The play suffered a long painful death at the hands of censors, actors and critics, and was never performed on the national stage for which it was designed.[69] It was savagely ridiculed not just by Sedaine's dramatic rivals and traditional opponents in the press, but by ardent *Encyclopédistes* such as Voltaire and also actors, particularly Le Kain, whom the young poet Sedaine had idolised and whom he wished to play the role of Marcel.[70] Even Diderot's response to the play, expressed in a letter to Sedaine, was lukewarm.[71] Censors, too, hated the play, and its first drafts were thoroughly savaged. Court officials also did everything in their power to prevent performances of the play.[72] The reasons for this mixed protest were not merely that Sedaine had chosen provocative subject matter – the battle for sovereignty over Paris at a politically unstable moment – at a time when the Maupeou coup and tensions within the *parlements* had rendered such subject matter hypersensitive,[73] but that the

---

[67] The play is set in 1358, and Sedaine's sources for this particular episode were the *Chroniques* of Froissart (see the edition edited by Baron Kervyn de Lettenhove (25 vols, Brussels: V. Devaux, 1867–77), VI); another possible source was François Eudes Mézeray's *Abrégé chronologique ou extraict de l'histoire de France* (3 vols, Paris: D. Thierry, 1657), II, pp. 351 and passim.

[68] On prose tragedy see Gustave Lanson, *Esquisse d'une histoire de la tragédie française* (New York: Columbia University Press, and Paris: Hachette, 1920); François Moreau, 'Le vers tragique en jugement aux XVIIIe siècle', *Revue de l'histoire du théâtre*, II–III (April–September 1993), pp. 35–48.

[69] On *Maillard ou Paris sauvé* see Ledbury, 'Greuze and Sedaine', pp. 199–239; Rayner, 'Sedaine's Dramatic Work', pp. 160–74; Lennart Breitholtz, *Le Théâtre historique en France jusqu'à la Révolution* (Uppsala Universitets Årsskrift, 1952, II, no. 12) (Uppsala: Lundequist; Wiesbaden, Harrassowitz, 1952), pp. 239–59.

[70] See the letter from Lekain to Henri Rieu, 9 April 1775, published in *Correspondance de Voltaire*, ed. Theodore Besterman (Geneva and Oxford: Voltaire Foundation, 1965), no. 18295. See also Count Gabriel Mareschal de Bièvre, *Le Marquis de Bièvre: sa vie, ses calembours, ses comédies 1747–1789* (Paris: Plon, 1910), p. 133. Sedaine's poem on Le Kain is *A M. Le Kain, acteur de la Comédie Française représentant Orosmane dans Zaire* in *Pièces fugitives de M. S**** (n.p. [The Hague and Paris: Durand?], 1752), p. 69.

[71] Diderot–Sedaine, undated [April 1771] in *Correspondance*, ed. George Roth and Jan Varloot (Paris: Editions du Minuit, 1955–70), V, no. 666, pp. 22–4.

[72] On the history of the play's censorship and the succession of problems that prevented its performance, the best guide is Rayner, 'Sedaine's Dramatic Work', pp. 165–74.

[73] See Sedaine's own account of the play's misfortunes in 'Quelques réflexions', p. 515; idem, *Maillard ou Paris sauvé* (Paris: Prault, 1788), 'Préface', pp. xi–xv. For literature on the *parlements* crisis, see especially Julian Swann, *Politics and the Parlement of Paris*

internal conventions of the genre were ruptured. The real objection to the play was generic: here was a determinedly 'mixed' tragedy, written not just in prose but in a peculiar idiom, which deployed proverb, Rousseauist discourse on wet-nursing, and rough-hewn, violent epithet in disconcerting alternation, and cared nothing for the fine decorums of the French tragic tradition. It also incorporated scenes which could only be described as Shakespearean in inspiration, involving cohorts of dark conspirators brandishing knives and swearing black revenge.

All this prompted a response from Voltaire (his sensitivity to the whiff of the Shakespearean heightened by the Shakespeare celebrations which had taken place in 1769)[74] who, on hearing of Sedaine's play in 1770, wrote: 'On m'a parlé d'une tragédie en prose qui, dit-on, aura du succès. Voilà le coup de grace apporté aux beaux-arts.'[75] He became yet more apocalyptic in later correspondence, claiming 'il nous manquait une tragédie en prose, nous allons l'avoir. C'en est fait, le monde est fini, l'antichrist est venu.'[76] Voltaire's second letter, written after Sedaine's play was officially accepted for performance, showed that his real anxiety was not so much about the existence as about the public success of such a drama. Having admired Sedaine's dramatic writing, Voltaire knew Sedaine had the ability to set precedents. It is clear that Voltaire's influence was instrumental in swaying Le Kain and others against the play, keeping the play off the stage for reasons of aesthetic politics. If an ambitious and confident Sedaine had decided that tragedy as a genre could be modernised, reformed and mixed, then the Comédie-Française, the literary establishment and even Sedaine's allies, the *encyclopédistes*, had reinforced the sacrosanct nature of tragedy by denying this experiment. The genre opposition had again proved powerful, even insuperable. Indeed, one might see this period of the 1770s as the moment of reassertion of generic structures after a brief period in which Sedaine and others had seemed to make a real impact on the way dramatic and visual genre was understood. It saw the advent of the D'Angiviller regime to the *Bâtiments du Roi*, the spread of Winckelmann's ideas in the visual arts and the marginalisation of dramatic

---

under Louis XV, 1754–1774 (Cambridge: Cambridge University Press, 1995), esp. pp. 314–51; William Doyle, 'The Parlements of France and the Breakdown of the Old Regime', *French Historical Studies*, VI (1970), pp. 415–58.

74 On Voltaire and the Shakespeare anniversary, see Haydn Mason, 'Voltaire versus Shakespeare. The *Lettre à l'Académie française*', *British Journal for Eighteenth-Century Studies*, XVIII (Autumn 1995), pp. 173–85. See also Jean Jusserand, *Shakespeare en France sous l'ancien régime* (Paris: Armand Colin, 1898).

75 Letter of 26 September 1770 in *Correspondance*, ed. Besterman, no. 15647.

76 Voltaire–Comte d'Argental, 5 September 1772, in ibid., no. 16838.

experiment such as that of Louis-Sébastien Mercier, after the anonymous publication of his treatise *Du théâtre* in 1773.[77]

The consequences of Sedaine's one generic experiment too far (which can be usefully compared to Greuze's 'failed' history painting, *Septime Sévère*)[78] were wide-ranging. The author was later to write aggressively and defensively about the play in both the preface and the dedication to its text, finally published in 1788. His bitterness and frustration spilled over into later dramatic works. Most directly, his experiences resulted in the satirical *Raimond V, comte de Toulouse* (written in 1778–9), a surprising response to a surprising commission for the Empress of Russia, Catherine II, engineered by Grimm.[79] Its troubadour exterior masked a clearly autobiographical drama based on Sedaine's post-*Maillard* experiences. The sour personal note pervaded even Sedaine's other large-scale prose drama, *Les Journalistes*, again commissioned by Catherine II. Catherine had specifically asked if she could have a play which reflected the *Sedaine gai* of the *opéras-comiques*, after being a little taken aback by the *amertume* of *Raimond V*,[80] but received a text that was replete with sardonic bitterness, and featured a strange half-gothic, half-farcical scene involving a savage beating administered with relish by one of the virtuous characters to a sniping journalist.[81] Bearing in mind the bitter words directed towards critics in the preface to *Aucassin et Nicolette*, written just before this drama, it is clear that Sedaine felt deeply misunderstood and betrayed by literary journalists, as well as by censors and actors.[82]

If we read the more complex musical dramas of Sedaine from the 1770s, and particularly *Félix ou l'Enfant trouvé*, considered at the time by Sedaine to be the most carefully written and constructed of his works,[83] the comedy seems drained of all but its satirical bite, and the text has a cynical, dark edge which all but swamps its seemingly uncontentious scenario. However, to say that self-

---

77 On D'Angiviller and new arts policy, see Thomas Crow, *Painters and Public Life in Eighteenth-Century Paris* (New Haven and London: Yale University Press, 1985); Jean Locquin, *La Peinture d'histoire en France de 1747 à 1785* (Paris: Laurens, 1912); on Mercier and *Du théâtre*, see Louis Béclard, *Sébastien Mercier* (Paris: Champion, 1903).

78 On this picture and its reception, see Edgar Munhall's entry on the image in Marie Catherine Sahut (ed.), *Diderot et l'art de Boucher à David* (Paris: Réunion des Musées Nationaux, 1984); see also Jean Seznec, 'Diderot et l'affaire Greuze', *Gazette des Beaux-arts*, LXVII (May–June 1966), pp. 339–56; Ledbury, 'Greuze and Sedaine', pp. 173–98.

79 On the commissioning of Sedaine's Russian plays, see Auguste Rey, *Notes sur mon village. La Vieillesse de Sedaine* (Paris: Champion, 1906), pp. 1–20. On *Raimond V*, see also Rayner, 'Sedaine's Dramatic Work', pp. 169–71; Ledbury, 'Greuze and Sedaine', pp. 267–75.

80 For details of the discovery of *Hinkelmann ou les journalistes*, see Ledbury, 'Greuze and Sedaine', Appx 1, pp. 370–88.

81 *Hinkelmann ou les journalistes*, Rondel Ms. 727, IV, p. ix.

82 See the full transcription in Chapter 9, pp. 262ff.

83 Sedaine, 'Quelques réflexions', p. 514.

conscious bitterness was the only result of the *Maillard* débâcle is to miss its subtler consequences. In Sedaine's post-*Maillard* works, one can chart what might be called a sublimated attempt to reform tragedy and to influence the high genre from 'beyond the grave' of practical failure. In the preface to *Les Femmes vengées* Sedaine discussed his stage experiment of showing three scenes simultaneously,[84] and suggests that tragedy (in this case *Britannicus*) might benefit from such scenic innovation. He would continue to make suggestions for improvements to tragedy, using the unlikely settings of his various prefaces, including *Le Mort marié* and *Aucassin et Nicolette*, constantly seeking to prove the transferability of dramatic skills across the unseen but powerful dramatic dividing line. I would suggest that the tone of these prefaces, which can seem pompous and self-aggrandising in the extreme, is profoundly affected by the haunting presence of Sedaine's failed tragedy. However, one might see how some of the ambitions and innovations undoubtedly achieved by Sedaine in the musical dramas (the scrupulous research for *Aucassin et Nicolette*, the vast scale and ambition of *Richard Cœur-de-Lion* or even the exploration of virtue, *patrie* and nation in *Guillaume Tell*) emerge from the frustrated tragic vision of the dramatist, channelled into further innovation. It was in the end the prodigiously and internationally successful *Richard Cœur-de-Lion* which opened the doors of the Academy to Sedaine – a work which combined the elements of medievalism, historical drama, pathos, serious tone, musical experiment and scenic innovation on which Sedaine had focused since *Maillard*.[85]

In the post-*Maillard* period Sedaine's crusade against the separation of the genres was to continue in unexpected, displaced ways in other aspects of his creative life. One of these was in architecture. When Sedaine was appointed as secretary of the Académie Royale d'Architecture in 1768, it was a piece of political manoeuvring following the *affaire de Wailly* in 1767, in which the architects had objected to Charles de Wailly being imposed directly as an architect *de la première classe* rather than being first accorded second-class status.[86] Sedaine was treated with something like contempt by his colleagues (except de Wailly himself and Antoine-Marie Peyre with whom he became

---

84 See the illustration by Charles-Nicholas Cochin for this play, Fig. 6, p. 162.

85 On *Richard Cœur-de-Lion* see especially Charlton, *Grétry*, pp. 226–42; Félix Gaiffe, *Richard Cœur-de-Lion* (Paris: Classiques Larousse, n.d.); Philippe Vendrix (ed.), *Grétry et l'Europe de l'opéra-comique* (Liège: Mardaga, 1992), esp. pp. 331–51.

86 On the Académie Royale d'Architecture, see especially Wolfgang Scholler, *Die Académie Royale d'Architecture. Anatomie einer Institution* (Köln and Weimar: Böhlau, 1993); on Sedaine at the Academy, see Ledbury, 'Greuze and Sedaine', pp. 253–7; the administrative business which occupied Sedaine in this period is chronicled in the *Procès-Verbaux de l'Académie Royale d'Architecture* (11 vols, Paris: J. Schemit, 1911–16), esp. VII–XI. Archival material relating to Sedaine's tenure at this academy is listed in 'A Sedaine Bibliography', Chapter 11 of the present work, Section A.

friendly);[87] but by the mid-1770s, although his relationships with some of the senior architects remained frosty, he had started to establish some kind of status for himself within the Academy, and was asked to speak on various aesthetic and practical matters. One such occasion occurred on 10 December 1776, when he gave a paper at an assembly of the architects entitled 'Refléxions sur les expressions du bon ou mauvais goût appliqués aux arts'.

The manuscript draft of this paper, now in the archives of the Institut de France, betrays many layers of refinements made as Sedaine tackled two issues close to his heart – taste and genre. If not widely known, this manuscript is of great interest.[88] It asserts the primacy of the artist's inspiration against the decorums of 'bon goût', and takes issue with another classic generic opposition which dominated thinking after the d'Angiviller regime had encouraged a strictly classical diet for architects and artists from the early 1770s, the opposition between the Gothic and the Greek:

> L'article goût en architecture inséré par le feu Blondel dans l'encyclopédie dit seulement que l'architecture gothique est de mauvais goût et que l'architecture grecque est du bon goût. Pour moi, ... je pense que même en architecture gothique il peut y avoir des choses d'un bon goût, et qu'en architecture grecque il est quelquefois arrivé d'employer des choses d'un mauvais goût.[89]

This particular heresy must have provoked a few raised eyebrows in the meeting hall of the Academy,[90] and although the whole document might simply be taken as adding to the growing body of evidence for claiming Sedaine as a pre-Romantic figure, I read its significance rather as a challenge to modes of

---

87 I have explored these relationships in '"Vous avez achevé mes tableaux": Michel-Jean Sedaine and Jacques-Louis David', *British Journal for Eighteenth-Century Studies*, forthcoming.

88 As far as I know, the only scholar to analyse this text was Jacques Guillerme, 'Über einige Wandlungen des Wahren in der Architektur', *Daidalos. Berlin Architectural Journal*, VIII (1983), pp. 38–47. I am presently preparing to publish it as part of a long article on Sedaine's experiences at the Académie Royale d'Architecture.

89 Sedaine, 'Réflexions sur les expressions du bon ou mauvais goût appliqués aux arts' [10 December 1776], Dossier B4, Archives de l'Institut, folio 3. The 'feu Blondel' to whom Sedaine is referring is Jacques-François Blondel (1705–74), whose influential articles in the *Encyclopédie* and his *L'Architecture française* (1752–6) and *Cours d'architecture* (1771–6) made him one of the most influential architectural authorities of the century.

90 Of course, the Gothic was not anathema in French architectural circles, and indeed Soufflot and Laugier had analysed aspects of Gothic architecture in favourable terms. See especially Marc-Antoine Laugier, *Essai sur l'architecture* (Paris: Duchesne, 1753), ch. 4, pp. 173ff. For a discussion of architectural theory in later eighteenth-century France, see Wolfgang Herrmann, *Laugier and Eighteenth-Century French Theory* (London: Zwemmer, 1962) and Walter Szambien, *Symétrie, goût, caractère* (Paris: Picard, 1986), which contains a very useful section on the questions of taste that Sedaine's paper raises.

generic understanding that had become even more oppositional and intransigent in academic circles in the course of the 1770s.[91] In expressing these opinions, though, Sedaine was reflecting a growing interest in the medieval, and had read widely in his preparations for *Maillard ou Paris sauvé*. He was also to use a much more thoroughgoing engagement with the medieval for his troubadour satire, *Raimond V, comte de Toulouse*. However, here the emphasis is not on extolling the Gothic *per se*, but on countering traditional modes of thinking about genres. In the same paper, Sedaine talks about the mechanisms of taste as afterthoughts, only superficially altering the products of creative imaginations. This was of course a deeply contentious thought to utter inside an Academy at a time when rules themselves were conceived as natural and innate.

An even more fascinating instance of Sedaine's need to challenge genre oppositions, and in particular to continue to make his repressed reforming zeal exercise influence, is to be witnessed through his remarkable relationship with the painter Jacques-Louis David. This relationship is only just beginning to attract the attention it deserves. It is known that David lived with Sedaine between 1769 and 1772, and probably until 1775, turbulent years for both men, and that, through Sedaine, David was put in contact with a wide range of intellectuals and reformers.[92] Less well known are the continuing relationships between Sedaine and David in the 1780s which my researches have charted.[93] One well-known account of Sedaine's influence over David's work is Alexandre Péron's anecdote concerning the genesis of one of David's most famous 1780s canvases, the *Oath of the Horatii*, describing an occasion in 1782 when Sedaine offered David advice on the creation of his image.

> L'action que tu as choisie, dit Sedaine le premier, est presque nulle; elle est toute en parole; c'est un excellent plaidoyer, favorables [sic] aux beaux mouvements oratoires, qui ont séduit Corneille et l'ont entrainé à faire un hors d'œuvre à sa tragédie. De plus, nos mœurs

[91] The notion of pre-Romanticism, and its manifestations in France, has been thoroughly examined and interrogated in Paul Viallaneix (ed.), *Le Préromantisme* (Actes et Colloques, XVII) (Paris: Klincksieck, 1975). On the Gothic revival and its sources in Europe, see Georg Germann, *Gothic Revival in Europe and Britain. Sources, Influences and Ideas* (London: Lund Humphries, 1972), in which Blondel's work to which Sedaine refers here is discussed on pp. 20–21. See also Lionel Gossman's book on La Curne de Sainte-Palaye, *Medievalism and the Ideologies of the Enlightenment* (Baltimore: Johns Hopkins University Press, 1968).

[92] See Thomas Crow, *Emulation. Making Artists for Revolutionary France* (New Haven and London: Yale University Press, 1995); Reed Benhamou, 'Diderot et l'enseignement de Jacques-Louis David', *Recherches sur Diderot et sur l'encyclopédie*, XXII (1997), pp. 71–86, 191–2.

[93] Ledbury, 'Greuze and Sedaine', pp. 279–319; idem, '"Vous avez achevé mes tableaux"'.

> françaises s'accommoderont-elles de l'autorité farouche d'un père, qui pousse le stoicisme jusqu'à excuser son fils du meurtre de sa propre fille? Non non, ajoute-t-il en ces propres termes, nous ne sommes pas assez *mûres* pour un pareil sujet.[94]

Sedaine's advice here, and the impact that it had on the painting, are worth lingering over. It is clear that Sedaine was here following his post-*Maillard* tendency of demonstrating the flaws in classical tragedy and suggesting how they might be improved. He stresses the importance of action and of *tableaux*, advice which owes much to his own dramaturgy, while his coda to the effect that his proposed scene would be too shocking for a French audience is surely inspired by his own experience in trying and failing to present material of a formally and thematically daring nature on the French stage.

Even if aspects of this anecdote are disputed, solid evidence points to the perhaps surprising fact that David himself may well have been a frequent recipient of important advice from Sedaine on the composition of both his painted images and his public image. In the development from the excessive and rhetorical in some early sketches to the compressed and pantomimic final versions that made his *Oath of the Horatii* (1785) and *Brutus* (1789) so emotionally effective and so universally acclaimed, some of Sedaine's advice quoted above seems to have come to fruition. I believe Sedaine had invested greatly in David's success, not only because of the real quasi-parental emotional bond that linked him to the painter,[95] but also because he saw a way of achieving his own tragic ambitions at one remove. The work of David in the 1780s, and its reception, can be more fully understood if we take seriously the possibility of Sedaine's continuing advice regarding the transformation of the

---

[94] Alexandre Péron, *Examen du Tableau du Serment des Horaces peint par David suivi d'un notice historique du Tableau lus à la société libre des Beaux-Arts* (Paris: Ducessois, n.d.), p. 28. For an examination of the circumstances of this discussion, and the controversy that surrounds it, see Crow, *Emulation*, pp. 31–6. I should add here some new information, which both muddies the waters and ties Sedaine's thinking on a possible plan for David's painting more firmly to his milieu. Bound with a copy of Noverre's ballet *Les Horaces* (dated Vienne en Autriche, 1773) in F-Pa, Rondel Rf. 1972, is an undated pamphlet entitled 'Introduction au ballet des horaces, ou petite réponse aux grandes lettres du Sr Angiolini' in which the anonymous author, presumed to be Noverre, but whose tone is very like Sedaine's, writes the following lines on Corneille's tragedy (pp. 1–2): 'Sa tragédie des Horaces, finit en quelque sorte avec le quatrième acte: Le cinquième est dénué d'action: c'est un magnifique plaidoyer en vers ... c'est un hors d'œuvre ...'. The echo of this analysis in Sedaine's words is remarkable, and one must conjecture either that Sedaine read this pamphlet and took his inspiration for his advice from it or, more likely, that Péron's anecdote mixes Sedaine's own words with citation from this pamphlet.

[95] On this bond, see especially Angélique de Vandeul, 'Notice historique sur Sedaine' in *Correspondance littéraire*, XVI (1797), esp. pp. 242–6; Jean-François Ducis, *Notice sur la vie de Sedaine* in *Œuvres* (3 vols, Paris: Nepveu, 1826), III, pp. 455–60. I explore it in 'Greuze and Sedaine', pp. 279–319.

highest genre, history painting, impacting on David. The success of the *Horatii* and the *Brutus* owes much to the dramaturgy of Sedaine with its multi-layered choreography (discussed in the preface to *Les Femmes vengées*),[96] its poignant intermixture of public and private. One might suggest that David's emphasis of the sewing-basket in the *Brutus*, and his daring exploitation of gaps and incoherences in the picture plane, owes something to the development of what might be called the pathos of objects and the use of ellipsis and poignant silence in Sedaine's drama.[97] Ironically, then, it is in the canvases of David, often perceived as the ultimate *exempla* of the revived high and noble style of French neo-classicism, that we might see achieved at one remove Sedaine's final ambition of a tragedy reformed by the infusion of the energy and appeal of lower, popular genres, an ambition he failed to fulfil in his own explicitly tragic work.

The Revolution, of course, had a profound effect on Sedaine personally. He, like others, greeted it as a liberation,[98] but in the course of the years 1792–4 watched in bemusement and some shock as many of his closest friends emigrated, as his son was called up, his Academic posts (and lodgings) were abolished, and his income was severely reduced by inflation.[99] However, there was no end to the popularity of his work on the French stages.[100] There are other ways in which Sedaine's tragic ambition achieved an unexpected and important afterlife. Much has been said about the conjunction of the Revolutionary political moment with the creation of a new genre, melodrama.[101] We also know through the researches of Emilio Sala and others

---

[96] See pp. 271–2 below.

[97] For an example of the emotional focus on objects, see the motif of the watch in *Le Philosophe sans le savoir* (Act II, sc. X).

[98] For indications of Sedaine's enthusiasm for the first stages of the Revolution, see for example his letter to the Comédie-Française of 4 February 1793, in F-Pcf, *Dossier Sedaine*. On Sedaine's problems in the later stages of the Revolution, see Rey, *Vieillesse de Sedaine*, pp. 61–9. However, Rey over-emphasises Sedaine's lack of enthusiasm for the Revolution, and explains *Guillaume Tell* as a necessary but contrived answer to the questioning of Sedaine's patriotism during the early stages of the Terror.

[99] Rey, *Vieillesse de Sedaine*, p. 68.

[100] For statistics on the performances of Sedaine's plays during the French Revolution, see Emmet Kennedy et al., *Theatre, Opera and Audiences in Revolutionary Paris: Analysis and Repertory* (Westport, Conn.: Greenwood Press, 1996).

[101] On this conjunction, see Peter Brooks, *The Melodramatic Imagination* (New Haven and London: Yale University Press, 1976); idem, 'Melodrama, Body, Revolution' in Jacky Bratton, Jim Cook and Christine Gledhall (eds), *Melodrama: Stage, Picture, Screen* (London: British Film Institute Publications, 1994), pp. 11–24. Among the most important historical studies of melodrama are: Alexis Pitou, 'Les Origines du mélodrame français à la fin du dix-huitième siècle', *Revue de l'histoire littéraire de la France* (April, 1911), pp. 256–96; James F. Mason, *The Melodrama in France from the Revolution to the Beginning of Romantic Drama* (Baltimore: J. H. Furst, 1912); Paul Ginisty, *Le Mélodrame* (Paris: Michaud, 1910); Eise Carel Van Bellen, *Les Origines du mélodrame* (Utrecht: Kemink en zoon, 1927).

that the musical and thematic blueprints for melodrama were created in the 1770s.[102] Sedaine's own bitterness, his opposition to the Comédie-Française, and his interest in non-French genres and theories all make him a key to an understanding of how experimental drama of the later eighteenth century and melodrama as understood by Brooks as a modern cultural discourse are linked. From *Le Déserteur* through *Félix* to *Guillaume Tell*, Sedaine's models of drama moved from tragicomedy with Shakespearean echoes through *Sturm und Drang* ever closer to the mode that Brooks would recognise as melodramatic in his modern, psychological and political sense, and in doing so showed how the emotion and portent of tragedy might be exploited by a genre of psychological and cultural immediacy. Sedaine's apparent failure to reform the high genre, tragedy, led him to experiments which cleared the path for the creation of a new and profoundly modern mode of theatrical creation. If this sounds too grand a claim, we should perhaps remember that Pixérécourt explicitly acknowledged his huge debt to Sedaine when explaining how he came to create the defining melodramas of the early nineteenth century.[103]

Ultimately, then, Sedaine did not win his battle with the structures of genre, and indeed the later verdicts of Hoffman and Geoffroy on his works showed how powerful the concept of genre and the idea of generic purity still remained in France through the Revolution, Directory and Empire periods.[104] However, his constant experiment did lay the foundations for all those forms of alternative theatrical and artistic practice which would eventually win the war with the rules. Sedaine's conscious experiments with generic modes and norms, his creation of a dramaturgy of intimacy, his combination of pastoral and irony, his awareness of the need for an 'effet du réel' and at the same time his acute sense of theatricality provided a blueprint for those practitioners in theatre, art and music-drama who, in the later nineteenth century, were responsible for what we now understand as the transition to modernism. The seemingly 'naïf' Sedaine should be viewed as a sophisticated, pre-modern man of the theatre, whose instincts and talents strained the frameworks of genre which underpinned French classicism, exposing fissures and frailties which were to be thoroughly exploited by modernist revolution.

---

[102] See Emilio Sala, *L'opera senza canto. Il mélo romantico e l'invenzione della colonna sonora* (Venice: Marsilio, 1995); idem, 'Mélodrame. Définitions et métamorphoses d'un genre quasi-opératique', *Revue de musicologie*, LXXXIV/2 (1998), pp. 235–46.

[103] Réné-Charles Guilbert de Pixérécourt, 'Dernières réflexions de l'auteur sur le mélodrame' in *Théâtre choisi* (4 vols, Paris and Nancy: Chez l'auteur, 1841–3), IV, pp. 493, 497.

[104] See Patrick Taïeb's essay, Chapter 8 in this volume, p. 173.

Chapter 2

Les Philosophes and *le savoir*: Words, Gestures and Other Signs in the Era of Sedaine

Sophia Rosenfeld

Historians of the theatre have long insisted that the dramatic works of the last decades of the *ancien régime*, and especially those commonly referred to as *drames*, placed a new and unusual emphasis on the visual.[1] For it is clear even to a late twentieth-century reader that the authors of these *drames* freely borrowed methods and conventions from other contemporary forms of visual spectacle – not only from painting and dance, but also from the various stages of Paris's fairgrounds, where wordless communication played such an important role throughout the eighteenth century. In this regard, the plays of Michel-Jean Sedaine are no exception. Even in his most famous 'serious' work, his first production to be mounted at the Comédie-Française, *Le Philosophe sans le savoir* (1765), Sedaine made use of silent *tableaux*, mimed actions, sudden gestures and facial expressions that were intended to reveal otherwise unarticulated emotions, together with a range of other techniques appropriated from less elevated theatrical settings, including those unofficial theatres prohibited from employing spoken words.[2] The playwright treated these visual forms of communication variously,

[1] On the eighteenth-century *drame* and, especially, its visual dimension, see the classic account of Félix Gaiffe, *Le Drame en France au XVIIIe siècle* (Paris: Armand Colin, 1910), as well as such recent works as: Scott Bryson, *The Chastised Stage: Bourgeois Drama and the Exercise of Power* (Stanford: Anima Libri, 1991), and Angelica Goodden, '"Une Peinture parlante": The *Tableau* and the *Drame*', *French Studies*, XXXVIII/4 (October 1984), pp. 397–413.

[2] On eighteenth-century French fairground theatres and their efforts to develop non-verbal theatrical practices in response to official restrictions on the use of spoken dialogue, see Marie-Françoise Christout, *Le Merveilleux et 'le théâtre du silence' en France à partir du XVIIe siècle* (The Hague and Paris: Mouton, 1965); Oscar Brockett, 'The Fair Theatres of Paris in the Eighteenth Century: The Undermining of the Classical Ideal' in M. J. Anderson (ed.), *Classical Drama and its Influence* (New York: Barnes and Noble, 1965), pp. 251–70; Henri Lagrave, 'La Pantomime à la foire, au Théâtre-Italien et aux boulevards, 1700–1789', *Romanistische Zeitschrift für Literaturgeschichte/Cahiers d'histoire des littératures romanes*, II (1979), pp. 408–43; Robert M. Isherwood, *Farce and Fantasy. Popular Entertainment in Eighteenth-Century Paris* (New

as silent *divertissements* between moments of focused dialogue and as complements to his characters' casual verbal exchanges and sputtering, ellipse-ridden speeches. The result, though essentially a moralising drama, has often served as a prime example of the new aesthetic hybridity of the 1760s.

For historians, however, such artistic products cannot but prompt the question: what inspired this up-and-coming playwright, like so many of his contemporaries, to poach across genres in this particular manner at this particular moment in the eighteenth century? And here too certain answers have become commonplace.[3] To explicate Sedaine's aesthetic decisions, commentators have not only pointed out that the playwright was an associate and disciple of Denis Diderot during the years in which the latter was engaged in imagining a novel synthesis of comedy and tragedy. They have also routinely invoked the fact that Sedaine himself got his start in the world of the fair theatres, writing the libretti for numerous *opéras-comiques* in the 1750s, as well as the fact that he was working on other kinds of projects, including a ballet scenario for the Opéra, almost simultaneously with the debut of his great *drame*, *Le Philosophe sans le savoir*. As is the case with his contemporary, the choreographer Jean-Georges Noverre, Sedaine's professional biography has routinely been offered as the obvious explanation for his mixing of popular and classical theatrical techniques in the context of his most serious work.

But can the rationale behind this deliberate fusing of mid-eighteenth-century conventions – high and low, verbal and visual – really be so easily explained in these terms? More specifically, can Sedaine's personal trajectory fully clarify why he chose to write a prose play, designed in his own words 'pour réconcilier le public avec l'idée du mot *philosophe*',[4] in which problems of misunderstanding and miscommunication figure so heavily and so much is conveyed through non-verbal signs? And if the connection is not immediately apparent, perhaps we need to ask anew: why did mid-eighteenth-century playwrights routinely utilise pantomime and other visual techniques common to fairgrounds, to the *opéra-comique* and, increasingly, to the ballet, in the service of that vehicle of the new philosophy that was the *drame* in prose?

York and Oxford: Oxford University Press, 1986); and Frederick Brown, *Theatre and Revolution: The Culture of the French Stage* (New York: Random House, 1989), pp. 40–64 ('The Speechless Tradition').

[3] On Sedaine's choices in the construction of this play, see the lengthy introductions to the following recently published editions: *Le Philosophe sans le savoir*, ed. Graham E. Rodmell (Durham: University of Durham, 1987); *Le Philosophe sans le savoir*, ed. Robert Garapon (Paris: Aux amateurs de livres, 1990); and *Le Philosophe sans le sçavoir*, ed. John Dunkley (Egham: Runnymede Books, 1993). See too the very interesting commentary in Mark Ledbury, 'Greuze and Sedaine', pp. 107–34.

[4] Sedaine, 'Quelques réflexions', p. 509.

To answer these questions, I contend that we need to look not only at the biographies of artists and writers who moved between high and low theatrical forms, but also at the larger meaning of the 'language of gesture' in mid-eighteenth-century Enlightenment culture and philosophy. For it is clear that Sedaine, like many of his intellectual and aesthetic allies, including Diderot, saw a close connection between non-verbal signs and the philosophic spirit. This chapter aims to demonstrate that the extra-linguistic communication which peppers Sedaine's most famous play was central not only to his efforts to establish a new form of dramatic theatre, but also to the project of defining for his public the attributes of his very modern hero: 'le philosophe sans le savoir'.

To make such a claim, however, one must first take a step back. Well before Diderot articulated his influential dramatic theories in his *Entretiens sur le Fils naturel* of 1757 and *Discours sur la poésie dramatique* of 1758, and well before Sedaine, among others, tried to put these theories into practice in the 1760s, questions about the nature of knowledge and the relative value of different modes of communication had already become central to Enlightenment philosophy.[5] The purpose of language, insisted eighteenth-century empiricist thinkers, was to paint the real world in an accurate fashion. This much was evident. But in the middle of the century it also seemed obvious to many people, especially adherents of sensationalism, that no language or sign system was entirely up to this task. In their comparative musings on the form and effectiveness of different kinds of signs – visual, vocal, natural, artificial – sensationalists accorded linguistic signs special importance as sources and conduits for all complex human ideas about the world. And the French language, that supposed pinnacle of civilisation, won particular praise as the premier vehicle for conducting the philosophical business of the contemporary world. But the words of modern languages, and especially the abstract terms common to French, were also faulted with some major shortcomings, failings that appeared to have serious consequences for modern perceptions of reality or truth.

Beginning with the abbé de Condillac's *Essai sur l'origine des connaissances humaines* (1745) and Diderot's early essay *La Lettre sur les sourds et muets, à l'usage de ceux qui entendent et qui parlent* (1751), the problem of the variable meaning of words, and consequently their susceptibility to misuse and misunderstanding, emerged as one of the key metaphysical issues of the era. John Locke had of course already paid considerable attention at the end of the previous century to what he called the dangers of the 'Abuse of Words', particularly in the

---

[5] On Enlightenment epistemology in general, see Sylvain Auroux, *La Sémiotique des Encyclopédistes: essai d'épistemologie historique des sciences du langage* (Paris: Payot, 1979); Ulrich Ricken, *Linguistics, Anthropology and Philosophy in the French Enlightenment: Language Theory and Ideology* (London and New York: Routledge, 1994); Elena Russo, *Skeptical Selves: Empiricism and Modernity in the French Novel* (Stanford and London: Stanford University Press, 1996), esp. chapter 1.

realm of philosophy, where the meaningless jargon of theologians had, he believed, severely compromised the possibility of arriving at secure truths.[6] But in the middle decades of the new century, Locke's anti-scholastic critiques were taken up with new enthusiasm in Enlightenment circles. And the negative consequences attributed to even the accidental *abus des mots*, as it came to be known, grew increasingly severe.

On the one hand, Diderot and Rousseau both pointed to the failure of everyday words, themselves generally arbitrarily chosen signs in modern languages, to convey true moral or emotional sentiments.[7] For both men, the abstractness of modern terminology was a key reason why poetry had become cold and sterile. And for Rousseau, as the critic Jean Starobinski has famously pointed out, the inadequacy of language also explained why sincere interpersonal expression had become impossible and social alienation had increasingly become the norm.[8] Many other encyclopedists and critics of contemporary society, on the other hand, faulted the ill-defined, loosely employed and vaguely understood terms of modern religion and politics for creating not only intellectual confusion but many of the great unresolved public controversies of the day. Examples of offending words ranged from *liberté* (in the case of Montesquieu) to *luxe* (in the case of the physiocrats) to *Dieu* (in the case of the circle around the Baron d'Holbach), but the consequences were thought to be the same.[9] As the philosopher Claude Adrien Helvétius put it in 1758, building on the ideas of Condillac as well as Locke,

> On voit quel germe éternel de disputes et de calamités renferme souvent l'ignorance de la vraie signification des mots. Sans parler du sang versé par les haines et les disputes théologiques, disputes presque toutes fondées sur un abus des mots, quels autres malheurs encore cette

6 See John Locke, *An Essay concerning Human Understanding* [4th ed., 1700], ed. Peter H. Nidditch (Oxford: Oxford University Press, 1990), chapter IX ('Of the Imperfection of Words'), pp. 475–90, and chapter X ('Of the Abuse of Words'), pp. 490–508.

7 In addition to Denis Diderot's *Lettre sur les sourds et muets* ([Paris]: n.p., 1751), see Jean-Jacques Rousseau's *Discours sur l'origine et les fondemens de l'inégalité parmi les hommes* (Amsterdam: Rey, 1755) and *Essai sur l'origine des langues où il est parlé de la mélodie et de l'imitation musicale* (Geneva: n.p., 1781) on the limitations of modern verbal languages.

8 See Jean Starobinski, *Jean-Jacques Rousseau: Transparency and Obstruction* (Chicago and London: University of Chicago Press, 1980), esp. pp. 304–22.

9 See, for example, Charles Louis de Secondat, Baron de Montesquieu, *De l'Esprit des loix* (2 vols, Geneva: Barrillot et fils, 1748), I, book 2, chapter 2, entitled 'Diverses significations données au mot de liberté'; Jean-François Melon, *Essai politique sur le commerce* (2nd ed., Amsterdam: F. Changuion, 1742), pp. 129–30, on the problem of vagueness in the use of the term *luxe*; and Paul-Henri Dietrich, Baron d'Holbach, *Le Bon-sens, ou Idées naturelles opposées aux idées surnaturelles* (London: n.p., 1772), preface regarding the varied and senseless meanings commonly attached to the word *Dieu*.

> ignorance n'a-t-elle point produits, et dans quelles erreurs n'a-t-elle point jetté les Nations?[10]

For many of the mid-century *philosophes*, in other words, misunderstandings born of the misuse and abuse of language seemed to be at the root of almost all modern social and political ills.

Could anything be done? In fact, few of these men of letters posited concrete solutions to this supposedly widespread socio-linguistic problem. Unlike the seventeenth century, the eighteenth produced little discussion or even hope of finding the perfect language, either Adamic or artificial. But in this climate of concern about the effects of the *abus des mots*, Condillac, Diderot, Rousseau and a host of other mid-century *philosophes* turned their attention to an old question, a question that the Bible was widely believed to have answered long before, namely, the origins of human language. Using the conceit that it would be beneficial to know how humans might hypothetically have gone about inventing a sign system without divine intervention, these men set out to rewrite, by means of reason alone, the story of language: both how it had developed from its initial primitive beginnings in the state of nature and how what we now call signifiers and signifieds (and they called *les mots et les choses*) had become so distant from one another in the course of time.

This task they accomplished in great abundance; there is, of course, a huge eighteenth-century literature on the subject of the history of language.[11] But it was on the very beginnings of the story that these writers lavished much of their attention. For many of these *philosophes* used the opportunity provided by this question to offer a sketch of an ideal idiom, a glimpse of the sign system that had ostensibly existed long before the advent of our duplicitous and faulty words. The hypothesis most commonly articulated, with various modifications, following the publication of Condillac's *Essai*, was that there had once, in the very distant past, been a language of nature, a universal language of bodily gestures and cries that, unlike arbitrary modern languages, was the product of sensation and instinct and thus immediately recognisable, and reproducible, by all human beings. Not only was this so-called *langage d'action* the product of direct and unmediated experience; it remained, when recalled, impossible to misunderstand or

---

10 Claude-Adrien Helvétius, *De l'Esprit* [1758] (Paris: Fayard, 1988), p. 48.

11 On the many eighteenth-century treatments of the problem of the origin of language (including those of Condillac, Diderot and Rousseau), see in particular Daniel Droixhe, *La Linguistique et l'appel de l'histoire, 1600–1800: rationalisme et révolutions positivistes* (Geneva: Droz, 1978), pp. 160–225; Hans Aarsleff, *From Locke to Saussure: Essays on the Study of Language and Intellectual History* (Minneapolis: University of Minnesota Press, 1982), pp. 146–209 and 278–92; and Downing Thomas, *Music and the Origins of Language: Theories from the French Enlightenment* (Cambridge and New York: Cambridge University Press, 1995).

misinterpret. As such, it soon became a common and enticing reference point in Enlightenment thought – and theatre – in many parts of Europe.

At first, certainly, the interest this model generated was purely speculative. After all, in the hands of most *philosophes*, it was presented either as a key feature of a hypothetical pre-history of human society or as a rhetorical tool, a fictional device for reflecting on the development of individuals and their institutions and the shortcomings of their modern equivalents. But in the course of the second half of the eighteenth century, the idea of an original gestural language – itself fuelled both by the reports of travellers to exotic places where pantomime still seemed to function as a viable form of rhetoric, as well as by recent efforts to uncover the silent declamatory practices of antique theatre – soon came to be thought of as a recoverable ideal. Indeed, the notion that there had once been a universal language of natural, iconic signs prompted a series of unusual semiotic experiments beginning in the late 1750s and early 1760s. Such efforts were essentially attempts to restore the timeless utopia predicated on the direct and unmistakable exchange of ideas described by Condillac and others. But this time, in the mid-eighteenth-century, these experiments were conducted neither in daily life nor in society at large but, rather, within the specialised confines of certain restricted spaces in *ancien-régime* culture. In particular, the notion of a long-lost universal pantomimic language, or *langage d'action*, encouraged the development in France of new kinds of theatrical spectacle in which communication would take place not only by means of the abstract, mediated verbal signs common to modernity but also by means of natural and universally comprehensible visual ones.

All of which takes us back, again, to Sedaine's contemporary, Noverre. Jean-Georges Noverre first began to articulate his vision of a *ballet d'action* or tragic pantomime drama in the late 1750s, following his own education in the world of the *opéra-comique* and in the techniques of the British actor David Garrick, as well as in the latest literature on ancient and contemporary theatre and aesthetics.[12] And like Diderot, Noverre announced his aspirations both in practice and in print. For in 1760, while ballet master at the Opéra in Lyon, Noverre published his seminal *Lettres sur la dance et sur les ballets*, in which he roundly criticised contemporary dance and offered a thorough plan of reform for the future. Central to his argument was the notion that opera ballet had become a purely decorative and thus meaningless spectacle. This was a waste, he insisted, because it was clear that dance had once been, and still had the potential to be, an imitative

---

[12] On Noverre and the influences on his work, see Deryck Lynham, *The Chevalier Noverre: The Father of Modern Ballet* (London: Sylvan Press, 1950); Manfred Krüger, *J. G. Noverre und das 'Ballet d'action'. Jean-Georges Noverre und sein Einfluß auf die Ballett Gestaltung* (Emsdetten: Lechte, 1963); Roland Virolle, 'Noverre, Garrick, Diderot: pantomime et littérature' in *Motifs et Figures* (Paris: Presses Universitaires de France, 1974), pp. 201–14; and Marian Hannah Winter, *The Pre-Romantic Ballet* (London: Pitman Publishing, 1974), esp. pp. 113–18.

art form, a means of representing and conveying human sentiments and emotions, just like poetry or drama. In order for choreographers and dancers to make ballets that spoke, and spoke eloquently, he continued, they had only to rediscover the universal art of painting the soul's passions through gestures and actions, or what the ancients called pantomime. '[L]a danse renferme en elle tout ce qui est nécessaire au beau langage,' Noverre explained,

> [et] qu'un homme de génie arrange les lettres, forme et lie les mots, elle cessera d'être muette, elle parlera avec autant de force que d'énergie et les ballets, alors, partageront avec les meilleures pièces du théâtre la gloire de toucher, d'attendrir, de faire couler des larmes ... .[13]

Yet it is important to note that Noverre never sought simply to perpetuate established theatrical forms, merely substituting gestures and visual signs for words. Neither was his principal aim simply to break down the rigid hierarchy of artistic genres. Rather, by restoring pantomime to dance, he hoped to institute a new kind of aesthetic experience, one that transcended the expressive limitations not only of painting, with its frozen images, but also of poetry and traditional drama, with their dependence upon successive but highly intellectualised and conventional words. Noverre, who was familiar with the aesthetics of the abbé Du Bos as well as Diderot's recent theory of the *drame*, believed that the visual, bodily expression of sentiments, passions and ideas could be absorbed by a viewer in a direct and profound manner that words simply could not imitate.[14] Words would become utterly superfluous in his new kind of theatre, he predicted, because communication by means of natural, visual signs always affected spectators more powerfully and more clearly than '[le] discours le plus véhément'.[15] Plus, he added, the universal language of gesture could never lie. And for Noverre, as for many of his contemporaries, such as Diderot and Mercier, it was this experience of unmediated and transparent communication, if directed towards moral ends, that could ultimately make possible the revival, at least in the theatre, of the kind of genuine conflict-free community that had supposedly disappeared with the demise of the original *langage d'action*. Noverre, in sum, certainly made good use of theatrical techniques that he derived from fair and then boulevard stages; but, as with Diderot and ultimately Sedaine, these borrowings were intended simply to be useful tools in their attempts to make the theatre serve a larger social purpose.

---

[13] Jean-Georges Noverre, *Lettres sur la dance* (Paris: Editions Lieutier, 1952), p. 98 (letter II in the original 1760 edition).

[14] Jean-Baptiste Du Bos, *Réflexions critiques sur la poésie et sur la peinture* (Paris: Mariette, 1719).

[15] Ibid., p. 140 (letter IX in the original 1760 edition).

Yet not everyone was convinced. Despite their forceful written articulation, these ideas of Noverre's were not immediately adopted in French theatres of any kind. Certainly, in the 1760s Noverre's fame grew to great proportions around Europe as he staged his pantomimed dramas for numerous noble and royal courts; but he was effectively barred from the most important of venues, the Opéra in Paris. And French intellectuals greeted Noverre's ideas with a combination of enthusiasm and scepticism, adulation and scorn, during these same years. Noverre's earliest backers in France included several well-known *philosophes* – Voltaire and the Baron Grimm among them – who insisted on the importance of the choreographer's innovations both as efforts at necessary theatrical reform and as experiments in devising new ways of conveying information and emotions.[16] Laments similar to that of the abbé Arnaud, who despaired that 'les signes, et si l'on peut s'exprimer ainsi, les hiéroglyphes de cet art [dance] ont perdu de leur noblesse et de leur importance', became a common feature of aesthetic criticism in the 1760s.[17] So did calls for the restoration of these *signes* to contemporary dance. But Noverre's ideas also generated considerable criticism once they were finally implemented in France in the 1770s. Indeed, they quickly became the subject of public debate, much like the quarrel about the relative merits of French and Italian opera that took place during these same years.

For most of the century, aestheticians like Du Bos and the abbé Batteux had been trying to catalogue the different ways in which different kinds of signs functioned and in what capacity, but they had never settled the question. Now the effectiveness of Noverre's *ballets d'action* provided a platform from which to assess the potential of the language of gesture as a conduit for knowledge in the modern world. Critiques tended to fall into one of two categories: some said that gestures were, in fact, less effective or only as effective as words in terms of their ability to convey clear, truthful ideas, and others proposed that gestures were so seductive and potent in comparison to words that they actually produced new kinds of deception. The economist and critic Ange Goudar, for example, argued that gestures were incapable of conveying anything but the simplest emotions and thus left audiences in an even greater state of confusion than did words, while the playwright and academician Jean-François Marmontel warned in the 1770s that gestures, because of their warmth and passion, could persuade one to believe

---

16 See, respectively, the *Œuvres complètes de Voltaire. Correspondance XI. Années 1763–1765* (Paris: Garnier frères, 1881), XLIII, p. 14 (October 1763), p. 195 (April 1764) and pp. 516–17 (April 1765), and the *Correspondance littéraire*, I (15 August 1761), pp. 451–5.

17 Abbé François Arnaud, 'Mémoire sur les danses chinoises d'après une traduction manuscrite de quelques ouvrages de Confucius' [1768] in *Variétés littéraires, ou Recueil de pièces, tant originales que traduites, concernant la philosophie, la littérature et les arts* (4 vols, Paris: Xhrouet, 1804), I, p. 425.

almost anything.[18] What remains interesting is less the specificity of the arguments on either side than the fact that this public debate about meaning and communication, with the ballet at its centre, spilled over into so many different realms.

How can we account for the common concerns at this particular moment of those whose business was words and those whose *métier* revolved around silent display? In effect, the generation of the encyclopedists and the key theatrical innovators of the mid-eighteenth century, including Sedaine, shared a fascination with what could or could not be conveyed in visual or verbal fashion, with how differently ideas might be framed and processed depending on the means used to relay them. In part, this was a question of intellectual fashion, an outgrowth of an increasingly popular sensationalist philosophy. But partly it stemmed from their mutual professional concerns as Enlightenment *gens de lettres*; for both the eighteenth-century *philosophe* and the man of the theatre saw his business as the successful navigation of the treacherous world of communication, from ideas to conversation to publication or performance.

Not surprisingly, a certain number of experiments with new forms of communication – including the language of gesture – took place within the confines of major institutions of Enlightenment sociability, like the learned society, the private classroom and the scholarly journal. But a significant number of these experiments occurred in the theatre. For in this protected social space the limits of language could be tested dramatically. Ideally, the deceptive semiotic practices of the present culture could be overcome, and the unmediated, unmistakable and forgotten practices of some distant past could be revived – all in preparation for their reintroduction to modern society as a whole.

Le Philosophe sans le savoir provides us with a perfect example of these processes. One of the most remarkable aspects of Sedaine's play is the way in which the author considers this question about the efficacy of different kinds of language in a play that is itself essentially constructed as an elaborate explication of a term (*philosophe*), much like an article in that ultimate eighteenth-century book of words, the *Encyclopédie*. From the beginning, the narrative turns on problems of knowledge and the sources of misunderstanding. In the very first scene, for example, the servant-girl Victorine tries, in conversation with her father, to make sense of a bit of gossip that she has overheard. But the conclusion of this initial scene is open-ended, as her father, Antoine, leaves her (and the audience)

---

[18] Among many works by Ange Goudar in which he discusses the ineffectiveness of pantomime, see *Observations sur les trois derniers ballets pantomimes qui ont paru aux Italiens et aux François, sçavoir: Télémaque, Le Sultan Généreux, la Mort d'Orphée* (n.p., 1759) and (under the name of his wife, Sara Goudar) *De Venise. Remarques sur la musique et la danse, ou Lettres de M. G*** à Milord P[embroke]* (Venice: C. Palese, 1773). For Marmontel's argument against gestural theatre, see his entry 'Pantomime' in the *Supplément à l'Encyclopédie* (4 vols, Amsterdam, 1776–7), IV, pp. 231–3.

with a rhetorical question: 'Et comment s'informer dans une grande ville?...' (Act I, sc. I).[19] Finally, in the last scene of the play, shortly after telling Vanderk, our *philosophe*, with a prearranged signal of three knocks, that his son has died in an ill-conceived duel, Antoine has to confront the fact that he has failed as an effective informant; he has seen recent events incorrectly as a result of a visual deception (the effects of distance have made a bullet piercing a hat look like a bullet through the head) and has arrived at a false judgement. Not only is life in the Vanderk household filled with strategic secrets, guesses and revelations. Sedaine, in this play, constantly keeps alive the idea that there are multiple sources of information and disinformation, multiple ways both of knowing and of being misled.

Indeed, this idea is central not only to the plot of the play but to character differentiation within it. The great virtue of Vanderk, Sedaine's *philosophe*-hero, is his special ability to grasp the significance of events around him, to arrive at sound and honest judgements, and to encourage others to do the same. Not that Vanderk is a man of letters or a savant, eager to explain problems of epistemology to his household. Sedaine deliberately makes his main character out to be a merchant, a practical man of the world. Thus what establishes Vanderk as a *philosophe* is not a question of the opinions he holds or the decisions he makes or the erudite knowledge he possesses; one interpretation of the title suggests that he is, in fact, without *savoir*. Rather, it is this character's particular way of thinking and expressing himself, combined with his personal integrity. Vanderk believes in reason (and the word crops up at numerous points in his speeches), but a reason based on what he has noted and analysed for himself and tempered by circumstance, social and moral considerations, compassion, and love of truth. And in this play the evidence Vanderk weighs comes in both verbal and non-verbal forms, one type of clue sometimes turning out to be more revealing or true than another.

In one crucial scene, for example, Vanderk *père* senses that something is the matter with his son. He bases this insight not on what his son says vocally but, rather, on his expressive body language. Thus the father immediately demands, 'Eh, mais, mon fils, quelle pétulance! quels mouvements! que signifie?...' (Act II, sc. IV). The audience is treated to a small joke when the son replies that he is only practising 'acting' or 'déclamation'; but the point of the scene changes as Vanderk *père* responds by warning his son against trying to fool or 'tromper' his own father and by encouraging him to speak his mind honestly so that Vanderk may once again take his son's word as the truth.

Of course, in this play, all such dialogue takes place in the tightly structured confines of one extended family's house in an unnamed French city; this is

---

[19] All citations from the play are taken from the 1766 edition, as edited by Graham E. Rodmell (see note 3).

essentially a domestic drama. Yet it is clear that Sedaine's horizons are wider than the home. Indeed, the fatherly businessman-as-*philosophe* offers guidelines not only for his own son's conduct, but also, as Sedaine makes clear, for the establishment of a cosmopolitan world devoid of the deception and miscommunication occasioned by the *abus des mots*, in short, for the true social harmony often associated with the long-lost state of nature. In a key line in the final act, Desparville, a former officer and an aristocratic client of Vanderk, announces: 'l'univers ne seroit qu'une famille, si tout le monde pensait comme vous' (Act V, sc. IV). This line can be read in many ways, of course. But the fact that Vanderk remains a 'philosophe sans le savoir', neither self-conscious about his philosophical way of seeing and analysing the world nor a savant, suggests the applicability of this model to men everywhere (and I use the word men deliberately, since standards for women, at least of lower social status, are quite different in this play), regardless of station or profession, and including even Sedaine himself.[20] Not only does Sedaine's own technique allow us to see the thought processes of his main subject in both theory and practice (after all, like any good definition, the play never makes use either of the actual word *philosophe* or any of its variants). But Sedaine has also constructed a drama in which the audience must be sensible and rational enough to weigh and judge the evidence with which the playwright has provided them: in brief, to think like unselfconscious *philosophes* too.

In fact, Sedaine does not simply make problems of communication central to the dialogue of his play. He also makes them central to the drama's formal structure, embodying different messages in different kinds of signs, from details of costumes to sound-effects to offhand gestures.[21] Certainly, Vanderk, like a traditional hero, is given the opportunity to convey his moral precepts in a few central speeches. But at other moments, Sedaine's technique for communicating with his audience seems closer to that of Noverre. At one juncture in this *drame*, as Vanderk *fils* tries to bid his father farewell, the reader is simply told of the ensuing physical actions that should transpire on stage:

---

[20] The question of who in French society was supposed to have the capacity and the need to act like a *philosophe* is an extremely important one that cannot be fully explored here. Diderot insisted that a playwright must be a *philosophe* in his own right so as to create characters capable of encouraging rational and moral conduct. But not all characters in either his or Sedaine's *drames* uphold this ideal themselves. In a crucial scene in *Le Philosophe sans le savoir*, for example, Victorine is encouraged by her father to be honest and wise but not so curious because *la curiosité*, as a trait, is inappropriate to her age and gender, not to mention her social station.

[21] On the significance of specific details of military costumes in *Le Philosophe sans le savoir*, see the edition of the play edited by Dunkley (cited in note 3), pp. 86n and 118n.

> Son père le repousse avec tendresse, et ne l'embrasse pas. Le fils fait quelques pas pour sortir; il se retourne, et tend les bras à son père, qui lui fait signe de partir (Act III, sc. XI).

Surely, the purpose of such purely visual scenes is not only to convey new information to the audience about these characters, but also to move the audience in the process, to use the universal language of gesture to create a common emotional bond among all assembled. As we have seen, the members of Sedaine's audience are expected to weigh the evidence and make sound judgements about characters and events, following the example of the *philosophe* himself. But they are also, like the spectators at one of Noverre's *ballets d'action*, given the opportunity to experience the heightened effects of a different kind of visual, physical communication in anticipation of a better, more transparent world to come.

How, then, is *Le Philosophe sans le savoir* related to the general project of the Enlightenment? Since the eighteenth century, the *drame* has often been described as a vehicle for forwarding the social and moral programme of the *philosophes*: for attacking contemporary prejudices and for supporting reformist causes. Sedaine himself, as is well known, declared in the middle of the Revolution that he wrote this play essentially as a meditation on the equality of estates, respect for commerce, the dangers of duelling, and freedom of religion; and one could easily add some additional Enlightenment themes, including the advantages of cosmopolitanism and the virtue of family, to his list.[22] Indeed, it is the combination of such elevated moral and 'philosophical' topics with stylistic conventions borrowed from the *opéra-comique* and other hybrid or base theatrical forms that is generally taken to be emblematic of the late eighteenth-century *drame*.

I propose, however, that this play is linked to the concerns of the *philosophes* not only by virtue of its didactic themes. The connection is also a consequence of the *drame*'s epistemological foundations. In an intellectual climate infused with faith in the power of words as well as fear of that same power, it is not surprising that the *philosophes* saw reasons to champion and to participate in the theatrical experiments of the second half of the eighteenth century. It is also not surprising that the creators of pantomimic spectacles – whether painted, danced or acted, whether silent or coupled with other kinds of vocal signs – often believed they were forwarding the larger goals of the Enlightenment and not simply finding new uses for baser and more visual theatrical forms. For in the mid-eighteenth century, philosophy and theatre both provided utopian venues in which the *abus des mots* could be overcome and novel solutions to questions of

---

[22] Letter from Sedaine to the officials of the Comédie-Française (4 February 1793), cited in the introduction to *Le Philosophe sans le savoir* (ed. Rodmell), p. 14.

savoir could be dramatised and tested. What linked these two pursuits most closely, in other words, was an obsession with discovering new, foolproof ways of knowing, communicating and understanding. *Le Philosophe sans le savoir* is one of the more successful efforts of the 1760s to bring this quest to life.

Chapter 3

The Representation of the Female in the Dramas of Sedaine

John Dunkley

Critics who attended the first performances of *Le Philosophe sans le savoir* appreciated that the role of Victorine was something quite new in the theatre, and the freshness and originality of the role was finely analysed by Sedaine's friend and fellow playwright, Antoine-Marin Lemierre.[1] It is of course tempting to remark that any novelty would have caught the attention of an audience at the Comédie-Française, which had, in the first half of the eighteenth century, been so starved of innovation. However, this critical reaction certainly indicates that Sedaine's conception of Victorine was perceived as innovative and justifies an investigation, pursued across a broader spectrum of his plays, of the female roles he created.

It is difficult to arrive at a general synthesis of the female roles in the work of a dramatist whose range is as wide as Sedaine's and which includes *opéra-comique*, tragedy, a *ballet-héroïque* and the model *drame* of the century. The different traditions operating in these disparate genres, which audiences expected to see upheld, to some extent inevitably obscure Sedaine's own perspectives in the texts which he produced.[2] Sensitivity to the expectations of the audience, in the context of productions at the Théâtre Italien or the Comédie-Française, implied sanitising or gentrifying material for the upper strata of Parisian society, with their particular norms, preoccupations, fashions and illusions. It is clear that the shepherds of *Rose et Colas* inhabit, if not exactly Arcadia, at least a countryside that never existed, and that Parisians

1 See *Mercure de France* (January 1766), p. 200; Antoine-Marin Lemierre and Michel-Jean Sedaine, *Discours prononcés dans l'Académie Françoise ... à la réception de M. Sedaine* (Paris: Demonneville, 1786), p. 20. See *Le Philosophe sans le sçavoir*, ed. John Dunkley (Egham: Runnymede Books, 1993), pp. 59–61.

2 For a discussion of the composition and the expectations of theatre audiences in eighteenth-century Paris, see John Lough, *Paris Theatre Audiences of the Seventeenth and Eighteenth Centuries* (Oxford and London: Oxford University Press, 1957); Henri Lagrave, *Le Théâtre et le public en France* (Paris: Klincksieck, 1972); idem, 'Privilèges et libertés' in Jacqueline de Jomaron (ed.), *Le Théâtre en France*, I: *Du Moyen Age à 1789* (2nd ed., Paris: Armand Colin, 1992), pp. 235–94; Martine de Rougemont, *La Vie théâtrale au XVIIIe siècle* (Geneva: Champion-Slatkine, 1988).

cultivated this illusion to contrast with the all too perceptible filth of the town. (In fact, the realities of peasant life were even more squalid.)[3]

But is the world of *Le Philosophe sans le savoir* in fact any more plausible? Is the *drame* a more accurate, because less traditional, reflector of Enlightenment world-views, and does the fact that the theorists of the *drame* advocated more faithful representation of contemporary conditions allow us to consider their productions as more socially accurate evocations of eighteenth-century society and its problems?

And what of the plays which are neither musical comedies nor *drames*, *La Gageure imprévue*, for instance – a comedy produced at the Comédie-Française? Are the female roles in these works significantly different from those in the works for the Opéra-Comique or the Théâtre Italien? Given that the female characters seem to take a more proactive role in spoken dramas, it is important to take account of the difference between *La Gageure imprévue* and those *opéras-comiques* such as *Les Femmes vengées* where female characters also play a prominent role.

There is an obvious difference between the dramas written for production by the Italiens and those written for the Comédie-Française, namely, the Italiens' ready acceptance of music and the Comédie-Française's extreme reluctance to include any. (One recalls the difficulties which Beaumarchais encountered with *Le Barbier de Séville* in this respect.[4]) But this difference, for all its obviousness, might be less fundamental than it first appears. Quite apart from its aesthetic value, the song constitutes a sign of the artificiality of the theatrical experience. But, if we say 'artificiality', we also imply an artifex whose optic on the real world is articulated through the totality of the dramatic work – for us, necessarily restricted to the text rather than the text transformed into performance.[5] Neither do the fundamental differences of house style obviate the fact that the same writer is writing for both audiences. It is not as if Sedaine laid aside his ethical and political perspectives on the world around him when he wrote for the Italiens, or assumed some when he wrote for the Comédie-Française. He is a *philosophe* in these respects, and the evidence

---

[3] Evidence of the poverty and hardship of peasant life in the period abounds, and the remark of François Lebrun, when he evokes the state of the west of France in the 1770s, is typical: 'la misère structurelle, fondamentale, désespérante, résultant du véritable sous-développement matériel et culturel [...]: alimentation insuffisante et mal équilibrée, hygiène lamentable, analphabétisme massif'. *Se Soigner autrefois* (Paris: Editions du Seuil, 1995), p. 178.

[4] On the complex genesis of the *Barbier de Séville*, see Emile Jules Arnould, *La Genèse du 'Barbier de Séville'* (Dublin: Dublin University Press; Paris: Minard, 1965).

[5] We do this while bearing in mind the caveats suggested by Anne Ubersfeld in her *Lire le théâtre* (4th ed., Paris: Editions Sociales, 1982), passim.

suggests that he did not cease thinking as one when he was writing the operatic pieces, or assume the mantle of one for the Comédie-Française.[6]

The Italien and Foire plays present a broad range of female roles, from the young to the very old and from the nobility to the peasantry. The settings into which the roles are integrated include castles (*Le Diable à quatre, Richard Cœur-de-Lion, Aucassin et Nicolette*), a farm near a village in a remote province (*Félix*), a village on the frontier of Flanders (*Le Déserteur*) and a painter's studio in Rheims (*Les Femmes vengées*). This is not simply a matter of convenience or convention, since Sedaine, unlike writers who situate plays 'à Paris, dans la maison de X', uses a precise setting to imply the social norms which govern its inhabitants and the mentality which an audience will expect them to exemplify, and then, within the parameters of those expectations, modulates and refines the roles as they interact.

As with most eighteenth-century comedies, the central problem around which the plays revolve is that of male/female relations in the context of courtship or post-marital dalliance. If Sedaine had limited himself, like many of his contemporaries, simply to offering variants on the *mariage contrarié/mariage forcé* theme (which typically involves a girl loving, and finally marrying, someone other than the partner whom either or both her parents has chosen for her) there would probably be little of note to distinguish his work from theirs. But, in some plays, he offers a number of interesting inflections on the trite formulae, both in terms of the plot and of the characters who drive it forward. The result is that, even in plays which seem superficially to be light entertainment, there is sometimes embedded a complex and coherent vision of the female personality as it integrates into, or accommodates with, or manipulates, the social structures of the period.[7]

This assertion must of course be qualified, because to claim the same subtlety of conception for all the dramas would be to overstate the case. The representation of female characters in *Le Roi et le fermier* (1762), for instance, offers a view which conforms largely to the norms both of the genre and of the period.[8] In this work, the peasant girl, Jenny, is cast as the victim of the lust of

---

[6] On the philosophical bases of *drame* writing, see Félix Gaiffe, *Le Drame en France au XVIIIe siècle* (Paris: Armand Colin, 1910); Jean-Pierre Sarrazac, 'Le Drame selon les moralistes et les philosophes' in de Jomaron (ed.), *Le Théâtre en France*, I, pp. 295–353.

[7] Recent historical research has done much to illuminate the construction of the female in early modern Europe. See especially Natalie Zemon Davis and Arlette Farge (eds), *A History of Women. Renaissance and Enlightenment Paradoxes* (Harvard: Harvard University Press, 1993). On the French Enlightenment construction of the female character, see also Lieselotte Steinbrügge, *The Moral Sex. Woman's Nature in the French Enlightenment* (Oxford: Oxford University Press, 1992).

[8] Unless otherwise stated, all references will bear on the texts given in *Œuvres choisies de Sedaine* (Paris: Hachette, 1860). In all cases, the spelling has been modernised. For views on *Le Roi et le fermier* which diverge from my own, see Michel Noiray, 'Quatre rois à la chasse: Dodsley, Collé, Sedaine, Goldoni', Chapter 5 in this volume, and also Marvin Carlson,

the aristocrat Lurewel (Richard says in scene IV that she has been 'enlevée, séduite, trompée'). Lurewel later tells a courtier that 'elle fait la sotte', which represents his view (a literary-aristocratic cliché) of her defence of her honour. In a sense, she is also the victim of Richard in that by demonstrating some of the characteristics which patriarchal society desired of the ideal woman at this period ('Ma Jenny est si douce, si timide': Act I, sc. V) she is validating the patriarchal mode by inviting domination. Where 'douceur' is a constant, the tendency is for others to take it for granted and not to strive unnecessarily to deserve it. And to be 'timide' implies a willingness to defer to a man for the sole reason of gender, which can mean environmental constraints or (deriving from them) lethargy in the face of choice. Richard, *qua* male, prizes these subservient characteristics because they are useful to him in that they reaffirm his patriarchal role, which he asserts by assuming the right to speak brusquely (to Betsy, who asks 'avec timidité' if it is indeed Richard that is entering the house, he responds 'Hé bien! me laisseras-tu en repos? Que me veux-tu?', Act I, sc. VI) and to give orders to women ('Allons, ma mère, vite, le couvert. Donne un siège, toi. Du jambon, une salade, tout ce que nous avons [...] Tiens, Betsy, porte cela et va tout de suite à la cave ...', Act III, sc. II) while showing the ultimate signs of deference to an upper-class male: 'Voulez-vous que je vous tire vos bottes?' Female deference and subservience are again foregrounded in Act III, scene IV. Here, La Mère sings a deferential (and, intellectually, barely coherent) *ariette* to the 'Monsieur', inviting him to eat, while none of the three women will join the men for the meal, two having already eaten and the other intending to eat later. This is an exclusion-marker, all the more emphatic because it involves *self*-exclusion, since Richard actually invites his mother to join them. The familiar hierarchical superiority of noble to peasant, and male to female, is quite clearly reflected here by Sedaine's conception of the roles.

Act III opens with a 'tableau' in which Jenny, Betsy and Richard's mother are spinning and sewing in the farmhouse. The conversation turns on their current situation but, more importantly, contains discourse-markers of its inherent femaleness ('Donnez-moi mon rouet ...'; 'Voulez-vous prendre votre dévidoir?') which double the visual ones – within the *interior* of a building – offered by the stage-directions.[9] In addition, when the men enter, the women

'Il re alla caccia and *Le Roi et le fermier*. Italian and French Treatments of Class and Gender' in Mary Hunter and James Webster (eds), *Opera buffa in Mozart's Vienna* (Cambridge: Cambridge University Press, 1997), pp. 82–97.

9 The educational and the purely fictional texts of the period typically associate females with the interior of houses, and males with the world beyond, with its connotations of experience, social contact and danger. This 'separation of spheres' has recently been the subject of much scholarly attention. See Sarah Maza, 'The Bourgeois Family Revisited. Sentimentalism and Social Class in Prerevolutionary French Culture' in Richard Rand (ed.), *Intimate Encounters. Love and Domesticity in Eighteenth-Century France* (Princeton: Princeton University Press, 1997), pp. 39–49. On the condition of the *foyer* in eighteenth-

literally cast their work aside, thus offering the visual signal that it is trivial by comparison with social intercourse with the males.

Briefly, then, one could say that *Le Roi et le fermier* exhibits signs of a stage fantasy with peasants: the visual component, the dialogue and the mentality which underpins it. We know from pictorial sources how the farmhouse was represented on stage: clearly, it functioned as a theatrical *sign* rather than a replica of real conditions.[10] But the mentality and the cast of the conversation which illustrate it appear to be based on observation of contemporary conditions rather than in arcadian fantasy.[11] Certainly, the dialogue is to be taken as authentic in the sense that it is not couched in the stage peasant language of, say, Lucas in Boindin's *Le Bal d'Auteuil*, with its characteristic popular pronunciations and grammatical errors.[12] Nor is any of the characters cast as the butt of satirical observation. Therefore, whereas the setting falls into the domain of *le vraisemblable*, the dialogue and the stage-directions align with *le vrai* in the way that Diderot was proposing for the *drame*.

If *Le Roi et le fermier* offers a representation of the female more or less in conformity with the prevailing conventions of the genre of light comedy, one can detect in *Le Déserteur* of 1769 something slightly different. In Act I, scene II, where all the peasant characters are conversing together, it is noticeable that La Tante and Jeannette, and sometimes Louise too, repeatedly give identical, sequentially delivered responses to Jean-Louis's information, and that all the responses are either simple sentences ('Il n'a pas parlé') or not sentences at all ('Dans son régiment!'; 'Dans quinze jours?'). The whole peasant group is presented (to the metropolitan audience) as simple. This is reinforced by the stage-direction, '*Il* [Jean-Louis] *a une baguette à la main, dont il niaise*', by Jean-Louis's phrase 'quand je lis dans mon gros livre' and by his admiring repetition of the duchess's subjunctive 'Que je ne doive en dire!' But, in this same context, we find the disingenuous question put into the mouth of Jeannette, when she reacts to Jean-Louis's cliché, 'Ah! c'est une belle chose que la guerre': 'Pourquoi est-ce que les garçons pleurent pour n'y pas aller?', to which the response comes: 'Taisez-vous, ça ne vous regarde

---

century France, see Annick Pardailhé-Galabrun, *La Naissance de l'intime. 3000 foyers parisiens XVIIe–XVIIIe siècles* (Paris: Presses Universitaires de France, 1988); see also Philippe Ariès and George Duby (eds), *Histoire de la vie privée* (Paris: Seuil, 1985–7), especially vol. III, *De la Renaissance aux Lumières*.

10 See below, Figs 9–10, pp. 168–9.

11 Bachaumont, Grimm and the *Mercure*, for instance, all praised the naturalness of Sedaine's dialogue; see our essay, '"Natural" dialogue in Sedaine's *Le Philosophe sans le savoir*' in John Dunkley and Bill Kirton (eds), *Voices in the Air: French Dramatists and the Resources of Language. Essays in honour of Charles Chadwick* (Glasgow: University of Glasgow, 1992), pp. 71–85 [74].

12 In Nicolas Boindin, *Quatre comédies (1701–1707)*, ed. John Dunkley (Paris: Société des Textes Français Modernes, 1997), passim.

pas.' Clearly, to impose silence is to admit that the question is unanswerable without denying the cliché. It cannot be insignificant, first, that the bluntly rational question is so strikingly at variance with the rest of a conversation so marked by the absence of intelligence and, secondly, that it is put by a female character who is silenced at once and who remains silent for the rest of the scene. While it would be unwise to attribute excessive significance to a single reply, it is clear that Sedaine is locating the antithesis of the cliché, and of the traditional discourse, in the mouth of a female character. It may also be noted that both the characters who initiate the action, the duchess, with her instruction, and Louise, who concludes it, are female. What is more, in her plea to the king, Louise uses the assertion of her inferior, female status as an instrument to obtain Alexis's release:

> Que suis-je, moi? moins que rien sur la terre,
> Trop faible hélas, pour travailler aux champs;
> Et mon amant pourrait aider mon père,
> Dans ses travaux au déclin de ses ans.[13]

But the use of female frailty as a source of strength is not a recurrent topos in Sedaine, except in so far as it is compensated for by an increased need for a female to use subtlety in order to impose her wishes. Scene X of *On ne s'avise jamais de tout* is an example of this.[14] In this scene, Lise plays along with Margarita's conservatism while at the same time keeping a lookout for Dorval (and here her behaviour differs from the more confrontational style of Rosine, placed in a similar situation in Beaumarchais's *Le Barbier de Séville*, Act I, sc. III). But subtlety is the second best, the coping strategy of the disempowered, and implies avoidance of overt conflict because it would be fruitless. It also implies a greater degree of intelligence than that needed simply to command.

Before coming to *La Gageure imprévue*, where female intelligence is a focal issue in a competitive context, it is worthwhile briefly to explore some of the other female roles from the broad range which Sedaine creates. Older women figure prominently, for example, in *On ne s'avise jamais de tout* (Margarita, the gullible duenna), in *Les Sabots* (Mathurine, the marriageable widow) and in *Rose et Colas* (La Mère Bobi, aged ninety-four). The prominence of their roles varies. That of La Mère Bobi is caricatural. She appears in scene II with the *ariette* 'La Sagesse est un trésor', a nonsense song in which she recounts how she is the butt of children's teasing. The song opens with a cliché and a *lapalissade* which function as character-signs. Her 'On pense que je radote' is echoed in the following scene by Rose's commentary, 'Voyez quel radotage!' As in her song, she returns in scene XV with more

---

13 See Act III, sc. VI.

14 Edition printed by P.-R.-C. Ballard, 'par exprès commandement de Sa Majesté', 1770, vol. II.

complaints about young people and more homespun observations, along the lines of 'c'est la négligence des pères qui dérange les enfants', 'A père négligent, enfant libertin', 'à présent ce sont les enfants qui conduisent les pères', and so on.

Although the role is a purely functional one, it is interesting to note that its content of popular wisdom, a certain tendency to violence and the regret for times past is not simply connoted with old age but also with stupidity. While great significance should not be attached to the indicators provided by this minor role in itself, it offers a notable contrast to the remarks of Maturin about his daughter: 'Oui, elle me gêne, elle me gêne ... plus que feue ma femme. Si je bois, si je jure, si je dis quelque drôlerie, elle me reprend: c'est comme ma femme, et pis encore; car il faut respecter la jeunesse' (sc. VIII). This is in a sense a revolutionary remark in that contemporary society generally respected age, not youth, and, contrasted with a portrayal of old age connoted with stupidity (in fact more typical of the *seventeenth* century), it may assume the dimension of a *prise de position*. Moreover, this conjecture would be supported by the evidence of *Le Philosophe sans le savoir*, where the young are to be taken seriously (as Vanderk does) and where the congener of La Mère Bobi, La Tante, figures as a foil to her idealised brother and as an object of ridicule, again associated with the trappings of tradition.

Age seems not, in itself, to be a significant determinant of sagacity or stupidity in Sedaine's dramaturgy for it can be inferred, from the age of Vanderk's children, that La Tante and Mathurine, in *Les Sabots*, are conceived as being of a comparable age. Using the same procedure as he had to present La Mère Bobi, Sedaine introduces Mathurine in scene II, and the basic traits of the role are presented immediately – in this case a jovial, down-to-earth rationality. She enters laughing at the sight of Lucas striking himself and remarks: '... je ne voudrais pas être votre femme. Si vous vous battez vous-même, que lui feriez-vous donc?' In fact, she *does* end by marrying him, and his appraisal of her has an equally practical ring to it: 'elle n'est pas sotte, Mathurine; elle est encore fraîche, cette femme-là; elle vous a un œil éveillé! c'est qu'elle se porte bien' (sc. VI). This evaluation would be true for the real peasant society of the day, where physical frailty represented a serious burden and robust health a materially important advantage.[15]

The outcome of the plot is presented as suitable in that Colin will marry Babet, and Lucas, Mathurine. Each partner will be of the same age-group, therefore. But an important point enters the picture here, and that is the strong interest which Lucas has taken in Babet and which his marriage to Mathurine will allow legitimately to continue. Lucas's prudent realisation that 'Jeune fille

[15] Little, if any, change had occurred since the time of Vauban's *La Dîme royale* of 1707. See the summary and comments of Wendy Gibson in *Women in Seventeenth-Century France* (London: Macmillan, 1989), pp. 124–5.

et barbe grise / Me paraissent peu de mise', which comes in the closing vaudeville, is a rationalisation of his position in the light of Babet's emphatic and natural preference for Colin, but his reason for proposing to Mathurine is only incidentally and conveniently her qualities, and, far more clearly, his continuing interest in Babet:

LUCAS:	Comment! je ne verrais plus Babet?
MATHURINE:	Non.
LUCAS:	Non, non! Non, c'est inutile; j'aime trop Babet. Si je ne la voyais plus, je mourrais. Il y a un biais à tout; tenez, Mathurine, marions-nous; et si je ne peux faire l'amour à Babet, je peux lui faire du bien un jour à venir.
BABET:	Et je vous aimerai bien comme mon beau-père.
LUCAS:	Qu'en dites-vous, Mathurine?
MATHURINE:	Hé mais! compère, c'est faisable.
LUCAS:	Oui, c'est faisable. Ils sont tous chez nous pour souper, on ne se moquera pas de moi. Je verrai Babet; car, tenez, Mathurine, satigué, tatigué, toute cette ardeur-là ne se passera qu'avec vous. (scene XIII)

No female voice is raised against this arguably incestuous and certainly insulting arrangement, but perhaps this is a case where the exigencies of the genre are less strictly moral than they would be in a *drame*.

Sedaine seldom foregrounds so prominently the emotional links between older men and younger women, and yet one such link is present in several plays and librettos: that of father and daughter. This appears in the visually lively episode of scenes XII–XIV of *Rose et Colas*.[16] Here, Colin visits Rose, entering by the skylight, which then closes and prevents his leaving. He is perched on the sill when Rose's father enters and picks up the ball of thread which Rose had earlier thrown to signal her presence to Colin. She snatches it back, while her father teases her about her carelessness. Follows the story about Colas's being sent away at that very moment. The father continues:

> Ah! tu es curieuse! ah, tu boudes, tu ne dis mot! Oui, hein? ah, tu boudes! ah, c'est cruel! Ah, quelle douleur! Ha, ha, ha! tout cela m'ennuie, tout cela me donne envie de dormir. Oui, on va la marier, une paresseuse, qui n'est capable de rien ...[17]

---

16 The process of courtship among the peasant classes is described by François Lebrun in *La Vie conjugale sous l'Ancien Régime* (Paris: Armand Colin, 1975), p. 25. Sedaine is here extending the more tentative traditional processes.

17 Sc. XIII.

and he goes on to tease her, mingling criticisms of her ('une paresseuse ... capable de rien ... une vaniteuse' and so on) with forced yawns in order to draw out the story (verbal torture) that Colas is being sent away for being 'un libertin, un vagabond, qui est amoureux de toutes les filles, qui en conte à toutes celles qu'il voit ...'. The whole scene is finely calculated to be self-annihilating in the two senses that, firstly, an audience knows from the genre of the play what the outcome will be and, secondly, that it would be so overtly cruel if taken seriously that excess itself is a sign that its meaning is the very opposite of its outward appearance. It becomes therefore a sign of closeness and of love.

Le Mort marié of 1771[18] contains a similar relationship between Monsieur Desbarres and his daughter.[19] Angélique has been corresponding with her lover, Déternois, while she was still in the convent. (So much for its morally educative value.) Angélique pretends to her father that she thought it was permissible to write to Déternois from the convent, although he had in fact forbidden the sending and receiving of letters except between Angélique and her sister because only the lovers' youth was an obstacle to their marriage, and for other reasons which he had not made explicit. Therefore, Angélique argues (in keeping with late eighteenth-century legal theory), writing to Déternois was permitted because it had not been expressly forbidden. Her father rejects this piece of logic-chopping: 'Il y a mille choses que je ne vous ai pas défendues, et que je ne vous défendrai jamais; parce que je ne présume pas qu'une honnête fille puisse les faire.' The conversation continues, and Monsieur Desbarres refers to Déternois as an *étourdi*, whereas Angélique sees in his acceptance of a challenge to a duel an indication that he loves her. Desbarres returns:

> Qu'il m'aime! Voilà encore une autre raison. Sitôt que les filles ont dit, Il m'aime, tout est dit: c'est un homme qui a toutes les qualités requises, toutes les vertus sociales: il est sage, prudent, fidèle, économe; c'est un homme comme il n'y en a pas. Il m'aime, il m'aime, tout est dit; il m'aime.

After a ludic contest of wills Angélique says she will return to the convent. And Desbarres:

> Ah, je vous entends; vous ferez tout ce que je voudrai, pourvu que je vous ordonne de faire ce qu'il vous plaît, n'est-ce pas? (*Angélique sourit.*) Oui, je vous entends. Venez avec moi, je suis trop bon; venez .... (Act II, sc. X)

---

18 Paris: Hérissant, 1771.

19 It also refers in passing to maternal love for a son which, if it runs true to form, will mean that the mother-in-law will be jealous of her daughter-in-law until the grandchildren arrive (Act II, sc. III).

This is certainly an illustration of the *philosophes*' view that parents should set out to be their children's friends but, for the girl, it is more significant. She is shown, in that context, to understand how to *interpret* a paternal rule rather than simply obey it, and the father clearly understands how to operate paternal authority with implicit, tacitly accepted, limitations – a system which could not operate without mutual confidence but which, when it does operate, has the effect of developing female self-assurance, the very opposite of the *timidité* discussed above. Sedaine develops the more subtle, intuitive, hence sensitive relationship only in evocations of the more socially elevated strata.

This drama has several features in common with *Le Philosophe sans le savoir* and the father/daughter relationship is similarly structured in both. It is more subtly presented in *Le Mort marié* and does not make the daughter appear slightly puerile, as Act I, scenes VI–IX of *Le Philosophe* do to Sophie. A further significant, ancillary element from *Le Philosophe* are the amiable relations of father-in-law and son-in-law, in Act I, scene X, for example, where Vanderk jokes: 'Vous allez, Monsieur, épouser une jolie personne ...' etc.

A stronger reflection of this cordiality appears in *Thémire*, the pastoral of 1770,[20] where Palémon, the father of the shepherdess Thémire, uses a knowledge of what Sedaine sees as female nature when he advises his daughter's lover, Timante, to pretend to love another shepherdess, Doris, in order to overcome Thémire's refusal to respond to his courtship. The stratagem succeeds, of course, but perhaps the capital question of exactly who is more successfully manipulating whom is left unanswered. It takes two males acting in concert to overcome Thémire's stonewalling, but on the other hand they play on what is presented as a natural weakness, her propensity to jealousy, incidentally by reifying Doris. In neither of these two cases is the female a victim, and yet the male hegemony is strongly affirmed by the implication that the female is being 'handed on' by one generation to the next, which resembles it in every respect – which is in fact no more than a reflection of the contemporary situation.

In *Les Femmes vengées* of 1775 the action is orchestrated by the wife of a painter, Madame Riss, who is being courted by the husbands of La Présidente and Madame Lek acting in concert. Because 'cet amour en commun', as she calls it, appears laughable to her, she informs their wives whom she dissuades from the hasty reaction of going public or making a scene because this will simply bring them personal discredit by provoking gossip in their provincial environment. In other words, the usual constraints operate on women, while men can get away with misbehaviour. Like the princesse de Clèves, Madame Riss has spoken of the situation to her husband who, unlike the prince de Clèves, laughs with her about the affair. The parallel is only partial, of course, since to have two importunate lovers at once is a burlesque situation rather

---

20 Edition printed in Paris by P.-R.-C. Ballard, 1770, vol. II.

than a tragic one, and Madame Riss does not reciprocate. But the real novelty here is the foregrounding of mid- to late-eighteenth-century companionate marriage, which contrasts with the jealous, tragic and aristocratic mode of earlier times. Madame Riss will receive the two suitors, but they will need to hide in a 'cabinet' when, as prearranged, Monsieur Riss arrives 'unexpectedly' home. Monsieur Riss will then flirt with their wives while they watch, impotent in their enforced concealment. This all takes place as planned, and the play closes with a general reconciliation and a song and a dance.[21]

The immediate conclusion might be that men (either by nature or because they have so organised the social formation that they can get away with it) are inveterate flirts, that women, albeit aided by an 'enlightened' man, can show up male foolishness by a more subtle and circumspect reaction (necessary subtlety again) than head-on confrontation, and that, as the closing vaudeville puts it: 'Pour rendre agréable la vie, / N'y regardons pas de trop près.' And it may be unjustifiable to press interpretation any further than to see this drama as an illustration of traditional clichés, with minor additions like the scorn for provincial rank snobbery (scene II). Because of the *opéra-comique*'s almost mathematical symmetry, both in the interplay of relationships and especially in the use of theatrical space, it has the imprint of a board-game played with traditional pieces. And if one then asks: 'why choose these particular traditional pieces?', the only reasonable answer may be that their familiarity is calculated precisely to divert the eighteenth-century spectator's typical attention away from reflection on the characters and towards the structural novelty of the play. Indeed, Sedaine's remark about the possibilities for the compartmentalised staging of *Britannicus*, which Racine had not used, and its potential effect on a spectator, would tend to support this.[22]

Ingeniousness and novelty of plot and characterisation may, at least in part, account for the success of *La Gageure imprévue*, the only one of Sedaine's plays, apart from *Le Philosophe*, to be performed at the Comédie-Française.[23] *La Gageure* tells us perhaps more than any other play about Sedaine's conception of women.[24] Along with *Le Philosophe*, it in fact

---

21 Sedaine returned to foreground companionate marriage in *Le Comte d'Albert* (1787), and Grétry's responses to the text in *Mémoires*, I, pp. 398–415, are revealing.

22 For the text of this remark, see p. 261. Other research which I have carried out confirms this point by indicating that audiences after about 1750 tended to show a preference for short comedies of a kind which offered a novel handling of characterisation, plots and stagecraft.

23 Regularly revived throughout the period covered by Joannidès's inventory, it received, for example, 80 performances between 1774 and 1790, 132 between 1801 and 1830 and 39 between 1861 and 1868; it was recently revived (1998) at the *Théâtre de la Monnaie*. See A. Joannidès, *La Comédie-Française de 1680 à 1900. Dictionaire général des pièces et des auteurs* (Paris: Plon, 1921), pp. 96–7.

24 See the discussion in the Introduction to Robert Niklaus's edition of the text (Exeter: University of Exeter, 1970).

foregrounds femaleness, not in terms of dramatic topoi, but as what Diderot had called a *condition*. Femaleness is not, then, to be understood just as a set of natural attributes, like intelligence turned to manipulativeness or a tendency to jealousy, or even socially induced or reinforced ones, like parasitic snobbery or self-effacement. It becomes a personality, formed by the action of rank, function and milieu in exactly the same way as maleness does. With *La Gageure*, Sedaine is not using traditional conceptions, which are implied by established genres, but is, within the context of a comic plot, exploring the situation of women in contemporary society. Obviously this is not a *drame*, and it could therefore justifiably be argued that the social mission is absent, but on the other hand the absence of commitment to a social programme does not in any sense exclude a serious evaluation of *condition* even in a ludic context.

The very first scene raises serious issues when Gotte, the servant, reflects that suffering the whims and mood-swings of masters at least prevents the boredom to which servants like her are subject despite, or because of, their intelligence, and she comes to the paradoxical conclusion that the more intelligent one is, the fewer resources one has for staving off boredom. One is therefore better off being a 'sot' because one thus has the possibility of finding everything amusing. But the idea 'vivent les sots pour s'amuser de tout', which she *appears* to be adopting for herself (but can one be sure?), is not a solution to the marquise's situation but only to the paradox, because, if she *is* intelligent, the marquise will require intellectual challenges which 'sots' would be unable to cope with (Gotte's reactions to her mistress's machinations alternate between puzzlement and admiration; see particularly scene XVIII), and because 's'amuser de tout' is positively the hallmark of stupidity. This is borne out when the marquise *invents* the game with her husband of naming all the components of a door. A game is *essentially* unproductive and represents intellectual exercise for its own sake (intellectual in this particular case, but the same would be true of a physical game, of course). An essential feature of games is their gratuitousness. Typical of her class and its non-productive (is Sedaine, not uncharacteristically, implying 'superfluous'?) social role, the marquise is oriented towards games generally; she plays another game as well, this time with her identity and with Détieulette's social prestige, when she has him told that her name is the comtesse de Wordacle, who is physically ugly and quite unlike the marquise. To frequent *her* would undermine Détieulette's social credibility.[25]

The debate about female intelligence permeates the whole play, but it is difficult to pin down. For instance, in scene XVIII, Gotte tells La Fleur of her admiration for her mistress, whom she rates above the marquis for intelligence.

---

[25] Sedaine does not pursue here the problems associated with the valuation of female attractiveness and the social importance of physical attractiveness generally. On this issue he seems simply to accept current norms.

At this point, Gotte says of herself 'je ne suis pas sotte', which seems to be a direct contradiction of what she implied about herself in scene I. Moreover, she is talking to La Fleur (with whom she has the traditional sentimental link, but whose dismissal in scene XXVI provokes only a token protest), who boasts of his own cleverness but finally loses his position, apparently proving the rightness of what Gotte is telling him, namely, that he is less intelligent than their mistress. He is drawn as fatuous, and it is in the end lack of intelligence, in going too far, being 'bête et malin', that gets him dismissed. So it would appear that the marquise is indeed more intelligent. On the other hand, 'malin' is a broad term, and the marquise herself is being 'maligne' vis-à-vis her husband – in which case, the difference is not so much one of intelligence as of power.

As the marquise and Détieulette leave the dining-room (sc. XIX), she is putting the case for female superiority, based on talents developed as a result of the social constraints placed on women:

> Oui, Monsieur, notre sexe trouvera toujours aisément le moyen de gouverner le vôtre. L'autorité que nous prenons marche par une route si fleurie, la pente est si insensible, notre constance dans le même projet a l'air si simple et si naturel, notre patience a si peu d'humeur, que l'empire est pris avant que vous vous en doutiez. [...] Dès l'enfance on nous ferme la bouche, on nous impose silence jusqu'à notre établissement; cela tourne au profit de nos yeux et de nos oreilles. Notre coup d'œil en devient plus fin, notre attention plus soutenue, nos réflexions plus délicates; et la modestie avec laquelle nous nous énonçons donne presque toujours aux hommes une confiance dont nous profiterions aisément si nous nous abaissions jusqu'à les tromper.

Détieulette also takes up the argument when he attributes to the marquis opinions he purportedly aired, in male company, about female intelligence. (He knows at this point that he is attributing statements to his hostess's husband, while she is unaware that he knows who she really is.)

> Les femmes, disait-il, n'ont d'empire que sur les âmes faibles; leur prudence n'est que de la finesse, leur raison n'est souvent que du raisonnement; habiles à saisir la superficie, le jugement en elles est sans profondeur: aussi n'ont-elles que le sang-froid de l'instant, la présence d'esprit de la minute, et cet esprit est souvent peu de chose; il éblouit sous le coloris des grâces, il passe avec elles, il s'évapore avec leur jeunesse, il se dissipe avec leur beauté. Elles aiment mieux [...] réussir par l'intrigue que par la droiture et par la simplicité; secrètes sur un seul article, mystérieuses sur quelques autres, dissimulées sur tous. Elles ne sont presque jamais agitées que de deux passions, qui même n'en font qu'une, l'amour d'un sexe et la haine de

> l'autre. [...] Défendez-vous [...] de leur premier coup d'œil; ne croyez jamais leur première phrase, et elles ne pourront vous tromper.

But although this apparent male commentary (also a game) is superficially impressive, thanks to the rhetorical techniques deployed and to Détieulette's knowledge of the situation, it really amounts to pure ratiocination. It is meaningless 'esprit', and hence is self-destructive and undermines male pretentions to superior intelligence. For intelligence, the advantage *seems* to go to the marquise, even though she is being fooled at this point, for what she says corresponds to contemporary female experience, whereas he is articulating the particular, disguised as the general and couched in pretentious clichés. And, bearing in mind the importance of impression when one is confronted with the ongoing movement of a drama, this is in itself significant.

The opening scene of the play raises other real issues too. There is the absolute dependency of servants (later illustrated by La Fleur's summary dismissal for divulging information). There is the forced inactivity of noble women, whose husbands typically neglect them in favour of male-only pursuits (in this instance, hunting, but it could be almost any activity, aristocratic or professional). There are the socially risky activities they may engage in in order to fill their empty lives (including anything between mild flirting and adultery), to which the only alternatives are embroidery, insipid visiting, solitary music-making, writing letters or reading 'approved' books, like the *Essai sur l'homme*![26] All these activities suggest profound isolation, an enforced and fundamental loneliness out of which it is dangerous to break because all exits attract at least disapproval and possibly real penalties (like the convent).

It is notable that when the marquis de Clainville does finally appear, in scene XXII, his wife is '*sur sa chaise longue, et faisant des nœuds*'. His first conversational contribution is to talk about his hunting, and his second is to talk about mechanical arts. The binary opposition between the conditions of males and females is encapsulated in her statement 'nous sommes bien ignorantes' and his 'je me suis donné une éducation si singulière'. These words indicate a whole world of enforced ignorance and inactivity on the one hand, opposed to an involvement with active leisure, sociability and modern technology on the other. (*Le Philosophe sans le savoir* illustrates this too, though less overtly.) And this could be seen by contemporaries in the context of the debates about education which were pursued with particular intensity from the 1750s onwards. The enforced idleness of the marquise's condition induces her frustrated intelligence to find trivial but risky outlets, while her husband, and to a lesser extent Monsieur Détieulette, can control his whole environment simply by having access to information. Indeed, the whole play can be viewed as a competition between intelligence and the control of

---

[26] Pope's poem (1733) had undergone several translations into French by 1768.

information. Moreover, it is in large part because she is (somewhat improbably – but this is a fantasy) denied information at various points in the play about the identity of Mademoiselle Adélaïde and Détieulette that she is exposed to personal embarrassment and, potentially, to social disgrace. The play ends on the refrain 'point de finesse' and praise of household management and making a husband happy. But this ideal female role, which the Enlightenment defined in order to occupy and confer value on women in the absence of a more egalitarian and competitive educational programme (which might well have undermined patriarchal hegemony), does nothing to answer the multiple and complex questions which the play raises.[27]

Clearly, *Le Philosophe sans le savoir* does not pursue the question of female identity to the same depth as *La Gageure* does.[28] It has been rightly pointed out, in fact, that Vanderk's role crushes all the others. Madame Vanderk, a rather marginal character, has in common with the marquise de Clainville that she accepts hegemonic control. The marquise, whose role can only be perceived as implying a waste of a natural attribute, is induced to renounce 'finesse', hence to return to conventionally conceived domestic activity (of a kind with a depressingly long future in front of it), and Madame Vanderk assumes the role of an invalid in need of her husband's protection. The only female role that stands out is that of Victorine. Her closeness to her father and his mixture of moderate brusqueness (which seems, over the spectrum of Sedaine's work, to be characteristic of lower-rank men towards women, for obvious reasons) and occasional gentle irony are of a kind already noted in other plays. Her intense interest in, or love for, Vanderk *fils* is clearly revealed to young Vanderk himself, to Vanderk *père* and to Antoine, but it remains undeveloped. In Sedaine's society, there was no way it could be otherwise. For one in Victorine's position, silence, restraint and keeping busy were the only choices open, and we see her attempting to follow that route. This role was, as we have seen, recognised as novel and interesting when the play was first performed. If it had a future, it was not one which Sedaine could give it.[29] And it is perhaps worth adding too that, if Sedaine's only *drame* leaves us with little that can be construed as important or novel in his representation of women, other *drames* are generally even less innovatory, perhaps because the Enlightenment's programme for women was basically paternalistic and repressive.

What conclusions, then, does this brief survey suggest? One could conclude that Sedaine's Italian and *Foire* comedies in general place heavy

---

[27] Socially, this is a 'faultline': issues are raised which cannot be resolved without envisaging changes from which the writer recoils; see Alan Sinfield, *Faultlines. Cultural Materialism and the Politics of Dissident Reading* (Oxford: Clarendon Press, 1992).

[28] Dunkley, 'Introduction' to *Le Philosophe sans le sçavoir* (see n. 1), pp. 58–9.

[29] George Sand's sequel, *Le Mariage de Victorine*, was first produced at the Théâtre du Gymnase-Dramatique in 1851.

reliance on traditional, trite conceptions of the female role, and that this is in part a response to audience expectations. Nevertheless, it is clear that one can detect significant inflections of the many traditional types of comic drama. For all their passivity and timidity, Sedaine's female characters are made capable of reflection and, if need be, of action; but the social formation is recognised as more generally promoting passive and victim roles and as stifling assertiveness in the name of female nature and correct behaviours. At the peasant level, assertiveness is exceptional. Elsewhere, enforced passivity is shown as fostering subtlety and a need for manipulation, but not the suppression of desires.

It is also noteworthy that Sedaine's women characters below middle age are usually drawn as more intelligent than older ones, and this may reflect a broader intuition on Sedaine's part that real young women from the 1760s onward had been bred to be a more reflective and assertive generation. In Sedaine's plays, it is also noteworthy that intelligence has nothing to do with social rank (Mathurine is more intelligent than La Tante), though with that one exception higher-ranking women are not portrayed as foolish, whereas peasants sometimes are. This characterisation of course corresponded to the perceptions of metropolitan audiences (and to the tendency of metropolitan writers), even where 'metropolitan' can be extended to include larger provincial towns (Rheims for example).

Further, particular emotional ties exist in Sedaine's dramas between older men and younger women, often in a father–daughter relationship, and the females derive advantage from this, though the relationship is presented as being based on mutual understanding and does not involve manipulation in any destructive or hostile sense. Women at all levels of society are in a subordinate role and, even when their intelligence appears to justify something better, Sedaine so structures his plots that he forces them into 'philosophical' domesticity. Marriage is their goal and their fulfilment, and the modern, bourgeois companionate marriage is foregrounded and implicitly approved in *Les Femmes vengées*, and to a lesser extent in *Le Philosophe.* Sedaine is, then, largely a traditionalist, with occasional but notable departures in his minor plays, and in his two major ones he subscribes to the contemporary discourse on woman's condition (as wife and mother),[30] ultimately recoiling before the conclusion that more innovative possibilities needed to be opened in order to divert their intelligence into channels already available to men.

[30] Sedaine's tragedy, *Maillard ou Paris sauvé*, is one of the rare plays in which he focuses on motherhood, and certainly shows him to be in conformity with a well-known ideology of natural and heroic motherhood. One of its more controversial scenes was a discussion of the pleasures and benefits of breast-feeding, directly deriving from contemporary theory, and particularly from the advocacy of breast-feeding in Rousseau's *Emile.* See *Maillard ou Paris sauvé* (Paris: Prault, 1788), Act I, sc. XIV. On the cultural representation of the breast-feeding mother in eighteenth-century France, see Carol Duncan, 'Happy Mothers and Other New Ideas in French Art', *Art Bulletin* , LV (December 1973), pp. 570–83.

PART II

Transformations

Chapter 4

Aline, reine de Golconde: une bergère d'opéra-comique à l'Académie Royale de Musique

Manuel Couvreur

Boufflers et le conte

Dans *Aline, reine de Golconde*, créée à l'Académie Royale de Musique de Paris, le mardi 15 avril 1766, Sedaine s'était inspiré d'un conte écrit en 1761 par le chevalier de Boufflers. Cet opuscule, tout en demeurant profondément original, se référait aux multiples formes de contes qu'avait vues se développer le XVIIIe siècle: *La Reine de Golconde* 'tient de la fraîche pastorale, du conte oriental, du conte de fées, du conte onirique, du conte galant, voire licencieux, du roman d'aventures, du conte philosophique, et même, à la fin, du conte moral'.[1]

Cependant, une référence explicite au *Bélier* d'Antoine Hamilton inscrivait avant tout *La Reine de Golconde* dans le genre du conte oriental parodique et de fantaisie, veine pourtant alors presque tarie. Celle-ci avait été suscitée par la 'traduction' des *Mille et une nuits* publiée par Antoine Galland à partir de 1704. Le succès avait aussitôt entraîné imitations et parodies, mais aussi des pastiches, comme ceux d'Hamilton, déjà mentionné, ou ceux moins connus de Choisy et de Moncrif. Le plus souvent, il s'agissait de récits initiatiques, caractérisés par une accumulation de péripéties invraisemblables se déroulant dans un cadre oriental. L'un des instruments de la parodie était de jouer sur le parallélisme entre les schémas narratifs des contes orientaux ou pseudo-orientaux de Galland avec ceux de la mythologie gréco-romaine ou des anciens romans médiévaux.[2] Ce procédé littéraire ne pouvait manquer

---

[1] Jacqueline Hellegouarc'h (éd.), *Nouvelles françaises du XVIIIe siècle: De Marmontel à Potocki* (2 vol., Paris: Livre de Poche, 1994), II, p. 191.

[2] Sur la part de création originale de Galland, voir Georges May, '*Les Mille et une nuits' d'Antoine Galland ou Le chef-d'œuvre invisible* (Paris: Presses universitaires de France, 1986). Sur la veine du conte oriental qu'elle suscita, voir Marie-Louise Dufrenoy, *L'Orient*

d'induire des rapprochements avec les livrets d'opéras et, plus particulièrement, avec ceux de Quinault qui avait puisé à ces deux sources.

Le conte parodique connut un nouvel apogée en 1744 avec *Acajou et Zirphile* de Charles Pinot-Duclos.[3] Carl-Gustaf de Tessin, ambassadeur de Suède à Paris et admirateur inconditionnel de l'opéra français, était l'auteur d'un petit conte qu'avait illustré François Boucher, alors décorateur à l'Académie Royale de Musique. La suite d'estampes donna l'idée à trois auteurs d'inventer chacun un conte qui pût également leur servir de support. Si ceux de Caylus – grand amateur de musique et qui avait déjà collaboré avec Moncrif – et de Voisenon – apparenté au surintendant de l'Opéra, Bombarde de Beaulieu, familier de Voltaire et futur collaborateur de Favart – n'ont pas été publiés, celui de Duclos connut un succès foudroyant: c'est dans ce courant qu'il convient de replacer la parution d'*Angola* de La Morlière en 1746 et des *Bijoux indiscrets* de Diderot en 1748.[4]

Comme on le voit, il existe une continuité entre ces auteurs de contes orientaux parodiques et le monde de l'opéra. *Le Bélier* d'Hamilton (1730) avait en outre fourni, dès 1749, la matière au *Prince de Noisy* de Rebel et Francœur sur un livret de La Bruère, ouvrage repris à l'Académie Royale de Musique en 1760. Favart, au début de sa carrière, avait souvent puisé à cette source, comme en témoigne son *Acajou* de 1744. A la fin de sa vie, lorsqu'il collaborera régulièrement avec Voisenon, on verra se multiplier les livrets tirés de ce type de contes: tel est le cas de *La Fée Urgèle*, inspirée du récit en vers de Voltaire *Ce qui plaît aux dames*, et mise en musique par Duni en 1765.[5] Voisenon, seul cette fois, empruntera à Hamilton la donnée de *Fleur d'épine*, mise en musique en 1776 par Emmanuelle Bayon, épouse de l'architecte Victor Louis.

Bien que beaucoup plus jeune, Stanislas de Boufflers avait entretenu des relations privilégiées avec ces illustres prédécesseurs. Élevé à la cour du roi de Pologne Stanislas Leszczynski – son parrain – le chevalier de Boufflers avait pu rencontrer Voltaire et Moncrif, tant à Lunéville qu'à Nancy. Le second était aussi lecteur de la reine de France, Marie Leszczynska, fille de son protecteur. À Paris, où il fréquenta assidûment le duc de Choiseul et le prince de Conti,

---

romanesque en France (1704–1789), I–II (Montréal: Beauchemin, 1946); III (Amsterdam: Rodopi, 1975).

3 Voir Jacques Barchilon, *Le Conte merveilleux français de 1690 à 1790* (Paris: Champion, 1975); et Raymonde Robert, *Le Conte de fées littéraire en France de la fin du XVIIe à la fin du XVIIIe siècle* (Nancy: Presses universitaires de Nancy, 1982).

4 Voir l'excellente préface de Raymond Trousson à la réédition d'*Angola*, dans l'anthologie *Romans libertins du XVIIIe siècle* (Paris: Laffont, 1993), p. 355–483.

5 Voir la préface de François Moureau à son édition de Charles-Simon Favart, *La Fée Urgèle*, précédée de *La Répétition interrompue* (Paris: Cicero éditeurs, 1991).

Boufflers put faire la connaissance de Voisenon.[6] Il est à la fois amusant et révélateur qu'adressant à Favart un exemplaire du livret d'*Aline, reine de Golconde*, Sedaine le 'prie d'en envoyer un exemplaire à M. l'abbé de Voisenon' et de le remercier 'de ce qu'il est venu à notre répétition'.[7]

La recrudescence soudaine du genre du conte oriental parodique et la présence massive du merveilleux exotique sur les scènes lyriques, ne pouvaient manquer d'éveiller l'attention de Sedaine. Dès sa publication en 1761, *La Reine de Golconde* avait été saluée par la critique, pour une fois presque unanime: Voltaire et Sade ne lui ménagèrent pas leurs compliments. L'ouvrage, d'une haute tenue littéraire, séduisit immédiatement un large public. Son succès ne devait pas connaître d'éclipse et *La Reine de Golconde* a conservé jusqu'à aujourd'hui son statut de chef-d'œuvre rare, mais incontournable. Quelle anthologie de contes français du XVIIIe siècle oserait y renoncer?[8] Malgré son extrême concision, l'œuvre a même eu les honneurs de deux éditions philologiques.[9]

Aux yeux d'un librettiste, *La Reine de Golconde* garantissait l'intérêt des spectateurs et, dès lors, la bienveillance des directeurs de l'Opéra. Si, à nos yeux, l'encadrement onirique, la structure répétitive, ou l'étalement temporel du conte semblent rendre impossible son adaptation à la scène lyrique, lors de la création, les critiques saluèrent le choix judicieux de Sedaine. Ainsi des *Mémoires secrets*: 'Le drame est tiré en partie d'un joli conte du chevalier de Boufflers. [...] Au reste, l'auteur n'a pas su tirer le parti qu'il aurait dû de ses situations.' Lors de la reprise de 1779, Bachaumont soulignera qu'en raison de 'sa variété, la multitude des décorations et des ballets qu'il exige naturellement', ce sujet est un de ceux 'qu'on puisse mettre au théâtre le plus heureux'.[10] Grimm partageait ce sentiment: 'la *Reine de Golconde* est un peu

[6] En ce qui concerne la biographie de Boufflers, on se reportera à l'excellent ouvrage de Nicole Vaget Grangeat, *Le Chevalier de Boufflers et son temps. Étude d'un échec* (Paris: Nizet, 1976).

[7] Citée dans Antoine Pierre Charles Favart (éd.), *Mémoires et correspondance littéraires, dramatiques et anecdotiques de C. S. Favart* (3 vol., Paris: Léopold Collin, 1808), III, p. 97.

[8] Le texte de Boufflers figure dans l'anthologie de Jacqueline Hellegouarc'h (éd.), *Nouvelles françaises du XVIIIe siècle*, II, p. 194–209, ainsi que dans celle d'Angus Martin, *Anthologie du conte en France (1750–1799). Philosophes et cœurs sensibles* (Paris: 10/18, 1981), p. 218–33.

[9] Stanislas de Boufflers, *Aline, reine de Golconde*, texte présenté et annoté par Simon Davies (Exeter: University of Exeter, 1977); et Stanislas de Boufflers, *Contes*, texte établi, présenté et annoté par Alex Sokalski (Paris: Société des textes français modernes, 1995), p. 125–206. Cette dernière édition fondée sur une étude minutieuse des éditions anciennes, enrichie de notes, d'une introduction et d'une bibliographie exhaustive, fait désormais autorité. C'est à elle que nous renverrons par la suite.

[10] *Mémoires secrets*, III (14 avril 1766), p. 23, et XIV (8 juillet 1779), p. 125.

libre, mais à cela près, le plus joli ouvrage qui ait paru en ce genre depuis longtemps. [...] Ce sujet était charmant à placer sur le théâtre.'[11]

Entre Grands et Philosophes

Plus que des raisons d'ordre esthétique, c'est peut-être un certain opportunisme politique qui incita Sedaine à s'intéresser à Boufflers. Le chevalier, par sa naissance et son esprit, avait vu s'ouvrir toutes les portes,

> à Versailles où les membres de sa famille sont les intimes de madame de Pompadour et du duc de Choiseul et à Paris où les parents et amis de sa mère forment la société que l'on voit chez le duc d'Orléans, chez le prince de Conti, chez le duc de Choiseul, chez le prince de Beauvau, chez le duc de Nivernais ou chez madame du Deffand.[12]

La duchesse de Mirepoix, le prince et la princesse de Beauvau, étaient en effet ses oncle et tantes. Or ces personnages avaient formé, autour du duc de Choiseul, le cercle très restreint des intimes de madame de Pompadour et de Louis XV. La comtesse de Boufflers, cousine de sa mère, était la maîtresse du prince de Conti, autre proche de Choiseul. Boufflers servit d'agent et d'espion à Choiseul et lui envoya lettres et poèmes. Après la disgrâce de son protecteur en 1770, Boufflers tenta en vain d'obtenir de la comtesse Du Barry le pardon du ministre. Les deux hommes partageaient en outre un anticléricalisme viscéral.

Durant ces mêmes années, Choiseul affiche un intérêt soutenu pour le monde du spectacle et s'immisce dans les affaires de l'Académie Royale de Musique. Même si rien ne permet d'affirmer qu'il ait été à l'origine du projet de Sedaine et Monsigny, il est certain qu'il le soutint de toute son autorité:

> [L'ouvrage] n'est pas annoncé favorablement, les directeurs répugnaient même à le jouer, mais un grand ministre l'a pris sous sa protection. Mr. le duc de Choiseul, malgré ses importantes occupations, est allé à six répétitions de suite, et s'intéresse fortement au succès de ce drame: il a exigé de Rebel et de Francœur qu'ils n'épargnassent rien pour sa réussite. Ils ont tout épuisé pour la pompe du spectacle, la richesse des habits, la magnificence des décorations. On assure qu'ils ont fait 30 000 livres de dépense.[13]

---

11 *Correspondance littéraire*, VII (1er mai 1766), p. 31.

12 Grangeat, *Boufflers et son temps*, p. 33–4.

13 *Mémoires secrets*, III (14 avril 1766), p. 23.

Choiseul demeura mal satisfait. Avec l'aide du prince de Conti, il contraignit tout d'abord Rebel et Francœur à la démission en 1767 et réussit ensuite à éliminer Dauvergne au profit de Trial et Berton. Si l'on en croit Bachaumont, l'intérêt du ministre peut s'expliquer par des raisons plus pressantes que celles de son amitié pour Boufflers:

> M. le duc de Choiseul a voulu qu'on reprit la *Reine de Golconde* à l'Opéra: ce qui s'est exécuté hier jeudi. La tendre affection qu'a ce grand seigneur pour ce drame, confirme le bruit qu'il en est le père. Les paroles sont assez mauvaises pour être de lui.[14]

L'image de Choiseul, à l'époque comme aujourd'hui, était très contrastée, en particulier auprès des philosophes. En cette même année 1769, Voltaire lui dédie ses *Scythes*, avec une préface flagorneuse qui 'sent l'homme qui a envie de revenir à Paris et qui fléchit le genou devant le tout-puissant pour obtenir cette grâce'.[15] En revanche, Diderot, qui déteste le scepticisme et la morgue de Choiseul, sait que celui-ci le hait.[16] Alors aux prises avec l'une des crises les plus graves de l'*Encyclopédie* – à peine envoyés à Versailles, les volumes ont été retirés aux souscripteurs – Diderot n'a certainement pas plus envie d'aider que d'irriter un Choiseul encore puissant.

A ce moment, Boufflers a également le vent en poupe auprès des philosophes. Jeune abbé, il avait contribué, dès 1757, au tome VII de l'*Encyclopédie*, en rédigeant partiellement l'article 'Généreux, Générosité'. En 1761, choqué par l'hypocrisie du clergé, il avait renoncé à une brillante carrière ecclésiastique. Il s'en était vigoureusement expliqué dans une lettre à son ancien précepteur, missive que la *Correspondance littéraire* s'empressa de faire lire à ses abonnés.[17] C'était d'ailleurs au temps où il moisissait au séminaire de Saint-Sulpice que Boufflers avait rédigé sa *Reine de Golconde*. Les pudibonds s'en étaient offusqués, ou du moins, l'avaient prétendu. Le *Mercure de France* se donna le ridicule d'une version expurgée, à la grande colère de Grimm qui en publia la version intégrale, en février 1765.[18] La verve anticléricale de Boufflers se manifestait encore par de nombreux poèmes, si

---

14 Ibid., III (27 février 1767), p. 169.

15 Ibid., III (5 avril 1767), p. 197.

16 Voir notamment la lettre qu'il adresse à Falconet, le 15 mai 1767, dans Denis Diderot, *Correspondance*, éd. George Roth et Jacques Varloot (Paris: Éditions de Minuit, 1955–70), VII, p. 56–7.

17 Grangeat, *Boufflers et son temps*, p. 28–31.

18 Les diverses versions du conte ont été excellemment étudiées par Alex Sokalski dans de nombreux articles. On en trouvera la substance dans l'introduction de son édition critique (*Contes*, p. 23–70).

amusants que Voltaire ou Diderot prenaient la peine de les copier à leurs correspondants.[19]

Tout ceci laisse à penser que Sedaine a élaboré son livret sous l'influence conjointe des cercles du pouvoir et des philosophes. Sans doute est-ce ce qui explique que l'utopie politique de Golconde y soit plus appuyée. Alors que dans le conte, Aline est l'image de la femme sous tous ses avatars, l'humilité de son origine sociale est soulignée par le livret. Boufflers ne lui faisait subir aucune épreuve qui la qualifiât pour régner sur ses sujets. Sedaine, tout au contraire, se réfère à une thématique royale inspirée des tragédies en musique de Quinault où Alcide, Thésée ou Persée traversent des épreuves qui les autorisent à régner. Cependant, si l'origine divine – traduisons, royale – de ces héros était parfois inconnue au départ, celle-ci se révélait par leur capacité même à accomplir ces hauts faits.[20] A l'inverse, dans *Aline, reine de Golconde*, c'est parce qu'Aline est devenue l'amour de ses peuples que ceux-ci l'ont placée sur le trône. Tout est changé: l'existence et non plus l'essence, les actions et non plus le droit divin, légitiment le monarque. Celui-ci doit être pacifique, juste et généreux, qualités qui font de lui un 'père du peuple'.[21] Un même renversement thématique se produira avec *Fleur d'épine* d'Hamilton, récit qualifiant à reconnaissance finale. Dans le livret de Voisenon, cette donnée est respectée. En revanche, dans l'adaptation de Beaumarchais pour Salieri, Tarare devient le héros éponyme d'une série d'épreuves qualifiantes, mais sans reconnaissance, et nourries des idées qui étaient celles des philosophes.[22]

Une telle transformation de la célébration royale ne pouvait déplaire aux philosophes. Notons au passage que Sedaine adresse son éloge du bon gouvernement à une femme, au moment où Catherine II se montre fort généreuse à l'égard de son ami Diderot. Cette conception nouvelle devait correspondre également à l'image que la cour voulait donner d'elle-même. C'est ce qui explique sans doute que l'opéra ait été souvent 'joué à la cour pour des fêtes de mariage',[23] tel celui du comte de Provence en 1771, ou lors de

---

[19] Grangeat, *Boufflers et son temps*, p. 127–9.

[20] Sur ces transformations de la thématique monarchique à la fin de l'Ancien Régime, voir notre article 'La tragédie en musique comme instrument de la politique royale', dans Antoine Hennion (éd.), *1789–1989. Musique, histoire, démocratie* (3 vol., Paris: Maison des Sciences de l'Homme, 1992), II, p. 265–70.

[21] Selon Nicole Vaget Grangeat, le royaume de Golconde serait une véritable utopie philosophique (*Boufflers et son temps*, p. 146). Il nous semble cependant que Jacqueline Hellegouarc'h force un peu le trait en avançant que la reine de Golconde met en pratique certaines des idées physiocratiques de Quesnay: *Nouvelles françaises*, II, p. 191.

[22] Sur *Tarare* (1784) voir Pierre-Augustin Caron de Beaumarchais, *Œuvres*, éd. Pierre Larthomas (Paris: Gallimard, 1988), p. 493–596 et 1427–75.

[23] Sedaine, 'Quelques réflexions', p. 510.

visites officielles, comme celle du 'comte du Nord' en 1782. Seul Bachaumont semble s'étonner de cette faveur:

> L'Académie Royale de Musique a remis aujourd'hui *Aline ou La reine de Golconde.* C'est un opéra qu'on a choisi pour être joué devant Sa Majesté danoise, on ne sait pourquoi; car ce n'est assurément pas le meilleur ouvrage du magasin.[24]

Par contre Gondot, en bon parodiste, souligna ce qui aurait pu avoir échappé. Au-delà de l'amusante proximité phonétique, *Nanine, sœur de lait de la reine de Golconde* établissait un parallèle avec la pièce de Voltaire, *Nanine*. Sous-titrée *Le Préjugé vaincu*, cette comédie met en scène un aristocrate se résolvant à déroger par amour pour une jeune paysanne. En fin de compte, sous leurs allures oniriques, ni le conte de Boufflers ni l'opéra de Sedaine ne disent autre chose, même s'il semble que ce soient moins les vertus de l'héroïne que ses faiblesses qui retiennent le héros ...

L'art de la citation

La donnée de Boufflers avait encore subi d'autres modifications. Pouvait-il en être autrement? Le conte est vert et s'attarde sur certains détails piquants. Comme le remarque justement le *Mercure de France*, 'l'auteur du poème d'opéra les a supprimés. Ceux qui connaissent le conte en sentent bien la raison; mais il faut le connaître pour entendre le drame.'[25] La décence interdisait en effet de rappeler que la reine de Golconde n'était qu'une prostituée reconvertie. Bien conscient des règles de la bienséance, Sedaine s'expliqua sur certains silences, en tête du livret:

> Le joli conte d'*Aline* m'a paru si répandu dans le public, et si digne de l'être, que je n'ai point hésité de le mettre au théâtre. Le sujet en est si connu, qu'il pourrait se passer de programme.[26]

---

[24] *Mémoires secrets*, XIX (4 octobre 1768), p. 27–9. Ce contenu politique pourrait expliquer que, légèrement modifié par Favières, le livret ait si bien survécu au XIXe siècle (voir le chapitre 'Du conte au livret' qu'Alex Sokalski consacre aux diverses adaptations postérieures du conte de Boufflers, *Aline*, p. 73–92).

[25] *Mercure de France* (mai 1766), p. 167.

[26] [Sedaine], *Aline, reine de Golconde, ballet-héroïque, en trois actes, représenté pour la première fois, par l'Académie Royale de Musique, le jeudi 10 avril 1766* (Paris: De Lormel, 1766), p. 8. Voir au chapitre 9 pour le texte intégral, p. 250–51.

Sedaine installait ainsi lecteurs et spectateurs dans un jeu raffiné de références au modèle: ce faisant, il en récupérait la dimension critique, comme l'a fort justement observé Michel Noiray.[27]

Le caractère parodique est sensible dans la désinvolture face aux règles élémentaires de la vraisemblance. Voici comment, dans l'avis au lecteur, Sedaine se joue des circonstances absurdes qui émaillent la destinée de ses protagonistes:

> Quelques années après, par un de ces événements qui n'a pas besoin de preuve, *Aline* devint reine de Golconde. [...] Par un événement, peut-être aussi singulier, *St Phar* quitte la France, passe dans les Indes, et est nommé ambassadeur vers la reine de Golconde.[28]

Si l'on pouvait rendre presque chaste ce conte grivois, il était impossible de lui donner une vraisemblance contre nature. Dès lors, le librettiste s'est amusé. À une époque où, chaque fois qu'ils introduisent un personnage s'exprimant dans une langue étrangère, dramaturges et romanciers s'expliquent longuement sur les circonstances qui ont permis au dit personnage d'apprendre le français, Sedaine nous montre Saint-Phar conversant, sans truchement, non seulement avec la reine de Golconde – qui est Française – mais aussi avec tous ses Golcondais. Le *Mercure de France* attribua ces invraisemblances à la médiocrité du librettiste:

> Ce Français, plus tendre que curieux, s'empresse de renouveler à son *Aline* les protestations les plus vives de son feu, sans s'inquiéter comment et par quel prodige il retrouve à Golconde cette bergère, le hameau qu'elle habitait en France, et son propre château [...]
>
> Beaucoup de spectateurs se sont étonnés ici de ce que *Saint-Phar* ne l'est pas davantage d'entendre parler ainsi de son *Aline*, et de ce qu'il ne soupçonne pas quelque mystère singulier dans tout cela; mais nous n'entreprenons que de rendre compte de cet ouvrage, et non pas de l'examiner [...]
>
> 'La fortune a fait un prodige / Pour en faire hommage à l'amour.' Ces deux seuls vers sont toute l'explication que l'auteur a cru devoir donner de son sujet et de l'intrigue de son drame.[29]

---

27 Michel Noiray, '*Aline, reine de Golconde*' dans Stanley Sadie (éd.), *The New Grove Dictionary of Opera* (4 vol., Londres: Macmillan, 1992), I, p. 88.

28 [Sedaine], *Aline, reine de Golconde*, p. 8.

29 *Mercure de France* (mai 1766), p. 176–81.

Aucun spectateur ne crut que tant d'invraisemblance pût être volontaire. Pourtant, grâce à ce 'flou', Sedaine avait réussi à préserver les qualités essentielles du conte: l'ironie et l'onirisme.

Le jeu de références était rendu plus complexe par le fait que Boufflers, lui-même, avait usé du procédé. Dès l'épître en vers, il donnait le ton en convoquant Dinarzade, personnage qui renvoyait à *Fleur d'épine*: Hamilton, dans ce conte, avait raillé le rôle ridicule que Galland avait fait jouer à cette sœur de Shéhérazade, celui de relancer, chaque nuit, le récit entamé la veille. Quant à Moulineaux et au bélier, ils venaient tout droit d'un autre conte d'Hamilton: *Le Bélier*. L'épître en vers est, en elle-même, un hommage à cet écrivain qui commence toujours ses contes de cette manière. L'influence est cependant plus essentielle et pourrait faire penser ici à un pastiche, que ce soit par la similitude des deux scènes initiales (le héros s'égare au cours d'une chasse) ou par la proximité du nom des deux héroïnes (la nymphe Alie devient Ali[n]e).

Boufflers multipliait encore les allusions.[30] Fréron avait déjà signalé la parenté avec *Candide*: l'utopie de Golconde rappelle celle d'Eldorado; Aline, comme Candide, se fait chasser par ses parents; les deux récits s'achèvent par un éloge du travail des champs. Chez les deux auteurs, la conclusion montrant le bonheur des deux protagonistes devenus âgés est, elle-même, une allusion au mythe de Philémon et Baucis, venu d'Ovide, mais plus sûrement de La Fontaine: on ne peut qu'être frappé par le fait que Sedaine s'empara aussitôt de *Philémon et Baucis* pour son second opéra.[31] Voltaire ne cachait pas sa dette envers les textes bibliques, et la *Genèse*, en particulier. Boufflers, lui aussi, multiplie les allusions: lors de sa première rencontre avec le narrateur – élue d'un dieu qui est ici celui d'amour –, elle lui offre à boire, comme Rébécca à Éliézer. Le parcours d'Aline, prostituée puis ermite, n'est-il pas celui de la Madeleine pénitente?

La Reine de Golconde, par son seul titre, suffisait à renvoyer le lecteur vers le célèbre roman libertin de La Morlière, *Angola*, dont l'héroïne, Luzéide, est, elle aussi, princesse de Golconde. Chez aucun des deux auteurs, l'évocation de ce royaume indien n'était fortuite. C'est Jean-Baptiste Tavernier qui, au siècle précédent, avait révélé ce 'bon pays, abondant en blé, riz, bœufs,

---

[30] Sur ce point, voir la préface de Jacqueline Hellegouarc'h, *Nouvelles françaises*, I, p. 191–2.

[31] Voir Louise Parkinson Arnoldson, *Sedaine et les musiciens de son temps* (Paris: l'Entente Linotypiste, 1934), p. 164–6; et Clarence D. Brenner, *Dramatizations of French Short Stories in the Eighteenth Century with Special Reference to the 'Contes' of La Fontaine, Marmontel and Voltaire* (University of California Publications in Modern Philology, XXXIII/1) (Berkeley: University of California Press, 1947), p. 1–34.

moutons et poules et autres choses nécessaires à la vie'.[32] Mais, comme le rappelle Nicole Vaget Grangeat,[33] la Golconde évoquait surtout le pays des mines de diamants et les feux du 'Kohinour' que le Grand Mogol avait montré au voyageur. Les richesses naturelles de Golconde seront au cœur du divertissement du premier acte où Zélis présente deux bouquets, l'un de fleurs, l'autre de diamants.

Cependant, si Voltaire déclarait que 'Tavernier n'apprend guère qu'à connaître les grandes routes et les diamants',[34] c'est qu'il l'avait lu un peu rapidement. Le voyageur avait mis en avant le bon gouvernement 'd'un roi bienfaisant qui tous les jours sur les quatre heures après midi [...] donne du pain et le pilaf à tous les pauvres qui se présentent'. Mais son utopie avait un revers qui n'avait pas manqué de titiller les imaginations:

> Il y a une si grande quantité de femmes publiques [...] qu'on fait conte qu'il y en a plus ordinairement plus de vingt mille écrites sur le livre du Deroga, sans quoi il n'est pas permis à aucune femme de faire ce métier-là. [...] Le soir, à la fraîcheur, on les voit devant les portes de leurs maisons [...] et quand la nuit vient, elles mettent à la porte pour signal une chandelle ou une lampe allumée.

Les prostituées ne payaient pas d'impôt, mais devaient, tous les vendredis, venir danser pour le roi... L'*Encyclopédie* rappelait ces faits, non à l'article 'Golconde', mais à celui de sa capitale, 'Bagnagar'. Il est vraisemblable pourtant que c'est directement chez Tavernier que Boufflers a puisé son inspiration. Outre les éléments déjà mentionnés et qui se retrouvent dans l'*Encyclopédie*, on peut encore signaler d'autres ressemblances. Tout d'abord, si la capitale s'appelle Bagnagar – 'jardin de Nagar' –, c'est parce que la ville avait été fondée par le roi 'à la sollicitation d'une de ses femmes qu'il aimait passionnément et qui s'appelait *Nagar*'. Pour entrer dans la ville, il faut franchir une rivière 'sur un grand pont de pierre qui n'est guère moins beau que le Pont-Neuf à Paris'. Afin de prouver qu''il y a de la vertu et de la générosité

---

32 Jean-Baptiste Tavernier, *Les Six voyages en Turquie, en Perse et aux Indes*, chapitre X, 'Du royaume de Golconda' (2 vol., Paris: Claude Barbin, 1676), II, p. 103 *sqq*. Les chapitres X–XXII du Livre II sont entièrement consacrés aux mines de diamants de Golconde. Sur l'image de l'Inde en France au XVIIIe siècle, voir Zenobia Bamboat, *Les Voyageurs français aux Indes aux XVIIe et XVIIIe siècles* (Paris: Jouve, 1933); Guy Deleury, *Les Indes florissantes. Anthologie des voyageurs français (1750–1820)* (Paris: Laffont, 1991); et Florence D'Souza, *Quand la France découvrit l'Inde. Les écrivains-voyageurs français en Inde (1757–1818)* (Paris: L'Harmattan, 1995).

33 Grangeat, *Boufflers et son temps*, p. 145–6.

34 Voltaire, *Essai sur les mœurs*, chapitre CLVII, cité par Charles Joret, *Jean-Baptiste Tavernier* (Paris: Plon, 1886), p. 244.

aux Indes comme il y en a dans l'Europe', Tavernier en donne 'un illustre exemple en la personne du roi de Golconda'. Enfin, un peu plus loin, le voyageur fait mention 'de la reine de Bornéo, et non pas du roi: la raison est, que dans ce royaume, ce sont les femmes qui gouvernent et non pas les hommes'. Ce qui lui paraît fort judicieux car un homme n'a jamais la certitude absolue d'être le père de sa progéniture... En s'emparant de ces divers éléments, Boufflers a su préserver toute l'ambiguïté du regard européen sur le royaume indien: la vision utopique est sapée par la référence sous-jacente à cette prostitution d'état et à l'infidélité des souveraines. Par ricochet, le livret de Sedaine récupérait cette double dimension.

Le librettiste alla plus loin et s'amusa, à son tour, à convoquer de nouvelles références littéraires. Pour souligner le bon gouvernement des Golcondais, Sedaine rendit hommage à Montesquieu et donna au principal ministre de la reine le nom d'Usbek qui, dès cet époque, était devenu commun pour désigner un sage étranger. L'intertextualité s'étend encore au personnage de Saint-Phar qui, chez Boufflers, demeurait un narrateur anonyme: Saint-Far est le personnage principal du *Bonheur*, qu'Antoine Bret venait de faire paraître, précisément en 1765, dans son *Essai de contes moraux et dramatiques*.[35]

La vie est un songe

Plus que le sel répandu sur tout l'ouvrage, un passage surtout fascina les lecteurs: celui où le narrateur retrouve Aline, dans le parc de Golconde où elle a reconstitué le vallon de ses premières amours.[36] Pour une fois, Fréron vit clair:

> Ce morceau est admirable. C'est celui de tout l'ouvrage qui fait le plus honneur à l'écrivain; il lui appartient; il est neuf pour l'imagination, et cependant il est dans la nature. C'est un trait de

---

[35] Dans la parodie *Nanine, sœur de lait de la reine de Golconde* (voir au note 41), le nom du héros devient Saint-Phal. Ce nom fut pris comme pseudonyme par le célèbre acteur Étienne Meynier qui débuta à la Comédie-Française en 1782. Il n'était pas non plus sans rapport avec celui de l'actrice Saint-Val ou Sainval: Sainval est le nom de l'amant d'Aline dans l'*Histoire des amoureux de Quimpercorentin*, version remaniée du conte que le marquis de Paulmy fit paraître en 1777 dans la *Bibliothèque universelle des romans* (Sokalski (éd.), *Contes*, p. 55, note 6). On notera que le nom de Saint-Phar est encore celui que les traducteurs français de *La Bohème* de Puccini donneront au conseiller d'état.

[36] Sur le succès de cet épisode, voir Sokalski (éd.), *Contes*, p. 55–7.

> *génie du cœur*, si je puis risquer cette expression. Le génie, en effet, n'est autre chose que le sentiment porté au suprême degré.[37]

C'était la 'scène à faire' et Sedaine le savait. Aussi est-ce autour d'elle qu'il construisit son livret. S'il avait voulu respecter les règles de la progression dramatique, il aurait dû placer cette scène de reconnaissance au dernier acte. Il la mit cependant au centre du second acte, comme axe central de l'ensemble. En cela, il suivait son modèle, dont il parvint, grâce à divers aménagements, à préserver la construction ternaire: la jeunesse en France, de la campagne à Paris; la maturité dans la capitale de Golconde avec, en incrustation, l'épisode de reconnaissance dans le vallon initial; la vieillesse, retirée à la campagne. Cependant, alors que le conte affirme son caractère cyclique, le livret affirme une progression dramatique de type initiatique. C'est par sa fidélité sans faille que l'ambassadeur de France devient roi de Golconde: Aline, selon Sedaine, 'fait pour *St Phar* ce qu'*Angélique* a fait pour *Médor*'.[38] Cette dernière référence renvoie bien sûr à l'Arioste, mais plus encore à Quinault que Sedaine s'était donné pour modèle:[39] la construction symétrique, plus architecturale que dramatique, du livret d'*Aline, reine de Golconde*, rappelle en effet celle des anciennes tragédies lullystes. Faut-il y voir un hommage à un illustre prédécesseur, ou plutôt une continuité esthétique entre ces deux librettistes-architectes?[40]

La scène était si célèbre que même les parodistes n'osèrent y toucher, crainte du sacrilège. Si sa Nanine est rabaissée au statut de 'riche héritière', si son Saint-Phal n'est plus ambassadeur, mais cornette de dragons, si ses Golcondais se réduisent à 'une douzaine de valets, frotteurs, palefreniers', Gondot change de registre lorsqu'il aborde l'épisode central: le piquant et le trivial font place à une versification délicate.[41] Notons cependant que l'héroïne

---

37 *L'Année littéraire* (1761), V, p. 269.

38 [Sedaine], *Aline, reine de Golconde*, p. 8.

39 Sedaine, 'Quelques réflexions', p. 510.

40 Sur l'influence des théories de l'architecture classique sur Quinault – oncle et tuteur de Germain Boffrand – voir notre ouvrage *Jean-Baptiste Lully. Musique et dramaturgie au service du prince* (Bruxelles: Vokar, 1992) p. 325–42.

41 *Nanine, sœur de lait de la reine de Golconde; parodiée, par imitation, sur les plus jolis airs connus, en trois actes, et quelques vaudevilles* (Genève et Paris: Veuve Duchesne, 1768), p. 34. Contrairement à ce qu'affirment les bibliographes, l'édition de 1773 (*Nanine, sœur de lait de la reine de Golconde; pastorale en trois actes; en ariettes et vaudevilles choisis* (Genève et Paris: Veuve Duchesne)) est loin d'être une simple réédition. Tout en reprenant largement le texte initial, cette seconde version adopte un ton nettement plus corsé et comprend en outre de très nombreuses suppressions, modifications et ajouts. En outre, ces deux parodies anonymes posent un problème d'attribution, actuellement insoluble. L'abbé Joseph de La Porte et Sébastien-Roch-Nicolas de Chamfort (*Dictionnaire dramatique* (Paris: Lacombe, 1776), II, p. 290) attribuent l'édition de 1773 à François-Fouque Deshayes, *dit*

chante sur l'air 'Toujours seule, disait Ninon', la chanson par laquelle Saint-Phal a réussi à lui ravir son pucelage: si cette Ninon-Nanine annonce certaine Nina, folle par amour, c'est surtout, pour le parodiste, une manière d'opposer l'active, mais peu chaste, Aline à la passive et fidèle Ariane qui, abandonnée par Thésée, mourut aux bords où elle avait été laissée. La seconde version de cette parodie, quoique beaucoup plus pimentée, ne touchera pas non plus au poétique deuxième acte. Toutes deux choisissent même la scène de retrouvailles pour sujet de leur frontispice.

Mais quelles sont les raisons du succès de la scène de vallon français? Au thème – qui continue d'émouvoir – du temps vaincu par l'amour, se superpose celui, religieux, du paradis perdu et celui, moral, de la campagne opposée à la ville et à ses perversions, incarnées par l'opéra et la prostitution. La scène centrale joue sur le réel. Le conte la plonge dans un brouillard onirique. Boufflers identifie héros et narrateur, empêchant le lecteur de prendre ses distances et de décider s'il s'agit ou non d'un rêve. Le livret de Sedaine, en revanche, prend le spectateur pour complice. Dès le premier acte, nous savons

---

Desfontaines de Lavallée. Ils précisent en outre que la musique était de Jean-Joseph Rodolphe et que l'ouvrage fut donné devant la cour à Fontainebleau en 1773. Ce fait semble établi aux yeux de la critique contemporaine (Franz Stieger, *Opernlexikon, Titelkatalog* (Tutzing: Schneider, 1975), II, p. 849; Elisabeth Cook et Michel Noiray, 'Rodolphe, Jean-Joseph', *New Grove Dictionary of Opera*). On notera cependant que *Nanine* n'est pas reprise parmi les œuvres attribuées à Desfontaines et à Rodolphe par La Porte et Chamfort. Cette attribution, absente de l'édition de 1775 du *Dictionnaire dramatique*, ne figure pas non plus dans la réédition de 1784. C'est sur cette base que Clarence D. Brenner (*A Bibliographical List of Plays in the French Language, 1700–1789* (Berkeley: University of California, 1947)) attribue la version de 1768 à Desfontaines. On notera que Desfontaines collabore alors avec Rodolphe pour *L'aveugle de Palmyre* (1767) et pour *Isménor* (1773). En revance, aucune des œuvres de Desfontaines publiées à l'époque ne relève du genre de la parodie. Tout en mentionnant l'attribution à Desfontaines, Joseph-Marie Quérard attribue l'ouvrage, dans sa version de 1768, à un certain Pierre-Thomas Gondot, 'commissaire des guerres, secrétaire des gardes-françaises et du duc de Biron' (*La France littéraire* (Paris: Didot, 1829), III, p. 407). Antoine-Alexandre Barbier attribue lui aussi l'œuvre a été écrite 'par Gondaut' (*Bibliothèque dramatique de monsieur de Soleinne* (Paris: Alliance des arts, 1844), III, p. 249, no. 3487). Jusqu'en 1777, la parodie est presque l'unique genre auquel se soit livré cet auteur mal connu. Il serait tentant d'attribuer la première version à Gondot et la seconde mouture à Desfontaines. Cependant, le ton très vert de la version de 1773 de *Nanine* est celui qu'affectionne Gondot. D'autre part, ce dernier avait l'habitude de réécrire ses parodies au gré des reprises: c'est le cas de son *Castor et Pollux*, paru à Bruxelles en 1754, et retravaillé pour la Comédie-Italienne sous le titre *Les Geméaux* (Paris: Duchesne, 1777). La question continue de diviser les bibliographes. Alexandre Cioranescu ne tranche pas (*Bibliographie de la littérature française du XVIIIe siècle* (Paris: CNRS, 1969), I, p. 648, no. 23216; II, p. 873, no. 31.433). Pierre M. Conlon l'attribue à Desfontaines, mais signale l'attribution à Gondot (*Le siècle des lumières. Bibliographie chronologique*, XV (1767–69) (Genève: Droz, 1995), p. 253, no. 68:779). Pour achever d'embrouiller les pistes, mentionnons encore que ces deux livrets ont fait l'objet de divers tirages et de contrefaçons, notamment bruxelloises.

qu'Aline est Aline et qu'elle a reconstitué le vallon d'amour dans ses jardins. Lorsque les spectateurs y retrouvent le héros, au second acte, ils savent qu'ils sont dans le réel. Saint-Phar, par contre, hésite sur la nature de ce qu'il voit: 'Rêvé-je? Où suis-je?... dans quels lieux?' (acte II, sc. I). Son songe est-il réellement le monde ou le monde est-il un songe? Sedaine renoue avec le thème, cher au baroque, du grand théâtre du monde et de ses illusions.

Il convient de se demander s'il s'agit ici d'une référence volontaire. Nous avons noté que, sur ce point, Sedaine a modifié la donnée de Boufflers. A-t-il songé à Shakespeare, chez qui cette thématique est évidemment très présente? Peut-être, mais il ne semble pas que cette facette de son génie intéresse alors les dramaturges français en quête de 'sublime'. En France même, les exemples ne manquaient pas. Au témoignage de Grimm, Sedaine et Monsigny se mirent au travail dès le printemps 1764,[42] au moment où Voltaire publiait ses *Commentaires sur Corneille.*[43] Certes, c'est sans aucun doute l'image du Corneille classique qui l'emportait. Seuls les spectacles à machines *Andromède* et *La Conquête de la toison d'or* faisaient l'objet d'une notice. Voltaire retient *Le menteur* et sa *Suite*, comédies inspirées de l'espagnol, mais de facture classique. Il bannit les comédies antérieures qui mêlaient comique et tragique. Rien non plus sur *L'Illusion comique* qui entre dans la thématique baroque qui nous intéresse. En revanche, Voltaire souligne la dette de l'*Héraclius* de Corneille envers Calderón. Pour trancher la querelle de paternité, Voltaire s'était procuré, non sans peine, la pièce espagnole. Son titre seul – *En esta vida todo es verdad y todo mentira* – trahit l'esprit baroque qui nous intéresse ici. Voltaire avait fini par la traduire presque intégralement et par la commenter. C'est évidemment Shakespeare qui sert de parangon. Voltaire leur trouve ce même mélange de grandeur et de bassesse qu'il rejette, tout en demeurant fasciné par le fait qu'ils atteignent, au même degré, au sublime. Voltaire vitupère cependant le caractère purement romanesque des pièces historiques de Calderón, alors que Shakespeare se voit célébré pour sa fidélité historique. Le commentaire s'achève par un éloge de l'*Arte nuevo de hacer comedias* de Lope de Vega.[44]

Sans doute cela donna-t-il envie d'en savoir plus. Prenant pour modèles les ouvrages de Brumoy sur le théâtre grec et ceux de La Place sur le théâtre anglais, Linguet décida de publier, en 1770, quatre volumes de *Théâtre espagnol.* La préface est un éloge dithyrambique des dramaturges espagnols, auxquels les auteurs français doivent plus qu'à ceux de l'Antiquité ou d'Italie.

---

[42] *Correspondance littéraire*, VII (1er mai 1766), p. 31.

[43] Voltaire, *Commentaires sur Corneille*, éd. David Williams, dans *Œuvres complètes* (Oxford: Voltaire Foundation, 1974–5), vol. LIII–LV.

[44] Voir la remarquable étude que David Williams consacre à 'Shakespeare and Calderón', *Commentaires sur Corneille*, LIII, p. 275–301.

Au milieu d'une production immense et encore peu perfectionnée, Linguet aperçoit 'des étincelles du génie le plus admirable'. Sa lecture induit des conclusions audacieuses. Il démontre le caractère purement conventionnel et relatif de l'unité de temps:

> Si nous avons pu étendre par tolérance jusqu'à vingt-quatre heures une action qui n'en occupe réellement pas plus de deux à la représentation, pourquoi ne serait-il pas permis aux Espagnols de reculer aussi un peu les bornes qu'ils se sont prescrites, et de prendre huit jours, quinze jours, au lieu de trois qu'ils ont annoncés? Cette réflexion pourrait mener loin.[45]

En effet ... Linguet stigmatise ensuite l'arbitraire de la séparation des genres, fondé sur une distinction sociale obsolète:

> Ils prennent indifféremment pour interlocuteurs, des rois, des princes, des ministres, des paysans, des bourgeois, et même la scène plaisante se passe souvent entre les premiers, tandis que l'attendrissement et l'infortune qui le produit, tombent sur les autres.[46]

La *comedia* espagnole lui apparaît comme la planche de salut des dramaturges en panne d'imagination:

> Le raffinement du goût, ou, si l'on veut, sa dépravation, ne permet plus aux poètes de se borner à la simplicité qui a fourni tant de chefs-d'œuvre à leurs prédécesseurs. Il faut aujourd'hui de grands mouvements sur la scène. Il faut des actions intriguées; on cherche à affecter les yeux et l'esprit, plus encore que le cœur. Les pièces espagnoles sont des trésors inépuisables de ces espèces de ressources, dont le génie peut tirer un très grand parti. Les jeunes gens qui se plaignent que les situations leur manquent, et que rien n'est si difficile que d'en trouver de neuves, n'ont rien qu'à lire, surtout, les comédies de Calderón; ils verront bientôt qu'ils se trompent.[47]

Autant d'idées qui montrent combien le retour à Calderón s'inscrit dans les préoccupations qui sont celles de Diderot et consorts à l'époque.[48]

---

[45] Simon-Nicolas-Henri Linguet, *Théâtre espagnol* (4 vol., Paris: De Hansy, 1770), I, p. xxiv.

[46] Ibid., I, p. xxv.

[47] Ibid., I, p. xiv.

[48] Voir Ana Maria Martin, 'Ensayo bibliografico sobre las ediciones, traducciones y estudios de Calderon de La Barca, en Francia', *Revista de literatura*, XVII (janvier–juin 1960), p. 52–100.

Linguet va même jusqu'à établir un lien entre le théâtre espagnol et l'opéra-comique. Une traduction de la pièce de Robert Dodsley *Le Roi et le meunier de Mansfield*, publiée en 1756 par Patu dans son *Choix de petites pièces de théâtre anglais*, avait immédiatement inspiré les dramaturges français. Collé en avait tiré la matière de *La partie de chasse de Henri IV* et Sedaine celle de son livret *Le Roi et le fermier*, mis en musique par Monsigny en 1762. Certes, 'les auteurs français ont eu la bonne foi d'avouer qu'ils avaient imité un Anglais qu'ils croyaient l'inventeur original de ce sujet: mais l'auteur anglais n'a pas dit qu'il l'avait pris d'un Espagnol'. Linguet démontre ensuite sans équivoque que Dodsley n'a fait que démarquer la *comedia El sabio en su retiro y villano en su rincón*, écrite au siècle précédent par Juan de Matos Fragoso:

> On pourra comparer ce diamant brut avec les pierres si bien mises en œuvre par messieurs Sedaine et Collé [...]. J'aurais mieux aimé pour eux et pour nous, qu'ils eussent obligation à l'original, qu'au copiste anglais.[49]

Le conseil fut suivi. Dalainval adapta la traduction de Linguet et en tira une comédie mêlée d'ariettes parodiées.[50] Les succès de Sedaine et de Collé prouvaient tout le profit qu'il y avait à retourner à Calderón, 'génie singulier, dont on ne prononcerait le nom qu'avec vénération, s'il était né Grec, et qui aurait laissé très peu de chose à faire aux Corneilles et aux Racines, s'il était né Français'.[51]

Réformer l'opéra

En 1762, Sedaine avait en effet réussi à emporter les suffrages avec *Le Roi et le fermier*. Son livret élevait en dignité le genre de l'opéra-comique, en mettant en scène des personnages historiques, dans une intrigue touchante. Il s'agissait bien d'une audace: Philidor se défila et laissa à Monsigny le soin d'essuyer les plâtres. Trois ans plus tard, Sedaine triomphait à la Comédie-Française avec *Le Philosophe sans le savoir*. Ces ouvrages novateurs avaient créé une attente: 'La

---

[49] Linguet, 'Avertissement' au *Sage dans sa retraite*, dans *Théâtre espagnol*, IV, n.p. Pour d'autres sources littéraires proposées, voir au texte suivant par Michel Noiray, p. 103–5.

[50] *Le sage dans sa retraite, comédie en cinq actes et en prose mêlée d'ariettes, traduit de l'espagnol, mise au théâtre français par Mr. Dalainval, musique de Grétry, représentée pour la première fois au Théâtre français de La Haye, pour le bénéfice de Mr. de Bray* (La Haye: Constapel, 1782).

[51] Linguet, *Théâtre espagnol*, I, p. xli.

réputation et les succès des auteurs du poème et de la musique, sur d'autres scènes, donnent naturellement la plus vive curiosité de voir cet ouvrage sur le théâtre de l'Opéra.'[52] Il ne restait plus qu'à s'attaquer au bastion de l'Académie Royale de Musique.

Ce qui peut avoir séduit Sedaine et les encyclopédistes dans le sujet de *La Reine de Golconde*, ce sont les possibilités qu'il offrait d'opérer une réforme en douceur. Il fallait certes saper la vieille esthétique lullyste, mais en sauvant les apparences. Sedaine en était parfaitement conscient:

> J'étais cependant satisfait d'avoir fait un poème qui remplissait tout le spectacle avec deux acteurs seulement, et les personnages étant français, sans baguette, sans féerie, nulle magie, point de combats, ni dieux, ni diables; et, cependant, il fit plaisir.[53]

Avec *Aline, reine de Golconde*, Sedaine avait renoncé au merveilleux que tous les théoriciens, de Charles Perrault à Cahusac, avaient imposé à l'opéra français.[54] On sait que Diderot appelait de ses vœux le dramaturge philosophe qui, réformant la poésie lyrique, 'la fasse descendre des régions enchantées sur la terre que nous habitons'.[55] Le *Mercure de France* saisit parfaitement l'enjeu d'*Aline, reine de Golconde* et s'interrogea sur la valeur de cette 'nouvelle forme qu'occasionne nécessairement le nouveau genre de musique que l'on tente aujourd'hui d'étendre de l'Opéra bouffon à l'Opéra héroïque'.[56] Ayant remarqué la disparition du merveilleux, le journaliste condamna

> ces changements subits de l'intérieur à l'extérieur d'un lieu, sans qu'il y ait le temps idéalement vraisemblable pour que les acteurs puissent s'y transporter, vraisemblance qui ne peut guère avoir lieu que par les entractes, toutes les fois que le pouvoir surnaturel ne les opère pas.[57]

Si le livret d'*Aline, reine de Golconde* trahit l'influence des encyclopédistes, force est de constater que la réforme était bien timide. Tout d'abord, Sedaine n'avait pas osé attaquer de front la tragédie en musique. Son *Aline, reine de Golconde* relève en effet d'un sous-genre bâtard, celui du ballet-héroïque. Bien que le mot ballet ait pu être parfois utilisé à l'époque pour désigner un véritable

---

52 *Mercure de France* (avril 1766), p. 182–3.

53 Sedaine, 'Quelques réflexions', p. 510.

54 Voir Catherine Kintzler, *Poétique de l'opéra français de Corneille à Rousseau* (Paris: Minerve, 1991), p. 181–352.

55 Denis Diderot, *Entretiens sur le Fils naturel*, dans *Œuvres complètes*, éd. Jules Assézat et Maurice Tourneux (Paris: Garnier, 1875–7), VII, p. 156–7.

56 *Mercure de France* (mai 1766), p. 182.

57 Ibid., p. 184.

opéra – *Platée* est un 'ballet héroïque' – chez un dramaturge novateur comme Sedaine, il ne peut s'agir d'une appellation floue, mais bien d'un choix de genre nettement affirmé. Sous tout rapport, *Aline, reine de Golconde* était, en fait, une 'pastorale héroïque', genre ancien qu'avait fondé l'*Acis et Galatée* de Lully. C'est vers le milieu du siècle que l'ancienne appellation – encore très commune chez Rameau jusqu'à *Daphnis et Eglé* en 1753 – fut remplacée peu à peu par celle de 'ballet héroïque'. Ce dernier genre avait été initié par plusieurs librettistes de Rameau: Fuzelier, Pellegrin et surtout par l'encyclopédiste Cahusac qui en avait usé pour *Naïs*, pour *Les Fêtes de l'Hymen et de l'Amour ou Les Dieux d'Égypte*, et pour *Les Fêtes de Polymnie*.

Un spectateur aussi malveillant que Collé épingla le manque d'audace: 'il n'a fait qu'une pastorale de ce conte singulier et gaillard'.[58] La parodie de Gondot, *Nanine, sœur de lait de la reine de Golconde*, dans sa seconde mouture, se présentera également comme une 'pastorale en trois actes'. A l'occasion de la représentation du 16 mai de 1771 à Versailles, Ballard publia un livret portant un nouvel intitulé: '*La reine de Golconde*, opéra en trois actes'. La suppression du prénom Aline effaçait l'allusion à l'humble origine de l'héroïne: la bergère disparaissait pour faire oublier la pastorale. La référence au genre de l'opéra évitait de se situer dans la hiérarchie des genres français. Peut-être soulignait-elle d'autre part l'italianisme de la musique.

Le ballet, dans *Aline, reine de Golconde*, constitue bien la part principale de l'ouvrage, tant en durée qu'aux yeux des spectateurs. Lors des reprises, seules ces parties firent l'objet de modifications importantes.[59] A chaque fois, on fit appel à des chorégraphes de renom: rien moins que Gardel, Vestris et Noverre, pour les représentations de 1779. Or, dans ces ballets, on ne voit rien qui puisse particulièrement répondre aux conceptions des encyclopédistes. Le ballet d'action se limite à une danse du premier acte:

> Les gens de la flotte et les soldats français viennent se mêler à la fête, qu'ils troublent; d'autres plus raisonnables les arrêtent. Ils se joignent tous aux contredanses générales qui finissent cet acte.[60]

Seules quelques didascalies précisent les mouvements que les protagonistes doivent effectuer durant ces danses, ceci afin d'éviter une trop grande coupure

---

58 Charles Collé, *Journal et mémoires*, p. 85.

59 Lors de la reprise de 1768, Bachaumont écrit qu''on a cru dédommager le public par les ballets qui font aujourd'hui la partie brillante de ce spectacle': *Mémoires secrets*, XIX (4 octobre 1768), p. 27–9.

60 [Pierre-Alexandre Monsigny et Michel-Jean Sedaine], *Aline, reine de Golconde, ballet-héroïque en trois actes, par Mr. ***, représenté pour la première fois par l'Académie Royale de Musique, le mardi 15 avril 1766* (Paris: Hérissant, s.d.), p. 103.

avec le reste de la pièce. La tentative était trop timide pour convaincre un adversaire aussi radical que Grimm:

> C'est le comble de la barbarie et du mauvais goût de mêler ensemble deux arts d'imitation, et si vous étudiez les premiers éléments du goût, vous sentirez que celui qui imite par le chant ne doit jamais se trouver dans la même pièce avec celui qui imite par la danse, l'unité d'imitation n'étant pas moins essentielle que l'unité d'action.[61]

Malgré son habilité, Sedaine n'avait convaincu ni les tenants de l'ancien opéra, ni les partisans d'une réforme. Le public, en revanche, se pressa en foule.[62]

Un même accueil mitigé fut réservé à la partition de Monsigny. Tant du point de vue musical que littéraire, le but avait été de transposer sur la scène de l'Académie Royale de Musique les procédés de l'opéra-comique. Monsigny était regardé

> comme l'homme le plus propre à opérer une révolution sur le théâtre de l'Opéra, et à faire la transition de ce vieux et misérable goût qui y règne à un nouveau genre, sans trop choquer les partisans de la vieille boutique et sans trop déplaire aux amateurs de musique.[63]

Ici aussi, la tentative parut trop timide à Grimm qui ne vit qu''un opéra français dans toute la rigueur du terme' et défia 'les plus rigoristes de lui reprocher la moindre innovation, la plus petite hérésie'.[64] La part prépondérante des ballets, la symbolique monarchique, la construction symétrique, les ariettes réservées aux divertissements, l'abondance des chœurs, tout ce que Grimm détestait dans l'opéra français était là. Quant à Diderot qui préférait de loin Philidor à Monsigny, il ne tint pas, pour le coup, à soutenir la tentative de son ami Sedaine. En revanche, tant Boufflers que Choiseul devaient préférer Monsigny, d'origine noble, et fort introduit dans la bonne société.

La musique de Monsigny, sans être révolutionnaire, témoignait d'une volonté de rénovation, discrète sans doute, mais incontestable. Venimeux et perspicace, comme à l'accoutumée, Collé ne s'y trompa pas:

> La musique de cet opéra, que l'on avait annoncé pour avoir un caractère de singularité qui devait surprendre tout le monde, n'a rien qui la distingue de la musique des pièces à ariettes de notre Comédie

---

61 *Correspondance littéraire*, VII (15 mai 1766), p. 41.

62 Voir *Mercure de France* (avril 1766), p. 182–3; (juin 1766), p. 196.

63 *Correspondance littéraire*, VII (15 mai 1766), p. 38.

64 Ibid., p. 39.

> Italienne; à moins qu'on ne trouve peut-être cette différence dans une plus grande monotonie et un ennui plus marqué.[65]

Nombre d'auditeurs perçurent la nouveauté de la partition et, en particulier, l'usage renforcé de la musique périodique qu'avaient promue les tenants des Bouffons et, à leur suite, les encyclopédistes comme Rousseau, Grimm, Diderot ou d'Alembert. En revanche, les admirateurs de Lully et de Rameau vitupérèrent les 'romances' que Monsigny avait tenté d'introduire dans la texture même des scènes:

> On peut juger si la coupe qu'exige ce style de romance dans la versification est aussi favorable à la liaison nécessaire du dialogue, à l'expression la plus naturelle des nuances et même des grands mouvements qui se varient et qui se contrastent quelquefois d'un moment à l'autre dans les passions? si les ariettes, qui tranchent subitement et qui se découpent sur le fond général d'une scène, sont plus satisfaisantes pour le goût que ces airs mesurés qui paraissent naître et se former du sein même de l'ancien récitatif auquel ils se marient?[66]

Monsigny n'utilise guère le récitatif 'simple', lui préférant le récitatif accompagné. Il se sert de celui-ci avec subtilité: il s'agit tantôt de très brèves sections insérées au sein d'une scène, tantôt d'une forme plus large qui conduit à l'arioso. Du point de vue compositionnel, seul l'usage de reprises ou de *da capo* permet de distinguer l'arioso d'un air proprement dit. Les retrouvailles d'Aline et de Saint-Phar, à la seconde scène de l'acte II, fournissent un bon exemple de ce mélange de techniques: la scène s'ouvre par un 'andante', en récitatif accompagné lorsque le héros décrit l'arrivée d'Aline. Leur premier dialogue, en récitatif simple, conduit à un 'andante' en récitatif accompagné: celui-ci est interrompu par un silence après la phrase de reconnaissance 'c'est Aline'. Sans transition, Aline chante une romance. Après un nouveau récit mesuré, la scène s'achève par un duo marqué 'amoroso', avec *da capo*. Sans doute est-ce dans l'usage intensif des formes intermédiaires, telles que le récit mesuré et l'arioso, que réside la part la plus novatrice de la partition: parmi les pages relevant de ce style mixte, signalons l''amoroso' d'Aline 'Sous cet ombrage, arrêtez un moment' (acte II, scène III), ou le 'lamentabile', avec basson et hautbois solos, de Saint-Phar, qui ouvre le dernier acte. Il est évident que la musique de Monsigny répondait d'assez près aux vœux que Diderot avait exprimés dans le *Troisième entretien sur le Fils naturel.* Notons

---

65 Collé, *Journal et mémoires*, III, p. 86–7.

66 *Mercure de France* (mai 1766), p. 189–90.

cependant que les airs *da capo* demeurent le plus souvent des airs de 'maximes' – 'L'Amour fuit les lambris dorés' d'Usbek (acte II, sc. IV) – plutôt que des peintures d'affects, comme le voulaient Chastellux dans son *Essai sur l'union de la poésie et de la musique*, ou Grimm, dans l'article 'Poème lyrique' de l'*Encyclopédie*, tous deux parus en 1765, en pleine élaboration d'*Aline, reine de Golconde.*

Comme on le voit, tout en étant perceptible, l'influence de Diderot et de ses amis demeure réduite. La pantomime, qui leur était si chère, est utilisée avec beaucoup de parcimonie. Le plus souvent, elle se limite à des didascalies qui précisent les mouvements de scènes se déroulant pendant une symphonie:

> Sur un des côtés et sur le devant de la scène est une tente magnifique, Usbek, en sort au commencement du lever de l'aurore, la tente s'enlève à un signal qu'il fait, il emmène les deux soldats qui gardaient la tente.[67]

On sait que le théâtre de Diderot, si verbeux soit-il, confère au silence un rôle expressif. Sedaine lui fait également place à coups de '...' de '?' ou de '!'. Monsigny use de ces silences d'une manière originale en créant des 'trous' dans la continuité du flux sonore, chère à l'esthétique française. C'est le cas lorsque, par trois fois, il interrompt le récitatif par des points d'orgue surmontés de la mention 'silence' (acte I, sc. III). Ailleurs encore, le compositeur se contente d'indiquer simplement, sans notation musicale, 'un petit silence' (acte III, sc. II). Les auteurs en tirent des effets très expressifs. Ainsi du silence qui suit la reconnaissance d'Aline par Saint-Phar, dont nous avons déjà parlé, ou encore, au finale, lorsque les bergers hésitent à se présenter devant celle qui est devenue leur reine: après l'annonce musicale du divertissement, la partition indique un silence avec la didascalie 'Ils avancent quelques pas et s'arrêtent, ils n'entrent sur la scène que lorsque la reine le leur dit.' Effet expressif qui a dû plaire à Diderot. L'originalité de cette écriture directement inspirée du drame bourgeois, surprit, comme en témoigne sa parodie dans *Nanine, sœur de lait de la reine de Golconde*:

> Tout ce que le cœur peut sentir
> Pour l'objet qu'il adore ....
> Ce que, dans l'excès du plaisir,
> Il se dit .... ces pleurs du sentiment,
> Ces transports .... ce délire ....
> Non, cela ne peut aisément
> Se peindre, ni se dire.[68]

---

67 [Pierre-Alexandre Monsigny et Michel-Jean Sedaine], *Aline*, acte II, sc. I.

68 [Gondot], *Nanine* (1773), p. 9.

Voir *Aline*

Pour terminer, tentons d'imaginer comment, visuellement, *Aline, reine de Golconde* a été représentée sur la scène de l'Académie Royale de Musique. Nous avons vu déjà que Choiseul avait exigé des directeurs une dépense dont l'importance s'explique par la réalisation de nombreux décors et costumes nouveaux. L'ampleur de la tâche prit la direction de court:

> Les soins et les recherches multipliées que l'on a employées pour ne rien laisser à désirer dans le spectacle de *la Reine de Golconde*, ont fait suspendre la représentation de ce nouvel opéra jusqu'au dimanche, 13 du mois.[69]

Ces recherches avaient visé

> à rendre l'exacte vérité du costume dans les habits, lesquels ont été faits sur des dessins exacts même sur des modèles tirés du pays même. On a parfaitement bien représenté la magnificence et la richesse asiatique, jusque sur les vêtements des nombreux cortèges qui forment la pompe de cette représentation.[70]

Sans doute étaient-ils dû à Louis-René Boquet qui, en 1758, avait succédé à Jean-Baptiste Martin, comme costumier de l'Académie Royale de Musique.[71] Au second acte, tous les personnages dansants et chantants 'sont vêtus à la française, dans le genre de la bergerie galante'.[72] Il est possible qu'un dessin de costume dû à l'atelier de Boquet et représentant un 'vieillard paysan' ait été destiné à ce personnage chantant d'*Aline, reine de Golconde*.[73] Un certain

---

[69] *Mercure de France* (avril 1766), p. 194.

[70] *Mercure de France* (mai 1766), p. 187–8.

[71] Sokalski (*Contes*, p. 71) reproduit une gravure de Jean-Baptiste Martin portant la lettre 'Africain, dans *Aline, reine de Golconde*'. Il s'agit d'une planche tirée du *23e Cahier de costumes français. 19e Suite d'habillements à la mode en 1779*. Étant donné qu'il n'est jamais fait état d'Africains dans cet opéra, même lors de la reprise de 1779, et que Martin avait quitté l'Opéra depuis près de vingt ans, il est vraisemblable qu'il s'agisse d'une simple remise au goût du jour d'une gravure ancienne. Celle-ci figure en effet, tantôt sans la lettre, tantôt avec la seule mention 'Africain' dans le recueil de vingt costumes publié par Martin en 1763. Un état, rehaussé d'aquarelle et d'or, est reproduit, en noir et blanc, dans Carlos Fischer, *Les Costumes de l'opéra* (Paris: Librairie de France, 1931), p. 73; et, en couleur, dans Jérôme de La Gorce, *Féeries d'opéra* (Paris: Éditions du patrimoine, 1997) n° 147.

[72] *Mercure de France* (mai 1766), p. 173. Voir les renseignements *infra*, p. 279–80.

[73] F-Po, D 216, reproduit dans François Lesure, *L'Opéra classique français* (Genève: Minkoff, 1972), planche 77.

'réalisme' qui caractérise ce costume n'est pas sans rappeler les 'paysans galants' et les 'paysannes galantes' du recueil de Martin. Nous pouvons également nous faire une idée du style des costumes exotiques. L'Opéra conserve un dessin à la plume qui, selon Fischer, pourrait être destiné au costume d'Aline.[74] Coiffée d'un turban à plumes, elle porte un manteau agrafé sur un corsage plat, large et fermé, et formant traîne. La robe renonce aux paniers à coudes, suivant ainsi la mode dominante à la ville depuis 1763. Bien qu'il porte la signature de Boucher, ce dessin rappelle, jusque dans certaines maladresses, la manière de Boquet. Tel est également le cas d'un second dessin représentant un fort exotique porteur de flambeau, 'tout de satin jonquille et argent, manteau de satin cerise, turban blanc garni de pierreries', qui ne dépareraient pas la cour de Golconde.[75] Boquet nous a encore laissé un projet pour le costume porté par Dauberval au troisième acte: l'habit d'indienne, simplement noué à la ceinture, le turban emplumé et la perle à l'oreille témoignent d'un véritable souci d'exotisme.[76] La chorégraphie se contentait malheureusement de reproduire les pas traditionnels au lieu de travailler elle aussi dans 'un caractère étranger'.[77] *Mutatis mutandis*, il semble bien que Boquet ait déjà esquissé pour *Aline, reine de Golconde* cette 'vérité du costume' qu'il devait développer après 1770, sous l'influence de Noverre.[78]

La réalisation de deux décors avait été confiée à François Boucher. Celui-ci avait déjà travaillé pour l'Académie Royale de Musique entre 1737 et 1739, puis de 1744 à 1748, avant d'y prendre la relève de Pietro Algieri en 1761.[79] Le *Mercure de France* nous apprend qu'il avait donné notamment l'idée du 'salon intérieur du palais, construit, orné et meublé très exactement dans le goût indien'.[80] A la même époque, Boucher travaillait aux cartons des *Fêtes chinoises*, pour lesquels il s'était inspiré des dessins du père Attiret, missionnaire en Chine depuis 1737. On peut imaginer que le décor indien

---

[74] Fischer, *Les Costumes de l'opéra*, p. 66.

[75] Reproduit dans Max Aghion, *Le Théâtre à Paris au XVIIIe siècle* (Paris: Librairie de France, s.d.), p. 427.

[76] Reproduit dans Fischer, *Les Costumes de l'opéra*, p. 91.

[77] *Mercure de France* (mai 1766), p. 187.

[78] La Gorce, *Féeries d'opéra*, p. 23.

[79] En l'absence d'une étude approfondie sur le travail de Boucher à l'Opéra, l'approche la plus fouillée figure dans *François Boucher (1703–1770), catalogue de l'exposition du Grand-Palais à Paris* (Paris: Réunion des Musées Nationaux, 1986), notice 47. La participation de Boucher à la création d'*Aline* y est cependant omise. On se reportera également à l'exposé succinct mais précis de La Gorce, *Féeries d'opéra*, p. 21. Sur les décors par Boucher pour l'entreprise de Monnet à L'Opéra-comique, voir aussi l'article d'Alisdair Laing, 'Boucher ou l'invention d'un langage' dans *Boucher: exposition du Grand-Palais*, p. 62–77; Ledbury, 'Greuze and Sedaine', p. 65–70.

[80] *Mercure de France* (mai 1766), p. 178–88.

d'*Aline, reine de Golconde* fut réalisé dans le même souci de vérité. Bien que cette démarche soit fort éloignée de la conception moderne de reconstitution,[81] elle démontre, chez Boucher et ses comparses demeurés anonymes, une volonté, quasi pédagogique, de réalisme dans l'exotisme, dont témoignaient également les costumes de Boquet:

> Les mêmes soins et la même dépense ont été prodigués pour les décorations. Une place publique, un kiosque élevé sur le bord de la mer, une salle, où tout ce qui la meuble est copié d'après des objets réels du pays, un extérieur de palais, un jardin et un kiosque dont l'effet est charmant et qui transporte le spectateur dans le sein de l'Inde, enfin, tout peint avec noblesse et agrément la nature et l'art d'un climat étranger et fort différent du nôtre.[82]

Est-il exclu que leur 'conseiller scientifique' ait été le célèbre orientaliste Abraham Anquetil-Duperron, qui, dès son retour en 1762, avait confié au *Journal des savants* une *Relation abrégée du voyage fait dans l'Inde*? Cet intérêt pour l'Inde peut surprendre à un moment où la France, se désintéressant de ses anciennes possessions, avait laissé le champ libre aux Anglais. Malgré son affaiblissement politique, la France poursuivait néanmoins ses échanges commerciaux: c'est à cette époque que la Compagnie Française des Indes Orientales atteignit l'apogée de sa prospérité.

Le second décor confié à Boucher était celui du fameux vallon d'amour. Si l'on en croit le *Mercure de France*, l'artiste s'en tira avec bonheur:

> [Les décorations] du bocage européen, terminé par le plus agréable paysage, ont été peintes d'après des dessins et esquisses du célèbre M. Boucher, premier peintre du roi; on doit juger ce que cela ajoute, au mérite d'une fidèle et savante exécution.[83]

Le décor champêtre conçu par Boucher pour la reprise d'*Issé* en 1741 peut donner une idée de ses réalisations dans le genre de la pastorale: des châssis pittoresques dissymétriques dégagent largement un vaste paysage peint sur la toile de fond.

---

81 C'est en effet surtout l'invention et la fantaisie qui dominent dans ces tapisseries, comme l'a montré Denys Sutton, *François Boucher (1703–1770): catalogue de l'exposition de Tokyo* (Tokyo: Nippon Television Network Corporation, 1982), p. 231–2.

82 *Mercure de France* (mai 1766), p. 188.

83 Ibid.

On peut affirmer, sans risque, que Diderot n'aimait guère Boucher:[84] 'Ne me tirerai-je jamais de ces maudites pastorales?' s'écriait-il, excédé par ses tableaux exposés au Salon de 1765.[85]

> Je vous défie de trouver dans toute une campagne un brin d'herbe de ses paysages [...]. Il est dans ses paysages d'un gris de couleur et d'une uniformité de ton qui vous ferait prendre sa toile, à deux pieds de distance, pour un morceau de gazon ou d'une couche de persil, coupé en carré.[86]

Et Diderot de souligner que l'artiste, au lieu de prendre la nature pour modèle, ne fait que transposer sur ses toiles, le monde faux des bergers d'opéra-comique:

> La grâce de ses bergères est la grâce de la Favart dans *Rose et Colas* [...][87]
> Au centre de la toile une bergère, Catinon en petit chapeau qui conduit un âne [...].
> À droite, sur le devant, toujours la bergère Catinon ou Favart couchée et endormie.[88]

Diderot n'était pas seul à penser que Boucher était incapable d'opérer, en profondeur, une réforme du décor à l'Académie Royale de Musique. Afin de souligner l'impossibilité d'adapter les formes musicales et littéraires de l'opéra-comique au grand genre, le *Mercure de France* use d'une comparaison

---

84 Voir Roland Mortier, 'Diderot contre Boucher ou le refus du rococo', *Etudes sur le XVIIIe siècle*, XVIII (Bruxelles: Editions de l'Université de Bruxelles, 1991), p. 151–7.

85 Denis Diderot, *Salon de 1765*, éd. Else Marie Bukdahl et Annette Lorenceau (Paris: Hermann, 1984), p. 66.

86 Ibid., p. 54, 57.

87 Ibid., p. 54. La variante du texte inclus dans la *Correspondance littéraire* donne ici *Annette et Lubin* au lieu de *Rose et Colas* (voir *Salon de 1765*, p. 54 et note 116). Il peut y avoir deux raisons à ce changement. Madame Favart n'a pas joué le rôle de Rose dans le *Rose et Colas* de Sedaine en 1764 (le rôle est pris par Mme Laruette), et Grimm voulait peut-être mettre de l'exactitude dans le texte de son ami. Mais il peut y avoir une autre raison. Diderot, dans ce passage acerbe, met l'accent sur l'artifice des toiles de Boucher (qu'il compare défavorablement au naturel de Chardin, Vernet et Greuze), en prétendant que les bergères des toiles de Boucher ressemblaient aux actrices Mme Favart (née Duronceray, 1727–72) et Mlle Foulquier ('Catinon') dans des rôles de théâtre. Il se peut que Grimm ait corrigé le texte de son ami, pour ne pas associer *Rose et Colas* de Sedaine (qui à ce moment-là était étroitement lié aux philosophes, et dont Grimm aimait à louer le 'naturel') avec l'artifice des toiles de Boucher.

88 Ibid., p. 60–61. 'Catinon' débuta en mars 1751 à la Comédie-Italienne, prenant les rôles de Nanette et Une batelière dans *Les Amants inquiets* de Favart.

éclairante et se demande 'si le pinceau d'un excellent paysagiste, ou celui de l'admirable peintre du *Père de famille*, sans changer de manière et de génie dans la composition, eût été également ou même plus propre à peindre les batailles d'*Alexandre*, les amours des dieux et des bergers héroïques, que celui des *Lebrun*, des *Mignards*, des *Lemoine*'.[89] C'est au salon de 1755 que Greuze avait exposé son *Père de famille expliquant la Bible*, soit trois ans avant la publication du *Père de famille* de Diderot.[90] Diderot devait vouer à l'artiste une admiration presque sans réserve jusqu'à l'échec, prédit ici, de son tableau historique *Les reproches de Sévère à son fils Caracalla* exposé au salon de 1769.

Gageons que pour le coup, Diderot et Choiseul se seraient accordés s'ils eussent été libres de leur choix: les collections de Choiseul comptaient de nombreux tableaux de Greuze. C'est l'époque où celui-ci peint *Les Deux amis* ou encore *La Laitière*. Tous deux renvoient à La Fontaine. En 1770, *Les Deux amis* devaient inspirer à Diderot – ainsi qu'à nombre de ses contemporains – un conte moral: *Les Deux amis de Bourbonne*. Quant à *La Laitière*, elle rappelle bien entendu Perrette, mais annonce aussi l'épisode de *Jacques le fataliste*, où celui-ci donne deux gros écus à une pauvre mère de famille dont la cruche d'huile vient de se briser. L'une des scènes les plus célèbres du conte de Boufflers est celle où Aline – autre Perrette et nouvelle référence à La Fontaine – cassait sa cruche et versait, de manière aussi grivoise que symbolique, son lait. Greuze n'avait pu montrer Aline sur la scène de l'Opéra, mais il lui consacra son tableau le plus célèbre: *La Cruche cassée*.[91]

---

[89] *Mercure de France* (mai 1766), p. 190.

[90] Voir Jean Ehrard, 'Tableaux de famille: *La lecture de la Bible*', dans Antoinette et Jean Ehrard (éd.), *Diderot et Greuze* (Clermont-Ferrand: Université de Clermont II-Adosa, 1986), p. 77–90.

[91] Rapprochements établis par Simon Davies (voir au note 9), *Aline*, p. 26.

Chapter 5

Quatre rois à la chasse: Dodsley, Collé, Sedaine, Goldoni

Michel Noiray

Dans l'avertissement qui précède son livret du *Re alla caccia*, Goldoni écrit:

> L'argomento di quest'Opera è fondato sopra un'antica tradizione, che tuttavia si mantiene e passa per un'istoria. L'hanno posta gl'Inglesi sopra la Scena, di là l'hanno tratta i Francesi, l'Autore Italiano se ne vale pel suo Paese. Ciascheduno l'ha vestita alla sua maniera; le cose principali si trovano in tutti, e le invenzioni si possono rilevar dal confronto.[1]

Le chapitre que voici tentera de répondre au vœu de Goldoni et de 'confronter', dans leur succession chronologique, quatre œuvres dramatiques qui présentent un évident rapport de filiation: une pièce de théâtre anglaise, *The King and the Miller of Mansfield* de Robert Dodsley, donnée à Drury Lane en 1737; une comédie de Charles Collé, *La Partie de chasse de Henri IV*, représentée pour la première fois à Bagnolet en juillet 1762; une 'comédie mêlée de morceaux de musique' de Sedaine, *Le Roi et le fermier*, représentée pour la première fois à la Comédie-Italienne en novembre 1762; et *Il re alla caccia, dramma giocoso* de Goldoni déjà cité, écrit à Paris pour le livret mais mis en musique par Baldassare Galuppi à Venise en 1763. Chacun à sa manière, les trois derniers auteurs ont reconnu leur dette envers Dodsley, qu'ils pouvaient lire dans une traduction française, *Le Roi et le meunier de Mansfield*, ordinairement attribuée à Claude-Pierre Patu et publiée à Paris en 1756.[2] On dispose ainsi d'un

---

1 'The argument of this opera is based on a traditional story which nevertheless is still current and passes for fact. The English put it on stage, the French have taken it from there, and the Italian poet makes use of it for his own country. Each one has dressed it in his own way; the main traits are present in all, and the variations may be drawn out by comparing them': 'A chi legge', dans *Tutte le opere di Carlo Goldoni*, éd. Giuseppe Ortolani (14 vol., s.l.: Mondadori, 1935–56), XII, p. 163. Cette édition se fonde sur le livret original, *Il re alla caccia* (Venise: Bassanese, 1763).

2 Patu (1729–57) est désigné comme traducteur dans la nécrologie parue dans Jean-Marie Clément et Joseph de La Porte, *Anecdotes dramatiques* (3 vol., Paris: Veuve Duchesne, 1775), III, p. 381 (réimp. Genève, 1971, p. 398). Avant sa mort prématurée, Patu

ensemble de textes homogène par ses motifs dramatiques mais disparate par les genres et les fonctions qui leur sont attribués; c'est l'occasion pour nous d'observer les variations dans le traitement d'un sujet exemplaire à bien des égards, d'un pays à l'autre, du théâtre parlé à l'opéra, d'un genre d'opéra à un autre.[3]

Le tableau qui suit donne une présentation synoptique des quatre pièces, non pas dans l'ordre adopté par Dodsley mais dans celui qu'ont adopté ses trois imitateurs, dont on verra bientôt qu'ils ont unanimement rejeté les incessants changements de décor exigés par leur modèle. Les chiffres en caractère gras désignent les morceaux en musique du *Roi et le fermier* et les *pezzi chiusi* du *Re alla caccia*; pour ce dernier, l'acte III tout entier, sans équivalent chez les auteurs précédents, est détaillé en bloc à la fin du tableau. Les noms des personnages qui chantent un air ou un ensemble sont soulignés. La deuxième ligne du tableau donne les équivalences entre les noms des personnages lorsqu'ils passent d'une pièce dans une autre.

Le Roi et le meunier de Mansfield	*La Partie de chasse de Henri IV*	*Le Roi et le fermier*	*Il re alla caccia*
'A Dramatick Tale' en un acte. Londres, Drury Lane Theatre, 29 janvier 1737 trad. Patu, 1756	Comédie en 2 actes. Bagnolet, 8 juillet 1762 En 3 actes, Bagnolet, 25 décembre 1764	Comédie mêlée de morceaux de musique. Paris, Comédie-Italienne, 22 novembre 1762 (Monsigny)	Dramma giocoso. Venise, Teatro San Samuele, automne 1763 (Galuppi)
Le Roi	Henri IV, roi de France	Le Roi	Il Re (Enrico IV, re d'Inghilterra)
Richard	Richard	Richard	Giorgio
Peggy	Agathe	Jenny	Giannina
Catherine	Catau	Betsy	Lisetta
Lurewell	Conchiny	Lurewel	Milord Fidelingh
Le Meunier	Michau	—	—
Marguerite	Margot	La Mère	—
—	Lucas	—	Pascale

avait vécu à Londres. Dodsley (1704–64) était à la fois écrivain et éditeur, et sa pièce est restée au répertoire de Drury Lane de 1737 à 1794: voir Ben Ross Schneider, Jr, *Index to The London Stage* (Carbondale etc.: Southern Illinois University Press, 1979), p. 245–6.

3 Une première approche de ce sujet se trouve dans John van Eerde, '*The King and the Miller* in England, France and Italy', *Francia*, XXXVIII (1981), p. 41–51. Voir aussi note 42.

Le Roi et le meunier de Mansfield	*La Partie de chasse de Henri IV*	*Le Roi et le fermier*	*Il re alla caccia*
	Fontainebleau		*Bosco spazioso*
	Acte I (ajouté en 1764)		I, I Coro **(1)** Fidelingh **(2)** I, II–III + Miledi, Re **(3)** I, IV + Riccardo **(4)** I, V Miledi **(5)**
	Forêt de Sénart	*Une forêt*	*Bosco con collina praticabile*
	II, I–II Lucas, Catau II, III–IV Lucas, Agathe		
La ville de Mansfield			
IV Richard lit la lettre de Peggy	II, V Richard, Lucas	I, I Richard **(1)** I, II Richard, Gardes	I, VI Giorgio **(6)**, Pascale
		I, III Richard, Betsy I, IV Richard, Rustaut **(2)** I, V Richard **(3)**	I, VII + Lisetta
		I, VI Richard, Betsy **(4)**	I, VII (suite), Lisetta **(7)** I, VIII Giorgio

Le Roi et le meunier de Mansfield	*La Partie de chasse de Henri IV*	*Le Roi et le fermier*	*Il re alla caccia*
Chambre dans une maison de Mansfield			
V Peggy, Phébé			
VI Peggy et Richard		I, VII + Jenny I, VIII Richard, Jenny **(5, 6)**	I, IV Giannina **(8)**, Giorgio **(9)**
			I, X Giannina, Lisetta I, XI + Pascale. Giannina **(10)** I, XII Lisetta, Pascale (= Collé II, I–II) I, XIII Pascale **(11)**
		I, IX–X Richard, Jenny, Betsy **(7)**	I, XIV Giannina, Giorgio, Lisetta, Pascale **(12)**
La forêt de Sherwood			
I Quatre courtisans	II, VI–VII Courtisans II, VIII + un Paysan	II, I Rustaut, Charlot **(8)**	II, I Giorgio, Pascale **(13)**
II Roi seul	II, IX Henri II, X + Braconniers	II, II Roi **(9)**	II, II Re **(14)**

Le Roi et le meunier de Mansfield	*La Partie de chasse de Henri IV*	*Le Roi et le fermier*	*Il re alla caccia*
III Roi, Meunier	II, XI Henri, Michau	II, III + Richard	II, III Re, Giorgio **(15)**
X Gardes			
		II, IV Lurewel, Courtisan **(10)** Lurewel **(11)**	II, IV Miledi II, V + Riccardo et Fidelingh
XI Gardes, courtisans		II, V + Rustaut, Charlot. Quatuor **(12)**	II, VI + Guardie, Pascale **(16)** II, VII + Fidelingh **(17)**
			II, VIII Pascale **(18)**, Miledi II, IX Guardie, Miledi **(19)**
Le moulin	*Maison du meunier*	*Une ferme*	*Cortile di Giannina*
VII Marguerite et Catherine	III, I Margot, Catau	III, I Betsy, Jenny, La Mère **(13)**	II, X Giannina **(20)**, Lisetta, Giannina **(21)**
VIII + Richard	III, II + Richard	III, II + Richard, Le Roi	II, XI + Re, Giorgio Giannina **(22)**
IX + Le Meunier, le Roi	III, III–X + Michau Henri flirte avec Catau.	III, II (suite)-3 III, IV La Mère **(14)**	

Le Roi et le meunier de Mansfield	*La Partie de chasse de Henri IV*	*Le Roi et le fermier*	*Il re alla caccia*
XII Roi, Meunier, Marguerite, Richard, à table XIII + Joseph	III, XI Les mêmes. Souper.	III, V Jenny, La Mère, Betsy **(15)** III, VI–VII III, VIII Jenny, Betsy **(16)** III, IX Richard, Jenny **(17)**	II, XII–XIV Re, Giannina, Lisetta, Giorgio. II, XIV Giorgio **(23)**
XIV + Peggy	III, XII + Agathe et Lucas	III, X–XII Jenny **(18)** Richard **(19)** Le Roi **(20)**	II, XV Re, Giannina, Lisetta **(24)** II, XVI + Giorgio
XV + Gardes et Courtisans	III, XIII + Garde-chasse III, XIV + trois Seigneurs	III, XIII–XIV + Gardes, Lurewel, Courtisan septuor **(21)**	II, XVII + Pascale, Guardie, Fidelingh, Riccardo
XVI + Peggy Le Roi rend sa justice.	III, XIV (suite) Henri dédommage Agathe et il dote Catau.	III, XIV (suite) + Jenny Le Roi anoblit Richard et dote Jenny. Il sort.	II, XVII (suite) Finale **(25)** Le roi anoblit Giorgio.
		III, XV–XVI chœur **(22)** vaudeville **(23)**	**(25)** (suite)

Acte III de Goldoni (*Recinto ombroso che introduce nel bosco*):
I Re, Pascale **(26)**; II Re, Riccardo **(27)**
III Miledi; IV + Fidelingh; V Fidelingh, Miledi **(28)**
VI Giannina **(29)**, Giorgio; VII + Lisetta **(30)**
VIII Giorgio, Giannina sont scandalisés par Lisetta.
IX Re leur refuse de nouvelles faveurs **(31)**.
X Giorgio, Giannina acceptent leur sort; + Pascale.
XI Giorgio, Giannina **(32)**; XII Tous **(33)**, ballet. Trois mariages.

L'*'antica tradizione'* à laquelle se réfère Goldoni dans son avertissement au *Re alla caccia* fait l'objet d'une explicitation par le même auteur dans ses *Mémoires*: 'La source véritable de tous ces sujets [de Dodsley, Collé, Sedaine et lui-même] se trouve dans *L'Alcaïde de Zalamea*, Comédie Espagnole de Calderón. Dans la Pièce de l'Auteur Espagnol il y a beaucoup d'intrigue: une Fille violée, un Pere vengé, un Officier étranglé, et l'Alcaïde est juge et partie, et bourreau en même tems.'[4] A la fin de la pièce, le personnage de l'Alcade déclare que 'l'auteur met fin à cette histoire véridique',[5] ce qui explique probablement la remarque de Goldoni sur ce sujet qui '*passa per un'istoria*', c'est-à-dire pour un fait historiquement advenu. Dans son résumé, Goldoni omet de signaler la présence d'un roi, que les spectateurs espagnols des années 1640 pouvaient aisément identifier comme Philippe II, ce qui situe l'anecdote une soixantaine d'années avant la représentation de la pièce de Calderón. Le personnage du Roi n'intervient qu'à la dernière minute, pour prendre la défense de l'Alcade, qui se trouve être aussi le père de la jeune fille déshonorée, et le justifier d'avoir fait exécuter un soldat sans foi ni loi, quoique de rang aristocratique. Au-delà des violentes péripéties de l'action, la morale de la pièce est donc la victoire du droit sur la force et l'affirmation du caractère indivisible de la justice, quelle que soit l'appartenance sociale des parties en conflit.

Cet excursus concernant *El alcade de Zalamea* pourrait apparaître comme une digression gratuite, dans la mesure où il n'est pas prouvé que Dodsley, Collé ou Sedaine aient pu s'en inspirer. La pièce espagnole mérite cependant sa place à la périphérie d'une étude centrée sur *Le Roi et le fermier*, car sa réception dans la France du XVIIIe siècle nous permet de mieux cerner les enjeux politiques soulevés par l'intervention royale. En effet, *L'Alcade de Zalamea* paraît en traduction française en 1770, dans le tome II d'un *Théâtre espagnol* dont le traducteur n'est autre que Linguet, avocat et publiciste protestataire, embastillé en 1779 puis agitateur virulent sous la Révolution française.[6] Mais les choses n'en restèrent pas là puisque l'adaptation de Linguet, publiée d'abord sous le titre du *Viol puni*, fut arrangée à Marseille par

---

4 Carlo Goldoni, *Mémoires* [1re éd. Paris: Duchesne, 1787] dans *Tutte le opere di Carlo Goldoni*, I, p. 496.

5 Pedro Calderón de la Barca, *El alcade de Zalamea* dans Robert Marrast (éd.), *Théâtre espagnol du XVIIe siècle* (2 vol., Paris: Gallimard, 1994 et 1999), II, p. 1112. Les informations reproduites ici sur cette pièce proviennent de la 'Notice' de Marrast, *Théâtre espagnol*, II, p. 1836–43.

6 Simon-Nicolas-Henri Linguet (1736–94); son *Essai philosophique sur le monarchisme* était un 'best-seller' clandestin. Voir Robert Darnton, *The Forbidden Best-Sellers of Pre-Revolutionary France* (Londres: HarperCollins, 1996), p. 63–5. Linguet pensait que Dodsley avait pris comme source *El sabio en su retiro* de Juan de Matos Fragoso: voir l'article de Manuel Couvreur, p. 85–6 du présent volume.

le dramaturge et acteur Jean-Marie Collot d'Herbois (1750–96), qui en publia sa propre version en 1778 sous le titre provocateur de *Il y a une bonne justice, ou Le Paysan magistrat.* Installé à Paris, Collot d'Herbois fit représenter sa pièce au Théâtre de la Nation en 1789, au moment où il embrassait la carrière politique que l'on sait: passant de la théorie à la pratique, il devint ensuite membre du Comité de Salut Public, et entra dans l'histoire comme l'un des symboles de ce que la Terreur a produit de plus sanglant et de plus sommaire en termes d'exercice de la justice. Entre-temps, le librettiste Louis-François Faur avait fait représenter en 1783 et 1784, au Théâtre-Italien, une comédie mêlée d'ariettes intitulée *Isabelle et Fernand, ou l'Alcade de Zalamea*, mise en musique par Stanislas Champein. Dans une longue préface au livret, Faur explique en détail la manière dont il se démarque de son modèle espagnol, dont il n'a conservé ni le viol de la jeune fille, ni l'exécution cruelle du soldat coupable: 'nos mœurs sont trop pures pour imiter une pareille hardiesse'.[7]

Il est cependant une modification dont Faur ne parle pas dans sa Préface: il a fait disparaître le personnage du Roi. Et c'est précisément dans la place attribuée à la figure royale que se situe l'originalité du *dramatick tale* de Dodsley, ainsi que des trois pièces qui ont été faites à son imitation. Certes, on trouve aussi, chez Dodsley, Collé, Sedaine et Goldoni comme chez Calderón, le thème du roi qui rend la justice en faveur d'une classe défavorisée (un meunier et son fils, dans *The King and the Miller of Mansfield*), au détriment d'un aristocrate (le libertin Lurewell) ayant abusé d'une paysanne. Mais l'important est la perspective inédite imaginée par Dodsley, qui élève le Roi au rang de protagoniste, et ce dès le début de la pièce (scène II, correspondant à l'acte II, scène II de Sedaine). Loin d'être un *deus ex machina* extérieur à l'action, le Roi de Dodsley permet d'introduire une foule de thèmes nouveaux, tels que la solitude du souverain, la bassesse de ses courtisans, la valeur heuristique que procure l'expérience de l'incognito, la générosité des simples paysans, et, en fin de compte, l'égalité de tous les hommes lorsqu'ils se rencontrent au milieu de la nuit en pleine forêt. Patu a donc raison, dans son 'Avertissement du traducteur' (non paginé), d'attirer l'attention sur la forte charge morale du 'conte dramatique' de Dodsley, 'bien différent de ces Auteurs qui donnent hardiment le titre de Comédie à ce qui le mérite si peu'; point de vue repris par Goldoni, dans ses *Mémoires*, lorsqu'il désigne l'originalité de Dodsley par les catégories de 'politique' et de 'critique' (critique sociale, s'entend),[8] tant la pièce anglaise va loin dans la mise en cause d'une aristocratie à la fois corrompue et corruptrice, à laquelle s'oppose la droiture d'une paysannerie joviale mais prête à faire valoir son bon droit lorsque son

---

[7] Louis-François Faur (c.1746–[?]), 'Préface', *Isabelle et Fernand, ou l'Alcade de Zalamea* (Paris: Prault, 1784), p. x.

[8] *Mémoires*, I, p. 496.

honneur a été bafoué. Comme pour *L'Alcade de Zalamea*, on ne sera pas surpris de voir ces thèmes resurgir chez des auteurs français, malgré l'assagissement qu'entraînaient aussi bien des contraintes politiques – sur lesquelles on reviendra – que des impératifs dramaturgiques: il suffit de parcourir le tableau comparatif donné plus haut pour mesurer l'éclatement des lieux scéniques du *King and the Miller*, puisque non seulement Dodsley transporte l'action en deux endroits de la ville de Mansfield (scènes IV et V–VI), mais il opère un surprenant va-et-vient entre le moulin du Meunier (scènes VII–IX, puis XII–XVI) et la forêt de Sherwood (scènes X–XI).

The King and the Miller, nous dit son traducteur Patu, met en scène le roi Henri VI, 'de pieuse mémoire', suivi en cela par Collé.[9] Bien que la pièce de Dodsley ne fasse aucune mention de sa source, une filiation établie par Suzanne Aspden la révèle clairement:[10] l'épisode retenu par Dodsley provient de 'A pleasant Ballad of King Henry IId, and the Miller of Mansfield', parue dans deux collections imprimées à Londres, datant de 1723 et 1737.[11] Patu se trompait donc de Monarque, peut-être parce que le texte de Dodsley ne fait référence qu'au 'good King Harry' ou simplement à 'King Harry' (par exemple avant la chanson à boire chantée au moulin). Mais Patu devait nécessairement savoir que la pièce avait un message politique fort, et qu'elle était immédiatement devenue un spectacle très couru, voire 'One of the most popular [plays] of the century'.[12] Dodsley lui-même, et les productions littéraires de son propre commerce (il était un éditeur de premier rang) ont été identifiés avec l'opposition au premier ministre anglais Walpole et à la corruption de son entourage. La carrière de Dodsley présente d'étonnants parallèles avec celle de Sedaine: il commence comme apprenti bonnetier, travaille à Londres comme valet de pied, écrit des poèmes qui sont publiés (*A Muse in Livery*, 1732), trouve l'appui de plusieurs protecteurs (y compris

[9] [Patu], *Choix de petites pièces du théâtre anglois* (Londres et Paris: Prault, 1756), p. 88. Voir Charles Collé, *Journal historique inédit pour les années 1761 et 1762*, éd. Adolphe Van Bever (Paris: Mercure de France, 1911), p. 346 (octobre 1762): 'M. Dosdley [sic] a mis pour son roy un Henri VI, qui est en vénération chez les Anglois.'

[10] Suzanne Aspden, 'Ballads and Britons: Imagined Community and the Continuity of "English" Opera', *Journal of the Royal Musical Association*, CXXII (1997), p. 24–51, en particulier p. 32, 35, 48.

[11] *A Collection of old Ballads. Corrected from the best & most ancient copies extant ... The Second Edition* (3 vol., Londres: J. Roberts, 1723), I, p. 53; *A Collection of Miscellany Poems, Never before Publish'd* (Londres: W. Warne, 1737), p. 180. Henry II (1154–89) a pu imposer un régime stable après vingt ans de violence exceptionelle, et il 'travelled unceasingly over his domains': Arthur Leslie Morton, *A People's History of England* (London: Lawrence & Wishart, 1976), p. 73.

[12] Harry M. Solomon, *The Rise of Robert Dodsley. Creating the New Age of Print* (Carbondale etc.: Southern Illinois University Press, 1996), p. 55. Des rééditions régulières du texte de Dodsley ne cessèrent de paraître qu'en 1909.

Alexander Pope), et réussit comme auteur dramatique dans le style satirique et critique; et il jouit aujourd'hui encore d'un certain renom, quoique comme éditeur plutôt que comme écrivain.

Les spectateurs français, quant à eux, pouvaient difficilement lire l'adaptation de Patu sans penser à Henri IV, dont le culte bénéficia du formidable succès de *La Henriade* de Voltaire, incessamment rééditée depuis sa première édition de 1723.[13] On ne sait au juste quelle pouvait être la forme originale de *La Partie de chasse de Henri IV* de Collé, qui a d'abord porté le titre du *Roi et le Meunier*; mais il est clair que dès sa conception cette pièce a été délibérément centrée sur la figure d'Henri IV; voici ce qu'en dit l'auteur lui-même dans son journal, à une date qui fait remonter une première version de l'ouvrage au mois d'août 1760:

> Le 15 je fus dès le matin à Bagnolet, où je dînai, après avoir lu à M. le duc d'Orléans, le *Roi et le Meunier* qui me parut lui faire une grande impression, et lui plaire beaucoup. Il étoit presque déterminé à jouer cette petite comédie cet hiver, lorsque je fus le premier à lui faire observer que, malgré la circonspection la plus minutieuse dont j'avois été en traitant ce sujet, on pourroit cependant faire des comparaisons du temps de Henri IV au temps présent, qui ne seroient sûrement pas à l'avantage de notre siècle. Cette réflexion, et quelques autres que nous fîmes ensuite, ont fait remettre la représentation de cette comédie à la publication de la paix.[14] Un Anglais qui liroit ma comédie du *Roi et du Meunier*, et qui entendroit les raisons qui font différer de la jouer, diroit bien que nous sommes de vils esclaves, et il n'auroit pas tort.[15]

Nous voilà donc à nouveau en pleine 'politique', pour reprendre le terme de Goldoni. Les appréhensions exprimées par Collé en 1760 se vérifièrent au-delà de tout ce qu'il pouvait redouter: si *La Partie de chasse de Henri IV* fut bien créée en juillet 1762 au théâtre de société du duc d'Orléans, à Bagnolet, le passage du domaine privé à la Comédie-Française se fit attendre pendant non moins de vingt-deux ans.[16] En décembre 1764, Collé se 'flatte, peut-être sans

---

[13] Voir Jean-Claude Bonnet, *Naissance du Panthéon. Essai sur le culte des grands hommes* (Paris: Fayard, 1998), p. 224. Cet ouvrage fait fréquemment référence au culte d'Henri IV, en particulier aux pages 106–7, 260 et 370 note 47.

[14] Collé fait sans doute allusion à ce qui fut ensuite appelé la Guerre de Sept Ans, et qui se termina en février 1763.

[15] Charles Collé, *Journal et mémoires*, II, p. 256–7. Collé ajoute que Dodsley lui a fourni 'le fond de mon *Henry Quatre*': *Journal historique*, p. 346.

[16] Le texte de *La Partie de chasse de Henri IV* (1re éd. 1766) est reproduit dans Jacques Truchet (éd.), *Théâtre du XVIIIe siècle* (2 vol., Paris: Gallimard, 1972–4), II, p. 599–655; cette édition contient une 'Notice' de Truchet, II, p. 1459–65. Voir aussi l'entrée que Pierre Frantz consacre à cette pièce dans Jean-Pierre de Beaumarchais et Daniel Couty

raison, que la principale difficulté a été aplanie par la mort de Mme de Pompadour, qui a empêché elle seule, il y a deux ans, que cette comédie fût alors représentée [à la cour].'[17] Mais rien n'y fit; Louis XV resta inébranlable dans son hostilité à la présentation scénique de son ancêtre, et, pour citer encore Collé, 'la pièce n'a été donnée sur le théâtre de Paris qu'après sa mort. Je forçai les Comédiens d'attendre la fin de son deuil. Ils l'eussent jouée après qu'il fut à Saint-Denis, si je ne les eusse arrêtés.'[18] Ailleurs en France, et dans la sphère privée à Paris même, ce spectacle est cependant devenu après 1766 l'objet d'une popularité exceptionelle. On raconte, par exemple, que le public de Verdun a manifesté au théâtre son dévouement à 'l'immortel Henri' 'en chœur et à haute voix'.[19]

Etait-il donc si dangereux pour Louis XV de risquer une comparaison voilée avec Henri IV? Comme on l'a déjà fait avec l'implication des figures de Linguet et de Collot d'Herbois dans la réception en France de *L'Alcade de Zalamea*, la tentation est grande de lire l'histoire de l'Ancien Régime à rebours, ou du moins de la situer dans la perspective quasiment inévitable de 1789. C'est une démarche de cet ordre qu'adopte Roger Chartier, avec les précautions et les nuances qui s'imposent, dans un chapitre intitulé 'La désacralisation de la monarchie'[20] qui traite des années ayant suivi l'attentat de Damiens contre Louis XV, en 1757. Et quel roi a le mieux donné l'image de la pure et simple humanité que Henri IV, du moins tel que la légende l'a constitué à l'époque des Lumières? Prenons par exemple cet épisode de *La Henriade* de Voltaire où Henri, encore prince de Navarre, fait naufrage à Jersey et se voit offrir un 'festin champêtre' par un vieillard qui vit en ermite dans une forêt:

(éd.), *Dictionnaire des œuvres littéraires de langue français* (4 vol., Paris: Bordas, 1994), III, p. 1474–5. Favart, qui assista à une représentation à Bagnolet en janvier 1763, rapporte que 'Monseigneur le duc d'Orléans a joué le rôle du meunier avec une vérité qu'aucun comédien de profession ne peut atteindre' (lettre à Durazzo, dans *Mémoires et correspondances littéraires, dramatiques et anecdotiques de C. S. Favart*, éd. Antoine-Pierre-Charles Favart (3 vol., Paris: Léopold Collin, 1808), II, p. 54–5.

[17] Collé, *Journal et mémoires*, II, p. 390.

[18] Ibid., II, p. 392. Louis XV mourut en 1774; les 'Comédiens' dont parle Collé sont les Comédiens-Français.

[19] Clément et La Porte, *Anecdotes dramatiques*, II, p. 39–40 (réimp., p. 166–7).

[20] L'expression vient de Dale Van Kley, *The Damiens Affair and the Unraveling of the Ancien Régime* (Princeton: Princeton University Press, 1984); voir Roger Chartier, *Les Origines culturelles de la Révolution française* (Paris: Editions du Seuil, 1990), p. 145–8.

Le prince à ces repas était accoutumé:
Souvent sous l'humble toit du laboureur charmé,
Fuyant le bruit des cours et se cherchant lui-même,
Il avait déposé l'orgueil du diadème.[21]

Quelle que soit l'œuvre où apparaisse le roi Henri IV dans la seconde moitié du XVIIIe siècle – discours académique, statue, récit historique, peinture d'histoire – son exemplarité fait naître les mêmes éloges, dont le souverain en exercice pouvait difficilement sortir indemne; en voici un témoignage parmi d'autres, tiré de l'entrée que Chamfort et La Porte consacrent à *La Partie de chasse d'Henri IV* dans leur *Dictionnaire dramatique*: 'Cette Comédie ingénieuse & intéressante, présente un tableau si vrai, si naïf, & en même tems si simple & si sublime du caractère & des mœurs du grand Henry, & du duc de Sully, son Ministre, que l'on ne peut assister à ce Spectacle, sans une vive émotion de plaisir & de tendresse.'[22] On conçoit mal un meilleur exemple de 'désacralisation', en effet, que ce 'héros en déshabillé',[23] naturel et bon enfant, qui n'a pas besoin pour asseoir son autorité des attributs régaliens du pouvoir, mais qui manifeste sa vraie grandeur par la considération qu'il accorde aux plus humbles de ses sujets. En outre, la sévérité d'Henri IV envers le libertin Conchiny, dans la pièce, contrastait ironiquement avec l'image que les Français se faisaient de leur roi, dont le comportement ouvertement adultère était devenu depuis les années 1740 un objet de scandale toujours croissant.[24]

Désireux d'enrichir son cadre historique, et peut-être de se démarquer du livret de Sedaine, apparu en 1762, Collé ajouta au canevas fourni par Dodsley un premier acte entièrement de son cru, dont la création eut lieu à Bagnolet en 1764.[25] On y fait plus ample connaissance avec l'Italien Concini, alias Conchiny, qui ajoute à la vilenie et aux penchants libertins de Lurewell toute l'épaisseur des intrigues politiques qui se tramaient dans le dos d'Henri IV et qui menèrent à son assassinat – à l'instigation des félons du clan italien, si l'on

---

[21] Voltaire, *La Henriade* [1re éd. 1723] dans *The Complete Works of Voltaire*, éd. O. R. Taylor (Genève: Institut et Musée Voltaire, 1970), II, p. 377 (chant I, vers 215–18); Taylor remarque (note 42) que les deux derniers vers cités proviennent d'*Esther* de Racine, acte I, scène I.

[22] [Nicolas de Chamfort et Joseph de La Porte], *Dictionnaire dramatique* [...], (3 vol., Paris: Vve Lacombe, 1776), II, p. 384–5. Le commentaire de Goldoni se situe dans la même ligne: 'il suffit qu'il y soit question de ce bon Roi, pour qu'il plaise aux François, et soit approuvé par tout le monde' (*Mémoires*, I, p. 496).

[23] Collé, 'Avertissement', *La Partie de chasse de Henri IV*, dans *Théâtre du XVIIIe siècle* (voir note 16), II, p. 599.

[24] Michel Antoine, *Louis XV* (Paris: Fayard, 1989), p. 485 *sqq.*; Darnton, *Forbidden Best-Sellers*, p. 232–43.

[25] Collé, *Journal et mémoires*, II, p. 389, et *Journal historique*, p. 303–5, où Collé se montre conscient dès 1762 des problèmes politiques inhérents à son sujet.

en croit une note de l'édition des *Mémoires* de Sully sur laquelle Collé s'est appuyé.[26] Le bon Sully apparaît également en personne, sans que Collé ait pu prévoir les manifestations d'enthousiasme que sa présence devait déchaîner deux décennies plus tard par identification à Necker. En effet, c'est en mai 1781, après l'annonce du renvoi du ministre de Louis XVI, que le personnage de Sully fut véritablement ovationné sur la scène de la Comédie-Française: 'Les Comédiens ont été s'excuser auprès de M. le lieutenant de police d'avoir donné lieu à une scène si touchante mais dont on pouvait leur savoir mauvais gré.'[27]

Ce n'est cependant pas dans l'ajout de la longue préhistoire constituée par le nouvel acte I qu'il faut chercher l'essentiel des innovations de Collé, mais bien plutôt dans des aspects à la fois dramaturgiques et anecdotiques qui enlèvent à la fable anglaise ce qu'elle pouvait avoir, pour un censeur français, de moralement choquant et de théâtralement irrecevable. La recherche d'une mise en scène sur plusieurs lieux simultanés disparaît, comme on pouvait s'y attendre chez un auteur qui, pour avoir été longtemps boudé par la Comédie-Française, ne s'en tenait pas moins à des canons théâtraux autrement plus conventionnels que ne le permettait la scène londonienne. En contrepartie, Collé élève un garde-chasse au rang de personnage de plein droit, nommé Lucas, afin qu'il forme avec Catau, la sœur de Richard, un second couple d'amoureux; ce renforcement de l'effectif dramatique, dont Sedaine n'a pas vu la nécessité, a pour principale fonction d'instituer le niveau d'une paysannerie infantile et patoisante, une humanité subalterne à laquelle Richard et Agathe échappent aussi bien par leur langage que par leurs valeurs morales. Richard, du reste, est le fils du 'plus riche meunier de ce royaume' et 'a fait ses études à Melun', où il a appris le latin (II, III). Agathe, de son côté, a été élevée chez la 'signora Galigai', autre personnage historique, puisque cette Italienne intrigante et sulfureuse fut la maîtresse de Concini. Collé ne pousse cependant pas jusqu'au bout son tableau de la corruption des mœurs de la cour, car il s'attache soigneusement à diminuer les conséquences de l'enlèvement d'Agathe: non seulement la durée de sa disparition a été notablement réduite – de 'plusieurs années' chez Dodsley à six semaines – mais l'issue n'a pas été fatale pour elle, puisqu'elle a réussi à résister aux avances du libidineux marquis de Conchiny. Alors que Peggy, l'héroïne anglaise, s'était donnée par dépit à son tortionnaire, Collé sauve Agathe de l'humiliation suprême: la morale est sauve, mais la pièce y perd le cruel réalisme qui faisait toute la force de Dodsley.

---

[26] *Mémoires de Maximilien de Béthune, duc de Sully* (3 vol., Londres: sans éd., 1745), III, p. 240, note 23. Collé se réfère à ces *Mémoires* dans son 'Avertissement', II, p. 600.

[27] *Correspondance littéraire* (mai 1781), citée par Bonnet, *Naissance du Panthéon* (voir note 13), p. 260.

Comparé avec *La Partie de chasse de Henri IV*, le livret de Sedaine pourrait paraître au premier abord politiquement timoré, et Collé ne s'est pas privé d'attirer l'attention sur la 'délocalisation' à laquelle s'est livré son rival de la Comédie-Italienne:

> M. Sedaine n'a pas osé mettre, comme je l'ay fait, un de nos rois, sur le théâtre; la police, sans doute ne l'eût point passé. Mais, du moins, il devoit ne point mettre la scène en Angleterre; il pouvoit, au contraire, la faire soupçonner être en France; aller même jusqu'à donner à entendre que c'étoit Henry IV, sans le nommer; multiplier des circonstances qui l'auroient fait deviner. Au lieu de cela, il a présenté un Roy froid, hautain, moraliste et ennuyeux.[28]

Mais Sedaine eut beau désactiver, partiellement du moins, la charge politique de sa pièce, il n'en eut pas moins des ennuis avec la censure, puisqu'il ne put pas en faire jouer une scène, même s'il présente le texte imprimé comme étant complet.[29] De quelle scène pouvait-il s'agir? probablement de l'acte II, scène III, qui met pour la première fois face à face Richard et le Roi; mais la fin de la scène X de l'acte III ferait elle aussi une bonne candidate à la censure, avec une fin particulièrement percutante, cette chute d'une vigueur à laquelle Collé, en dépit de tout son attirail historique, ne s'est pas risqué:

> RICHARD: J'ai vû ce qu'un Roi n'est pas toujours à portée de voir.
> LE ROI: Quoi?
> RICHARD: Des hommes.

Coupées ou non à la Comédie-Italienne, ces répliques n'étaient encore pas le genre de chose que la cour de France était prête à entendre, en 1762, ce qui explique le changement de dernière minute que nous rapporte Sedaine dans ses 'Quelques réflexions': *Le Roi et le fermier* 'devait en première représentation être donné à la cour; mais les fausses interprétations données au titre et à quelques scènes, en empêchèrent'.[30]

Sedaine eut-il connaissance de la pièce de Collé avant d'écrire son livret? Aucun document ne permet de l'avancer avec certitude, mais force est de constater que les deux ouvrages présentent un plan d'un surprenant parallélisme: les actes I et II de Sedaine se déroulent dans la forêt, tandis que l'acte III, d'une longueur presque égale aux deux premiers ensemble, est situé dans la demeure de Richard. La clarté de la construction est cependant nuancée par un certain nombre de procédés qui rappellent, par leur tendance

[28] Charles Collé, *Journal historique*, p. 346–7.

[29] Voir l''Avertissement' de Sedaine, p. 242–3 du présent volume.

[30] Sedaine, 'Quelques réflexions', p. 508.

systématique au flou et à l'approximation, le décousu si caractéristique de Dodsley. D'une part, la 'liaison des scènes', qui constitue l'une des bases de la dramaturgie classique, y est particulièrement malmenée, notamment au cours de l'acte II: les personnages y apparaissent et disparaissent avec l'irrationalité d'une scène nocturne, au point même de laisser le spectateur en suspens au milieu d'une conversation: 'Pourquoi?', demande le Roi à Richard à la fin de la scène III de l'acte II, tandis que la réponse nous restera à jamais inconnue. Les beaux esprits contemporains de Sedaine, si prompts à lui reprocher ses multiples 'irrégularités', n'auront pas manqué non plus de noter la bizarrerie d'une référence au troupeau volé à Jenny (III, III) alors qu'on n'a pas entendu Richard en parler avec le Roi.

Si l'on regarde de plus près les modifications apportées par Sedaine à l'intrigue de Dodsley, la volonté d'anoblissement du Tiers Etat, tous rôles confondus, apparaît comme une caractéristique majeure. La première innovation, d'importance capitale, est la fusion en la personne de Richard de deux figures différentes chez Dodsley et chez Collé, celle du père (le 'meunier') et celle du fils menacé de perdre sa fiancée. Ce redoublement de l'image fait à la fois de Richard le héros de l'intrigue sentimentale et le représentant de la moralité paysanne, fort de la pureté de ses mœurs autant que de son sens de la justice. Il n'est sans doute pas fortuit que le rôle ait été confié non pas à Clairval, le jeune premier de la troupe de la Comédie-Italienne, mais à Caillot, un excellent acteur dont la voix de 'concordant' était capable de couvrir le double registre du ténor et de la basse.[31] Du côté de l'héroïne, Sedaine n'a pas été en reste puisqu'il a doté Jenny d'un statut moral à la hauteur de son partenaire: la durée de sa captivité a encore diminué par rapport à celle que lui fixe Collé, pour se réduire aux quelques instants passés en la compagnie d'une entremetteuse à la solde de Lurewell. L'alerte a été chaude, mais l'honneur de la jeune fille n'a jamais été mis directement en danger; ainsi se justifie du même coup la rapidité avec laquelle Richard accepte le récit de Jenny à la fin du premier acte, sans s'étendre sur des soupçons qui auraient confiné à l'insensibilité. Nougaret et Collé ont ironisé sur cette réconciliation sans délai,[32] mais on peut précisément y voir une intention morale forte, celle de refuser la convention des chamailleries et du dépit amoureux, et d'affirmer à leur place un amour suffisamment vrai pour que des expressions de méfiance aient paru hors de propos.

La respectabilité du 'fermier' et de sa fiancée s'étend logiquement à la famille de Richard tout entière: sa mère et Betsy, sa sœur, témoignent pour Jenny d'une authentique compassion où à aucun moment n'entre la crainte du

[31] Voir le texte de Raphaëlle Legrand, dans ce volume, p. 130–31.

[32] [Pierre-Jean-Baptiste Nougaret], *De l'art du théâtre en général* (2 vol., Paris: Cailleau, 1769), I, p. 196; Collé, *Journal historique*, p. 347.

qu'en-dira-t-on. Tandis que Collé donne à la sœur d'Agathe, la malveillante Catau, tous les dehors de la mesquinerie pudibonde, Sedaine peint une paysannerie sans tache, dont les valeurs dépassent les usages fatalement restrictifs de la vie en société pour atteindre à la simple humanité. L'*ethos* de la classe inférieure est certes encore présent, sous la forme d'une gaucherie bien pardonnable en la présence d'un gentilhomme – le Roi, comme on sait, ne révèle qu'*in extremis* son identité réelle; mais l'empressement embarrassé de la Mère et de Betsy ne rend que plus palpable l'hospitalité authentique d'un milieu encore indemne de l'hypocrisie en vigueur chez les aristocrates. L'idylle de Dodsley s'accomplit sur un fond sinistre d'innocence perdue; celle de Sedaine sauve par avance ses héros de la flétrissure d'un monde cynique et faux.

On comprend dès lors que *Le Roi et le fermier* fasse l'économie du souper, scène capitale chez Dodsley (scène XII), dont Collé fait par ailleurs ses choux gras (III, XI), et qu'il reproche à Sedaine de ne pas avoir exploitée.[33] Point donc de louange publique du roi Henri, éliminé d'entrée de jeu par Sedaine – même si le spectateur, on peut le supposer, suppléait par l'imagination à ce décalage sur l'identité du Roi. Point non plus de libertinage visible de la part du Roi, auquel Collé permet de donner libre cours à ses penchants de 'Vert-galant', alors que son flirt avec Betsy, dans *Le Roi et le fermier*, ne trouve sa place que sur le mode du récit, formalisé dans un bref air narratif (III, VIII). S'il est vrai que Sedaine fait dire à Richard 'des choses fort au-dessus de son état', comme le remarquait Collé non sans aigreur,[34] il était bien naturel que le refus de la trivialisation s'étende au souverain lui-même, paré par Sedaine d'une générosité d'autant plus exemplaire qu'elle est délivrée de toute association trop précise.

Ces éléments à la fois idéologiques et dramaturgiques sont sans nul doute à l'origine du jugement, formulé par Bachaumont quelques jours après la création du *Roi et le fermier*, selon qui il s'agissait là d'un 'opéra-comique de grande manière'.[35] Du point de vue de l'expressivité, cette 'manière' se fait jour dès la première ariette, sur laquelle commence l'opéra en l'absence de tout dialogue ni numéro musical explicatif. Richard y est présenté en proie au plus violent désarroi, sans toutefois que la raison de ses tourments soit jamais dévoilée: cinq quatrains défilent ainsi, sur une musique tendue et pathétique, mais dont l'objet reste perpétuellement repoussé dans le non-dit. Les

---

33 Collé, *Journal historique*, p. 348.

34 Ibid.

35 *Mémoires secrets*, I, 18 novembre 1762. C'est aussi ce que laisse entendre Sedaine lui-même dans son 'Avertissement' lorsqu'il évoque la difficulté que lui posa la recherche d'un 'ami qui voulût bien risquer un genre nouveau en musique' (voir p. 243 et Raphaëlle Legrand, p. 120).

conversations de Richard avec les trois Gardes et avec Betsy ne nous en apprennent pas davantage, et il faut attendre la scène IV pour connaître la cause d'un tel désordre. Puis vient encore un air de Richard, narratif celui-là (scène V), un rondeau significativement qualifié 'amoroso' dans la partition de Monsigny, qui parachève une entrée en matière entièrement colorée par l'affectivité du héros. Bien moins originale est l'exposition de Collé, où deux paysans jargonnants détaillent laborieusement les tenants et les aboutissants de la situation. Chez Sedaine, au contraire, le projecteur est résolument braqué sur le 'Fermier', tandis que le Roi doit attendre le début de l'acte suivant pour retrouver la place qu'il occupe dès le début chez Dodsley: voilà un indice supplémentaire prouvant que Sedaine change délibérément de terrain par rapport à son modèle, en focalisant d'abord toute l'attention sur le drame sentimental de Richard, les implications sociales de la donnée dramatique étant réservées pour un stade ultérieur de la pièce. Quant à Goldoni, dont on examinera plus loin la version avec davantage de détails, on remarquera tout de suite que l'entrée en scène de Giorgio, dans *Il re alla caccia*, produit un effet semblable à celle de Richard chez Collé: non seulement son premier air annonce sans ambages ce qui cause son tourment ('*La molinara m'ha abbandonato*'), mais le spectateur a déjà été amplement éclairé par les cinq scènes introductives. Le héros souffrant, chez Collé comme chez Goldoni, a perdu son aura de mystère, et rien ne dit que le gain en clarté compense cette abolition du suspens dramatique.

Si Richard se taille la part du lion dans la phase d'exposition, les deux autres personnages principaux ont eux aussi eu droit à un soin infini dans la mise en scène de leurs sentiments dominants. Jenny reproduit le chemin de Richard en sens inverse, commençant par une ariette narrative pour enchaîner presque immédiatement – sans même un air intercalaire d'un autre personnage – sur un 'amoroso' qui fait pendant à celui de son fiancé. Sedaine va tout aussi loin dans la présentation du Roi, dont le monologue initial, qui occupe entièrement la scène II de l'acte II, s'articule en un 'récitatif mesuré' et une ariette de dimensions véritablement royales.

Ces quelques références à la partition font déjà apparaître à quel degré le livret de Sedaine est calculé en fonction d'un impératif 'dramatico-musical' – pour reprendre une expression que David Charlton a repérée sous la plume de Grétry.[36] Cette 'musicalisation' du texte se traduit d'abord par l'attribution de fonctions très variées aux morceaux chantés, dont la plus remarquable, en comparaison de la pratique italienne qui faisait loi dans le reste de l'Europe, est la fonction narrative. Ce n'était pas là une invention de Sedaine, mais au

---

[36] David Charlton, '"L'art dramatico-musical": An Essay' dans Nigel Fortune (éd.), *Music and Theatre: Essays in Honour of Winton Dean* (Cambridge: Cambridge University Press, 1987), p. 229–62.

contraire l'exploitation d'un *topos* de l'opéra-comique généralement lié à l'idée de séduction; on en trouve des exemples dans deux livrets de Poinsinet, *Gilles garçon peintre, z'amoureux-t-et rival*[37] (scène II, Gilles narre une rencontre faite en revenant du cabaret) et *Sancho Pança*, où un homme et une femme racontent successivement la même histoire dans deux romances appariées.[38] Un autre librettiste, La Ribadière, emprunte un chemin semblable avec le récit de Toinette dans *Les Aveux indiscrets* (scène II) et, dans *Les Deux sœurs rivales* (représentées deux semaines après *Sancho Pança*), avec les airs appariés de Babet et de sa sœur Colette (scène II). Dans *Le Roi et le fermier* c'est l'air de Betsy au troisième acte (scène VIII) qui se situe le plus clairement dans cette tradition comique, tandis que celui de Jenny, à l'acte I (scène VIII), interrompu par un saisissant passage en récitatif, représente l'inflexion vers le drame qui fait la caractéristique du livret de Sedaine par rapport à ses prédécesseurs.

Il en va de même pour les quatre chansons de l'opéra (aux scènes I et XII de l'acte III), qui répondent à la convention désormais bien établie, à l'opéra-comique, de donner aux personnages des airs qu'ils chanteraient tout aussi bien dans la vie réelle, pour ainsi dire. En s'en tenant toujours à quelques échantillons antérieurs au *Roi et le fermier*, on pourrait citer l'ariette de Fanchette 'Les filles de ce hameau' à la scène IX du *Jardinier et son seigneur* (sur un livret de Sedaine, 1761), notée avec l'indication 'en chantonnant', ou encore, aux tous débuts de la comédie avec ariettes, l'air strophique de Ninette dans *Ninette à la cour* de Favart (I, IV), 'Je vois du plus beau jour briller l'aurore', que l'héroïne chante 'en faisant semblant de travailler' pendant que le roi Astolphe l'observe avec convoitise.[39] L'argument proposé par Dodsley fournissait à Sedaine une situation idéale pour le placement de tels morceaux, à l'occasion de la scène du souper; dans la pièce parlée, Dodsley y fait même intervenir un personnage épisodique, Joe (Joseph), aux seules fins de le faire chanter (scène XIII). Collé, pour sa part, se livre à une véritable débauche de chansons (III, XI), auxquelles il ajoute le piquant de les faire rouler sur le

[37] Dans cet exemple comme dans ceux qui suivent, les sources consultées sont des opéras-comiques en partition gravée, dont voici les compositeurs et les années de création: Jean-Benjamin de La Borde (*Gilles garçon peintre, z'amoureux-t-et rival*, 1758), Philidor (*Sancho Pança*, 1762), Monsigny (*Les Aveux indiscrets*, 1759) et Robert Desbrosses (*Les Deux sœurs rivales*, 1762).

[38] David Charlton, 'The *Romance* and its Cognates: Narrative, Irony and *Vraisemblance* in Early Opéra Comique' dans Herbert Schneider et Nicole Wild (éd.), *Die Opéra comique und ihr Einfluß auf das europäische Musiktheater im 19. Jahrhundert* (Hildesheim: Georg Olms, 1997), réimp. dans *French Opera 1730–1830: Meaning and Media* (Aldershot: Ashgate Publishing, 2000), p. 43–92 [80–81].

[39] *Le Jardinier et son seigneur* (1761), partition de Philidor; *Ninette à la cour* (1755) est un centon de morceaux de musique de divers auteurs mais le *Catalogue de la musique imprimée avant 1800 conservée dans les bibliothèques publiques de Paris* de François Lesure (Paris: Bibliothèque nationale, 1981) le fait figurer au nom de Duni.

caractère du roi Henri IV, lequel en est le premier destinataire. La différence entre les deux auteurs français, cependant, est que Sedaine a pris la peine de montrer au spectateur, dans un ensemble d'action à la fin de l'acte II, l'arrestation des courtisans par les Gardes (suivant en cela l'exemple de Dodsley, scène XI) alors que Collé n'a pas préparé avec autant de soin la réapparition de ses courtisans. Les trois chansons qui se succèdent dans *Le Roi et le fermier*, acte III, scène XII – la romance de Jenny et les ariettes de Richard et du Roi – ont donc clairement pour fonction de susciter l'attente, de faire monter la tension à l'approche du dénouement: plus la petite fête chez Richard sera étirée en longueur, plus spectaculaire sera l'entrée des Gardes-chasse accompagnés du scélérat voué à la royale punition.

L'intégration réaliste de la musique est encore plus évidente à la première scène de l'acte III, qui montre Betsy, Jenny et la Mère en train de chanter tout en se livrant à des tâches de couture et de filage – là encore à l'imitation de Dodsley, où la mère et la sœur de Richard sont occupées à tricoter. C'est probablement une situation de ce genre qui inspira la phrase suivante à Lemierre, dans le discours qu'il prononça pour la réception de Sedaine à l'Académie Française: 'Vous avez su tirer les plus grands effets des sujets les plus humbles, & dans une ferme ou dans une place de village causer des émotions telles que les favoris de Melpomène n'en excitent guère de plus vives dans les Palais des Rois.'[40] Mais on voit bien que ces 'effets' n'auraient pas eu lieu si Sedaine n'avait su tirer le meilleur parti de la composante musicale, au point de l'intégrer à son livret de façon indissociable. L'entracte qui relie les actes I et II, par exemple, n'est concevable qu'accompagné de son illustration sonore: sonneries de chasse, effets imitatifs liés à l'évocation de la tempête, bourrasques de vent, coups de tonnerre, tout est prévu pour porter l'illusion théâtrale à son point extrême.

A l'inverse, Sedaine peut assigner à la musique une tâche beaucoup plus complexe, celle de renforcer des moments d'intense théâtralité. Le plus connu de ces moments est le septuor au cours duquel se produit la reconnaissance du Roi, qui a déjà fait l'objet de nombreux commentaires, à commencer par ceux de Sedaine lui-même dans sa préface à *Rose et Colas* (1764). L'action s'y arrête, suspendue par la grâce de tous ces procédés qui sont interdits au théâtre parlé: l'extension de la durée par la répétition du texte, la lenteur du débit chanté comparé à la simple parole, la possibilité de combiner à l'infini des voix différentes, concordantes ou antagonistes. Mais ce morceau, qui constitue en quelque sorte le prototype de ce que les musicologues appellent 'ensemble contemplatif', ne doit pas faire oublier tous les numéros musicaux où l'action est au contraire prise en charge par la musique, transposée par des motifs, des

---

[40] *Discours prononcés dans l'Académie Françoise, le Jeudi XXVII Avril M.DCC.LXXXVI, à la réception de M. Sedaine* (Paris: Demonneville, 1786), p. 21–2.

modulations et des couleurs orchestrales. Le dialogue parlé, véhicule habituel de telles situations, laisse alors la place à une véritable mise en scène musicale, comme dans le duo comique des deux Gardes-chasse au début de l'acte II ou, à la fin du même acte, le quatuor où ces mêmes Gardes-chasse s'affrontent aux deux Courtisans. Comme pour les airs narratifs, qui empiètent délibérément sur le territoire normalement réservé à la simple parole, Sedaine élargit le champ d'action de la musique sur une échelle qui relève de l'intention novatrice plus que de la reproduction de modèles existants.[41]

Il re alla caccia de Goldoni résulte de la transplantation d'un livret conçu pour un genre précis, l'opéra-comique, dans un genre différent, quoique apparenté, le *dramma giocoso*.[42] Ce ne sont donc pas seulement les variantes de détail qu'il faudra relever entre *Le Roi et le fermier* et le livret de Goldoni mais des traits génériques spécifiques à deux traditions dramatiques possédant chacune ses conventions propres.[43] La preuve en est déjà, à grande échelle, la longueur bien supérieure de la pièce italienne, dictée par le simple fait qu'elle devait remplir un spectacle entier alors que les opéras-comiques n'étaient jamais représentés, à la Comédie-Italienne, qu'en combinaison avec une autre pièce, comédie parlée ou opéra-comique. Il n'y a pas à chercher plus loin la raison des deux intrigues secondaires du *Re alla caccia*, qui font intervenir deux couples supplémentaires, l'un d'aristocrates, l'autre de paysans. Fidelingh (Lurewell chez Sedaine) est en effet pourchassé, chez Goldoni, par une certaine Miledi Marignon, dont l'existence dérive d'un personnage d'entremetteuse qui n'apparaît pas directement chez Sedaine ni chez Collé: il s'agit,

[41] Sur les ensembles du *Roi et le fermier*, voir Elisabeth A. Cook, *Duet and Ensemble in the Early Opéra-Comique* (New York et Londres: Garland, 1995), p. 133, 158–60, 178–81, 185, 272–3.

[42] L'article de Marvin Carlson, '*Il re alla caccia* and *Le Roi et le fermier*: Italian and French Treatments of Class and Gender' dans Mary Hunter et James Webster (éd.), *Opera buffa in Mozart's Vienna* (Cambridge: Cambridge University Press, 1997), p. 82–97, n'était pas paru lorsque notre article fut présenté au colloque de Londres. Une discussion de la thèse de Carlson passerait par un examen approfondi de ce qui, chez Goldoni, est attribuable aux conventions musico-dramatiques du *dramma giocoso*, par opposition à ce qui pourrait se dégager comme une vision proprement goldonienne (ou 'italienne') des classes et des sexes. Une telle discussion nous éloignerait ici de Sedaine, qui se trouvait à la Comédie-Italienne devant une combinatoire formelle moins contraignante que celle de l'opéra *buffa* italien.

[43] Sur les livrets de Goldoni, voir Ted Emery, *Goldoni as Librettist. Theatrical Reform and the 'Drammi giocosi per musica'* (New York: Lang, 1991) (Studies in Italian Culture, Literature and History, III), et Françoise Decroisette (éd.), *Musiques goldoniennes. Hommage à Jacques Joly* (s.l.: Outre-monts/Circé, 1995). Sur Goldoni en France on consultera l'ouvrage collectif *Goldoni in Francia* (Rome: Accademia Nazionale dei Lincei, 1972), Jacques Joly, *L'altro Goldoni* (Pise: Edizioni Techniche Scientifiche, 1989), 'Goldoni à Paris', *Revue d'histoire du théâtre*, XLV (1993), n° 1 (numéro entier), et Andrea Fabiano, *I 'buffoni' alla conquista di Parigi. Storia dell'opera italiana in Francia tra 'Ancien Régime' e Restaurazione (1752–1815)* (Turin: Paravia/De Sono, 1998).

considérablement transformée et anoblie par Goldoni, d'une femme que Jenny se borne à mentionner dans son récit de l'acte I, scène X, et que Collé, comme on l'a vu plus haut, identifie à 'Léonore Galigaï', âme damnée de Concini et ennemie jurée d'Henri IV. Ces deux aristocrates ont leur pendant bouffe, non seulement avec Lisetta, sœur de Giorgio, mais aussi en la personne de son fiancé, le rustique Pascale (le Lucas de Collé, sans équivalent chez Sedaine). L'impératif de la durée dramatique se double donc d'un retour aux rôles types du *dramma giocoso*, les deux *parti serie* et les deux *parti buffe* de rigueur, pour reprendre la terminologie même du livret de Goldoni.

La mise en conformité avec les types de rôles constitutifs de l'opéra bouffe vénitien s'accompagne naturellement de conséquences profondes, comme la longue exposition centrée sur Miledi (acte I, scènes I–V), et surtout par l'invention d'un troisième acte entièrement original où le héros et l'héroïne, Giorgio et Giannina, exploitent la situation créée par Fidelingh pour tenter d'extorquer au Roi de nouveaux avantages afin de s'établir à Londres et d'y mener grand train. Au snobisme aristocratique de Miledi, qui tance Fidelingh pour s'être amouraché de Giannina, '*una donna vulgar*' (I, V), répond donc le ridicule encore plus grave, car plus longuement exposé, de deux paysans prêts à renoncer à toutes les valeurs morales qui ont fait leur prestige lors des deux premiers actes. En cela Goldoni se situe délibérément du côté de Collé, donnant comme lui en spectacle des paysans ridicules par essence, irrémédiablement tirés vers le bas par l'humilité de leurs origines. Alors que dans *Le Roi et le fermier* Betsy n'accepte l'argent du Roi qu'avec une naïveté enfantine, dont témoigne son air de l'acte III, sa contrepartie vénitienne Lisetta trahit une cupidité et un cynisme que Sedaine s'était bien gardé de lui donner: non seulement elle s'arrange pour détourner dans sa propre bourse l'argent que le Roi destinait à Giannina (II, XV) mais, en conformité avec son modèle Catau, chez Collé, elle pousse la sécheresse de cœur jusqu'à tenter de détourner son frère Giorgio de l'alliance avec Giannina, prétendument souillée par le bref enlèvement dont elle a été victime. Mais il faut dire que sa future belle-sœur le lui rend bien, puisque de son côté Giannina, devenue l'épouse d'un Giorgio anobli, s'oppose au mariage de Lisetta avec Pascale car elle ne saurait tolérer une mésalliance dans sa famille. Enfin, pour noircir encore le tableau, si Giannina et Giorgio renoncent à aller s'établir à Londres, c'est uniquement par peur d'être rejetés par une société dont ils ne comprennent pas les rouages.

L'âme paysanne, pour Goldoni, n'est donc immunisée ni contre le pharisaïsme ni contre la puissance de corruption que suscite la proximité du pouvoir. C'est pourquoi aucun des personnages bouffes n'échappe à la bassesse de langage indissolublement liée à leur condition. Bien loin de Richard est le Giorgio qui sacre '*corpo di Bacco!*' (I, VI – pour les premières paroles de son rôle), bien différente de la douce Jenny est la Giannina qui se targue de pouvoir griffer comme un chat (I, IX), avant de se lancer avec Giorgio dans une scène de dépit amoureux où elle répond à ses questions soupçonneuses avec la plus totale bonne conscience.

Toutes ces différences entre Goldoni et Sedaine, où affleurent peut-être, mêlés aux particularités génériques, des points de vue éthiques propres aux deux auteurs, n'empêchent pas *Il re alla caccia* de reproduire fidèlement un certain nombre d'idées 'dramatico-musicales' venues en droite ligne du *Roi et le fermier*.[44] Le duo comique de Giorgio et Pascale dans le noir (II, I) est la réplique fidèle de celui de Rustaut et de Charlot (au même endroit), et bien d'autres morceaux du *Re* témoignent d'une semblable émulation: citons le quatuor final de l'acte I, parcouru par les sonneries de chasse et les coups de tonnerre, ou le duo entre Giannina et Lisetta où les deux jeunes filles, encore unies par l'incertitude de leur sort, chantent fraternellement tout en brodant ou en cousant (n° 20, II, X). Il est un endroit, cependant, où Goldoni ne s'est pas risqué à suivre son modèle: la scène de reconnaissance du Roi est prudemment rendue en récitatif, l'ensemble final ne prenant son envol qu'une fois la situation clairement rétablie.

On touche là du doigt la profonde hardiesse de Sedaine, pour qui la nouveauté du matériau dramatique semble avoir été une incitation à l'innovation plutôt qu'à la prudence. Non seulement l'esprit de sérieux qui domine toute sa pièce prend un poids supplémentaire lorsqu'on compare *Le Roi et le fermier* avec la pièce équivalente de Collé ou avec le livret de Goldoni, tous deux marqués par la persistance de stéréotypes sociaux défavorables à la classe inférieure, mais c'est dans la souplesse et la liberté de la composition dramatique que Sedaine donne le plus pleinement la mesure de son originalité. Il est vrai qu'il se trouvait pour cela dans une situation de collaboration idéale avec Monsigny, profitant de la nouvelle dynamique qu'avait entraînée la récente fusion de la Comédie-Italienne avec l'Opéra-Comique. Goldoni, de son côté, a peut-être été inhibé par l'absence de communication directe avec son musicien, puisqu'il était alors établi à Paris alors que Galuppi n'avait pas quitté sa Venise natale. Mais réduire les différences entre les deux livrets à de simples déterminations extérieures serait injuste pour Sedaine comme pour son musicien: *Le Roi et le fermier* répond clairement à une ambition esthétique raisonnée et assumée, celle de la 'grande manière' d'où est sortie une lignée ininterrompue d'opéras-comiques français.

---

[44] Partition consultée: Baldassare Galuppi, *Il re alla caccia*, F-Pn (Mus), D. 4293.

Chapter 6

'Risquer un genre nouveau en musique': l'opéra-comique de Sedaine et Monsigny

Raphaëlle Legrand

> Le drame est de l'invraisemblance la plus extravagante (ce qui est vrai pour la donnée première), mais il offre des détails touchants et des scènes du plus grand effet. J'allai à la première représentation et j'avoue que j'y versai des torrents de larmes.[1]

L'émotion ressentie par la jeune Stéphanie-Félicité de Genlis durant la représentation du *Déserteur* de Sedaine et Monsigny trouve un écho chez une personne d'une autre génération, Marie du Deffand, qui écrit à Voltaire: 'ce Sedaine a un genre qui fait grand effet. Il a trouvé de nouvelles cordes pour exploiter la sensibilité: il va droit au cœur.'[2]

Le public du *Déserteur* – la longue et élogieuse critique de Grimm le confirme[3] – comprend qu'il y a là une nouvelle sensibilité dramatique à l'œuvre: l'esprit, le goût, la finesse des réparties, l'habileté de la construction (qualités d'un Favart ou d'un Marmontel) sont délaissées au profit du naturel du dialogue, de situations touchantes sommairement préparées mais longuement développées, du pathétique qui parle directement à l'âme, bref – pour reprendre le terme commun à madame de Genlis et à madame du Deffand – de l'*effet*. Sedaine étonne la critique, d'abord déroutée par son mépris des règles et par son style 'dur et raboteux',[4] puis emporte l'adhésion des cœurs.

---

1 Stéphanie-Félicité de Genlis, cité par Arthur Pougin, *Monsigny et son temps* (Paris: Fischbacher, 1908), p. 130.

2 Lettre à Voltaire du 16 juillet 1769, dans Marie Anne du Deffand, *Correspondance complète* (Paris: Michel Lévy, 1866), I, p. 245.

3 *Correspondance littéraire*, VIII (1er avril 1769), p. 314–21.

4 Ibid., IV (1er déc. 1761), p. 502.

On décèle les mêmes traits dans *Le Roi et le fermier*, écrit également par Sedaine pour Monsigny, et que l'on peut considérer comme le premier opéra-comique en trois actes où ce ton nouveau se fait sentir. La carrière de Sedaine librettiste est en effet divisée en trois périodes, associées chacune au nom d'un musicien. Après *Le Diable à quatre* puis une série de pièces comiques en un acte – comme *Blaise le savetier* ou *Le Jardinier et son seigneur* – écrits pour Philidor et montées sur les théâtres de la Foire, Sedaine entame une fructueuse collaboration avec Monsigny, qui coïncide à peu près avec l'absorption de la troupe de l'Opéra-Comique de la Foire par la Comédie-Italienne.[5] Aux côtés de pièces en un acte comme *On ne s'avise jamais de tout* ou *Rose et Colas*, trois grands opéras-comiques, *Le Roi et le fermier*, *Le Déserteur* et *Félix ou l'Enfant trouvé* semblent le fruit d'une ambition nouvelle: développer des intrigues plus longues où le comique cède le pas à l'émotion.[6]

Pour l'aider à réaliser ce projet, Sedaine trouve en Alexandre Monsigny un artiste possédant à bien des égards des qualités comparables aux siennes, compensant son manque de formation technique par un très sûr instinct du théâtre et une grande originalité dans l'invention mélodique et dans la construction des airs. Les trois opéras-comiques en trois actes qu'ils écrivent ensemble préparent la dernière période de Sedaine, marquée par la production d'œuvres de vastes dimensions mises en musique par Grétry, et troquant souvent les figures de paysans et de bourgeois propres au genre pour des personnages historiques ou issus d'un moyen-âge imaginaire (*Aucassin et Nicolette*, *Richard Cœur-de-Lion*, *Raoul Barbe-Bleue*, etc.).

---

[5] *On ne s'avise jamais de tout*, opéra-comique en un acte créé à la Foire Saint-Laurent le 17 septembre 1761, est la première œuvre née de la collaboration de Sedaine et Monsigny. Elle fut jouée moins de cinq mois plus tard, le 3 février 1762, lors du spectacle d'inauguration qui consacrait la réunion des deux troupes, ou plutôt l'intégration dans le personnel de la Comédie-Italienne des cinq meilleurs acteurs forains, précisément ceux qui avaient créé les rôles principaux dans cette même œuvre de Sedaine: voir Charlton, chapitre 9, p. 220–21. La première représentation du *Roi et le fermier* eut lieu le 22 septembre de la même année 1762. Clairval tenait le rôle du Roi, Laruette celui de Rustaut et Mademoiselle Deschamps celui de la Mère. Dans la distribution du *Déserteur*, en 1769, on retrouve encore Laruette (Jean-Louis) et Mademoiselle Deschamps devenue Madame Bérard (la Tante). Clairval triomphe dans le rôle de Montauciel. En 1777, cet acteur tient le premier emploi dans le rôle-titre de *Félix*.

[6] Pour le présent travail, nous nous référerons aux livrets suivants: M.-J. Sedaine, *Le Roi et le fermier, Comédie en trois actes mêlée de morceaux de musique* (Paris: Hérissant, 1762); *Le Déserteur, Drame en trois actes, en prose mêlée de musique* (Paris: Hérissant, 1769); *Félix ou l'Enfant trouvé, Comédie en trois actes, en prose et en vers mis en musique* (Paris: Ballard, 1777). Les partitions consultées sont: *Le Roi et le fermier* (Paris: Hérissant, s.d.); *Le Déserteur* (Paris: Hérissant, s.d.); *Félix ou l'Enfant trouvé* (Paris: Bailleux, s.d.). Cette dernière partition ne contient pas l'ouverture, publiée séparément: *Ouverture de Félix arrangée pour le clavecin ou le forte piano avec accompagnement de violon par M. Cesar* (Paris: Boyer, s.d.).

Dans cette perspective, *Le Roi et le fermier*, *Le Déserteur* et *Félix ou l'Enfant trouvé*, créés à la Comédie-Italienne respectivement en 1762, 1769 et 1777, occupent une place importante dans la carrière de Sedaine et, plus largement, dans l'évolution du genre de l'opéra-comique. Malgré les années qui les séparent, ces œuvres possèdent de nombreux points communs et l'on peut, à travers elles, observer la mise en place d'un système dramatique encore simple mais très efficace, résolvant de façon originale et novatrice le problème, dans une œuvre longue, des rôles respectifs du dialogue parlé et de la musique, bref, des modalités de cet art 'dramatico-musical' que Grétry va bientôt illustrer et théoriser.[7]

Grimm et La Harpe, entre autres, ont remarqué que les drames de Sedaine ne doivent pas se juger à la lecture mais au théâtre, lorsque la musique et les jeux de scène viennent réaliser pleinement le projet dramaturgique.[8] Pour en comprendre la portée, il s'agit donc d'aborder les trois œuvres qui nous occupent à travers une étude conjointe du texte et de la musique, tant sur les plans de l'économie générale de l'intrigue, du choix des personnages, du rôle de la musique et des moyens formels et stylistiques qu'elle met en œuvre.

La force d'une intrigue élémentaire

Ce qui frappe en premier lieu dans ces trois opéras-comiques, c'est l'extrême simplicité de l'intrigue.[9] Rapidement exposée, elle est aussi vite dénouée. Le dénouement ne constitue d'ailleurs pas une surprise. Annoncé longtemps à l'avance, il est aisément prévu par le spectateur. Les péripéties et les scènes de liaison, enfin, sont réduites à peu de chose, au risque de confiner à l'invraisemblance.[10] Tout est sacrifié pour mettre en valeur quelques situations

---

[7] Voir David Charlton, '"L'art dramatico-musical": An Essay', dans Nigel Fortune (éd.), *Music and Theatre. Essays in Honour of Winton Dean* (Cambridge: Cambridge University Press, 1987), p. 229–62.

[8] A propos d'*On ne s'avise jamais de tout*, Grimm remarque: 'Cette pièce [...] est charmante; mais en la lisant il est impossible de sentir l'effet qu'elle fait au théâtre': *Correspondance littéraire*, IV (1er déc. 1761), p. 502. Il est rejoint par La Harpe: 'il est impossible de soutenir la lecture de la plupart de ses ouvrages [...]. Son talent ne peut absolument se passer ni du théâtre ni de la musique, et pourtant n'est point méprisable': Jean-François de La Harpe, *Lycée, ou Cours de littérature ancienne et moderne* (Paris: Agasse, an IX), XII, p. 387.

[9] Cf. les trois tableaux en annexe. Les numéros entre parenthèses et les distributions en gras signalent les pièces musicales. Etablis pour la commodité de nos lecteurs, ces numéros n'apparaissent ni sur la partition, ni dans les livrets.

[10] Dans *Le Déserteur*, l'apparition de Montauciel tient à une simple méprise du geôlier. 'Oh ciel!' s'exclame Alexis dans sa prison. 'Ah, vous connaissez Montauciel' réplique le gardien, 'je vais vous l'envoyer'. Sedaine, *Le Déserteur*, p. 16. Les critiques de F. B. Hoffman à ce sujet

intéressantes, dont on sait qu'elles étaient le moteur de l'invention de Sedaine.[11] Le statisme dramatique qui en résulte devient un atout, car il permet de développer les situations sur le plan émotionnel, c'est-à-dire de laisser agir la musique.

On pourrait d'ailleurs observer des parentés entre les trois intrigues. Toutes trois mettent en scène un couple d'amants. Dans les deux premières, le jeune homme croit la jeune fille infidèle, mais sa jalousie est tôt ou tard désarmée par des explications soulignant l'intervention néfaste d'une tierce personne. La réconciliation des héros a lieu aussitôt. Un obstacle subsiste pourtant à l'union des amants: léger dans *Le Roi et le fermier* (il manque à Jenny une dot), plus considérable dans *Félix* (le statut social de cet enfant trouvé), terrible dans *Le Déserteur* (la condamnation à mort d'Alexis). On prévoit cependant très tôt la façon dont cet obstacle sera levé. Dès le milieu du deuxième acte du *Roi et le fermier*, Richard rencontre le Roi dans la forêt, sans le reconnaître. On comprend que cet hôte de marque défendra la fiancée du jeune homme contre les entreprises du Lord qui la persécute et favorisera son mariage avec Richard. A la fin du deuxième acte du *Déserteur*, Louise court implorer la grâce d'Alexis. Si l'on est prévenu de la façon dont le jeune homme pourra échapper à la mort, le troisième acte se passe dans l'attente de cette grâce, et l'on se demande si elle arrivera à temps. C'est également à la fin du deuxième acte de *Félix* que le dénouement se dessine. Gourville reconnaît dans le jeune homme celui qui l'a récemment sauvé d'une attaque de brigands. Il ne se présente pas encore comme le père de cet enfant trouvé, mais apparaît déjà comme le personnage providentiel qui lui prouvera sa reconnaissance en le défendant contre ses frères adoptifs.

Pour retarder le dénouement, Sedaine ne cherche pas à introduire des péripéties: il prévoit pour les héros des numéros musicaux développant le pathétique de la situation, et pour les personnages secondaires des airs caractérisés, souvent comiques, n'ajoutant rien à l'action sinon un effet de variété. Dans les intrigues élémentaires de Sedaine, le mélange de comique et de tragique (qui étonnait et séduisait tant Grimm)[12] est donc nécessaire au même titre que la présence de la musique.

---

sont résumées au chapitre 8.

[11] Dans son 'Avertissement' placé en tête du livret du *Magnifique*, opéra-comique centré sur la fameuse scène de la rose, Sedaine note: 'ce conte m'a paru propre au genre de l'Opéra-Comique; il promettoit des situations sur lesquelles la Musique pût s'arrêter': voir texte intégral, chap. 9, p. 259. Voir aussi André-Ernest-Modeste Grétry, *Mémoires, ou Essais sur la musique* (3 vol., Paris: Imprimérie de la République, An V; repr. New York, 1971), I, p. 247, 255, 398. Selon Ladislas Günther, on pourrait, dans chaque pièce de Sedaine, trouver 'une scène qui a donné naissance à tout l'échaffaudage': Ladislas Günther, *L'Œuvre dramatique de Sedaine* (Paris: Larose, 1908), p. 135.

[12] 'Si j'écoute le plus grand nombre de nos juges, ils me diront presque tous que *Le Déserteur* est une espèce de monstre dramatique, et que ce mélange du tragique et du comique est

Des personnages caractérisés

La construction de l'opéra-comique est ainsi liée aux personnages choisis par le librettiste. Ici encore, Sedaine ne cherche pas à approfondir leur psychologie mais au contraire à la simplifier. Aux héros – les deux amants – agités de passions diverses (tendresse, jalousie, désespoir), il oppose une galerie de caractères de second plan mûs chacun par un mobile unique et traités respectivement sur des tons divers, sérieux, comique ou satirique.

On rencontre ainsi plusieurs types d'aristocrates: le pervers et machiavélique Lord Lurewel (qui séquestre Jenny dans *Le Roi et le fermier*) et le grossier Versac (promis à Thérèse dans *Félix*) dont les vices contrastent avec la noblesse et la bonhommie du Roi (*Le Roi et le fermier*). L'uniforme apparaît dans les trois pièces, avec les figures comiques des gardes forestiers du *Roi et le fermier*, le joyeux Montauciel du *Déserteur* ou le brutal Morinville de *Félix*. Sedaine excelle à brosser en quelques répliques pleines de naturel des portraits de jeunes filles: la naïveté enfantine de Betsy et de Jeannette, la fraîcheur attendrissante de Manon.[13] Pour les autres personnages, une vieille femme radoteuse, un ecclésiatique égoïste, un paysan benêt, quelques reparties suffisent à en brosser la caricature. Pour chacun, Sedaine prévoit un air, sans aucune utilité sur le plan de l'action, mais qui ménage au musicien de bonnes occasions de musique imitative.

La part de ces airs caractérisés diffère selon les œuvres. Dans *Le Roi et le fermier*, on peut citer l'air de Rustaud et le duo comique de Betsy et Richard, retardant l'explication entre les deux amants (acte I), les rôles des gardes et des Lords (acte II), les chansons qui émaillent le troisième acte (l'étonnant trio composé de refrains superposés, les airs de Jenny, de Richard et du Roi). Toutes ces interventions confèrent une grande variété musicale à l'ensemble, même si le troisième acte perd sur le plan du suspens ce qu'il gagne en pittoresque dans l'évocation d'un intérieur paysan.

Dans *Le Déserteur*, on observe moins d'éléments extérieurs à l'action. Sedaine et Monsigny parviennent à développer de plusieurs façons et dans de nombreux numéros musicaux la situation tragique d'Alexis. Les différents personnages secondaires sont peu sollicités musicalement et se tiennent en retrait au profit d'un seul, Montauciel, dont la présence ne se justifie pas

barbare; mais je ne déciderai pas aussi vite qu'eux une question aussi importante. Et d'abord, à ne consulter que le grand modèle, la nature, je vois qu'elle fait toujours comme Sedaine dans son *Déserteur*, qu'elle mêle constamment la tragédie avec la comédie, qu'elle offre rarement une scène pathétique ou terrible sans mettre à côté quelque chose de risible': *Correspondance littéraire*, VIII (1er avril 1769), p. 319.

[13] Ce personnage se nomme Marguerite dans le livret de *Félix ou l'Enfant trouvé*, Manon dans la partition de Monsigny.

au profit d'un seul, Montauciel, dont la présence ne se justifie pas dramatiquement, sinon pour entrecouper d'épisodes comiques l'expression du désespoir d'Alexis et de ses proches. Sedaine lui ménage trois numéros musicaux qui donnent beaucoup de consistance à ce personnage enjoué, et en font une sorte d'antithèse d'Alexis.

Dans *Félix ou l'Enfant trouvé*, les figures secondaires sont plus nombreuses. On trouve aux côtés du Père Morin, figure patriarcale du fermier vertueux, ses trois fils pervertis par la vie urbaine (un procureur, La Morinière, un militaire, Morinville, et un ecclésiastique, Saint-Morin), M. de Versac – dont la muflerie à l'égard de sa fiancée Thérèse n'a d'égale que sa passion pour la chasse – M. de Gourville qui se révélera être le père de Félix, et enfin la petite servante Manon. Versac, Morin, Saint-Morin, Morinville et Manon se voient attribuer des airs illustrant leur caractère, mais La Morinière et Gourville ne sont pourvus d'aucune intervention musicale propre. Quant à la peinture satirique des trois frères et du noble Versac, elle est aussi traitée dans de nombreuses scènes sans musique. L'équilibre très réussi ménagé dans *Le Déserteur* entre musique et dialogues parlés, épisodes secondaires et intrigue principale se rompt au profit d'un partage des tâches, l'action et la satire sociale se développant davantage dans le dialogue parlé, l'émotion et la dimension moralisatrice dans les numéros musicaux.

Les grandes articulations de la dramaturgie musicale

Dans l'économie générale d'un opéra-comique, la musique a pour fonction de marquer les grandes articulations du déroulement dramatique: l'ouverture, les entractes, les morceaux qui commencent et terminent les actes sont conçus notamment à cette fin. Monsigny est très conscient du rôle qui lui incombe et trouve souvent des solutions originales pour souligner la structure musicale de la pièce.

L'ouverture est délibérément associée à la pièce qu'elle introduit. Celle du *Roi et le fermier* est indissociable du premier numéro vocal. Elle est conçue en deux parties, l'une vive en *mi* bémol majeur, l'autre *andante allegretto* en *do* mineur; l'ariette de Richard, *allegro* et en *mi* bémol, constitue ainsi le troisième volet de la forme tripartite de type italien. L'ouverture de *Félix* exploite l'air militaire de Morinville, 'Je t'attends à la caserne' (n° 9). Celle du *Déserteur* est la plus novatrice, annonçant le chœur final et résumant l'action moins par un rappel de thèmes que par une succession de climats.[14]

---

[14] Voir Patrick Taïeb, 'L'ouverture d'opéra-comique de 1781 à 1801, Contribution à l'histoire du goût musical en France à la fin du XVIIIe siècle', Doctorat de Musicologie, U. François-Rabelais de Tours, 1994, p. 14–15.

Les entractes musicaux imaginés par Monsigny sont également fort intéressants. Ils possèdent un rôle dramatique et ne sont jamais gratuits: ainsi *Félix*, qui se déroule dans une parfaite unité de lieu et de temps, n'en comporte pas. Les deux entractes du *Roi et le fermier*, en revanche, contribuent à brosser le décor forestier de l'œuvre. Le premier représente un orage qui a éclaté durant le dernier numéro vocal du premier acte (le duo de Richard et Jenny) et qui s'apaise au début du second acte (pour le duo comique des deux gardes qui précédera le récitatif et l'ariette du Roi). On se trouve ainsi en présence d'un vaste ensemble de cinq numéros musicaux s'enchaînant sans interruption, dans la ligne du procédé qui reliait la première ariette à l'ouverture.[15] Le second entracte marque un changement de lieu. Cet air de chasse, succédant au quatuor des gardes et des Lords, fait encore partie du décor extérieur de la forêt. Mais il pourrait aussi bien être entendu de l'intérieur de la maison de Richard, où se déroule le dernier acte.

Les entractes du *Déserteur* sont les plus étonnants: rappelant ou anticipant d'autres numéros musicaux, ils évoquent les actions de Louise en dehors de la scène. Le premier entracte reprend l'air initial 'Peut-on affliger ce qu'on aime?' Entendu pendant l'entracte qui suit la scène de la désertion, il sonne comme le rappel de l'inquiétude prémonitoire de la jeune fille qui, au moment où on l'entend, ne connaît pas encore le sort de son amant. Le second entracte annonce un passage de l'air de Courchemin, où le soldat raconte comment Louise s'est jetée aux pieds du Roi. Evoqué sous forme de récit au milieu du troisième acte, cet événement a effectivement eu lieu au moment où l'entracte musical y faisait référence (cf. tableaux en annexe).

Sedaine et Monsigny confèrent un rôle dramatique particulier au premier numéro vocal de leurs opéras-comiques. Tous trois commencent par un air qui a pour fonction plonger immédiatement le spectateur dans un climat pathétique. On ne connaît pas encore la raison du désespoir de Richard ('Je ne sais à quoi me résoudre') et de Louise ('Peut-on affliger ce qu'on aime?'), alors que la partie centrale de l'air de Félix ('Non, je ne serai point ingrat') donne davantage de détails sur son sort. Mais il s'agit à chaque fois d'une sorte d''exposition musicale', d'ordre affectif, de la situation dont on n'aura une explication précise que dans les scènes parlées qui suivent.

La fin des actes est marquée par des ensembles, duos, quatuors ou 'quinques'.[16] Le chœur n'intervient qu'au dénouement qui prend la forme d'un

---

[15] Se succèdent le duo n° 8, l'entracte n° 9, le duo n° 10, le récitatif et l'air du Roi n°s 11 et 12. Cf. tableau en annexe.

[16] Voir Elisabeth Cook, *Duet and Ensemble in the Early Opéra-Comique* (New York: Garland, 1995). Voir aussi idem, 'Developments in Vocal Ensemble Composition in the Opéra-Comique, 1750–1775' dans Philippe Vendrix (éd.), *Grétry et l'Europe de l'opéra-comique* (Liège: Mardaga, 1992), p. 113–29.

ensemble multipartite à la française dont les sections enchaînées obéissent davantage à la succession des événements dramatiques qu'à un pur souci de construction musicale.[17]

La fusion de tous les éléments du dénouement dans un ensemble entièrement mis en musique n'est pas encore opérée dans *Le Roi et le fermier*. Un septuor peint la stupéfaction générale lorsqu'on découvre l'identité du Roi. Les explications sont alors données dans une scène parlée où le Roi rend sa justice. Le monarque et les courtisans sortent, laissant les autres personnages chanter un simple chœur de reconnaissance auquel s'enchaîne le traditionnel vaudeville.

Dans *Le Déserteur*, en revanche, de nombreuses entités musicales se succèdent dans un final purement dramatique: l'ariette d'Alexis faisant ses adieux dans sa prison à Louise évanouie, le récitatif accompagné de la jeune fille revenant à elle, le chœur derrière la scène acclamant le roi, le changement de décor (représentant maintenant une place publique), le dénouement chanté par les protagonistes et commenté par la foule et enfin le dernier chœur en rondeau qui ressemble à une version dramatique et élargie d'un vaudeville.

Félix ou l'Enfant trouvé se termine de façon étonnante: après la reconnaissance de Félix par son père Gourville, où alternent solos et ensembles, Manon intervient pour annoncer l'approche d'une foule menaçante: Versac à la tête d'une troupe de chasseurs et Saint-Morin conduisant un groupe de villageoises viennent pour tenter d'empêcher le mariage de Félix. Leur irruption provoque de nouvelles explications et une réconciliation générale, scellée par un chœur dont Thérèse et Félix chantent les couplets et prétexte à une danse collective. Ce dernier épisode semblerait bien gratuit s'il ne permettait d'élargir l'ensemble final et de compléter le spectacle par la mise en scène d'une foule en liesse.

Si les éléments musicaux suivent donc les événements dramatiques dans ces scènes terminales, on comprend aussi qu'à l'inverse de tels dénouements ne peuvent être conçus en l'absence de leurs dimensions visuelle et sonore. Peu vraisemblables à la lecture, ils restent extrêmement efficaces à la scène et servent de pendant à l'exposition musicale de l'intrigue située dans le premier air.[18]

---

[17] Arnold Jacobshagen, *Der Chor in der französischen Oper des späten Ancien Régime* (Perspektiven der Opernforschung, V) (Frankfurt am Main: Lang, 1997), p. 39–44, 54–9.

[18] Confronté au problème du dénouement de *Richard Cœur-de-Lion*, Sedaine, après plusieurs essais infructueux, ne peut que se ranger à une solution similaire, l'intérêt musical et spectaculaire primant sur la vraisemblance. Dans le genre qu'il développe, Sedaine semble condamné à l''effet'. Cf. Grétry, *Mémoires*, I, p. 376 : 'Enfin *Sedaine* adopta le siége qui concilie tout [...] et qui présente un beau spectacle, seule ressource qui restoit après avoir intéressé aussi vivement dans le second acte.' Voir Charlton, *Grétry*, p. 248–50.

Le rôle dramatique des numéros musicaux

A l'intérieur du cadre structurel formé par les ouvertures, les entractes, les airs introductifs et les ensembles terminaux, les pièces vocales sont investies de plusieurs rôles dramatiques. En effet, dans un genre qui fait alterner scènes parlées et numéros musicaux, leur intervention doit trouver une justification.

La musique peut participer directement à l'action dans de petites scènes chantées par un ensemble, comme le quinque du *Déserteur* montrant la désertion d'Alexis (n° 8) ou le quatuor du *Roi et le fermier* où l'on voit les gardes capturer les Lords (n° 15). Pour Sedaine, l'écriture musicale permet alors de faire entendre avec vraisemblance plusieurs voix simultanément mais ce procédé comporte un inconvénient majeur, les paroles des divers protagonistes pouvant perdre de leur intelligibilité.[19]

Cet obstacle est levé lorsque l'action apparaît sous forme de récit chanté par un seul personnage: Jenny raconte son évasion (*Le Roi et le fermier,* n° 6), Courchemin relate l'épisode où Louise implore la grâce du roi (*Le Déserteur*, n° 19). La musique permet alors d'actualiser la narration en l'enrichissant d'une dimension imitative et affective.

Une façon plus courante d'intégrer la musique à l'action consiste à la faire intervenir en fin de scène, selon une distinction des tâches propre au genre de l'opéra-comique: le dialogue parlé expose la situation puis cède la place au chant qui apporte un surcroît d'émotion dans l'expression des sentiments. Le passage d'un idiome à l'autre – parfois périlleux sur le plan de la vraisemblance dramatique – est particulièrement bienvenu lorsqu'il s'agit d'un ensemble permettant aux protagonistes de s'exprimer simultanément, comme dans les duos d'amour du *Roi et le fermier* ('Ah! Richard, ah mon cher ami', n° 8) et de *Félix* ('Adieu Félix, adieu Thérèse', n° 11) ou l'étonnant trio fugué du *Déserteur* ('O ciel! quoi tu vas mourir', n° 14).

Les airs solistes, nous l'avons vu, sont de nature différente selon les personnages auxquels ils sont dévolus. Les deux héros principaux expriment les passions qui les agitent dans des ariettes qui représentent, avec les ensembles que

---

19 Sedaine est fort conscient du problème. Il prône l'ensemble musical dans le cas du dénouement du *Roi et le fermier*: 'La Tragédie ou la Comédie eût été forcée de le prolonger, de faire parler les Acteurs l'un après l'autre, & d'affaiblir la situation pour la rendre nettement avec noblesse ou décence: & la musique, en les faisant parler ensemble, a le droit de fixer le tableau, & de le tenir plus longtemps sous les yeux': Sedaine, 'L'auteur au lecteur', *Rose et Colas*. Mais Sedaine pose le problème de l'intelligibilité dans le quinque du *Déserteur*. 'Il est vrai que j'aurois dû, suivant ma coutume, faire débiter l'Ouvrage le jour même de la représentation, j'avois même cette fois-ci une raison très-forte. J'ai placé des parties d'exposition dans un *Quinque* [n° 8], dont les paroles sont perdues, sur-tout les premiers jours': Sedaine, 'Préface', *Le Déserteur*. Voir les textes intégraux au chapitre 9, p. 245–6 et 253–5.

nous venons d'évoquer, les sommets pathétiques de la pièce. Dans *Le Roi et le fermier* comme dans *Félix*, ces ariettes sont concentrées au début de l'opéra-comique.[20] La réussite du *Déserteur* tient notamment à la distribution équilibrée des airs passionnés dans toute la pièce.[21] A travers les six solos d'Alexis qui jalonnent l'ensemble de l'opéra-comique, Sedaine et Monsigny parviennent à évoquer sans redite les différents aspects de la jalousie et du désespoir du jeune homme. Cet exploit est rendu possible par la présence d'épisodes comiques, liés aux personnages de Jeannette, de Montauciel et de Bertrand, et qui introduisent des moments de détente.

Prévus pour les personnages secondaires, les airs caractérisés, sous leur apparente gratuité, ont pour fonction de retarder l'évolution de l'action et l'intervention du dénouement, tout en apportant une nécessaire variété entre les numéros pathétiques. Nombreux dans *Le Roi et le fermier* et dans *Félix*,[22] ils sont réduits aux deux interventions de Montauciel dans *Le Déserteur*.[23]

Il faut signaler enfin les chansons: parfaitement justifiées sur le plan de la vraisemblance dramatique (puisqu'il s'agit du seul cas où la présence de la musique est absolument nécessaire), elles sont en général étrangères à l'action. Elles abondent dans le troisième acte du *Roi et le fermier* où elles ont pour double fonction de peindre le caractère des personnages qui les chantent et de retarder le dénouement.[24] Elle sont absentes dans *Félix*, Morinville tentant en vain d'entonner un vaudeville assez leste que son père interrompt immédiatement.[25] Dans *Le Déserteur* (n° 15), on peut citer les deux chansons successives de Montauciel et de Bertrand, superposées ensuite dans un duo très comique, suivant un procédé qui rappelle le trio du *Roi et le fermier*. Mais la chanson de Jeannette, au premier acte, est également une réussite, tant par son charmant ton pastoral que par son insertion ingénieuse dans l'intrigue: on l'entend une première fois en entier lors de la

---

[20] L'angoisse puis la jalousie de Richard, enfin la tendresse de Jenny font l'objet des airs n°s 2, 4 et 7 du *Roi et le fermier*. Après la réconciliation des amants, la situation n'appelle plus d'air passionné de la part des deux héros. Dans *Félix*, on peut citer les ariettes de Félix (n°s 1 et 7) et de Thérèse (n°s 2 et 4). La situation des jeunes gens n'évolue guère au cours des actes II et III mais Sedaine ne peut prévoir, sous peine de redondance, de nouveaux airs passionnés. Il a alors recours aux ensembles (duo n° 11, trio n° 16).

[21] Airs de Louise n° 2 et 13, airs d'Alexis n°s 4, 10, 18, 20, 21, auxquels il faut ajouter le récitatif accompagné n° 7.

[22] Dans *Le Roi et le fermier*: airs de Rustaut (n° 3), du Roi (n° 12), de Lurewel (n° 14), de la Mère (n° 18) et de Betsy (n° 20). Dans *Félix*: airs de Versac (n°s 3, 9), de Saint-Morin (n° 5), de Morinville (n° 9), de Manon (n° 13), de Morin (n° 15).

[23] Airs n°s 11 et 17.

[24] Trio n° 17, superposant les chansons de Jenny, de Betsy et de la Mère; chansons de Jenny (n° 22), de Richard (n° 23) et du Roi (n° 24).

[25] Acte I, sc. IV, sur l'air 'du Mirliton'.

'répétition' avec Jean-Louis (scène III), puis par bribes lorsque la jeune fille, suivant à la lettre les instructions données, cherche à toute force à terminer ses couplets avant de répondre aux questions pressantes d'Alexis (scène VI).

Si l'on peut ainsi rapprocher les choix dramaturgiques de Sedaine dans les trois opéras-comiques qui nous intéressent, il semble que *Le Déserteur*, sur le double plan du rôle des numéros musicaux et de leur distribution dans l'intrigue, reste un modèle inégalé d'habileté et d'équilibre.

La forme musicale au service du projet dramatique

Tandis que Sedaine ménage, dans son drame, une place essentielle à la musique, Monsigny met tout en œuvre pour rendre sa musique théâtrale. Son inventivité se manifeste notamment dans la forme de ses ariettes et dans ses techniques d'imitation musicale.

Profondément pragmatique, Monsigny écrit pour une troupe et exploite les capacités vocales et théâtrales de chacun (cf. la liste des interprètes infra).[26] Il choisit la tessiture d'un rôle et en façonne les airs en fonction des aptitudes du chanteur qui devra l'incarner. Ainsi, deux artistes qui n'ont ni la même voix ni les mêmes qualités d'acteur, Caillot et Clairval, se succèdent dans des emplois similaires d'amoureux: le premier crée les rôles de Richard (*Le Roi et le fermier*) et d'Alexis (*Le Déserteur*), le second, le rôle-titre de *Félix*. Monsigny écrit pour eux des airs de forme et de style tout à fait distincts.

Joseph Caillot possédait une belle voix de basse-taille, très étendue dans l'aigu, jusqu'à atteindre le registre de haute-contre.[27] C'était également un extraordinaire acteur, d'abord voué aux rôles comiques puis développant son talent dans les emplois sentimentaux. Grimm ne tarit pas d'éloges à son égard dans *Le Roi et le fermier*:

> Quand on se souvient avec quelle finesse Caillot jouait ce rôle; comme on voyait dans tout son maintien un homme qui avait reçu de l'éducation; comme on voyait à travers ses brusqueries et sa mauvaise humeur envers les gardes-chasse la douceur naturelle de son caractère; avec quelle mesure il savait reprendre sa mère un peu ridicule, comme il souffrait son bavardage, avec quelle finesse il cherchait à la dérouter et savait affecter

26 Sur la troupe de la Comédie-Italienne, voir Pougin, *Monsigny*, p. 67–82; Clarence D. Brenner, 'Historical Introduction', *The Théâtre Italien. Its Repertory, 1716–1793* (University of California Publications in Modern Philology, LXIII) (Berkeley and Los Angeles: University of California Press, 1961), p. 1–43; et Charlton, *Grétry*, p. 13–16.

27 Cf. Grétry, *Mémoires*, I, p. 146.

de la gaieté pour ne pas la choquer; quand on se rappelle tout cela, on a le modèle d'un grand acteur dans la tête. [...]

Cet acteur était sublime sans aucun effort, et c'est peut-être de tous les talents le plus rare. [...] Garrick, l'ayant vu jouer pendant son séjour en France, lui apprit qu'il serait acteur quand il lui plairait. Ses essais furent des succès aussi étonnants que rapides.[28]

LES PRINCIPAUX INTERPRETES

	Le Roi et le fermier	*Le Déserteur*	*Félix*
Dessus			
Mlle La Ruette	Jenny	Louise	
Mme Trial			Thérèse
Mlle Deschamps	La Mère	La Tante	
Mlle Collet	Betsy		
Mlle Beaupré		Jeannette	
Mme Dugazon			Manon
Hautes-contre			
Clairval	Le Roi	Montauciel	Félix
Trial		Bertrand	La Morinière
Saint-Aubert	Un Courtisan		
Julien			Saint-Morin
Tailles			
Lejeune	Lurewel		
Desbrosses	Charlot	Un Garde	
Basses-tailles			
Caillot	Richard	Alexis	
Laruette	Rustaut	Jean-Louis	
Meunier			Versac
Narbonne			Morinville

28 *Correspondance littéraire*, X (15 déc. 1772), p. 121.

Caillot prit cependant sa retraite à quarante ans, en 1772, car sa voix présentait des signes de fatigue. Pour Grimm, 'à mesure que son jeu s'était perfectionné, sa voix s'était perdue. [...] Mais cette voix, soutenue du jeu le plus parfait, était suffisante pour nous faire du plaisir encore bien longtemps.'[29] Un jugement identique se trouve sous la plume de Grétry, à propos de la création par Caillot du rôle de Blaise dans *Lucile*, en 1769, c'est-à-dire l'année même où le chanteur incarnait Alexis dans *Le Déserteur*: 'Son organe commençoit à s'affoiblir, mais chaque jour il se montroit plus grand comédien.'[30]

Aux côtés de Caillot, Jean-Baptiste Clairval joua d'importants seconds rôles, comme le Roi dans *Le Roi et le fermier* et Montauciel dans *Le Déserteur*. Grétry lui confia le personnage d'Azor en 1770 et, après la retraite de Caillot, Clairval créa la plupart des grands emplois masculins, dont le rôle-titre de *Félix* et celui de Blondel dans *Richard Cœur-de-Lion*. Doué d'une belle voix de haute-contre, Clairval était également un remarquable acteur, dont Grétry louait le 'charme' et le 'goût exquis'.[31]

Chargée des rôles d'amoureuses, Marie-Thérèse La Ruette créa ceux de Jenny (*Le Roi et le fermier*) et de Louise (*Le Déserteur*). Marie-Jeanne Trial lui succéda dans son emploi et incarna Thérèse dans *Félix*. Toutes deux furent d'excellentes actrices, mais les contemporains évoquent surtout la sensibilité, la grâce et la décence de la première, tandis que la très belle voix de la seconde incitait les compositeurs à écrire pour elle des airs de bravoure.[32]

Plusieurs facteurs conditionnent alors la structure des ariettes de Monsigny: la fonction du morceau dans la pièce (les airs passionnés sont souvent plus complexes que les airs de caractère); les sentiments exprimés; la personnalité de l'interprète; l'évolution de l'écriture du compositeur qui, de 1762 à 1777, explore diverses solutions formelles.

Dans *Le Roi et le fermier*, la moitié des airs sont de forme *da capo*: il s'agit des ariettes caractérisant Rustaut (n° 3), le Roi (n° 12), la Mère (n° 18) et de chansons interprétées au troisième acte par Richard et par le Roi (n° 23, 24). La reprise de l'ariette de Lurewel est modifiée pour conclure de façon plus brillante

---

29 Ibid., p. 122.

30 Grétry, *Mémoires*, I, p. 176.

31 Ibid., I, p. 226–7, 370–71.

32 Sur madame La Ruette, cf. par exemple Grétry, *Mémoires*, I, p. 162, 188. Pour madame Trial, le compositeur écrivit un air de virtuosité dans *L'Amant jaloux*. 'L'air de bravoure qui commence le second acte, n'est pas celui que *d'Hele* ni moi avions destiné à cet endroit: l'ancien air n'étoit qu'en demi-caractère [...] et c'étoit ce qui convenoit à la situation; mais l'envie de faire briller le plus bel organe que la nature forma jamais; l'envie de contenter la plus douce, la plus honnête, la moins capricieuse des actrices, madame *Trial*, nous fit consentir à ce contre-sens dramatique, que les journaux nous reprochèrent avec raison': ibid., I, p. 322–3.

(n° 14), tandis que la belle simplicité de la ligne mélodique de l'air de Jenny ('Ce que je dis est la vérité même', n° 7) appelle une forme ABA élémentaire, pour traduire la droiture et la sincérité de la jeune fille. A l'inverse, la jalousie de Richard et ses alternatives de doute et de certitude ('D'elle-même et sans effort', n° 4) sont judicieusement exprimées par une forme rondeau.

Ailleurs, Monsigny construit des formes irrégulières, évitant les reprises strictes. La romance de Jenny ('Que le soleil dans la plaine', n° 22), écrite sur une basse de musette, combine les formes rondeau et ABA'. L'ariette de Betsy ('Il regardait mon bouquet', n° 20) est une fausse forme strophique, la ligne mélodique s'adaptant à chaque couplet aux nuances du naïf récit de la petite fille.

Mais les formes les plus complexes sont réservées aux héros principaux: la première ariette de Richard ('Je ne sais à quoi me résoudre', n° 2) et l'émouvant récit de Jenny ('Le Milord m'offre des richesses', n° 6) enchaînent de nombreuses parties dans deux combinaisons différentes de formes rondeau et ternaire, afin de suivre avec souplesse l'évolution des sentiments exprimés et de ménager des sections contrastantes tout en conservant une structure tonale claire.

Les airs du *Déserteur* explorent une autre solution au problème de la reprise du texte et de la musique. Certes, les simple formes ternaires *da capo* ou ABA restent nombreuses, auxquelles il faut ajouter les chansons de forme strophique (celle de Jeannette, n° 3) et binaire (celles de Bertrand et de Montauciel, superposées dans le n° 15). On peut également citer le rondeau irrégulier de l'ariette d'Alexis 'Mourir n'est rien' (n° 10).

Souvent, Monsigny ne cherche plus à varier la reprise mais à modifier l'équilibre de l'air en faisant précéder la forme ternaire d'une importante section initiale (structure ABCB). Plus mélodique qu'un simple récitatif, cette introduction permet de préparer musicalement le sentiment dominant de l'air, exprimé ensuite dans la partie reprise à la fin *dal segno*. Ce type d'ariette (n° 4, 20, pour Alexis, et n° 17, pour Montauciel) est surtout conçu comme une succession d'états affectifs différents.

Ainsi, la première ariette d'Alexis (n° 4) peint avec finesse le caractère exalté du jeune soldat, impatient de retrouver sa fiancée mais saisi d'inexplicables pressentiments. Une ritournelle instrumentale *allegro maestoso*, agitée par des arpèges ascendants puis des syncopes, montre l'arrivée d'Alexis hors d'haleine puis sert d'accompagnement à sa première intervention ('Ah! je respire'). Mais le ton change subitement, le jeune homme reconnaissant le lieu où il échangea des serments avec Louise ('Oui, le voici cet orme heureux'): la ligne mélodique se fait gracieuse, l'orchestre la soutient par les *pizzicati* des basses et les violons en contretemps. Dans un mouvement plus vif (*allegro*), Alexis entame alors la section principale de l'air ('Je vais la voir'), dont la mélodie joyeuse laisse bientôt place à un passage proche du récitatif ('Mais je frissonne') avant de conclure de façon brillante ('Ah! quel moment charmant'). Dans une nouvelle section librement déclamée, Alexis s'inquiète de l'absence de Louise, imagine leur réunion, cherche à se renseigner ('Mais pourquoi ne l'ai-je pas vue?') avant de reprendre 'Je vais la voir'. La structure en quatre parties de l'air regroupe donc en réalité une dizaine de changements de climat émotionnel, assortis à chaque fois d'une modification du style vocal.

Comme les autres interventions d'Alexis (le *récitativo obligato* n° 7 qui introduit le quinque; le rondeau 'Mourir n'est rien', n° 10, dont le deuxième couplet est occupé par la lecture d'une lettre de Louise; l'ariette n° 18, 'Il eut été si doux', où le jeune homme écrit à sa bien-aimée, dans une forme *da capo* dont la partie centrale est un récitatif; l'air n° 20, 'On s'empresse', dont la structure est proche de l'ariette que nous venons d'analyser; le dernier air, 'Adieu, chère Louise', n° 21, dont la reprise est écourtée, les soldats emmenant Alexis vers le lieu de son exécution), cette ariette initiale est manifestement dédiée à un Joseph Caillot au sommet de son art de comédien et qui pousse Monsigny à créer des formes originales, profondément théâtrales et pathétiques.

Dans *Félix*, en revanche, Clairval et madame Trial ont remplacé Caillot et madame La Ruette. Tous les airs sont de forme ternaire: la troisième partie reprend la première dans un *da capo* littéral omettant la ritournelle introductive ou, plus rarement, apporte des modifications à la reprise (n°s 2, 13, 15). En contrepartie, chaque section est plus développée et le style vocal plus complexe et brillant qu'auparavant.

Monsigny n'a pas renoncé aux effets de contraste entre des climats affectifs opposés: la partie centrale de la première ariette de Thérèse ('Quoi, tu me quittes', n° 2) tranche sur le *lamentabile* de l'ensemble par son tempo *allegro*; à l'inverse, celle de l'air comique de Versac ('Hé mes amis', n° 10) est un ironique *andante amoroso*. Mais ces oppositions restent intégrées dans des structures tripartites plus conventionnelles et ne conditionnent plus la forme.

Huit ans après les étonanntes expériences du *Déserteur*, Monsigny semble délaisser les recherches formelles pour se consacrer à l'élaboration d'un style vocal moins dramatique mais plus purement musical. Les interprètes sont successivement acteurs dans les scènes parlées et chanteurs dans les ariettes, où la difficulté de leur partie vocale les pousse à faire passer l'action théâtrale au second plan: Monsigny participe en cela à une évolution générale de l'opéra-comique, où la musique tient une place croissante jusqu'à rendre obsolète le terme de 'comédie mêlée d'ariettes'.

Les voies de l'imitation musicale

Si la place des numéros musicaux dans l'intrigue et leur structure interne sont d'une grande importance, la dramaturgie de l'opéra-comique repose également sur une étroite relation entre les situations et leur traduction dans une dimension sonore. Il s'agit moins de l'illustration servile d'un texte que de la double participation – verbale et musicale – à un projet expressif commun.

S'il est impossible d'entrer ici dans le détail des effets musicaux au service du drame, on pourra s'interroger brièvement sur la nature d'une imitation souvent hétérogène dans ses modalités, l'essor de l'opéra-comique mêlé d'ariettes, sous l'impulsion de Duni, Philidor et Monsigny, contribuant d'ailleurs largement, au milieu du siècle, à renouveler la palette expressive des musiciens lyriques.[33]

Se mêlent sous la plume de Monsigny des souvenirs de l'imitation baroque et des procédés liés à l'émergence d'une nouvelle sensibilité. Ici encore, il faut distinguer les situations et les personnages, l'expression changeant de nature selon qu'elle s'applique au pathétique ou au comique, aux héros passionnés ou aux figures secondaires.

Les émotions diverses qui agitent le couple d'amoureux sont traduites au premier chef par le profil mélodique, l'invention inépuisable de Monsigny lui fournissant des lignes amples et énergique pour exprimer le désespoir,

Le Roi et le fermier, Ariette no. 2

[33] Pour une analyse du style de Monsigny, voir Karin Pendle, 'L'Opéra-comique à Paris de 1762 à 1789' dans Philippe Vendrix (éd.), *L'Opéra-comique en France au XVIIIe siècle* (Liège: Mardaga, 1992), p. 123–32.

Le Déserteur, [Ariette] no. 10

Félix ou l'Enfant trouvé, Air no. 1

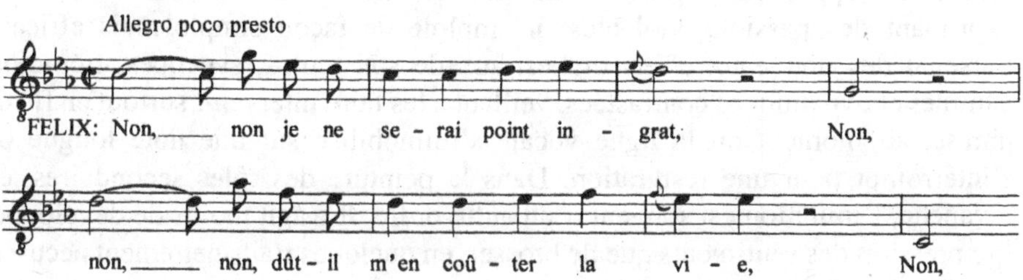

ou au contraire d'une simplicité charmante pour traduire la sincérité et la tendresse.

Le Roi et le fermier, Ariette no. 7

Le Déserteur, [Air] no. 13

Mais si Monsigny est d'abord apprécié comme mélodiste, il ne faut pas sous-estimer son apport sur le plan de l'accompagnement instrumental. Dans les airs exprimant des passions violentes, il emploie de façon simple mais efficace l'arsenal des nouveaux effets orchestraux de son temps, syncopes, trémolos, gammes et dynamiques contrastées, veillant à les faire intervenir surtout en fin de phrase, au moment où la ligne vocale s'immobilise sur une note longue ou s'interrompt pour une respiration. Dans la peinture des rôles secondaires, en revanche, l'imitation est souvent d'un autre ordre. Il s'agit moins de développer l'expression des sentiments que de brosser, en quelques traits nettement accusés, les contours d'une physionomie.

Lorsqu'il souhaite indiquer la fonction sociale d'un personnage, Monsigny emploie des rythmes emblématiques comme il était d'usage à l'époque baroque: l'aristocratie de Lurewel et de Versac est représentée par des airs de chasse (on reconnaît la mesure ternaire et les mélodies en arpèges des sonneries de trompes), l'état militaire de Montauciel et de Morinville par l'écho de marches guerrières (avec une mesure binaire et des rythmes pointés).

D'autres figures secondaires sont évoquées dans une situation comique. La ligne mélodique peut imiter les gestes, comme dans l'amusante ariette de la Mère du *Roi et le fermier* (n° 18) où la vieille femme se confond en révérences soulignées par les cordes:

Le Roi et le fermier, Ariette no. 18

puis, perdant un peu la tête devant un hôte de marque, s'exclame sur un motif répété qui figure à merveille son radotage.

Le Roi et le fermier, Ariette no. 18

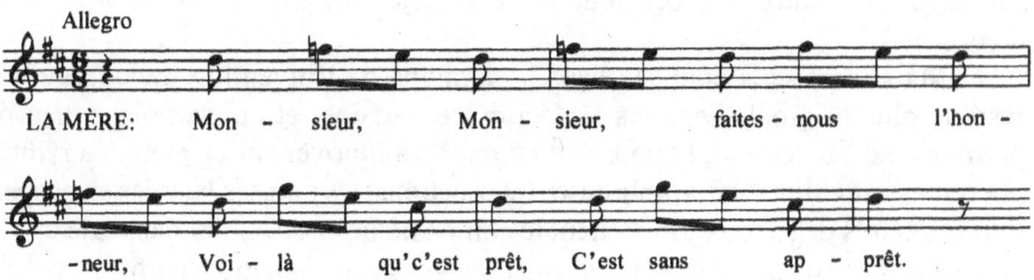

Monsigny aime répéter des interjections pour accentuer l'effet comique (les 'fi, fi' de Rustaut dans le n° 3 et les 'hi, hi' de Betsy tout en pleurs dans le n° 5 du *Roi et le fermier*) ou terminer un ensemble sur un *decrescendo* et un ralentissement progressif des rythmes pour figurer l'éloignement des personnages (duo de Rustaut et Charlot, n° 10 du *Roi*, quinque n° 6 et quatuor n° 14 de *Félix*), autant de procédés simples et efficaces qui soulignent le jeu théâtral.

De l'opéra baroque, Monsigny conserve parfois le souci de la peinture du mot: 'je tremble' est illustré par un motif de cordes (*Le Roi*, n° 13), 'vol' ou 'voler' par une gamme rapide (*Le Roi*, n° 14, *Félix*, n° 4), 'flamme' par un mélisme (*Le Roi*, n° 12), mais son imitation est en général moins directement liée au texte et peut se développer de façon autonome. Ainsi, dans le duo n° 8 du *Roi et le fermier*, Richard et Jenny entendent au loin dans les bois les appels de trompes et les galops des chevaux d'une chasse, puis les grondements de l'orage qui approche: il s'agit moins d'un récitatif accompagné par un orchestre illustratif que du commentaire chanté de l'évocation sonore des bruits de la forêt:

JENNY

Entends-tu les chiens, les chasseurs,
Les abois, les cris, les clameurs?

RICHARD

J'entends le galop des chevaux,
Le bruit des cors et les échos.

On pourrait signaler encore le petit motif de doubles-croches qui, dans le récitatif accompagné du Roi égaré, peint le mystère des bois silencieux et sombres ('Quelle nuit! quelle obscurité! / Personne en ce bois écarté') et que Monsigny reprend avec bonheur dans la partie centrale de l'ariette qui suit, lorsque le Roi évoque à nouveau 'ce triste et profond silence / La vaste horreur de ces forêts'. Dans ces tentatives de développement des procédés imitatifs, dès *Le Roi et le fermier*, Monsigny se montre un précurseur des recherches que Grétry va bientôt étendre et théoriser.

Mais c'est sans conteste dans le domaine de l'invention mélodique qu'il reste le plus original. Les vers si décriés de Sedaine, et qui semblent bien peu harmonieux à la lecture, le poussent en réalité à innover sur ce plan: les rythmes poétiques irréguliers, les nombreuses interjections, les phrases laissées en suspens, tous ces effets de rupture empêchent le compositeur de se couler dans une carrure et une symétrie de phrases trop systématiques.[34] La déclamation, parfois proche du récitatif, s'entremêle aux mélodies les mieux découpées et confère au style vocal de Monsigny une souplesse, une certaine forme de 'naturel' qui répondent parfaitement au projet esthétique du librettiste.

Dans sa collaboration avec Monsigny, Sedaine se montre donc le promoteur d'un nouvel équilibre dramatique au sein de l'opéra-comique. Il rejette le titre de 'comédie à ariettes' au profit d'autres, tel que 'drame' (*Le Déserteur*), 'comédie mêlée de morceaux de musique' (*Le Roi et le fermier*), ou 'comédie en prose et en vers mis en musique' (*Félix*).[35] La musique en effet n'intervient pas comme un ornement mais devient intimement liée à la conception et à la réalisation du drame.

Le librettiste semble s'effacer[36] et servir le compositeur en réduisant l'intrigue au minimum, en partageant l'action entre les dialogues parlés et les

---

[34] 'Si *Sedaine* n'est pas le poëte qui soigne le plus les vers destinés au chant, les situations qu'il amène [...] sont si impérieuses qu'elles forcent le musicien à s'y attacher pour les rendre. Il dit presque toujours le mot propre, et il se croit dispensé de l'embellir par des tours poëtiques. Il force donc le musicien à prendre des formes neuves pour rendre ses caractères originaux': Grétry, *Mémoires*, I, p. 254. F.-B. Hoffman jette un regard rétrospectif sur l'apport de Sedaine sur ce plan: 'Peu à peu on s'habituait à sa manière brusque, mais animée; à son style barbare, mais plein de mots heureux; à ses fautes grossières, mais qui produisaient des beautés inattendues': F.-B. Hoffman, *Œuvres* (10 vol., Paris: Lavigne, 1834), VI, p. 531. Je remercie vivement Patrick Taïeb qui m'a fait connaître ce texte, dont on trouvera l'analyse aux p. 173–91 de ce livre.

[35] Pour une allusion à ce procédé par Sedaine lui-même, voir au chapitre 9, p. 246. Le phénomène en générale est discuté par Manuel Couvreur et Philippe Vendrix, 'Les enjeux théoriques de l'Opéra-Comique' dans Vendrix (éd.), *L'Opéra-comique*, p. 213–81 [259–60]; et par Corinne Pré, 'Le Livret d'opéra-comique en France de 1741 à 1789', Doctorat ès Lettres, Université de Paris III, 1982, p. 85–9.

[36] Voir les préfaces du *Déserteur* et du *Magnifique*, plus loin, aux p. 253 et 259.

épisodes musicaux, en imaginant des personnages secondaires aux caractères tranchés, propices à l'illustration musicale. En retour, la musique permet de développer le pathétique des situations imaginées par Sedaine.[37] Elle décuple la charge émotionnelle de l'œuvre théâtrale: c'est elle qui plonge d'emblée le public dans le registre du sentiment, registre que Sedaine saura exploiter et soutenir jusqu'à un dénouement deviné, prévu, désiré, longtemps différé par des interventions comique, pittoresques ou attendrissantes, et réalisé enfin dans une scène à grand spectacle, peu vraisemblable mais d'une grande efficacité théâtrale.

Cette abdication partielle du librettiste a pu être critiquée sur le plan littéraire.[38] Elle n'en constitue pas moins l'acte fondateur d'une nouvelle esthétique de l'opéra-comique, remportant un énorme succès auprès d'un public avide d'émotion et ouvrant la voie aux chef-d'œuvres de Grétry.

Pour y parvenir, Sedaine devait s'associer à un musicien doué d'un grande sensibilité théâtrale et capable d'endosser à son tour le rôle du dramaturge. Avant Grétry, avec lequel il réalisera des œuvres plus complexes et plus ambitieuses, Monsigny saura être cet artiste que Sedaine remerciait dans son 'Avertissement' placé en tête du *Roi et le fermier*:

> Il falloit que je trouvasse un grand Artiste, un Musicien habile qui voulût bien avoir un peu de confiance en moi, enfin un ami qui voulût bien risquer un genre nouveau en musique.[39]

---

37 A propos des ensembles: 'La musique, en les faisant parler ensemble, a le droit de fixer le tableau, & le tenir plus longtemps sous les yeux': Sedaine, 'L'auteur au lecteur', *Rose et Colas* (voir n.19).

38 Cf. Hoffman (voir n. 34) qui plaide pour un retour à un genre plus purement comique.

39 Voir aussi plus loin, p. 245.

LE ROI ET LE FERMIER

(1)		**Ouverture**	
(2)	I, I	**Richard: 'Je ne sais à quoi me résoudre'**	Angoisse de Richard
	I, II–IV	Richard et les gardes	Exposition: le roi chasse dans la forêt, Jenny est chez Lord Lurewel
(3)	I, IV	**Rustaut: 'Ami, laisse là la tendresse'**	Air comique du garde
(4)	I, V	**Richard: 'D'elle-même et sans effort'**	Jalousie de Richard
(5)	I, VI	**Richard, Betsy: 'Non, vous ne m'avez jamais'**	Duo comique: impatience de Richard, pleurs de Betsy
(6)	I, VII	**Jenny: 'Le milord m'offre des richesses'**	Récit de Jenny
(7)	I, VIII	**Jenny: 'Ce que je dis est la vérité même'**	Amour sincère de Jenny
(8)	I, X	**Richard, Jenny: 'Ah! Richard, ah mon cher ami'**	Duo d'amour, réconciliation des amants
(9)		**Entracte: orage**	
(10)	II, I	**Rustaut, Charlot: 'Tu résistes, tu défends'**	Duo comique des gardes
(11–12)	II, II	**Le Roi: 'Je me suis égaré / Dans les combats'**	Récitatif et air du Roi égaré dans la forêt
	II, III	Richard, le Roi	Richard offre l'hospitalité au Roi
(13)	II, IV	**Lurewel, le Courtisan: Ah! ciel, ah si c'était le roi'**	Duo comique des lords
(14)	II, IV	**Lurewel: 'Un fin chasseur'**	Air caractérisant Lurewel

(15)	II, V	**Rustaut, Charlot, Lurewel, le Courtisan: 'Avance'**	Quatuor comique, les gardes s'emparent des deux lords
(16)		**Entracte: air de chasse**	
(17)	III, I	**Betsy, Jenny, la Mère: 'Lorsque j'ai mon tablier blanc'**	Intérieur paysan. Trio: trois chansons superposées
	III, II–III	Richard, le Roi, la Mère, Betsy, Jenny	Hospitalité de Richard, le dénouement se dessine
(18)	III, IV	**La Mère: 'Monsieur, monsieur'**	Air comique de la mère
(19)	III, V	**Betsy, Jenny, la Mère: 'Ah! ma tante'**	Espoir de Jenny
(20)	III, VIII	**Betsy: 'Il regardait mon bouquet'**	Air caractérisant Betsy
(21)	III, IX	**Richard, Betsy: 'Un instant / Il m'attend'**	Duo des amants
	III, X	Richard, Le Roi, Jenny	Richard donne son opinion sur la vie de cour
(22)	III, XII	**Jenny: 'Que le soleil dans la plaine'**	Chanson (romance) de Jenny
(23)	III, XII	**Richard: 'Ce n'est qu'ici'**	Chanson de Richard
(24)	III, XII	**Le Roi: 'Le bonheur est de répandre'**	Chanson du Roi
(25)	III, XIV	**Le Roi, Richard, Betsy, la Mère, Rustaut, Lurewel, le Courtisan: 'Le Roi, le Roi'**	Septuor. Dénouement: l'identité du Roi est découverte, le Roi confond Lurewel
(26)	III, XVI	**Chœur: 'Que du ciel la bonté suprême'**	Réjouissance finale
(27)	III, XVI	**Vaudeville: 'Ne perdons jamais l'espérance'**	

LE DESERTEUR

(1)		**Ouverture**	Annonce du chœur final et résumé de l'action
(2)	I, I	**Louise: 'Peut-on afffliger ce qu'on aime?'**	Tristesse de Louise
	I, II	Louise, Jean-Louis, la Tante, Jeannette, Bertrand	Préparatifs pour la mystification d'Alexis
(3)	I, III	**Jeannette: 'J'avais égaré mon fuseau'**	Répétition: air pastoral de Jeannette
(4)	I, IV	**Alexis: 'Ah! je respire'**	Sentiments mêlés d'Alexis: joie, impatience, sombres pressentiments
(5)	I, V	**Marche**	La fausse noce passe
	I, VI	Alexis, Jeannette	Jeannette informe Alexis de la fausse nouvelle du mariage de Louise
(6)	I, VI	**Jeannette, Alexis: 'Serait-il vrai?'**	Désespoir d'Alexis
(7)	I, VII	**Alexis: 'Infidèle'**	
(8)	I, VIII	**Alexis, 3 Gardes, Courchemin: 'Fuyons ce lieu'**	Quinque: désertion d'Alexis
(9)		**Entracte**	Rappel du n° 2: tristesse de Louise
	II, I	Le Concierge, Alexis	Alexis en prison
(10)	II, II	**Alexis: 'Mourir n'est rien'**	Douleur d'Alexis lisant la lettre de Louise
(11)	II, III	**Montauciel: 'Je ne déserterai jamais'**	Air caractérisant Montauciel, le joyeux soldat
(12)	II, VI	**Alexis, Louise: 'O ciel! puis-je te voir ici'**	Duo des amants

(13)	II, VIII	**Louise: 'Dans quel trouble te plonge'**	Louise détrompe Alexis et l'assure de son amour
(14)	II, X	**Jean-Louis, Alexis, Louise: 'O ciel, quoi tu vas mourir'**	Louise et son père ont appris la condamnation d'Alexis
	II, XIV	Le Concierge, Louise	Louise supplie le concierge: annonce du dénouement (elle va implorer le roi)
(15)	II, XVII	**Montauciel, Bertrand: 'Tous les hommes / Vive le vin'**	Intermède comique: deux chansons successives puis superposées
(16)		**Entracte**	Annonce du n° 19 (Louise supplie le roi)
	III, I–II	La Tante, Jeannette, Bertrand, Alexis	Désespoir comique des amis d'Alexis
(17)	III, IV	**Montauciel: 'V, o, u, s'**	Air comique de Montauciel apprenant à lire
(18)	III, IV	**Alexis: 'Il eut été si doux'**	Douleur d'Alexis: lettre à Louise
(19)	III, VI	**Courchemin: 'Le roi passait'**	Récit de Courchemin, annonce du dénouement
(20)	III, VII	**Alexis: 'On s'empresse, on me regarde'**	Douleur d'Alexis
(21)	III, X	**Alexis: 'Adieu, chère Louise'**	Evanouissement de Louise. Adieux d'Alexis
(22)	III, XI	**Louise: 'Où suis-je?'**	Réveil de Louise, restée seule
	III, XII–XIII	**Ensemble et chœur**	Changement de décor (place publique). Dénouement: Alexis est grâcié par le roi

FELIX OU L'ENFANT TROUVE

		Ouverture	Annonce le n° 9
(1)	I, I	**Félix: 'Non je ne serai point ingrat'**	Douleur et résolution de Félix
	I, II	Félix, Thérèse	Exposition: Thérèse va épouser Versac, Félix veut partir
(2)	I, III	**Thérèse: 'Quoi, tu me quittes'**	Douleur et amour de Thérèse pour Félix
	I, IV–IX	Morin, Morinville, St-Morin, La Morinière, Thérèse, Versac, le Tabellion, Manon	Préparation du mariage, portraits des trois fils de Morin et de Versac
(3)	I, IX	**Versac: 'Courir les bois'**	Air caractérisant Versac
	I, X		On entend des coups de feu dans les bois
(4)	I, XI	**Thérèse: 'Hélas! où peut-il être?'**	Inquiétude de Thérèse
(5)	I, XIII	**Saint-Morin: 'Qu'on se batte'**	Air comique de Saint-Morin
	I, XIV–XV	Morin, Morinville, St-Morin, La Morinière, Versac, M. de Gourville	On soigne Gourville, délivré des brigands
(6)	I, XVI	**Manon, Morinville, St-Morin, La Morinière, Versac: 'Finissez donc'**	Quinque: Morinville lutine Manon, encouragé par ses frères et Versac
(7)	II, I	**Félix: 'Il faut que je les quitte'**	Douleur de Félix
(8)	II, II	**Morin, Félix: 'Non, je pars demain'**	Adieux de Félix à Morin
	II, IV	Félix, Morinville	Félix s'engage dans le régiment de Morinville
(9)	II, V	**Morinville: 'Je t'attends à la caserne'**	Air caractérisant Morinville

	II, VI–VIII	Morin, Morinville, St-Morin, La Morinière	Morin veut restituer son bien à Gourville, contre le gré de ses fils
(10)	II, IX	**Versac: 'Hé mes amis, que faut-il donc'**	Air caractérisant Versac
	II, X–XII	Morin, Morinville, St-Morin, La Morinière, Versac	Menaces et complot contre le projet de Morin
(11)	II, XV	**Félix, Thérèse: 'Adieu Félix, adieu Thérèse'**	Duo des amants, Gourville, caché, reconnaît en Félix son libérateur
(12)	III, I	**Chœur: 'A la chasse'**	Air de chasse, en relation avec Versac
(13)	III, III	**Manon: 'Ah, qu'une fille est à plaindre'**	Air caractérisant Manon
	III, IV	Morin, Félix, Gourville	Morin restitue son bien à Gourville
(14)	III, VI	**Morin, Morinville, St-Morin, La Morinière: 'O ciel, est-il possible'**	Colère des trois frères contre leur père
(15)	III, VII	**Morin: 'Il est dans le fond de mon âme'**	Vertu de Morin
(16)	III, IX	**Morin, Félix, Thérèse: 'Ne vous repentez pas'**	Piété filiale de Thérèse et Félix
	III, XI	Morin, Félix, Thérèse, Gourville, Morinville, St-Morin, La Morinière	Gourville lègue son bien retrouvé à Félix, son libérateur
(17)	III, XII	**Ensemble et chœur**	Dénouement: Gourville reconnaît en Félix son fils

PART III

The Public Image

Chapter 7

Sedaine et les images

Martine de Rougemont

I. Portraits

Messieurs, votre erreur est extrême:
Ce moi-là, ce n'est pas moi-même,
Ce ne sont là que mes portraits.[1]

Plus que pour aucun autre écrivain peut-être, les portraits que nous connaissons de Sedaine ont été faits par des amis. Ces amis sont aussi de grands artistes, ils sont assurément capables de proposer des images pénétrantes et inspirées de modèles qui leur sont étrangers, mais il me plaît de penser qu'ici l'échange entre le peintre ou le sculpteur et le poète, que le dialogue a été plus intime. Parfois plus complexe? Décrire dans la chronologie ces portraits ce sera donc aussi faire l'histoire de ces amitiés. Ce pari narratif, bien que peu 'scientifique', permet d'étayer ou de contester des attributions et des dates par des critères externes souvent utiles.[2]

Jean Siméon Chardin est né en 1699, vingt ans avant Sedaine. Leurs destins se ressemblent: fils de maîtres artisans (le père de Chardin ébéniste, celui de Sedaine entrepreneur), ils ont interrompu leurs études scolaires pour travailler et garderont tous les deux la marque de l'autodidacte, ils subiront également le mépris des savants, et ils feront la leçon aux savants à partir de leur place forte d'artistes-praticiens. Tous les deux, ils apporteront au cœur du dix-huitième siècle une découverte du réel, préférant les sujets familiers aux scènes mythologiques, 'petits' maîtres devant lesquels les esprits les plus brillants s'inclineront. 'Promis' à rien du tout, ils arrivent à la force du poignet aux honneurs, et quand ils sont vieux et ne peuvent plus s'imposer, on les jette l'un et l'autre au rebut, dit leur légende.

---

[1] Michel-Jean Sedaine, *Pièces fugitives de Monsieur S**** (n.p., 1752), 'Stances à S*** pour le prier de faire mon portrait'.

[2] Le point de vue 'scientifique' a été revu attentivement par Mark Ledbury, dont j'ai scrupuleusement intégré les rectifications et les compléments d'information. On se reportera aussi à son 'Iconography of Sedaine' dans ce volume, et à sa thèse, 'Greuze and Sedaine'.

Michel-Jean Sedaine a perdu son père, ruiné depuis trois ans, quand il en a seize; fils aîné, il lui faut assurer la subsistance de sa mère et de ses deux frères, ce sera en travaillant sur des chantiers comme tailleur de pierre, grâce aux anciennes relations paternelles. Il aurait environ dix-sept ans au moment que je vais laisser décrire à Mme Guieysse-Frère:

> Parmi les vieux amis de Jean Sedaine, un brave menuisier, fabricant des billards du roi, avait un fils, Siméon Chardin, qui admirait le courage simple et le dévouement de Michel Sedaine et qui venait aussi souvent s'asseoir auprès de lui pendant qu'il maniait son marteau. Chardin n'avait, lui, jamais poussé le rabot, mais tout petit, il aimait dessiner et 'tripoter' la couleur: tout seul il voulait apprendre à peindre, et, comme il le racontait à Sedaine, 'il mettait de la couleur jusqu'à ce que cela ressemble' à ce qu'il voyait. Chardin était simple et têtu comme un bon fils d'artisan et à force de regarder un poisson frais, 'une raie', un chaudron, une pomme, un pain, une brioche il était devenu un très grand peintre, exposant sur la place Dauphine, à la Fête-Dieu, et ne dédaignant pas même de faire un tableau 'en enseigne' pour un chirurgien-barbier, ami de son père. Ce brave homme l'avait aidé et placé chez Caze, un peintre du roi.
>
> Siméon Chardin était maintenant de l'Académie et, pour compléter son talent, s'essayait aux portraits. Tout en causant avec son jeune ami, il dessinait; puis il apporta sa palette et fit du tailleur de pierre, coiffé d'un chapeau mou, dans sa veste grise de travailleur, son marteau à la main, un portrait délicat et sans apprêts qui prouva combien l'étude des simples objets usuels avait été profitable à son talent.[3]

[3] La toile de Chardin [Fig. 1], connue sous les deux titres 'le Tailleur de pierre' ou 'Portrait de Sedaine', figure notamment dans le *Catalogue raisonné de l'œuvre de Chardin* d'Armand Dayot (n° 106) et dans le catalogue de l'exposition *Hommage à Chardin* (Paris, galerie Heim, 1959 n° 15), qui donne ses dimensions '0,465 × 0,380'; l'éditeur du catalogue, Georges de Lastic St Jal, prétend qu'elle fut peinte vers 1750–55, et offerte par Chardin à la sœur de Sedaine. J'inclinerais à la dater comme Mme Guieysse-Frère d'environ 1735–40, quand Sedaine était encore vraiment un travailleur manuel. Elle a été exposée en 1878, 1885, 1907, 1910 et 1959 et appartenait à une collection particulière à cette dernière date. (Je remercie Mme Geneviève Ponge du département des tableaux du musée du Louvre pour ces informations et Sandrine Roux et Catherine Guillot qui m'ont aidée dans cette recherche.) [Il faut pourtant de la prudence dans l'identification et du peintre et du sujet de ce portrait. Dans le catalogue raisonné de Georges Wildenstein (rev. ed. Daniel Wildenstein, Oxford: Cassirer, 1969), qui fait référence encore, ce tableau est mentionné dans l'appendice, où Wildenstein place des tableaux douteux (p. 237). Il est certain que George de Lastic St Jal se trompe dans son récit de l'histoire du tableau, dans la mesure où Sedaine n'avait pas de sœur survivante. M. L.]

Ce fut aussi un encouragement pour les études de Sedaine, et il se dit qu'il pourrait peut-être arriver, lui aussi, à manier la langue française comme son ami Chardin maniait son pinceau.[4]

Fig. 1: [Attribué à Jean Baptiste Siméon Chardin], portrait présumé de Sedaine. Huile sur toile, c. 1745–50. Collection privée. Photo: © Bibliothèque Nationale de France, Paris.

Le tailleur de pierre à la mèche rebelle et au poing serré que nous présente Chardin progresse dans le bâtiment, et lâche le marteau pour le compas et le crayon. Lentement. Il fréquente des écrivains et des artistes, il s'exerce à la poésie. A partir de 1748, âgé de vingt-neuf ans, il quitte l'entreprise de Buron, architecte et constructeur qui l'employait depuis dix ans, et il reçoit un logement et une rente de Le Conte, ancien Lieutenant criminel au Châtelet, qui lui permet de se consacrer presque entièrement à l'écriture. En 1752 paraît un petit recueil anonyme de *Pièces fugitives* dont le clou est une 'Epître à mon habit', habit neuf et de parade:

> Ce que je décidai fut le *nec plus ultra.*
> On applaudit à tout, j'avais tant de génie!
> Ah! mon habit, que je vous remercie!
> C'est vous qui me valez cela!

---

4 Emile Guieysse-Frère, *Sedaine. Ses protecteurs et ses amis* (Paris: Flammarion, 1907), p. 36. Les récits pittoresques de Mme Guieysse-Frère, qui habitait la maison de Sedaine à Saint-Prix, s'appuient surtout sur les travaux d'Auguste Rey (maire de Saint-Prix) mais aussi sur des recherches personnelles, qu'elle met une grande coquetterie à masquer. Ils sont certainement très imaginatifs.

C'est dans ces années qu'il fréquente les frères Saint-Aubin, quatre artistes-ornemanistes dont Gabriel, le plus talentueux, son cadet de cinq ans, l'accompagnera ou en sera accompagné pendant une vingtaine d'années. Dans le recueil de 1752 figurent déjà une 'Epître à M. de S.A.' et surtout des 'Stances à S*** pour le prier de faire mon portrait' que les éditions suivantes (1760 et 1780) adressent plus précisément à M. S.A.: cinq dizains assez désinvoltes sur 'Mon minois, que par conjecture, / J'estime moi-même assez laid'! Un 'Portrait présumé de Sedaine',[5] présumé de 1753 environ, marquerait le début de ce chemin [Fig. 2]. C'est un Sedaine dans un bel habit, avec des manchettes à faire pâlir Buffon, qui est évoqué ici comme écrivain, la plume à la main, la table couverte de livres et de papiers; il a de grosses mains noueuses, la fenêtre est ouverte ...

Fig. 2: Gabriel de Saint-Aubin, portrait de Michel-Jean Sedaine.
Pierre noire, c. 1752–4. Collection privée. Photo: Audap, Godeau, Solanct.

[5] Ce dessin de Gabriel de Saint-Aubin est passé en vente chez Audap, Godeau et Solanet le 11 mars 1987. Je remercie vivement Mark Ledbury de me l'avoir signalé (voir sa 'Greuze and Sedaine', p. 9–10).

Dans la deuxième édition de ces poèmes, qui porte la date de 1760, figure un frontispice daté, lui, de 1757, dessiné et gravé par Gabriel de Saint-Aubin,[6] assez fâcheux à vrai dire, avec un méli-mélo de petits amours mâles et potelés et d'allusions à l'auteur et à ses sujets, un compas à côté d'une houlette de berger, des livres encore, une pipe cassée, et dans un médaillon rond, un profil droit de Sedaine, presque invisible et méconnaissable, chauve et vieux. Voilà si l'on veut un portrait officiel et une médaille à l'antique; il marque un recul par rapport au dessin précédent, qui donnait un tel 'effet de ressemblance'.

Or de ces deux petits volumes de poche, pendant une douzaine d'années (1761–72), Gabriel de Saint-Aubin fera son carnet d'esquisses, remplissant les marges et les pages blanches de croquis souvent datés, coloriant et signant à nouveau le frontispice. 'Le "Sedaine" du musée Condé' est à Chantilly et les images publiées (toujours en noir et blanc) ne comportent pas ce frontispice qu'on espère amélioré. Mais on y trouve un amusant cul-de-lampe pour l''Epître à mon habit' qui propose un Sedaine à genoux, le nez long et la mèche alerte, baisant un habit couché sur le fleuron imprimé, que je crois plutôt le bel habit neuf que l'ancien, tandis qu'un quidam fait le geste théâtral de l'admiration.[7] La page de titre du second volume présente deux personnages vus de dos, au premier plan un 'monsieur' en habit et peut-être même en perruque, à moitié allongé sur une pierre plate mais accoudé sur une autre, tandis que le second, plus pâle et lointain, est à califourchon sur une pierre dressée, en vêtement de travail, coiffé de ce qui semble être un béret: le tailleur de pierres? Une inscription manuscrite pourrait se lire 'LE Pœte'.[8]

Le visage mûri, la mèche toujours aussi rebelle, encore attentif mais plus distant: c'est un dernier portrait de Sedaine par Gabriel de Saint-Aubin, profil gauche comme le premier qu'il rappelle en plus grave, daté de 1771.[9] Ecrit-il ou parle-t-il? Cette esquisse, toute légère, transparente, est touchante d'intimité [Fig. 3].

---

[6] Frontispice reproduit, ainsi qu'une version avant la lettre et avant le portrait dans Emile Dacier, *Gabriel de Saint-Aubin* (2 vol., Paris et Bruxelles: Van Oest, 1929–31), II: *Catalogue raisonné*, pl. XII.

[7] Dessin reproduit dans Emile Dacier, 'Le "Sedaine" du Musée Condé', *Revue de l'art ancien et moderne*, XXXVIII (juin 1920), p. 5–18 [9]; XXXIX (juillet–août 1920), p. 93–104. Emile Dacier donne une description assez détaillée de tous les dessins dans son *Catalogue raisonné* au n° 1071*.

[8] L'intérêt de ce dessin que Dacier décrivait comme 'deux croquis d'hommes étendus sur le dos', ce qui est manifestement faux, a été remarqué par Catherine Guillot.

[9] Dessin à la sanguine conservé dans les archives de l'Institut, découvert et photographié par Mark Ledbury. Voir son 'Greuze and Sedaine', p. 461. Le dessin est crayonné au recto d'une lettre qui appartient à la correspondance officielle de l'Académie Royale d'Architecture.

Fig. 3: Gabriel de Saint-Aubin, portrait de Sedaine.
Sanguine, 1771. Paris, Archives de L'Institut. Photo: © Mark Ledbury.

Tout autre est le portrait peint par Jacques-Louis David, l'année suivante s'il date bien de 1772.[10] Désormais l'on peut dire que Sedaine a réussi: le marquis de Marigny l'a nommé Secrétaire perpétuel de l'Académie Royale d'Architecture en 1768 et l'a logé au Louvre, les théâtres se disputent ses pièces et il peut se voir jouer à la fois dans les trois spectacles royaux, l'Opéra, la Comédie-Française et la Comédie-Italienne; seule l'Académie Française ne l'a pas encore accepté.

Marié depuis 1767, père de famille, Sedaine n'oublie pas qu'il a été un jeune orphelin dans la misère: c'est ainsi qu'il a aidé la mère de David, veuve

[10] Auguste Rey dans *La Vieillesse de Sedaine* (Paris: Champion, 1906) mentionne ce portrait paru à l'Exposition des Alsaciens-Lorrains de 1874; il appartenait alors au comte de Brisay, gendre de Sedaine. C'est lors d'une exposition de 1913 sur *David et ses élèves* qu'il a été photographié; on le trouve reproduit ensuite dans Jacques Maret, *David* (Monaco: Les documents d'Art, 1953), pl. 27. L'authenticité du portrait est attestée par la gravure; le seul doute porterait sur la date. David a aussi peint Mme Sedaine, sans doute à la même époque, leurs filles, sûrement plus tard, car l'aînée des deux est née en 1767 et c'est une grande jeune fille, voire une jeune femme, que le portrait représente, et leur fils Anastase Henry (vers 1774).

avec son garçon de neuf ans, puis qu'il accueille le jeune homme dans son vaste appartement du Louvre. Il l'introduit auprès des peintres qui habitent ou fréquentent le vieux palais, il le soutient tout particulièrement dans cette pénible année 1772 où pour la troisième fois David se voit refuser le Grand Prix de l'Académie de Peinture.[11]

Les portraits que David peint alors de Sedaine et de sa femme, dont on ignore les propriétaires actuels, sont des bustes 'de grandeur naturelle' qui ne manquent pas d'apprêt. Enfin, des portraits comme il faut, presque de face, le regard vers le spectateur, portraits posés. Sedaine cependant n'est pas en grande tenue, même si le jabot est strictement boutonné; il n'est pas non plus dressé, mais penché en arrière, le geste reposé: à la fois énergique et se montrant 'ce brave et sensible homme' que dit David.

Fig. 4: Pierre-Charles Levesque, d'après Jacques-Louis David, portrait de Michel-Jean Sedaine. Gravure, 1772. Photo: © Bibliothèque Nationale de France, Paris.

[11] Voir le récit autobiographique de David: comment il avait décidé de se laisser mourir de faim, et comment Sedaine le sauva avec l'aide de Doyen, dans Marie-Catherine Sahut et Régis Michel, *David: l'art et la politique* (Paris: Gallimard Découvertes/RMN, 1988), p. 130–33.

Gravée par Levesque dès 1772,[12] l'image prend vie et jeunesse, l'œil est aigu, la lèvre est plus sarcastique et le sourcil se lève pour ce portrait officiel, car c'en est un et il porte le titre du Secrétaire d'Académie [Fig. 4]. La gentillesse s'efface ici au profit de quelque chose d'un peu inquiétant qu'on devinait sur la toile de David et que le graveur fait ressortir – quelque chose que sans doute Sedaine a dû reconnaître et accepter, puisque c'est désormais son image *ne varietur*.

Mais autant d'amis, autant de visions de Sedaine. Voici une autre image encore, que nous offre Pajou[13] [Fig. 5]. C'est de nouveau un des protégés du dramaturge, si l'on peut en croire la bonne Mme Guieysse-Frère, racontant vers l'an 1738 ou 39 une conversation entre Favart, qui vient de découvrir le petit Philidor, et notre auteur:

> Ah! dit Sedaine pensif, moi aussi, je viens de voir un enfant bien remarquable; quoiqu'il n'ait encore que huit ou neuf ans, on ne sera pas longtemps sans entendre parler de lui. C'est le fils d'un ornemaniste du faubourg Saint-Antoine, Pajou, que nous employons; je suis allé tantôt voir son père et il m'a montré une série de bustes, de statues que le petit Augustin, 'son gamin', comme il me disait avec orgueil, avait faits, en cachette, avec la terre à modeler de son père.
>
> Que faut-il faire, monsieur Sedaine, me disait-il. Je vois bien que le gamin fera mieux que moi et pourra devenir un sculpteur comme M. Lemoyne, que j'ai vu dans son atelier, entouré de ses grands travaux. J'avais emmené le petit avec moi, c'est depuis ce moment qu'il a la tête tournée et que je ne lui vois plus le cœur à l'ouvrage, près de moi, comme l'année dernière, car voilà un an qu'il me sert d'apprenti; nous sommes très pauvres, vous le savez, le pain est si cher, je ne puis me passer de l'enfant.
>
> Ce pauvre diable de père me faisait de la peine, ajouta Sedaine, son fils lui est utile, je le sais, et cependant il faut absolument tirer parti des dons qu'il a reçus de la nature, je lui ai promis de m'en occuper.[14]

N'est-il pas amusant, ce 'monsieur Sedaine' qui n'a pas vingt ans et qui se pose en protecteur? La tirade est peu croyable, mais l'amitié entre les deux

[12] 'J.-L. David pin. P. Car. Levesque sculp.' Mark Ledbury a trouvé l'annonce de la gravure dans l'*Année littéraire* (1772), VI, p. 261. Jacques Maret la datait par erreur de 1778.

[13] Le buste en terre cuite (0,485 m × 0,460 m), signé et daté au dos, appartient au Victoria and Albert Museum. Il a fait partie de l'exposition *Augustin Pajou, sculpteur du roi*, au Louvre et à New York, en 1997–8, ainsi que le buste de Mme Sedaine fait par Pajou en 1781.

[14] Guieysse-Frère, *Sedaine*, p. 53.

hommes est ancienne, et ne faiblira jamais: en 1797, Pajou fera partie du petit cercle qui accompagne Sedaine à sa tombe.

Fig. 5: Augustin Pajou, buste de Michel-Jean Sedaine.
Terre cuite, 1775. © The Board and Trustees of the Victoria and Albert Museum.
Photo: V & A Picture Library.

En 1775, quand le sculpteur trace au verso la date, il a quarante-cinq ans, l'écrivain en a cinquante-six. Le beau portrait! tout de chaleur et de sympathie, pas trop formel avec son col ouvert, souriant certes, et l'œil se plisse, mais grave aussi, car l'œil pèse. Pajou ne rajeunit pas son ami, mais il lui donne plus de force et d'énergie que ne faisait David. Personne n'en ferait aujourd'hui la transcription écrite qu'osait Henri Stein en 1912:

> Michel Sedaine, cet homme paisible, gai et malicieux qui fut à la fois féru de poésie et de théâtre, secrétaire de l'Académie d'architecture, brave homme aussi, plein de vertus moyennes, médiocre en ses désirs comme en ses facultés, soucieux de gloire sans ambition fiévreuse, mêlé à toute la vie intellectuelle de son temps.[15]

Quelle condescendance! Ce buste permettait sans doute une lecture semblable, car c'est la bonté qui y domine. Mais on préférera le commentaire plus perspicace de James David Draper:

> Pajou se livre ici à une analyse de caractère extrêmement complexe dans laquelle se devinent l'énergie et la fierté du self-made-man. Les rides verticales de part et d'autre du nez ajoutent une pointe de ruse cependant que la bouche, pas tout à fait rieuse, est décidément généreuse tandis que les yeux sont pénétrants et peut-être même sceptiques. En somme, nous ne sommes pas surpris d'apprendre que le poète vivait un peu reclus tout en possédant à un degré rare le talent de l'amitié.[16]

On n'est pas trop loin de Pajou avec un portrait 'attribué à Fragonard'.[17] Celui-ci, Jean Honoré Fragonard, est voisin de Sedaine au Louvre, lui aussi, mais tient à lui bien moins étroitement que Pajou ou David. Dans trois livres consacrés à Fragonard, je n'ai trouvé qu'une référence à Sedaine – que David aurait fait guillotiner! – et les livres sur Sedaine ne mentionnent pas le peintre. La toile ne fait en tout cas pas partie de la grande série de portraits visionnaires autour de 1769 (dont relève un Diderot en extase), avec leurs grandes traînées de rouge et les cols et poignets blancs de fantaisie. Celui-ci serait beaucoup plus tardif, assez sage de couleur, dans un gros plan (si le cadrage de la photo est exact) attentif à la ressemblance. Sedaine? peut-être. Il est plus vieux, il

---

[15] Henri Stein, *Augustin Pajou* (Paris: Librairie Centrale des Beaux-Arts, 1912), p. 58.

[16] *Augustin Pajou, sculpteur du roi*, Catalogue de l'exposition au Musée du Louvre (Paris: RMN, 1997), p. 248.

[17] Publié dans *Les plus beaux manuscrits du théâtre français* (Paris: BNF/Robert Laffont, 1996), p. 163, avec la mention: 'Huile sur toile, attribuée à Fragonard, milieu du XVIIIème siècle. (Collection particulière.)'. Aucun catalogue de l'œuvre de Fragonard ne mentionne cette œuvre.

s'est empâté, ses paupières s'affaissent. La vivacité de la tête relevée pour mieux regarder, l'appui des mains sur le dossier d'une chaise ou d'un fauteuil, pose familière, sans apprêt, disent l'énergie contenue, mais c'est encore une fois la bonté qui prime. Le bon papa Frago nous offrirait un bon papa Sedaine ...

Nous n'omettrons pas qu'Auguste Rey donne en tête de son 'Mariage de Sedaine' la photo d'une miniature anonyme que la famille disait de l'auteur;[18] je ne le crois pas, non pas à cause de l'habit soigné et du beau jabot de dentelle ni même des cheveux poudrés à blanc, mais parce que le long visage maigre est très régulier, les sourcils courts, les lèvres droites et minces: tout le contraire de la gravure de Levesque qui est la seule effigie garantie, et qui ressemble à toutes les autres (même le pseudo-Fragonard).

Neuf images sur un demi-siècle, est-ce peu ou beaucoup? Qu'est-ce que cela pourrait nous apprendre sur la place de Sedaine parmi les écrivains du XVIIIe siècle? Il n'existe pas, à ma connaissance, d'études iconographiques comparatives en ce domaine; on se contente de saluer l'extraordinaire richesse et diversité des portraits et caricatures de Voltaire, certainement le poète le plus souvent représenté du siècle, et sans doute Jean-Jacques Rousseau le suit-il – d'assez loin. Tout écrivain français tant soit peu notoire a, par ailleurs, un portrait de base servant de frontispice à ses œuvres plus ou moins complètes: pas Sedaine. De même tout détenteur d'une charge publique est représenté dans le cadre de celle-ci: c'est la fonction de la gravure de Levesque d'après David.

Remontant cette liste à l'envers, on peut souligner la bizarrerie du statut de Sedaine comme Secrétaire perpétuel de l'Académie d'Architecture: fonction, finalement, plus honorable qu'honorifique? Sedaine n'est pas académicien parmi les architectes: il est le secrétaire de leurs travaux. Cela lui vaut une rente, des jetons, un logement, un travail, mais pas l'accession à un titre d'Architecte (avec la majuscule), pour lequel rien ne le qualifie. J'ignore si les Architectes Académisés faisaient solenniser leur grade par un portrait peint ou une gravure ornée: je le pense. En tout cas Sedaine semble n'avoir comme effigie que la gravure de 1772, de quatre ans postérieure à sa prise de fonction, ornée d'un minimum de feuilles de laurier et d'une très mince trompette. Certes, la qualité du portrait est remarquable, mais ses entours sont modestes.[19]

---

[18] Auguste Rey, 'Le Mariage de Sedaine', *Revue de l'histoire de Versailles et de Seine-et-Oise*, XI (1910), p. 5–15.

[19] Dans Jean-Louis Baritou et Dominique Froussard (éd.), *Chevotet, Contant et Chaussard. Un cabinet d'architectes au siècle des Lumières* (Paris: La Manufacture/Délégation artistique de la Ville de Paris, 1987) figurent les portraits peints de Chevotet (par Perronneau) et de Chaussard (par Valade) ainsi qu'une solennelle gravure ornée de Contant d'Ivry datée de 1770. Mark Ledbury me signale l'ouvrage de Wolfgang Scholler, *Die Académie Royale d'Architecture. Anatomie einer Institution* (Cologne et Weimar: Böhlau,

Et si l'écrivain, de son vivant, a fait l'objet d'une autre estampe depuis le déplorable frontispice de Saint-Aubin publié en 1760, nous l'ignorons, et cela n'est pas signalé dans les histoires de la littérature. Au XIXe siècle, c'est à de plates et mièvres banalisations d'après David que l'on procède.[20] Aucune belle gravure du XVIIIe avec ses légendes, ornements allégoriques et références aux œuvres ne nous a été transmise.

Il n'existe donc pour ainsi dire que des portraits privés de Sedaine. Et alors il est peut-être intéressant qu'il y en ait tant. Ils portent un double témoignage, sur la personnalité de Sedaine et sur son rapport privilégié avec certains artistes, qui est une de ses originalités comme écrivain. Tard élu en 1786 à l'Académie Française (à soixante-sept ans et, paraît-il, quatorze candidatures), il ne relève ni du 'High Enlightenment' ni de la 'low life of literature' dont parle Robert Darnton: il a une place à part. Issu d'un milieu d'artisans-artistes (ce qui le différencie du fils de pâtissier Favart), milieu dont il se réclame fortement dès ses premières œuvres publiées en 1752 ('C'est pour vivre que je suis Maçon: je ne suis Poète que pour rire'),[21] il restera toute sa vie lié à autant de peintres, graveurs et sculpteurs que d'écrivains. Son entrée dans le monde des mécènes est sous ce signe. S'il avait eu un carnet d'adresses, on y aurait aussi remarqué, d'ailleurs, les acteurs et les entrepreneurs de spectacles. Des hommes de lettres, certes, Grimm en particulier qui s'est dépensé pour promouvoir son œuvre, mais ils ne sont pas majoritaires. Ce n'est ni un littérateur ni un 'philosophe', et hormis les deux premières images de Gabriel de Saint-Aubin à ses débuts, il ne s'est pas fait ni n'a été représenté comme un homme de lettres, ni à la tâche ni inspiré. Et il n'a pas non plus investi dans la création d'un portrait solennel qui l'eût embelli pour la postérité, comme la magnifique effigie de Beaumarchais par Nattier.

Ce n'est alors pas, dans ses portraits, une image emblématique qui nous est transmise, mais l'image de quelqu'un, d'un homme particulier. Il ne dicte pas à ses portraitistes un discours codé, ce sont eux qui semblent vouloir se rendre compte, par les moyens qui leur sont propres, de la personne d'un ami singulier.

1993), et le fait que la gravure de Sedaine fut critiquée lors de sa parution par *L'Année littéraire*, journal de plus en plus hostile à l'auteur, pour son manque de noblesse. Il rappelle que Sedaine, qui était alors en pleine dispute avec Ange-Jacques Gabriel, le Premier Architecte du Roi, au sujet de son statut à l'Académie, avait peut-être de bonnes raisons de ne pas se montrer dans un cadre trop élaboré.

[20] Entre la série 'Portraits' du Cabinet des Estampes de la BNF et celle de la Bibliothèque de l'Institut, on trouve sept ou huit variations du XIXe siècle sur David, dont l'étude serait intéressante, car elles se répartissent en deux groupes bien distincts: les jeunes quadragénaires au teint fleuri et au sourire charmeur, et les ironistes mesquins ...

[21] Formule finale de la préface des *Pièces fugitives de Monsieur S**** de 1752, reprise dans les éditions de 1760 et 1780.

II. Théâtre

> Mais chez nous, peuple aimable, où les grâces, l'esprit,
> Brillent à présent dans leur force,
> L'arbre n'est point jugé sur ses fleurs, sur son fruit;
> On le juge sur son écorce.
>
> (Sedaine: 'Epître à mon habit')

Si l'on n'a pas ou presque de portraits officiels de Sedaine le maçon-poète, ni de Sedaine l'académicien-français, cela ne signifie pas que Sedaine ne se soit pas intéressé aux images, et ne se soit pas occupé de leur diffusion. Une chose est l'image de l'auteur, une autre l'image de l'œuvre. Nous entrons ici dans l'histoire des illustrations, où Sedaine joue un rôle notable.

L'illustration théâtrale est aujourd'hui un champ en voie d'exploration, de même que le portrait d'acteur et d'autres secteurs iconographiques qui ont beaucoup à nous apprendre sur l'histoire des représentations – mentales et théâtrales. Les images publiées avec les pièces de théâtre soulèvent deux ensembles de questions. L'un, très difficile à analyser pour les œuvres du passé, est général: il concerne les rapports entre l'auteur, le libraire (notre éditeur) et l'illustrateur, qui semblent souvent se présenter en deux couples distincts: l'auteur a affaire au libraire, le libraire commande une image à l'illustrateur. Le troisième couple, celui de l'auteur et de l'illustrateur, est attesté mais rare au XVIIIe siècle.

Les questions spécifiques, elles, concernent le rapport de l'image avec le texte et avec la scène, l'acte de lecture et d'interprétation qu'est l'image. Va-t-on privilégier l'imaginaire de la fiction (placer l'action dramatique dans un milieu 'réel', ou illustrer les récits et l'irreprésentable), ou va-t-on rappeler le souvenir d'une représentation théâtrale (d'un acteur, d'un geste, d'un décor, d'un 'tableau')? Les cas de figure que présente Sedaine sont tout à fait intéressants.

Remarquable spécialiste de la scène, il tient à utiliser le livre comme instrument non seulement de lecture mais de réalisation. Il lui arrive, contrairement à l'usage du temps, de publier ses pièces pour la date de la première, afin que le spectateur puisse y suivre, notamment, certains ensembles chantés dont la complexité échappe à la première audition. A plusieurs reprises, dans ses préfaces qui sont souvent brèves et fonctionnelles, il explique la multiplication des didascalies et la description précise des décors par le désir d'aider tous ceux (amateurs, provinciaux, étrangers) qui voudraient monter ses opéras-comiques.[22] Rien de plus naturel alors que d'utiliser

[22] Voir p. 235, 237, 243, 260, 261.

l'illustration, ce qu'il fait toutefois avec une relative parcimonie sur laquelle il sera peut-être nécessaire de s'interroger.

Fig. 6: C. Lingée, d'après C.-N. Cochin, frontispice des *Femmes vengées*. Gravure, 1775. Photo: © Bibliothèque Nationale de France, Paris.

L'exemple le plus significatif est celui des *Femmes vengées,* publiées chez Musier, qui n'a imprimé que cette pièce illustrée, unique, en 1775 [Fig. 6]. Quel sens peut avoir le recours à ce libraire-imprimeur qui n'est pas spécialiste de l'édition théâtrale? plus de liberté pour l'auteur? Le frontispice dessiné par Cochin a été gravé par Lingée, deux bonnes références.[23] Dans

[23] Mark Ledbury a spéculé que ce dessin peut être rapproché de l'intérêt de Sedaine pour le projet de la nouvelle Comédie-Française dessiné par ses amis Peyre et de Wailly. Voir son '"Vous avez achevé mes tableaux." Michel-Jean Sedaine and Jacques-Louis David', *British Journal for Eighteenth-Century Studies*, à paraître. Il estime surtout que l'existence de la gravure nous en dit plus que l'image elle-même. Charles Nicolas Cochin (fils) était aussi un des amis de Sedaine, et les deux hommes partageaient un vif intérêt pour le

cette pièce, Sedaine expérimente l'emploi d'un décor multiple où l'on joue simultanément 'trois Scènes à la fois, en trois lieux différents', et il précise dans son Avertissement: 'J'ai fait mettre une Gravure qui représente la situation de la Scène.' L'image est en effet à programme; elle compense difficilement, cependant, son format vertical en limitant l'action à la moitié inférieure de la page. Un autre exemple d'illustration en frontispice unique réalisé est celui du *Jardinier et son seigneur*, gravé en 1761 par Augustin de Saint-Aubin d'après un dessin de son frère Gabriel [Fig. 12, p. 241], qui répond au même principe d'évocation de la réalité scénique (et pose les mêmes problèmes de format).

Il en va tout autrement dans le cadre d'une opération de librairie dont les œuvres de Sedaine sont un des vecteurs principaux: la publication de livres de luxe richement illustrés, où une série de six gravures accompagne une pièce quelle que soit sa longueur. L'idée de l'entreprise est due à un graveur imprimeur, François Nicolas Martinet, qui assure avec d'autres membres de sa tribu la gravure et souvent l'impression et la commercialisation de ces suites, qui pouvaient se vendre séparément. Un descendant des Martinet, Louis Hautecœur, de l'Institut, indique dans une étude sur sa famille un rapport probable entre le choix des pièces illustrées et leur représentation récente et réussie à la Cour:[24] plusieurs volumes sont en effet dédiés à Papillon de La Ferté, l'Intendant des Menus Plaisirs du Roi, ce qui ne saurait être un hasard.

La liste des pièces publiées avec une série de six gravures, telle que Louis Hautecœur la donne, comporte vingt œuvres entre 1760 et 1772, dont quinze auxquelles participent Martinet ou sa sœur Thérèse comme dessinateurs ou comme graveurs. Plusieurs ont été rééditées, parfois avec des suites de gravures différentes. Dans cette liste, Sedaine est absolument l'auteur de prédilection avec sept pièces,[25] loin derrière lui arrivant Marmontel avec trois

---

renouveau de la scène française. Sur Cochin, voir Christian Michel, *Charles Nicolas Cochin et l'art des lumières* (Rome: Ecole Française de Rome, 1993), et surtout les p. 481–2 sur les rapports entre Sedaine et Cochin; Michel prétend que le frontispice pour *Les Femmes vengées* est tiré d'un projet antérieur de Cochin.

[24] Louis Hautecœur, 'Une famille de graveurs et d'éditeurs parisiens: les Martinet et les Hautecœur (XVIII et XIXème siècles)', *Paris et Île de France Mémoires*, XVIII–XIX (1967–8). Je remercie Claude Mengès de m'avoir communiqué son mémoire de DEA sur 'La Petite Galerie Dramatique entre 1796 et 1822' (Université de Paris I, 1986) qui m'a notamment fourni cette référence.

[25] Suites pour des opéras-comiques de Sedaine: *Blaise le savetier* (Ballard, 1762), *Le Déserteur* (deux séries, Hérissant, 1769), *Le Jardinier et son seigneur* (Hérissant, 1761), *On ne s'avise jamais de tout* (Hérissant, 1761), *Le Roi et le fermier* (Hérissant, 1761 et 1770), *Rose et Colas* (Hérissant, 1762), *Les Sabots* (Hérissant, 1762), liste établie à partir de Louis Hautecœur, 'Une famille de graveurs', p. 221–2, et du *Guide de l'amateur de livres à gravures du XVIIIème siècle* de H. Cohen et Seymour de Ricci (Rouquette, 1912). [Voir plus loin, au chapitre 10, notre liste plus complète, et de nouvelles recherches sur les suites de gravures Martinet qui mettent en doute les informations contenues dans Hautecœur et Cohen. M.L.]

œuvres sur une douzaine d'années. C'est évidemment pour les opéras-comiques de Sedaine la preuve d'un succès important [Fig. 7].

Fig. 7: Anon. (Grangeret, C. L. Desrais, J. V. Dupin, Thérèse Martinet), illustration pour sc. X de *Blaise le savetier*. Gravure, c.1762. Photo: © Photothèque des Musées de la Ville de Paris.

Il s'agit en effet d'opéras-comiques, c'est-à-dire d'œuvres de trois actes au maximum, souvent de deux voire d'un acte seulement. Dans les mêmes années, une tragédie ou une comédie en cinq actes, dont le statut littéraire est infiniment supérieur, n'ont jamais au grand plus qu'un frontispice, comme si la poésie se suffisait. On mesure aisément combien une suite de six illustrations pour une pièce courte, même si elle peut se passer dans plus d'un lieu (mais en général pas plus de trois), devient absurde au point de vue d'une information sur la mise en scène, et dérisoire par rapport à la fragilité du texte.[26] C'est que ces images sont des ornements de beaux livres, sans plus, prenant leur appui sur la réputation mondaine des œuvres. L'effet publicitaire est réciproque.

Sur la lancée de l'opération des Martinet, la formule des suites d'illustrations va être reprise par les auteurs de drames sérieux ou bourgeois, qui publient leurs œuvres (jouées ou non, c'est apparemment égal) avec des suites non de six mais de cinq gravures, c'est-à-dire un frontispice par acte. Ils veulent faire reconnaître le prestige de leurs drames, et c'est en réalité plutôt leur statut infra-littéraire qu'ils mettent ainsi en valeur. Aussi une des dernières séries citées par Louis Hautecœur, *Le Roué vertueux*, présente-t-elle en 1770, dans un quarto très élégant, six gravures (un frontispice général, une vignette, et un frontispice pour chacun des quatre chants), exécutées par Leprince, séparées par des pages où le texte se réduit à quelques interjections et beaucoup d''interponctuation'.[27] L'ère de la parodie est arrivée, et celle du beau livre de théâtre s'estompe – tandis que vont se multiplier les éditions complètes illustrées des classiques du XVIIe siècle, entreprises qui s'appuient sur la réputation désormais séculaire des œuvres autant que sur la modernité brillante des images.

Les pièces de Sedaine ont donc joué un rôle décisif dans l'entreprise commerciale des Martinet. Il se peut que l'auteur ait participé activement à la chose, et en ait été payé: on ne saurait lui en faire reproche. Pourtant je suis tentée de ne pas le croire. En effet, on peut noter d'abord l'existence d'éditions parallèles aux éditions de luxe, dont la publication peut être simultanée: ainsi *Le Jardinier et son seigneur* est publié la même année, 1761, avec une suite de six gravures Martinet, et avec un frontispice unique, dû à Gabriel de Saint-Aubin, manifestement destiné à montrer une situation scénique précise, et d'un artiste très lié avec l'auteur. Il y aurait une séparation claire entre l'édition de luxe et celle à laquelle l'auteur est associé. Il en va de même pour *On ne s'avise jamais de tout*, pour lequel Saint-Aubin avait gravé un frontispice,

---

26 On pourrait s'interroger sur la pertinence de ces suites d'illustrations par rapport à des moments musicaux, notamment les grands airs.

27 Voir la reproduction de certaines de ces illustrations dans Martine de Rougemont, *Paradrames* (Saint-Etienne: Lire le Dix-huitième siècle, 1998).

comme pour d'autres pièces telles *Le Faucon* qui n'a finalement pas été illustré.[28]

Et l'on peut noter d'autre part que les deux œuvres que Sedaine a pu faire jouer à la Comédie-Française, avec un très grand succès, *Le Philosophe sans le savoir* et *La Gageure imprévue*, n'auront de son vivant aucune illustration sous son contrôle. Il me semble donc vraisemblable, à la fois que Sedaine ait eu une véritable stratégie éditoriale, et qu'il ait voulu celle-ci modeste et précise, liée étroitement au destin scénique de ses œuvres. On retrouve l'idée d'un Sedaine précurseur du metteur en scène que Pixérécourt a contribué à former, l'idée d'un Sedaine homme de théâtre complet, mais parfaitement sensible à toutes les contraintes financières, lui qui sera avec Beaumarchais un des fondateurs et des organisateurs du Bureau de Législation Dramatique (notre S.A.C.D.).

Du destin scénique des œuvres, il existe d'autres témoignages iconographiques qui échappent complètement au contrôle de l'auteur de son vivant même. Leur succès au théâtre à travers les années est attesté par toute une gamme d'images qui se réfèrent directement à la représentation, et qui ne sont pas destinées au livre, comme accompagnement du texte, mais constituent des commémorations de la mise en scène. Les images de représentations acquièrent peu à peu un statut honorable, de 'scènes de genre', mais il faut rappeler que celles qui concernent les œuvres de Sedaine se caractérisent à la fois par leur nombre et par leur qualité [Fig. 8].

L'image la plus intéressante tant au point de vue artistique qu'au point de vue théâtral est assurément le dessin au crayon signé 'P.A. Wille filius' en 1767 [Fig. 9]. J'y ai vu, dans un article ancien, l'Image même du Théâtre du XVIIIe siècle.[29] Elle représente en effet une large vue de la Comédie-Italienne à l'ancien Hôtel de Bourgogne, baignée de lumière, avec tout son public au contact le plus proche avec la scène. Sur les planches, on reconnaît une scène du troisième acte de l'opéra-comique *Le Roi et le fermier*. Cinq ans plus tard, Wille reprenait le même sujet dans un dessin à l'encre rehaussé de lavis, au moins partiellement exécuté sur place lui aussi, dans la mesure où l'un et l'autre restituent fidèlement des états différents de la scène et des loges, modifiés entre 1767 et 1772 [Fig. 10].

Le premier dessin semble avoir constitué pour l'artiste, qui avait alors dix-neuf ans, une sorte de 'chef-d'œuvre'. Remarquablement fini, il est plus vivant que bien des illustrations, et donne à comprendre le rapport particulier entre le public et les acteurs qui jouent sur l'avant-scène, tout près des

---

[28] La gravure pour *On ne s'avise jamais de tout* et l'esquisse pour *Le Faucon* sont reproduites par Louise Arnoldson Parkinson, *Sedaine et les musiciens de son temps* (Paris: L'Entente linotypique, 1934).

[29] Martine de Rougemont, 'Deux images d'un théâtre, ou l'Image du Théâtre', *Quaderni di teatro*, III/11 (février 1981), p. 51–66.

Fig. 8: François Boucher, *Les Sabots*. Huile sur toile, 1768.
Art Gallery of Ontario, Toronto. Purchase, F. Wood Endowment, 1978.
Photo: © Art Gallery of Ontario.

premières loges sur le théâtre. Rien n'est montré de ce qui pourrait contribuer à une illusion théâtrale, et les éléments du décor (moins nombreux que dans la didascalie de l'auteur) ne figurent qu'un fond lointain sur lequel les acteurs se détachent. En 1772, quoique la scène soit moins profonde, l'effet persiste. Et peut-être ceci n'était-il pas ce que Sedaine voulait qu'on vît au théâtre, lui qui fait jouer un rôle au lieu dans *Les Femmes vengées* par exemple, et cela nous signifie-t-il un malentendu ou un décalage entre Sedaine et son époque? Aurait-il préféré les deux toiles exposées au musée de l'Opéra qui représentent des scènes de son *Déserteur*?

Fig. 9: Pierre Alexandre Wille (fils), scène jouée à la Comédie-Italienne: *Le Roi et le fermier*, Acte III (?). Crayon, 1767. Photo: © Bibliothèque Nationale de France, Paris.

Fig. 10: [Attribué à Pierre Alexandre Wille (fils) et à Gabriel de Saint-Aubin], scène jouée à la Comédie-Italienne: *Le Roi et le fermier*, Acte III (?). Encre, lavis sur pierre noire, 1772. Photo: © Bibliothèque Nationale de France, Paris.

Une nouvelle pratique d'iconographie théâtrale va paraître dans les années 1770. Inspirées des 'theatrical conversations' à l'anglaise, ce sont des images prises sur le vif (des instantanés, dira-t-on plus tard) d'un ou de deux acteurs, rarement trois, saisis dans un moment très précis d'une représentation, avec leur costume et leur maquillage de scène [Fig. 11]. L'image est accompagnée du nom des acteurs et des rôles, et d'une légende tirée du dialogue, qui permet d'identifier non seulement la scène, mais le mouvement exact qui correspond au mot. Contrairement à l'usage dominant dans l'illustration, l'enjeu est sans aucun doute la mémoire de la pratique théâtrale, l'individualité du comédien dans sa création éphémère.

Fig. 11: Dambrun, d'après Quéverdo, illustration d'Acte II, sc. V du *Déserteur*. Gravure, c.1770. Photo: © Photothèque des Musées de la Ville de Paris.

L'inventeur de ce genre d'images est Jean-Louis Faesch, artiste d'origine bâloise, qui passe un an ou deux à Londres d'abord, où il fréquente Garrick, le grand maître de la promotion théâtrale, et publie une série sur les acteurs anglais chez Robert Sayer; il vient ensuite à Paris.[30] Son entreprise juxtapose deux pratiques. L'une, plus artisanale, consiste à peindre à partir d'une esquisse des petites gouaches carrées d'une dizaine de centimètres, peut-être

[30] Sur Jean-Louis (ou Johann Ludwig) Faesch (ou Fœch, ou Fish comme écrit Garrick), 1738–78, voir de Maria Ines Aliverti, *Il Ritratto d'attore nel Settecento francese e inglese* (Pise: ETS Editrice, 1986), p. 127–33, et son intervention en juillet 1999 dans le cadre du réseau 'European Theatre Iconography' de la Fondation Européenne des Sciences (18 p. dact.).

en utilisant un système de transparents, qui fait que l'acheteur possède une œuvre originale, unique encore que répétable; l'autre, plus industrielle, consiste à graver une série d'images et à les publier, par exemple dans un petit cahier intitulé *Les Métamorphoses de Thalie et de Melpomène*, à partir des mêmes esquisses de base. Dans lesdites *Métamorphoses* datant de 1782, deux des huit scènes tirées de la Comédie-Italienne appartiennent à des opéras-comiques de Sedaine. D'autres gouaches et gravures renverront aussi à ses œuvres.

Sedaine, on le sait, reste un auteur très joué pendant les années révolutionnaires: Tissier, pour 1789–92, le classe dix-huitième, Kennedy, pour 1789–99, vingt et unième, c'est après les grands classiques et les propagandistes du jour.[31] Or à partir de 1796 la maison Martinet, de retour dans l'édition théâtrale, propose des séries beaucoup plus populaires que celles de Faesch: leur Petite Galerie Dramatique, à travers le XIXe siècle, va se monter à plusieurs fois plusieurs centaines de numéros. Leurs estampes sont coloriées à la main, du format d'un petit octavo, et saluent toutes les grandes créations et les grandes reprises; de qualité en général médiocre, elles présentent des acteurs en général seuls, avec des légendes détaillées, elles sont plus attentives au costume qu'au geste, et bien qu'elles le nomment elles se soucient peu de la physionomie du comédien. Telles quelles cependant elles constituent un tribut au succès, et l'on ne manque évidemment pas d'y retrouver les personnages de Sedaine remis à la mode du jour.[32]

Je n'ai encore que très partiellement dépouillé les multiples de Faesch et les nombreux microfilms de la Collection Martinet à la Bibliothèque Nationale: ce sondage indique bien qu'il y a là matière à toute une étude sur la réception du théâtre à travers l'imagerie. Il reste beaucoup à faire, au total, pour une iconographie théâtrale de Sedaine. Elle serait à approfondir par l'analyse et la comparaison systématique des illustrations contemporaines entre elles et avec les didascalies. Elle serait aussi à prolonger vers le XIXe siècle, pour mesurer l'ampleur de la popularité de Sedaine, et aussi les différents travestissements de son œuvre: à quel XVIIIe siècle, à quelles bergeries, à quelle époque troubadour vont renvoyer les mises en scène et les illustrations qui continuent d'apparaître? La question ne sera pas de la justesse de ces images, mais de la vision qu'elles nous révèlent.

Il y aurait aussi lieu de composer une biographie de Sedaine, en tentant de faire la part des choses dans les différents récits qui se succèdent ou se juxtaposent. On a raconté un Sedaine bien-pensant, plus ou moins loyaliste,

---

[31] André Tissier, *Les Spectacles à Paris pendant la Révolution. Répertoire analytique, chronologique et bibliographique* (Genève: Droz, 1992), et Emmet Kennedy et al., *Theatre, Opera and Audiences in Revolutionary Paris. Analysis and Repertory* (Westport, Conn.: Greenwood Press, 1996).

[32] Voir le mémoire de Claude Mengès cité note 24.

poète de bergeries à l'eau de rose; on raconté un Sedaine âpre, le maçon contestataire – le premier serait plus ou moins représenté par le livre de Mme Guieysse-Frère, le second par les articles d'Auguste Rey. On a beaucoup insisté aussi sur le côté artisanal, professionnel du dramaturge, avec une ambiguïté sensible chez Diderot, avec une vénération particulière chez Pixérécourt. Une conversation relatée comme toujours sans sources par Mme Guieysse-Frère révèle cette attitude; on est en 1789 chez les Necker:

> Un ancien recteur d'université, homme maigre, long, au teint bilieux, prit Bouilly à part et lui dit:
> Quel est ce vieillard au nez pointu, aux yeux de lynx, à la figure de renard que Mme de Staël semble écouter comme un oracle, malgré son air bourgeois et simple?
> – C'est Sedaine, répondit Bouilly, qui doit en ce moment lui exposer quelque nouveau canevas dramatique.
> – Quoi! C'est là ce maçon littéraire, ce fabricant de pièces de tréteaux, où le peuple qu'il flatte et qu'il prétend peindre a la sottise de courir.
> – Monsieur, répondit Bouilly indigné, Sedaine est un homme de génie, le charpentier de la scène française et depuis quarante ans est toujours applaudi.
> – Ne me parlez pas de tous ces faiseurs d'opéra-comiques, ce sont de véritables jongleurs, des charlatans forains, ce que, nous autres savants, nous appelons de la raclure littéraire.[33]

Œil de lynx, figure de renard ... portraits divers de Sedaine, avec leurs constantes et les traces en eux du regard de ses différents amis artistes. Il y aurait lieu, peut-être, de placer au cœur de sa biographie une physiognomonie de Sedaine. 'Ce ne sont là que [des] portraits'? ils ont cherché une vérité. Deux cents ans après sa mort, saurions-nous repartir à sa rencontre?

33 Guieysse-Frère, *Sedaine*, p. 324.

Chapter 8

Un jugement de François Benoît Hoffman sur Sedaine en 1812

Patrick Taïeb

Amis, Apollon nous menace
De faire aplanir le Parnasse;
Dès demain il doit le saper,
Et si plat il saura le rendre
Que Sedaine y pourra grimper,
Et qu'il nous y faudra descendre.[1]

Depuis l'admission controversée de Sedaine à l'Académie Française (1786) et surtout depuis la mort de ce dernier dans une période particulièrement troublée du Directoire (1797), le monde littéraire n'a eu que peu d'occasions de s'exprimer sur son œuvre jusqu'à cette date de 1812. Elle n'a pas encore fait l'objet d'une édition complète et aucun événement particulier, sinon des reprises accueillies avec éclat sous l'Empire, n'a donné lieu à une mise au point sur la position très singulière que Sedaine a pu occuper dans la production littéraire des Lumières. La vogue de ses opéras-comiques est pourtant bien solide pendant l'Empire. Certains de ses livrets remportent des succès réels à l'Opéra-Comique où les ouvrages issus de ses collaborations avec Grétry et Monsigny tiennent l'affiche avec une faveur inégale.[2] *Le Diable à quatre* (remis en musique par Jean-Pierre Solié en 1809) totalise 95 représentations en l'espace de quatre années (1809–13) et, sans doute, le public garde-t-il en mémoire les reprises triomphales de *Richard Cœur-de-Lion*

---

[1] Epigramme d'Hoffman écrite en 1786 lors de la nomination de Sedaine à l'Académie Française, cité par Louis Castel dans 'Notice biographique et littéraire sur F. B. Hoffman', *Œuvres de F.B. Hoffman précédées d'une notice sur sa vie* (10 vol., Paris: Lavigne et Ducollet, 1834), I, p. x.

[2] Neuf opéras-comiques sur des livrets de Sedaine ont été représentés durant la seule année 1812; le nombre des représentations entre le 1er janvier et le 31 décembre figure entre parenthèses: *Richard Cœur-de-Lion* (20), *Le Roi et le fermier* (19), *Les Sabots* (16), *Aucassin et Nicolette* (14), *Le Diable à quatre* (14), *Le Déserteur* (9), *Félix ou l'Enfant trouvé* (12), *Rose et Colas* (4), *On ne s'avise jamais de tout* (1). Un dixième livret est une adaptation de Favières pour Henri-Montan Berton de *Aline, reine de Golconde* (16). Statistiques établies d'après les registres de l'Opéra-Comique conservés à la Bibliothèque de l'Opéra.

(cinquante-trois représentations pour la seule année 1806) et de *Félix ou l'Enfant trouvé* (cinquante représentations pour les années 1807–8). Ce succès incontestable, obtenu dans un genre considéré comme secondaire par l'académisme littéraire et, de surcroît, en vertu d'une originalité qui place les livrets de Sedaine en marge même de l'opéra-comique, est sans doute la marque la plus spécifique de sa réputation posthume et, aussi, on va le voir, la plus difficile à assimiler pour une historiographie naissante. Car Sedaine est un auteur que les hommes de lettres n'ont jamais véritablement admis comme un des leurs. Son succès, principalement comme librettiste, le situe dans l'équivoque d'un talent supérieur mais consacré à un genre au statut indéfinissable, entre théâtre parlé et théâtre lyrique, entre opéra et, pour certains, spectacle de boulevard. La Harpe, dans son cours de littérature de 1801, lui consacre quarante-cinq pages au ton ambigu.[3] François Benoît Hoffman (1760–1828), librettiste et cadet de Sedaine d'une quarantaine d'années, est donc fondé à déclarer que 'cet auteur, qui n'était pas homme de lettres, n'a pas encore été ni bien connu, ni bien jugé'.[4]

En 1812 paraît une édition sélective de livrets d'opéra-comique qui fait suite à une série monumentale intitulée *Répertoire général du théâtre français composé des tragédies, comédies et drames.* C'est elle qui va donner lieu à l'un des tout premiers jugements posthumes sur l'ensemble de l'œuvre de Sedaine. Il s'agit d'une entreprise destinée à s'imposer comme une collection de référence pour le théâtre parlé et qui regroupe les pièces des grands auteurs entrées au répertoire de la Comédie Française depuis le XVIIe siècle. Pour autant que l'on en puisse juger par les états incomplets conservés actuellement dans les bibliothèques parisiennes, les soixante-sept volumes réunissant ce répertoire (vingt-sept pour les auteurs du 'premier ordre' et quarante pour ceux du 'second') appliquent une politique de sélection consistant à regrouper de quatre à sept pièces parmi les meilleures de chaque auteur, depuis Molière et Rotrou jusqu'à Beaumarchais, en passant par Marivaux, Crébillon, Marmontel ou Diderot. Chaque groupe est précédé d'une notice sommaire sur l'auteur indiquant la liste plus générale de ses œuvres. Pariant peut-être sur l'implicite légitimité d'un genre mêlant le parlé et le chanté – l'opéra n'est pas pris en compte – l'éditeur Nicole entreprend un appendice à son entreprise

[3] Jean-François de La Harpe, *Lycée, ou Cours de littérature ancienne et moderne* (16 vol., Paris: H. Agasse, an VII–XIII). Les pages sur Sedaine constituent la troisième section du chapitre VII intitulé 'De l'Opéra-Comique et du vaudeville dramatique qui l'a précédé' et situé dans le douzième volume, p. 386–431. Voir le texte de Raphaëlle Legrand dans le présent volume, p. 119 et note 8.

[4] *Journal de l'Empire* (24 mai 1812), troisième partie de la série de comptes rendus sur laquelle est fondé cet article: 'Variétés. Théâtre de l'Opéra-Comique ...'. L'article le plus récent sur la vie et les ouvrages de Hoffman, écrit par M. Elizabeth C. Bartlet, se trouve dans Stanley Sadie (éd.), *The New Grove Dictionary of Opera* (4 vol., London: Macmillan, 1992).

gigantesque en consacrant huit volumes à l'opéra-comique. Ce faisant, il ne pouvait pas ignorer Sedaine, un des auteurs dramatiques du siècle précédent qui figure en très bonne place parmi les librettistes restés au répertoire. Les huit volumes d'opéras-comiques paraissent en plusieurs livraisons au cours de l'année 1812 et sont annoncés par le très officiel *Journal de l'Empire* sous le titre suivant: *Théâtre de l'Opéra-Comique ou Recueil des Pièces restées à ce théâtre, pour faire suite aux Théâtres des auteurs du premier et du second ordre.*[5] Le compte rendu de cette partie est confié à Hoffman, librettiste reconnu qui s'est récemment reconverti dans une carrière de critique. Il s'y est forgé une réputation solide d'intégrité et de rigueur et occupe une position où il est redouté de ses contemporains.

Pour ses biographes, l'abandon du théâtre pour la critique, après le livret des *Rendez-vous bourgeois* (musique de Nicolas Isouard, 1807), résulte d'une décision consciente inspirée par une déontologie personnelle. D'après Louis Castel, qui aurait commencé à le fréquenter vers 1814, ce souci d'impartialité et d'indépendance contribue à la réputation de ses excellentes critiques couvrant un large éventail du savoir.[6] Au cours de ses presque vingt années d'exercice au service du *Journal de l'Empire*, où il a été appelé par l'académicien Charles Guillaume Etienne, il rend compte des ouvrages du docteur Gall sur la craniologie, des *Martyrs* de Chateaubriand, du *Cours de littérature dramatique* de A.-W. Schlegel sur le romantisme, ou de la somme théorique de Castil-Blaze intitulée *De l'opéra en France*. C'est donc un critique éclectique et avisé en même temps qu'un homme drapé dans sa position de juge impartial qui exprime l'un des tout premiers jugements sur Sedaine, publiés après sa mort, dans les colonnes d'un périodique officiel. A cette époque, Hoffman signe ses articles de la lettre 'H'. La paternité de ces textes ne fait cependant aucun doute car elle est attestée par la publication en 1834 des *Œuvres de F. B. Hoffman précédées d'une notice sur sa vie* en dix volumes (voir note 1), à laquelle Louis Castel a joint ce texte ainsi qu'une notice apportant des éclaircissements sur les diverses signatures employées par le critique pour conserver l'anonymat.

---

[5] *Journal de l'Empire* (8 février 1812).

[6] Hoffman ne s'écartera jamais de son principe: les deux livrets ayant servi après sa retraite du théâtre étaient dans ses tiroirs dès avant son changement de carrière. Il s'agit de *La Mort d'Abel* (musique de Rodolphe Kreutzer) représenté à l'Opéra, en 3 actes, en 1810 et repris en 2 actes en 1823; et du *Dilettante d'Avignon*, opéra-comique terminé par Léon Halévy (musique de Fromental Halévy) et créé en 1829. Voir Bartlet, art. cit. (note 4).

La légitimité du genre opéra-comique

Sept volumes de livrets sont annoncés dès le mois de février 1812, mais les quatre premiers seulement sont parus lorsque Hoffman livre la première partie d'une critique qui en comportera quatre.[7] Au jour de parution de la dernière, le 1er juillet, il semble que les trois volumes en attente n'ont toujours pas vu le jour et que l'éventualité d'un huitième est encore confidentielle. De plus, il apparaît clairement que, en dépit des annonces publicitaires accompagnant chacun des articles d'Hoffman, ils ne rendent compte précisément que du premier volume dont le critique donne explicitement le sommaire. Il est fort probable qu'il n'avait qu'une vague idée du contenu global des huit parus finalement: cela expliquerait le manque de régularité des articles, dont les deux derniers paraissent à des dates éloignées des deux premiers, ainsi que les promesses non tenues des premiers comptes rendus. Le 24 mai, il écrit: 'Dans un dernier article, je m'occuperai du style des opéras comiques qui ont paru depuis la révolution opérée par Sedaine.' Mais l'article du 1er juillet, le dernier, est entièrement consacré à Sedaine, encore, et à des vues historiques le concernant. D'autre part, on relève des différences entre les articles de 1812 et la version, en un seul texte, de l'édition de 1834. Elles tiennent en partie à la nécessité de supprimer les phrases de liaison inhérentes à la présentation en feuilleton et d'effacer des formulations publicitaires dues à la fonction initiale des articles de presse. Toutefois, certaines omissions de 1834 devront être signalées car elles ont pour effet, involontaire ou recherché, cela est difficile à dire, d'adoucir la charge.

Les huit volumes sont composés sur le modèle des précédents. Trente-cinq livrets illustrent la production de douze auteurs, parmi lesquels Sedaine (9 titres), Favart (8) et Marmontel (6) occupent la plus grande place (voir le sommaire, annexe 1). Après avoir salué la première véritable collection dramatique du siècle, Hoffman évalue la place du livret d'opéra-comique sous l'angle exclusif de la lecture. Il n'est pas indifférent que ce jugement sur Sedaine ait eu pour objet le compte rendu d'une telle édition car celle-ci autorise une approche critique différente de celle des comptes rendus de représentation. Hoffman l'annonce dès l'introduction de sa première livraison du 8 février:

> Un autre rédacteur rend compte tous les jours des pièces de ce théâtre, sous le rapport de la représentation; à cet égard je ne pourrais que répéter ce qu'il a dit: je n'envisagerai donc l'opéra-comique que dans ses ressemblances et ses différences avec le théâtre français; et, conformément à la tâche qui m'est imposée, j'aiderai le lecteur à

---

[7] Les quatre parties du compte rendu d'Hoffman ont été publiées aux dates suivantes: 8 février, 28 février, 24 mai, 1er juillet 1812. Dans les trois premières, les volumes en attente sont annoncés incessamment mais le quatrième article n'en dit plus rien.

> décider si l'opéra-comique mérite les honneurs de la bibliothèque, et s'il est digne de faire suite aux Théâtres du premier et du second ordres.

La première considération d'Hoffman tient en effet à la légitimité du genre dans une collection destinée à être lue. Car l'intérêt essentiel de l'entreprise gigantesque des éditeurs est bien à ses yeux de rassembler les ouvrages pour la scène exclusivement, émanant d'auteurs qui se sont illustrés dans d'autres genres et de les proposer sous la forme d'une collection homogène:

> Autrefois [...], il fallait se procurer les œuvres de presque tous les auteurs dramatiques, c'est-à-dire acheter en même temps un grand nombre d'ouvrages fort étrangers à la scène, comme, par exemple, dans Racine, ses Poésies sacrées, ses Lettres polémiques, etc.; dans Régnard, son roman de la Provençale, son voyage en Laponie, etc.: ouvrages estimables sans doute, mais qui grossissaient la collection, et n'avaient aucun rapport avec l'art dramatique. Il y avait disparité dans les éditions et dans le format, et, de plus, un mélange des chefs-d'œuvre avec les premiers essais des auteurs et des productions moins heureuses. Le Théâtre du premier et du second ordre remédie à tous ces inconvénients.[8]

D'emblée, Hoffman dénonce la faiblesse de cet appendice lyrique qui tient à des vices inhérents à l'opéra-comique, vices qui sont détaillés selon trois catégories. Le premier remonte aux origines du genre, situées implicitement par l'éditeur au milieu du siècle, lorsque l'opéra-comique relevait de la parodie et s'inspirait directement de l'*intermezzo* italien. Il s'agit d'un vice de style. Il apparaît clairement que le critère central de son évaluation, annoncé dès le premier article, sera cette question de la correction de l'écriture et qu'elle prépare le jugement sur Sedaine qui occupera plus de la moitié du compte rendu. L'art de parodier est 'très-difficile', si difficile qu'il est impossible de bien écrire sous la contrainte d'une musique préexistante:

> Dans cette opération presque mécanique, la poésie est sur le lit de Procruste; et ce tyran lui coupe ou lui allonge les membres, selon le caprice de la musique.

Hoffman détaille les manipulations impures qui contraignent le littérateur à produire du vers dans une quantité et une forme définies par des exigences musicales, cela au détriment de la correction du vers lui-même. En bon élève

---

[8] *Journal de l'Empire* (8 février 1812); ce paragraphe n'apparaît pas dans la version de 1834. Les citations suivantes laissées sans référence sont présentes dans les deux versions.

de Grétry, il rappelle l'épineuse contrainte des syllabes muettes et pleines, et l'irrégularité du nombre de pieds à laquelle le poète est contraint:

> La longueur et la mesure de ses vers dépendant de la phrase de chant, il est obligé de les faire de toutes dimensions, et souvent de former des alliances bizarres, comme des vers de trois, cinq et sept syllabes, après ceux de quatre, six et huit. Il est aisé de voir que des vers qui ont toutes les mesures n'ont aucune mesure réelle, et qu'ils sont à proprement parler de la prose, puisqu'une phrase de prose quelconque a six, sept, huit, neuf, dix syllabes, plus ou moins, et que tous ces nombres sont admis dans les vers parodiés.

Suit alors un exemple d'air extrait de la version française de *La Servante maîtresse* de Pierre Baurans qui illustre à merveille cette sorte de littérature chantée entremêlant des exclamations courtes et des onomatopées qui avait ravi l'auditoire de 1754 pour son naturel et qui, privée de la musique, produit un effet de repoussoir pour le lecteur:[9] 'Quel est, en effet, le lecteur un peu délicat qui prenne quelque plaisir à lire [de tels] vers'. Hoffman en tire une première conclusion qui vise au cœur le projet éditorial et révèle son incongruité en soulignant l'hybridité congénitale du genre.

> On m'objectera sans doute que de pareils vers ne doivent être jugés que relativement à la musique, j'en conviens; mais alors ne les en séparez pas, et ne me donnez pas à lire ce qui n'est pas lisible.

A ce premier grief qui, au fond, laisse la scène intacte et concerne le genre à ses origines, Hoffman ajoute des arguments d'une portée plus profonde pour dénoncer un vice affectant la construction dramatique.

Ces derniers dévoilent un versant de l'esthétique d'Hoffman qui n'est pas toujours illustré par son œuvre personnelle et qui s'exprime à travers un attachement aux règles du théâtre classique. Hoffman en tient non seulement pour un livret bien écrit, mais aussi respectueux des unités, observant du principe de liaison des scènes, et conduisant à un dénouement logique et entièrement fondé sur le discours. Or, la musique 'allège considérablement la tâche du poète', 'elle tient lieu de style, de liaison, de conclusion, chaque fois que le poète se trouve embarrassé'. Et même si Hoffman distingue les mauvais auteurs, auxquels incombe la plus grande responsabilité dans la médiocrité du genre, il souligne les facilités qui font qu''un opéra quelconque est [...]

---

9 Il s'agit de vers extraits du duo de Zerbine et Pandolfe 'Je devine', à l'acte I sc. II. Voir *La Servante maîtresse, Comédie en deux actes, mêlée d'ariettes, parodiées de la Serva Padrona, Intermède italien; représentée pour la 1re fois par les Comédiens Italiens Ordinaires du Roi, le 14 août 1754* (s.l., n.d.), p. 30–31.

toujours infiniment plus facile à faire qu'une comédie de quelque genre que ce soit':

> S'agit-il de terminer une scène? L'ariette fait sortir un acteur, la ritournelle en fait entrer un autre: un duo donne de la chaleur à un dialogue qui languit ...

Le blâme d'Hoffman est catégorique sur ce point. Le livret doit, en théorie, se conformer aux lois du théâtre et la présence de la musique doit laisser inviolée une sorte d'étiquette du dramaturge contraint d'admettre que 'toute situation comique ou intéressante, préparée et présentée convenablement, produira le même effet, soit en musique, soit en déclamation'. L'illégitimité du livret au sein du théâtre lu tient donc autant aux incorrections du style qu'à une construction dramatique qui pêche par le fait qu'elle ne garantit pas une qualité autonome au livret. Pour Hoffman, celui-ci n'a pourtant rien de spécifique qui pourrait l'autoriser à s'écarter des conventions habituelles du théâtre. La charge est surprenante, venant d'un auteur dont le succès le plus retentissant (*Euphrosine, ou le Tyran corrigé*, musique de Méhul, 1791) s'était constitué autour d'un duo rendu extrêmement dramatique par un motif fameux, et d'une action romanesque répartie, en première intention, dans cinq actes outrepassant les vingt-quatre heures,[10] et il faudra revenir sur cette étonnante discordance entre une partie de l'œuvre d'Hoffman et ses vues théoriques exposées *a posteriori*.

Les arguments de cette intransigeance littéraire sont des plus étonnants. Ils débouchent sur un dernier grief affectant les fondements même du genre lyrique. A certaines de ses formulations, on se sent étrangement renvoyé à plus d'un siècle en arrière, à l'époque où Saint-Evremond pourfendait l'opéra sur la base d'une opposition entre l'esprit, propre à la création littéraire, et la sensualité, propriété spécifique de la musique, et le qualifiait de 'travail bizarre de poésie et de musique, où le poète et le musicien [sont] également gênés l'un par l'autre'.[11] Certes, Hoffman ne reprend pas à son compte les arrière-pensées de ce critique du Grand Siècle et encore moins celles de Bossuet ou de Boileau. La musique n'est pas pour lui cette muse impure, vénéneuse, qui

[10] Le motif 'de la jalousie' que l'on considère parfois comme l'un des tout premiers exemples de leitmotiv. Voir la partition, *Euphrosine, ou le Tyran corrigé, Comédie en trois actes et en vers* (Paris: Cousineau, [1791]), acte II, sc. V, p. 111–32. L'opéra dut être remanié en trois actes après quelques représentations critiquées dans la version en cinq actes, et celle en quatre actes. Voir David Charlton 'Motive and Motif: Méhul before 1791', *Music & Letters*, LVII (1976), p. 362–9, réimp. dans *French Opera 1730–1830: Meaning and Media* (Aldershot: Ashgate, 2000).

[11] Charles de Saint-Evremond, *Lettre à M. le duc de Buckingham* (1677), citée dans Georges Snyders, *Le Goût musical en France aux XVIIe et XVIIIe siècles* (Paris: Vrin, 1968), p. 50.

attirait sur l'opéra naissant les foudres moralisatrices des ennemis du plaisir des sens. Au contraire, elle lui apparaît comme un agent du pathétique et du mystère, un art au pouvoir insondable qui 'se plaît beaucoup moins à rire qu'à pleurer':

> La preuve que cet art n'exclut pas le sérieux, la gravité, et même la tristesse, c'est qu'il accompagne nos cérémonies religieuses, nos mystères, et nos pompes funèbres.

Son association avec le drame n'est qu'une de ces 'invraisemblances convenues' définissant les limites des diverses formes d'art et il est clair que, à certaines conditions, le genre lyrique n'est pas condamnable en lui-même. Mais comme la musique agit par des moyens 'physiques' plutôt que 'moraux', les derniers étant du ressort de la littérature, le livret d'opéra-comique est en danger de médiocrité en raison non seulement des facilités qui se présentent au librettiste, mais à cause d'une rencontre dont les modalités peuvent concourir à la réussite esthétique comme à une faute de goût impardonnable.

> L'auteur lyrique ... a toujours à ses ordres ou l'harmonie imposante, ou la séduisante mélodie, qui déguisent ses défauts ou les font pardonner. [... Il] emprunte les ornements d'un art qui lui est étranger, ce qui est contraire aux règles du goût.

La critique ne porte donc plus sur le style ou sur les écarts des auteurs: elle vise le monstre littéraire né d'un mariage qui reste légitime à condition seulement de ne pas sacrifier les règles essentielles du théâtre à la recherche d'effets licencieux. Pour être clair, Hoffman se réfère aux excellents ouvrages de Grétry qui ont su plier la musique aux lois de la représentation. Un type d'écriture vocale proche de la prosodie, un certain art du dialogue en musique attestent que la musique 'pouvait suivre tous les mouvements de la scène, et s'approcher jusqu'à l'illusion, de la vérité du dialogue'. La position d'Hoffman est donc très clairement celui du lecteur et de l'homme de lettres qui admet parfaitement l'union de la musique et du drame mais qui ne souffre pas qu'une fois dépouillée des ornements étrangers à sa cohérence propre, une pièce dramatique laisse paraître le moindre signe d'une insuffisance.

> La musique emploie des moyens physiques pour plaire, et ... les ouvrages d'esprit ne doivent être que des productions de l'esprit, sans aucun secours physique et matériel.

Il s'en suit une sorte de palmarès des auteurs du genre opéra-comique inspiré par les trois critères du style, de la construction dramatique et de l'autonomie du livret, le dernier étant très longuement développé à travers un réquisitoire sévère centré sur les œuvres de Sedaine. Baurans est fustigé pour la platitude de son style parodié dans *La Servante maîtresse*, Favart a tous les honneurs pour l'esprit et la beauté du style, hormis dans son œuvre parodiée (*Ninette à la cour*), tandis que Marmontel et d'Hèle sont reconnus furtivement pour leur contribution à l'invention de la comédie en musique.

La révolution opérée par Sedaine

Sedaine est donc au cœur de la polémique esthétique à travers laquelle Hoffman développe implicitement sa propre conception du genre. L'intronisation académique est la cause des malentendus dont il convient de lever les équivoques. Cette reconnaissance par l'institution garante de l'usage de la langue est 'précisément [celle] que Sedaine ne méritait pas'.

> On lui attribue un talent qu'il n'avait pas; on fait à peine attention à un talent bien réel qu'il avait à un très haut degré, et quand on s'est moqué de son style (à la vérité bien barbare), on se croit en droit de mépriser ses ouvrages sous tous ses rapports.

Les pages que Hoffman consacre à son style sont certainement les plus sévères et, peut-être aussi, les plus déloyales qu'un homme de lettres ait jamais écrites sur un librettiste d'opéra-comique. Elles consistent en treize citations privées de leur contexte et choisies pour illustrer les reproches d'incorrection et de platitude de l'expression. Dans leur ensemble, elles sont fidèles aux textes originaux de la collection et, pour quelques cas, on peut souscrire aux remarques ironiques de leur censeur. Mais il est troublant que, à une exception près, la totalité ait été choisie dans les parties chantées et que Hoffman ne se soit pas montré fidèle à son argument principal selon lequel les médiocrités stylistiques de Sedaine auraient pu être mises au compte de l'imperfection de principe affectant l'irruption du vers chanté. Les deux dernières proviennent d'ailleurs des vaudevilles de *Félix* et de *Rose et Colas*, un genre de chanson strophique sans ambition expressive destinée à conclure en laissant chaque protagoniste exprimer à son tour la morale de son expérience individuelle. La citation de l'acte III scène IV de *Richard Cœur-de-Lion* est en fait une compilation de vers empruntés au chœur et au couplet de Marguerite (deuxième exemple dans le tableau en annexe). La première citation provient d'une pièce absente de la collection de 1812, *Le Magnifique*, citation dont La Harpe s'était déjà servi en 1800 dans son *Lycée* (p. 394). On peut donc raisonnablement interpréter ces écarts à une parfaite objectivité comme étant dictés par la volonté de nuire très spécifiquement à Sedaine. D'ailleurs, aucun éloge argumenté ne vient contrebalancer plusieurs pages d'ironie cinglante sur ces pièces 'mal écrites'.

Il semble pourtant qu'en 1812, les œuvres de Sedaine aient joui d'une certaine réputation en vertu de leur construction originale. Hoffman parle d'un 'dicton proverbial' vantant la 'charpente' de ses opéras-comiques. Mais celle-ci ne lui inspire pas plus d'égard et provoque au contraire une condamnation académique qui n'avait pas été encore exprimée dans des termes aussi définitifs:

> Il n'a jamais existé d'auteur qui se soit plus moqué des règles d'Aristote.

Hoffman souligne que Sedaine conçoit ses drames comme une succession de tableaux remplis d'effets de scène. Il parle à leurs sujets de 'comique matériel', de 'moyens physiques', de situations 'intéressantes' ce qui fait songer tout à la fois à Monsieur Pince bondissant de son armoire (dans *Blaise le savetier*, opéra-comique de Philidor, absent de la collection) et aux dénouements spectaculaires du *Déserteur* ou de *Richard Cœur-de-Lion.* Les nombreuses prisons dont Sedaine a usé dans *Le Déserteur*, *Aucassin et Nicolette*, *Richard Cœur-de-Lion*, *Le Comte d'Albert*, et *Raoul Barbe-Bleue* procèdent d'un genre de théâtre où l'intérêt visuel tient lieu de style.

> [Sedaine finit une pièce] par une porte que l'on fracasse [*Blaise le savetier*], une [autre] par une forteresse que l'on prend d'assaut en deux minutes [*Richard Cœur-de-Lion*]; une autre enfin ne se dénoue pas du tout, et l'on est obligé de faire quarante ou cinquante lieues pour trouver, non pas son troisième acte, mais sa suite qui n'a aucun rapport avec le sujet [*Le Comte d'Albert*].[12]

Hoffman loue l'extraordinaire talent instinctif de celui qui 'dans une foule de sujets ... a reconnu celui qui pouvait convenir au théâtre', et qui 'dans un sujet dramatique a ... vu quel était le point qui portait l'intérêt, qui devait former la situation principale, et qu'il fallait faire ressortir aux dépens de tous les autres':

> Il a ... fait connaître l'art d'y [à l'Opéra-Comique] présenter des situations très dramatiques, et d'y intéresser vivement le spectateur.

Mais il n'admet pas le primat de la scène et stigmatise, au nom des règles classiques, la conséquence de ces visions géniales qui conduisent à sacrifier l'écrit à la représentation.

---

[12] Voir le commentaire au chapitre suivant, et l''Avertissement' de ce livret, p. 267.

> [Sedaine] ne s'occupe jamais de liaison ... ses acteurs entrent par une coulisse, tandis que d'autres sortent, sans que rien prépare, motive, nécessite l'entrée de ceux-ci, ni la sortie de ceux-là.

Un autre grief intéressant porte sur les dénouements prévus dès le commencement de la pièce. Il met l'accent sur un point fragile de la dramaturgie en tableaux qui est particulièrement illustré par le livret de *Rose et Colas* dans lequel le mariage des deux jeunes gens est différé jusqu'à une échéance prévue à l'avance. Hoffman épingle cette esthétique:

> Il finit une pièce par un moyen prévu dès le commencement.

Plusieurs livrets de Sedaine présentent cette particularité. *Le Déserteur* est également incriminé, on le reconnaît à travers des remarques du type telles que celle-ci:

> Il saute à pieds joints du nœud sur le dénouement.

L'invraisemblance des conduites de ses personnages est un autre travers relevé dans *Le Déserteur* qui est 'un sot'. 'Il cause avec une petite fillette au lieu d'entrer chez sa maîtresse' et de déjouer la mise en scène fictive qui doit le décourager d'épouser Louise. Le seul intérêt que l'on prend au malheur d'un homme condamné à mort nous fait oublier de 'chercher comment il eût pu l'éviter'. Dans tous les cas, l'absence de conduite logique et la liaison des scènes négligée sont 'irrégulièrement' compensées par l'effet scénique à laquelle la musique prête son secours, ce qui permet à Hoffman de faire converger ses remarques dramatiques avec sa conception de la distinction des essences propres à la littérature et à la musique:

> Toujours des ressorts physiques, et, par cela même, bien plus puissants sur le vulgaire des spectateurs.

Mais sous ce double reproche d'incorrection du style et de la charpente, qui lui fait dire que Sedaine 'a fait disparaître la grâce, l'élégance, le style, et jusqu'à l'habitude d[e] parler français', il y a plus sans doute qu'une critique académique ravivant la polémique de 1786. Pour le comprendre, on doit prendre en compte les vingt-cinq années qui séparent la consécration contestée et le jugement d'Hoffman. En 1812, la scène lyrique a concédé depuis plusieurs années un droit de cité à un genre de spectacle nouveau qui préoccupe le public lettré des théâtres: le mélodrame. La dernière accusation, la plus grave, met en relation la dramaturgie de Sedaine et le genre nouveau qui fait recette aux boulevards, au grand dam des académiciens.

> … le comique matériel qui frappe les yeux sans intéresser l'esprit, qui substitue un meuble à une passion, un déguisement à un caractère, les décorations aux mœurs, le mouvement physique au mouvement moral; moyen grossier qui plaît à la foule, qui a d'autant plus de charmes qu'il est plus exagéré, qui ouvre la porte aux manœuvres, et qui a produit le mélodrame.

Ici, Hoffman apporte une précision historique qui reste à évaluer. Elle situe l'origine du mélodrame, entendu comme un spectacle fondé sur des situations intéressantes mais dénué d'action, au moment de la composition du *Comte d'Albert*, lequel aurait été reconnu précocement comme relevant de ce genre:

> Sedaine enfin a le malheureux avantage d'être cité comme l'introducteur du mélodrame à l'Opéra-Comique.[13]

En outre, Sedaine aurait joué un rôle prépondérant dans l'évolution du goût du public au point d'imposer à l'Opéra-Comique ce monstre, coupable de substituer au style l'intérêt des scènes spectaculaires.

> On s'habitua peu à peu à préférer l'action physique à l'action morale, le mouvement brusque et rapide à la marche un peu trop lente des pièces qu'on avait vues jusqu'alors, et l'effet des tableaux accumulés aux développements d'une scène tranquille.

Après avoir posé le cadre d'une critique globale de la légitimité du genre opéra-comique au sein de la collection, Hoffman concentre ses arguments sur ce qui lui paraît la partie la plus faible du répertoire envisagé sous l'angle du livre. Et s'il atténue la charge par des formulations équilibrées, comme celle-ci: 'la vérité me force à dire que cet auteur a perfectionné et en même temps corrompu le genre de l'opéra-comique', il pose un cadre critique impitoyable pour l'évaluation du livret. Au fond, ceux de Sedaine révèlent leurs défauts à la lecture. Le texte brut, dénué des ressources de la scène et de la musique apparaît comme un squelette sans chair, un canevas sans 'esprit' et sans logique qui fatiguera le lecteur surpris, peut-être, de voir la 'magie' du théâtre de Sedaine envolée.[14] Et ce désenchantement serait la preuve que la vogue du librettiste est une mode sans lendemain, comme si l'épreuve de la

---

[13] Emilio Sala a pu établir très clairement les origines de ce genre et son influence sur Sedaine, exprimée dans la préface de *Guillaume Tell*: *L'opera senza canto. Il mélo romantico e l'invenzione della colonna sonora* (Venezia: Marsilio, 1995), p. 41; idem, 'Mélodrame. Définitions et métamorphoses d'un genre quasi opératique', *Revue de musicologie*, LXXXIV/2 (1998), p. 235–46. Voir cependant d'autres précisions infra, p. 269–71.

[14] Les expressions entre guillemets sont d'Hoffman.

lecture préludait au jugement historique des auteurs. Ce dernier point est la pierre angulaire d'une dernière considération inspirant au critique un regard rétrospectif sur l'histoire du genre.

Révolution et contre révolution, la morale de la parenthèse Sedaine

Incontestablement, l'article d'Hoffman déborde le seul cas de Sedaine et de son inclusion dans une collection de référence du théâtre français: c'est bien le livret d'opéra-comique qui est mis en examen. Mais on ne peut pas oublier non plus que la plus grande partie de l'œuvre dramatique d'Hoffman est composée de livrets d'opéra-comique, et l'on a vu que le genre lui-même n'est pas mis en cause intrinsèquement. Hoffman adopte donc une stratégie plus subtile consistant à prendre position sur la perspective que l'édition de Nicole dessine implicitement par ses choix et à dresser un bilan en forme de diagnostic.

> Ce genre [l'opéra-comique] est tombé dans un tel discrédit, que les hommes même incapables de rien faire affectent de le dédaigner. Personne n'a recherché la cause de ce mépris.

Hoffman ébauche sa propre anthologie que l'on peut résumer de la manière suivante. L'opéra-comique est né sur les tréteaux de foire entre 'bateleurs et danseurs de corde'. Sous les plumes de Le Sage, Fuzelier ou d'Orneval, le fond en était souvent insignifiant mais les 'couplets bien tournés' et la facture de leurs auteurs qui se 'recommandent par le style' portent en germe des avancées de l'époque suivante. Favart est apprécié. Avec Marmontel et d'Hèle, l'opéra-comique en vaudeville devient la comédie en musique. Ces deux auteurs sont peu évoqués mais, par opposition, on comprend que le mal arrive lorsque Sedaine introduit le 'mélodrame' qui ouvre la porte aux expérimentations les plus hasardeuses, c'est-à-dire le drame – sans explications supplémentaires – et même, ce qui est le comble, la tragédie.[15] La terminologie d'Hoffman n'est pas toujours très aisée à interpréter. Il est clair cependant que la courbe est déclinante à partir de Sedaine et touche le point le plus bas pendant la Révolution, à l'époque où Hoffman entre dans la carrière et produit coup sur coup plusieurs dizaines de livrets en l'espace de deux décennies. Dans les toutes dernières années du siècle une 'contre révolution' se fait jour.

---

[15] On note que Hoffman est l'auteur de deux opéras-comiques basés sur des sujets antiques, traités en alexandrins: *Stratonice, comédie héroïque* en un acte (musique de Méhul, 1792), et *Médée, opéra en trois actes* (musique de Cherubini, 1797), qui retient un dénouement tragique.

> Des auteurs estimables vinrent au secours de l'opéra-comique, lorsqu'il luttait malheureusement contre les farces héroïques du boulevard.

Les pièces citées ne laissent aucun doute sur les auteurs et la nature de ce sursaut. Ce sont: *Le Prisonnier* (Alexandre Duval et Della Maria), *Adolphe et Clara* (Marsollier des Vivetières et Dalayrac), *Maison à vendre* (Duval et Dalayrac), *Une heure de mariage* (Etienne et Dalayrac), c'est-à-dire quelques-uns des très gros succès de l'Opéra-Comique sous le Consulat et l'Empire qui, d'après Hoffman, 'ramenaient la véritable comédie, et qui rappelaient les pièces du bon temps, telles que *L'Amant jaloux*, *L'Ami de la maison*, etc, etc, et l'on put, sans rougir, applaudir un opéra-comique'.[16]

Plus encore que les compositeurs Dalayrac et Della-Maria, ce sont les librettistes qui retiennent notre attention. Car si Marsollier est déjà un auteur du passé qui a incarné la permanence du comique pendant la Révolution, Duval et Etienne appartiennent à une nouvelle génération, proche d'Hoffman, qui réunira les principaux détracteurs du courant romantique pendant les années 1820–30 après leur promotion au rang académique.[17] On sent donc dans cette confession une pincée d'amertume affectant l'itinéraire personnel de son auteur, qui recoupe plusieurs tentatives historiographiques entreprises à la même époque, telle que celle de Jacques Daniel Martine. Pour Martine, dont la périodisation est essentiellement musicale, trois grandes époques sont à distinguer, articulées autour d'un âge d'or situé entre 1768 et 1789.[18] Avant, la tragédie lyrique est dans l'erreur et l'opéra-comique dans les limbes. Un art national, constituant un réservoir de classiques pour le nouveau siècle, a émergé avec l'arrivée de Grétry et la venue de Gluck, Piccinni et Sacchini, un art national au sens d'un répertoire excellent voué à rester aux programmes d'institutions reconnues par le privilège sous l'Ancien Régime et récemment distinguées au sommet de la pyramide établie par les décrets impériaux de 1806–7.[19] Puis une période de décadence est inaugurée avec la Révolution, qui appelle une régénération, un ressourcement dans les modèles de l'âge d'or identifié au règne de Louis XVI.

---

16 Pour une estimation chiffrée des succès de la période 1801–14, voir Raphaëlle Legrand et Patrick Taïeb, 'L'Opéra-Comique sous le Consulat et l'Empire' dans Paul Prévost (éd.), *Le Théâtre lyrique en France au XIXe siècle* (Metz: Éditions Serpenoise, 1995), p. 1–61. *L'Amant jaloux* était écrit par d'Hèle, *L'Ami de la maison* par Marmontel.

17 Voir, notamment, le texte fameux d'Alexandre Duval, *Lettre à M. Victor Hugo* (Paris: Dufey et Vézard, 1834).

18 [Jacques-Daniel] Martine, *De la musique dramatique en France* (Paris: Dentu, 1813), chapitre VIII, 'Tableau de la révolution musicale en France divisé en époques', p. 67–110.

19 Pour un résumé de ces décrets on consultera Nicole Wild, *Dictionnaire des théâtres parisiens au XIXe siècle* (Paris: Aux Amateurs de Livres, 1989), p. 13–14.

Que les catégories du jugement de Martine soient basées sur la musique n'empêche pas que sa périodisation recoupe celle d'Hoffman sur certains points et converge pour quelques arguments, au point qu'il faudrait approfondir la portée des articles d'Hoffman en termes de référence pour les écrits sur l'histoire de l'art dramatique à partir de 1812. L'hypertrophie de la musique, incriminée dans le jugement sur les œuvres de la Révolution, est l'argument central pour une échelle de valeurs plaçant les derniers opéras-comiques de Grétry avant 1789, ceux justement de la collaboration avec Sedaine, sous le signe d'une décadence. Que *Raoul Barbe-Bleue*, une œuvre particulièrement noire, compte au nombre des pièces de la Révolution qui 'n'ont pas toute la fraîcheur, toute la verve des précédentes' vient à la rencontre des conceptions développées par Hoffman.

Toujours en 1813 paraît un recueil d'*Œuvres choisies de Sédaine* [sic] précédées d'une notice signée par un collaborateur d'Hoffman au *Journal de l'Empire*, Louis-Simon Auger (1772–1829), futur académicien et autre pourfendeur des romantiques.[20] L'influence de la critique d'Hoffman se fait vivement sentir dans cette notice où l'on peut lire un condensé de son article de 1812:

> Il faut bien convenir qu'il y a, de la part de l'auteur dramatique, un talent peu commun d'intéresser et d'émouvoir. Ce talent consiste à saisir la nature, non pas dans les masses, mais dans les petits détails; à indiquer sans les approfondir, un grand nombre d'intentions dramatiques ou morales; enfin à jeter dans le dialogue de ces traits de vérité commune, mais frappante, qui saisissent fortement, et produisent un genre d'illusion souvent refusé aux moyens de l'art les plus recherchés et les plus délicats.[21]

On note également un développement intéressant sur la source principale de ce théâtre d'effets qui tourne le dos aux règles classiques, source que Grétry avait déjà relevée dans ses *Mémoires*,[22] le théâtre de Shakespeare:

---

20 Louis-Simon Auger (éd.), *Œuvres choisies de Sédaine* (Paris: Didot l'aîné et Firmin Didot, 1813), 'Notice sur la vie et les ouvrages de Sedaine', p. v–xii. Voir L.-S. Auger, *Discours sur le Romantisme prononcé dans la séance des quatre académies du 24 avril 1824* (Paris: Firmin Didot, 1824).

21 Auger, 'Notice', p. x.

22 Grétry, *Mémoires*, p. 400.

> Lorsque la traduction de Letourneur[23] vint à paraître, [Sedaine] n'eut rien de plus pressé que de la lire ou plutôt de la dévorer. Il en était dans l'extase, dans le ravissement; il parlait de Shakespeare à tout ce qu'il rencontrait.[24]

Le texte d'Hoffman – mais peut-être faudrait-il dire, les textes, car la critique de Sedaine serait utilement élargie à son abondante activité critique – attend une étude sur sa réception qui révélerait peut-être son importance dans la formulation des arguments de l'anti-romantisme émergeant quelques années plus tard.

Pour l'heure, Hoffman sent bien qu'un anathème aussi tranché comporte une fragilité essentielle si on le confronte à la popularité incontestable des ouvrages restés au répertoire de l'institution. Cette contradiction lui inspire une conclusion sociologique qui vient établir une relation entre révolution dramatique et Révolution. A quoi tient cette étonnante popularité si les pièces incriminées recèlent des faiblesses aussi criantes à la lecture? N'est-ce pas au fait que le public qui s'y intéresse est assez peu lecteur? Examinant les progrès de Sedaine à la fin de l'Ancien Régime, Hoffman observe que sa renommée s'est établie très progressivement. Les premières ont souvent été houleuses et il a fallu aux spectateurs un temps d'adaptation auquel il trouve au moins deux explications. La première réside dans l'histoire de l'institution elle-même qui aurait eu le très grand tort de mettre l'accent sur les opéras, au dépens du répertoire parlé. Cet événement se situe après 1789. La troupe d'acteurs non-chanteurs est dissoute.[25] Cela aurait eu pour conséquence de laisser l'opéra-comique hors de la comparaison avec le théâtre parlé, le bon théâtre.

> Dans les provinces, où l'on a conservé l'usage de jouer la comédie et l'opéra-comique sur le même théâtre, le public a toujours été plus sévère qu'on ne l'était à Paris: le style y était compté pour quelque chose et l'homme qui venait entendre *Le Tartuffe* ou *Le Misanthrope*,

---

[23] *Shakespeare traduit de l'anglais* (20 vol., Paris: Vve Duchesne, 1776–82). Mais l'intérêt de Sedaine pour Shakespeare est antérieur à cette traduction. On en trouve le témoignage dans un avertissement écrit en 1764: voir au chapitre suivant, p. 249.

[24] Auger, 'Notice', p. xi.

[25] Les comédiens se sentèrent obligés le 3 février 1790 de faire des économies: les dix acteurs qui ne jouaient que dans les pièces sans musique 'se retirèrent avec une pension': Arthur Pougin, *L'Opéra-Comique pendant la Révolution* (Paris: Savine, 1891; repr. Genève, 1973), p. 28; Clarence D. Brenner, *The Théâtre Italien. Its Repertory, 1716–1793* (University of California Publications in Modern Philology, LXIII) (Berkeley and Los Angeles: University of California Press, 1961), p. 34. Néanmoins, on continue à monter des spectacles parlés de temps en temps, y compris un drame de Hoffman lui-même (*Adélaïde, ou la Victime*), le 25 juillet 1793, qui tombe aussitôt. Voir André Tissier, *Les Spectacles à Paris pendant la Révolution. Répertoire analytique, chronologique et bibliographique* (Genève: Droz, 1992), p. 75–89; Emmet Kennedy et al., *Theatre, Opera, and Audiences in Revolutionary Paris. Analysis and Repertory* (Westport, Conn.: Greenwood Press, 1996).

> sifflait impitoyablement toute la pièce où la langue et le goût étaient trop maltraités.

Ce point de chronologie vient préciser la deuxième explication. Elle repose sur l'apparition d'un public nouveau au goût moins sévère, entré au théâtre avec la Révolution.[26]

> Comme les gens qui n'apportent au théâtre que des yeux et des oreilles sont infiniment plus nombreux que ceux qui y viennent avec du goût et de l'esprit, les romans dialogués, les pièces à processions, à prisons et à fracas, attirèrent bientôt la foule du peuple et même les gens d'esprit qui finissent souvent par penser comme le peuple, ou au moins par le suivre.

De cette évolution de la salle dépendrait celle du monde littéraire, et notamment des journalistes qui auraient abdiqué leur mission principale devant cette masse inquiétante:

> Les critiques ne s'occupent plus du style, qui est la partie la plus importante en littérature, et la seule qui fasse vivre les ouvrages.

Sedaine aurait été d'abord un habile calculateur qui aurait su utiliser son pur instinct sans talent pour rencontrer ce 'nombreux public qui ne juge que par sentiment, applaudit avec transport et imposa silence à cet autre public qui juge par principe'. Même *Richard Cœur-de-Lion* (1784), que l'on ne peut pas soupçonner d'avoir été écrit pour satisfaire les inclinations du public révolutionnaire, ni même pré-révolutionnaire puisqu'il fut interdit sous la Révolution en raison de la connotation royaliste de l'air de Blondel ('O Richard, O mon roi'), tomberait sous la coupe de cette accusation de l'avoir été pour un public sans exigence.

> On reprochait à Sedaine d'avoir pris cette pièce tout entière dans un fabliau, d'y avoir aussi copié la romance *Une fièvre brûlante*, et même les couplets du Sultan Saladin. Cela peut être vrai, répondait le bourgeois qui vient au théâtre pour s'amuser, mais je ne connaissais pas le fabliau, je ne l'aurais jamais lu, et cette pièce, au théâtre, me fait le plus grand plaisir.

---

[26] Cette observation sociologique a été établie par David Charlton, au sujet des livrets à 'délivrance' dont Sedaine a fourni plusieurs exemples: 'On Redefinitions of "Rescue Opera"' dans Malcolm Boyd (éd.), *Music and the French Revolution* (Cambridge: Cambridge University Press, 1992), p. 169–88 [172–3].

Tout le talent de Sedaine reposerait donc sur la conjonction d'une situation désastreuse pour le théâtre et d'une inspiration guidée par le souci de plaire au plus grand nombre.

> Travaillant pour la masse, son but était d'intéresser; il ne se trompait jamais sur le moyen, et quand il l'avait trouvé, il rejetait dédaigneusement toutes les observations, tous les conseils fondés sur la régularité, la vraisemblance, ou l'habitude.

L'insatisfaction d'Hoffman s'exprime finalement à travers la proposition de refondre la collection qui serait augmentée de pièces éventuellement 'dénuées d'intérêt dramatique' mais rattrapées par un style impeccable tandis que, implicitement, il écarte les ouvrages déclarés illisibles, au sens où la lecture révèle leur imperfection congénitale. Hoffman plaide en faveur d'une sélection d'ouvrages de Le Sage, Panard, Piron et Favart remontant aux origines du genre. Son plaidoyer est peu compréhensible s'agissant de Favart dont on peut dire qu'il est bien représenté, mais il est clair que la sélection de Nicole fait une large place à Sedaine qui totalise plus du quart des ouvrages et que les livrets d'avant 1750 sont totalement oubliés. Dans le second groupe, il jette pêle-mêle les opéras parodiés de l'italien et tout Sedaine.

> Cet auteur tient une grande place dans l'édition de M. Nicole, et si quelque puriste reprochait à l'éditeur d'accorder les honneurs de la bibliothèque à des ouvrages si peu littéraires, n'aurait-il pas le droit de répondre: Il n'appartient pas à un libraire d'être plus difficile que l'Académie.

Si l'on tient compte à la fois des considérations historiques et des critères de jugements fondés sur l'épreuve de la lecture, on voit se dessiner une conception alternative de l'anthologie qui écarte Sedaine de l'opéra-comique comme s'il s'agissait d'un accident, d'une contribution aussi passagère que la mode et qui aurait dévié momentanément le cours normal de son histoire. Celle-ci commence avec Le Sage et Piron, se poursuit avec Favart, Marmontel, d'Hèle, et, peut-être, Marsollier et Hoffman lui-même, avant de se réincarner après l'orage révolutionnaire, à travers Etienne et Duval. Et, derrière cette contre-proposition, pointe, à coup sûr, l'accusation d'une anthologie composée en vue d'un succès public, avec des visées commerciales.

En fait, le jugement sur Sedaine dépasse de beaucoup l'évaluation d'un auteur. Il sert de plaidoyer en faveur d'un genre en péril permanent. En premier lieu, l'opéra-comique est mis en danger par sa popularité. 'Il plaît plus qu'il n'est estimé', écrit-il, avant de déplorer que

> dans les coulisses de ce théâtre, *pièce froide* et *pièce bien écrite* sont deux expressions synonymes, comme s'il fallait être barbare pour intéresser, comme si le moyen de plaire aux Français était d'écorcher la langue française.

En second lieu, son indéfinition chronique sur le plan littéraire le place constamment en position d'emprunter aux genres voisins au risque de perdre son essence propre. Hoffman semble donc plaider pour un théâtre lyrique du juste milieu, contraint à une correction de style qui garantit sa valeur dans le temps et sa place dans les bibliothèques, et un théâtre remarquable par sa mobilité à condition de se démarquer des genres environnants dans lesquels il puise les apports indispensables à son renouvellement. Incidemment, Hoffman dessine un trait d'union entre l'innovation de Sedaine et le courant romantique auquel ses collaborateurs et modèles vont s'affronter, et propose une hypothèse sur les origines sociales et esthétiques du romantisme qu'il conviendrait d'approfondir en étudiant la réception de Sedaine au XIXe siècle.

ANNEXE 1

Sommaire des huit volumes du Théâtre de l'Opéra-Comique[27]

tome I	Notice sur Baurans; *La Servante maîtresse*; Notice sur Favart; *La Chercheuse d'esprit, Annette et Lubin, Ninette à la cour*
tome II	*La Fée Urgèle, Isabelle et Gertrude, Les Moissonneurs, L'Amitié à l'épreuve, La belle Arsène*
tome III	Notice sur Anseaume; *Les Deux chasseurs et la laitière, Le Tableau parlant*; Notice sur Poinsinet; *Le Sorcier*; Notice sur Sedaine; *Le Roi et le fermier, Rose et Colas*
tome IV	*Le Déserteur, Les Femmes vengées, Félix, On ne s'avise jamais de tout, Aucassin et Nicolette*
tome V	*Richard Cœur-de-Lion, Le Comte d'Albert, Suite du Comte d'Albert*; Notice sur Audinot; *Le Tonnelier*; Notice sur Lemonnier; *Le Cadi dupé, Le Maréchal ferrant*
tome VI	Notice sur Marmontel; *La Bergère des Alpes, Le Huron, Silvain, Zémire et Azor, L'Ami de la maison, La Fausse magie*
tome VII	Notice sur Fenouillot de Falbaire: *Les Deux avares*; Notice sur Laujon; *L'Amoureux de quinze ans*; Notice sur d'Hèle; *Les Fausses apparences,*[28] *Le Jugement de Midas, Les Evénements imprévus*
tome VIII	Notice sur Pezay; *La Rosière de Salenci*; Note sur Grenier; *La Mélomanie*; Notice sur Forgeot; *Les Dettes*; Notice sur De Jaure; *Lodoïska, Montano et Stéphanie*

[27] Ce sommaire a été établi à partir de deux collections incomplètes et complémentaires: F-Pn (Département des imprimés) et la Bibliothèque de la Sorbonne.

[28] Il s'agit de *L'Amant jaloux* dont le titre, lors de la création, était bien *Les Fausses apparences*.

ANNEXE 2

Répliques de Sedaine citées par Hoffman (suivant l'ordre de leur apparition dans le texte d'Hoffman)

	Citation d'Hoffman	Titre de la référence	Version dans l'édition de 1812
1	'C'est en vain que je m'applique A n'y réfléchir jamais'	*Le Magnifique*, I, II; air de Clémentine	absent du recueil[29]
2	'Comment savez-vous cette affaire? Ah! grand Dieu! mon cœur se serre!'	*Richard Cœur-de-Lion*, III, IV; répliques de Marguerite et de chevaliers combinées	'Chevaliers: Comment savez-vous ce mystère? Marguerite: Ah! s'il est vrai, quel jour prospère! Ah! grands Dieux … ah! mon cœur se serre De joie et de saisissement.' (V, p. 46–7)
3	'Un bouquet qu'unit un brin d'herbe'	*Le Roi et le fermier*, I, VIII; ariette de Jenny	(III, p. 206) citation exacte
4	'Ce nuage n'est qu'un passage'	*Le Roi et le fermier*, I, IX; duo de Richard et Jenny, réplique de Richard	(III, p. 210) citation exacte
5	'J'entends, la chasse se disperse; Le bruit des cors, tiens, comme il perce'	*Le Roi et le fermier*, I, IX; final, réplique de Richard	(III, p. 212) citation exacte

29 Cité dans La Harpe, *Lycée*, XII, p. 394

6	'Sa bouche Touche Cette quenouille Si joliment! Elle la mouille En la filant: Que je la baise! Et cette chaise; Ici tout est charmant.'	*Rose et Colas*, 12; ariette de Colas	'Sa bouche Touche Cette quenouille Si joliment, Tant joliment! Elle la mouille En la filant: Que je la baise! Et cette chaise; Ici tout est, tout est charmant.' (III, p. 300)
7	'Fléchissons-nous? il faut fléchir. – Non, réfléchissons à loisir.'	*Rose et Colas*, 15; duo de Pierre et Mathurin	'Mathurin: Fléchissons-nous? il faut fléchir. Pierre: Non, réfléchissons à loisir.' (III, p. 326)
8	'Est-il rien de plus cruel? Venir ici: l'infidèle! Et de ma douleur mortelle Paraître jouir! O ciel!'	*Le Déserteur*, II, VI; duo de Louise et Alexis, réplique d'Alexis.	'Est-il rien de plus cruel? Venir ici: l'infidelle! Et de ma douleur mortelle Paraître jouir! O ciel!' (IV, p. 33)
9	'Mais ta peine redouble Et semble s'augmenter.'	*Le Déserteur*, II, VIII; ariette de Louise, 2e couplet	(IV, p. 37) citation exacte
10	'Ah! s'il est quelque péril, Il s'y jette, il n'est pas maître De n'y pas voler; que fait-il? Ah! grands dieux! où peut-il être?'	*Félix ou l'Enfant trouvé*, I, XI; ensemble, réplique de Thérèse	(IV, p. 169) citation exacte

11	'Vivez ensemble long-temps, Vous Félix, et vous Thérèse. Ah, grands dieux, que je suis aise!'	*Félix ou l'Enfant trouvé*, III, XII; vaudeville final, réplique du chœur	(IV, p. 232) citation exacte
12	'Des regrets, quand le dieu d'hymen Dès demain vous donne ma main! Ah! si je savais que l'hymen Précédât le don de ma main!'	*On ne s'avise jamais de tout*, 13; compilation de répliques parlées de Lise et Dorval	'Dorval: Des regrets, quand le Dieu d'hymen Dès demain vous donne ma main. Lise: Ah! Si je savois que l'hymen précédât le don de ma main.' (IV, p. 266)
13	'Il m'est cher; vous, mon père, encor plus; Si nos jours ne coulaient ensemble, Ses désirs deviendraient superflus. Même nœud nous unit, nous rassemble, Et nos enfants seront en moi Pour vous la leçon la plus sûre; L'amour instruirait la nature Si jamais j'oubliais sa loi.'[30]	*Rose et Colas*, 17 Vaudeville final, couplet de Rose	(III, p. 330) citation exacte

30 Cité ibid., p. 394.

Chapter 9

Sedaine's Prefaces: Pretexts for a New Musical Drama

David Charlton

(a) Introduction

In the course of an almost forty-year career in musical theatre Sedaine changed the face of *opéra-comique* and so helped determine the course that Western opera as a whole would take. The only reason that he remains unsung in this wider respect is that musicology has so far not come to terms with Thalia, the muse of comedy, in considering eighteenth-century French opera. Fortunately, Sedaine left copious evidence of his intentions in the form of prefaces to his librettos, which are here made available together for the first time.

As a musical dramatist Sedaine embarked almost from the start on a trajectory of reform, following hard on the heels of two related but separate antecedents: the work of Favart and Vadé in the 1750s, establishing a new voice for vernacular musical pastoral and comedy; and the immensely strong impact of Italian *intermezzi* and *opere buffe* as brought to Paris by the Bambini troupe in 1752–4. His private account of his theatrical beginnings mixed the egocentric with the objective (rather like his prefaces),[1] while his publicly expressed credenda had been available to anyone who had read the endnote to page 192 of the 1760 edition of *Le Vaudeville, Poème didactique*, first published in 1756. This note amounts to an advance programme for Sedaine's career in music theatre.

> La musique depuis la tolérance des Ariettes, peut s'y employer au stile familier, étendre son Dictionnaire de mots, trouver des ressources inconnues à l'Opéra même, & qui tourneront à son profit; enfin sur ce Théatre les Auteurs ont un moyen de s'exercer dans le genre Comique, qui de plus que le Tragique, exige de joindre au génie une

---

1 'Quelques réflexions', pp. 501–4. See the discussion of this document by Mark Ledbury, p. 20.

> connoissance des mœurs & du cœur humain, plus délicate, plus étendue, & plus profonde.[2]

The existence of Sedaine's prefaces has been no particular secret, yet, in spite of their number and significance, systematic attention has been lacking. Seventeen such published prefaces exist; only eight published works for music lack a preface. The details of these works will be set out in section (d) below. These prefaces cover Sedaine's whole career from 1759 to 1793 and provide an unexpectedly rich source of information not just about his own philosophy and works but about other related topics, such as acting, performance and reception. As a whole they also amount to what one might call their author's 'agenda' for musical theatre, which includes a modest measure of musico-dramatic theory. The purposes of the present notes are, first, to contextualise Sedaine's work; second, to elucidate his idiosyncratic approach to preface writing; and, last, to fathom the nature of the public–private dialogue represented in these texts. I shall also trace the development of Sedaine's style of prefatory writing as it follows the path of a largely successful career in musical theatre. All this precedes an edition of all the known prefaces themselves.

This edition has entailed close examination of a substantial number of printed sources in order both to locate sometimes rare examples of prefaces themselves and also to verify various printings of a given preface. Because the detailed bibliographical study of these materials is in its infancy I have picked my way carefully and gone some distance towards providing extra information regarding the identification and dating of the earliest editions of these librettos themselves. This in turn has thrown up interesting questions reflecting back on Sedaine's decisions concerning the exact date of issue of librettos and their prefaces, enriching the interpretation of their content.

The editions of the prefaces are also provided with short commentaries pertinent to the works in hand, and these incorporate the often brief but equally often essential background information set out by Sedaine in 'Quelques réflexions', completed in 1778, and sundry other evidence.

Section (b) briefly introduces perceptions of Sedaine as a theatre practitioner, and also the 'Réflexions' themselves. Section (c) describes the existence of prefaces other than Sedaine's in *opéra-comique* librettos of the 1750s and early 1760s. Section (d) concerns the practicalities and bibliographical realities of librettos and prefaces; section (e) analyses Sedaine's prefaces as part of a discourse within the public sphere; section (f) summarises the categories of information in the prefaces, and this is followed by an

---

2 *Recueil de poésies de M. Sedaine. 2e édition* (London and Paris: Duchesne, 1760); *Le Vaudeville, Poème didactique* (n.p., 1756). On the nature of 'ariettes' see n. 88 below.

identification of Sedaine's own music-theatrical 'agenda' through their content (g), before the texts and commentaries conclude the proceedings in section (h).

I would like to make acknowledgements here, some of which relate to the prolonged incubation of this project.[3] Ensuing enquiries by letter to American academic libraries in 1993–4 elicited often very helpful replies in the search for missing prefaces, and I should like to thank the persons, named or otherwise, who thus replied.[4]

(b) Making theatre

Many, since the eighteenth century, have discussed the literary aspect of Sedaine's theatre;[5] his own prefaces bear witness to such discussions in his lifetime, and give his response to criticism. But early perceptions of Sedaine's work as innovative, varied music theatre included perspectives stemming from Sedaine's practical work. This experience lay behind the anecdotes related in the prefaces, and formed the theatre that gave rise to controversy.

'Quelques réflexions' provide an essential autobiographical dimension. Pixérécourt published this now-lost manuscript with a note to the effect that one of Sedaine's daughters had passed it to him after Pixérécourt had arranged a pension for her during his directorship at the Opéra-Comique (from April 1824 to August 1827).[6] The intended recipient may have been a biographer; the

---

3 Professor Reinhard Strohm gave me the chance to air the subject in a King's College (London) colloquium in 1990. Dr Elisabeth Cook provided a vital critique of my results at that time. I am grateful for the research resources furnished at my then institution, the University of East Anglia. Mr David Chadd assisted in the interpretation of Sedaine's Latin. Mr Peter Turner's scrupulous work as my assistant in the British Library is a pleasure to acknowledge. Mlle Monique Abud is thanked for allowing me to use her research on *Guillaume Tell*, and also for her researches on my behalf in Paris libraries. Professor Tim Carter scrutinised the complete text in draft and made many improvements. Royal Holloway (University of London) and the Research Committee of its Music Department kindly granted sabbatical leave. The Humanities Research Board of The British Academy awarded a complementary research leave.

4 University of California, Berkeley: Judy Tsou; University of Illinois, Urbana-Champaign: Leslie Troutman; Tulane University, New Orleans; University of Michigan, Ann Arbor, Special Collections: Calvin Elliker; University of Minnesota, Minneapolis; Harvard University, Mass., Eda Kuhn Loeb Music Library: William G. Thauer; New York Public Library, General Research Division and Music Division; New York Public Library for the Performing Arts, Music Division; Columbia University, New York, Rare Books and MSS Division: Rudolph Ellenbogen; University of Cincinnati, Ohio, Gorno Memorial Music Library: Robert Johnson; University of Pennsylvania, Philadelphia, Department of Special Collections.

5 A summary is provided in the Introduction to the present book.

6 Nicole Wild, *Dictionnaire des théâtres parisiens au XIXe siècle* (Paris: Aux Amateurs de Livres, 1989), p. 329.

internal dating (1778) is verifiable from details it gives of Sedaine's latest public work, *Félix ou l'Enfant trouvé.*[7] The papers were presumably returned to Sedaine at his own request, which is explicitly noted on pp. 515–16 of the eventual edition.

The attitude of dominance over composers that Sedaine's earlier prefaces reveal is also evident from this document (albeit, as we shall see, his prefaces by 1778 do reveal more accommodating stances). The assumption that the librettist might choose his composer, even by virtue of giving him a test piece to set to music, is central to the narrative of how François-André Danican Philidor came to compose *Blaise le savetier*. Sedaine credits himself with the right 'instinct' in requesting Philidor be sent to him by Julien Corby, then one of the four co-directors of the Opéra-Comique troupe.

> Amenez-le-moi. – M. Philidor vient, je lui propose de mettre en musique le morceau de *Blaise le savetier*, 'cet air interdit me dit, coquine'. [...] Je l'entends huit jours après, et mon instinct le trouva très-bon. (p. 504)

This sense of pride and even self-congratulation (although counteracted by other rhetorical strategies) is found in certain prefaces; it goes together with Sedaine's tendency to measure himself advantageously against predecessors. For example the 'Réflexions' relegates the pathbreaking comic opera *Les Troqueurs* (1753; text by Jean-Joseph Vadé, set by Antoine Dauvergne) to mere passing mention as an 'essai' even though he knew it was also a paradigmatic work which was still holding the boards (as it would for a full thirty years) and that its varied ensembles included an excellent concluding quartet with copious acting-instructions after Sedaine's own later style. By the same token, he inflates his own originality in conceiving the idea of action-laden ensembles, by using an invented or reconstructed piece of dialogue: 'le plaisir d'essayer de mettre toute une scène en musique, scène qui serait composée de plusieurs interlocuteurs mis en actions'. 'Ah! Monsieur, la grande, la belle idée', Corby is said to have replied, articulating that same authorial self-aggrandisement which irritated Sedaine's opponents when they were led to ironise or parody his prefaces.

Sedaine's total artistic conviction led him on the one hand – here and in his prefaces – to express fulsome appreciation of composers who stayed with him, and on the other to denigrate everyone, including (later) Philidor, whom he construed as enemies because they did not unreservedly support his projects. Philidor, he learns indirectly, has put aside *Le Roi et le fermier* in favour of *Le*

[7] On p. 514 of the Pixérécourt edition Sedaine apparently gives '1778' not '1777' for *Félix*, but provides the correct day and month of production. The following citations all stem from this edition.

Maréchal ferrant around 1761. Later, Sedaine detects dark influences behind Philidor's eventual disinclination to set the former piece at all:

> Philidor ... me l'avait rendu, en me disant qu'il le croyait infaisable. Il y a tout lieu de croire que quelqu'un l'avait dissuadé de le mettre en musique. (p. 507)

Inevitably, Sedaine's attitude to sectors of influence like the aristocracy was ambivalent. He refers to them sometimes with a certain conspicuous respectfulness (mercilessly mocked in a broadside against *Le Déserteur*; see (h) below), while at other times he cynically denigrates their taste and way of behaving. The comte de Maillebois, for one, thought he perceived Sedaine's true mind, or at least is reported to have quipped:

> Ce que j'aime à cet homme-là, C'est qu'il ne nous aime pas.[8]

Sedaine's prefaces, of course, can reveal only the politer tendency; and Sedaine was perhaps not in a position to argue when the Court increasingly asked to have first performances in advance of public showing. In 'Quelques réflexions' these attitudes to private premières could be expressed freely. *Rose et Colas* was asked for by the Duc de Fronsac:

> Je lui confiai le manuscrit, et ce que j'avais dit à M. Monsigny arriva. – Notre intéret, lui dis-je, est que le public en ait la première représentation et non M. le duc; nos gens de qualité vont lire ce manuscrit, le trouveront détestable et nous le rendront sans l'employer; ce qui fut. Mais le mal qu'ils en dirent, toujours à l'oreille, avait prévenu les hautes sociétés. (p. 508)

It is therefore rather ironic that a brief yet unique account of Sedaine on stage, actively preparing a new work and its accompanying libretto for public scrutiny, goes back to an *opéra-comique* for the Duc d'Orléans: it is Charles Collé's report of the author rehearsing his revised version of Collé's and Monsigny's *L'Isle sonnante* for the Comédie-Italienne. At this time (1762–72) Sedaine worked for the most part exclusively with Monsigny, who had replaced Philidor as the librettist's permanent partner.[9] Collé and Monsigny

---

[8] Quoted from Constance-Marie Pipelet's *Eloge historique de M. Sedaine* (1797) by John Dunkley (see n. 44 below), p. 69. On Maillebois, see n. 56 below. Sedaine's altercation at Fontainebleau with Papillon de La Ferté in 1786 is also revealing: Adolphe Jullien, *L'Opéra secret au XVIIIe siècle* (Paris: Edouard Rouveyre, 1880; repr. Geneva, 1978), pp. 51–3.

[9] Space forbids rehearsing the important theme of poet–musician partnership itself, which, following Sedaine's habit, became metaphorically construed as a faithful marriage-partnership in French discourses on opera. It is true that French lyric tragedy had long

were both part of the duc's close circle. When *L'Isle sonnante* was given at Villers-Cotterêts in August 1767 it failed and Collé asked Sedaine to make improvements. A timetable can be constructed: the changes were made between 18 and 20 December 1767; the first rehearsal took place on 25 December; and the first public performance ensued on 4 January.[10] In the meantime, presumably after final textual adjustments, Sedaine must have submitted the libretto to the censors: Marin signed his *approbation* on 2 January and the final *permis* authorising publication, unsigned, was dated 3 January.[11] Collé continues:

> Huit jours auparavant [27 December] je forçai M. Sedaine, qui s'en défendit longtemps et d'une manière très-honnête, d'accepter la moitié de mes honoraires. [...] il étoit juste, d'ailleurs, qu'il fût récompensé des peines qu'il s'est données, et il s'en est donné beaucoup. Il a répété et les acteurs et les actrices, a arrangé toutes leurs positions sur le théâtre; il a fait imprimer la pièce; bref, il m'a déchargé généralement de tous les détails, qui sont immenses à ce théâtre-là. Quant à son travail sur mon poëme, les changemens qu'il y a faits sont peu de chose ...

Collé also implies here that these activities in production and preparation were those normal for Sedaine in his capacity as librettist, even if on this occasion Sedaine was doing – and getting paid for doing – what Collé would as author otherwise have had to do. For Collé himself admits that he was not bothered to rehearse *L'Isle sonnante* even at Villers-Cotterêts, as a consequence of which the actors simply got it wrong:

> Le 9 du courant [August 1767] je reçus une lettre de M. de Monsigny qui revenoit de Villers-Cotterêts où je n'avois point voulu aller, comme je l'ai dit. Je dois me savoir gré à tous égards de m'être épargné ce voyage, puisque mon *Ile sonnante* est tombée tout à plat.

---

established a unique relationship between a literary text and its musical setting. But Sedaine's metaphor dignified the operatic ideal and made the notion itself take root: it implied mutual exploration of possibilities. The notion is satirised in *Correspondance littéraire*, VIII (1 Nov. 1768), p. 196: 'M. Sedaine s'est ainsi marié avec M. Monsigny', etc. Collé's lengthy account (see following note) hangs on this very concept of poet–composer fidelity. See also the commentaries to *Le Roi et le fermier* and *Le Magnifique* in section (h) below.

10 Collé, *Journal et mémoires*, III, pp. 180–81. Collé's given date for the première is of course independently verifiable.

11 These processes and terms are explained in section (d). See [anon.], *L'Isle sonnante, opera-comique en trois actes* (Paris: Claude Hérissant, 1768) (copy consulted: F-Pn (Mus) ThB.3605), p. 52. One should note that the libretto itself testifies to being issued some time during January, since the title-page (hereafter TP) states 'La Partition paroîtra au mois de Février.' In this particular case no *privilège* was sought.

> [...] les acteurs, que je n'ai point été à portée de faire répéter, ont joué sans gaieté et dans un sens directement opposé au genre de la pièce.[12]

And in closing his account Collé mentions a cardinal reason why he, like any *opéra-comique* librettist, should wish his audience to be furnished with a libretto on the first night, if the work contained new music:

> En général, même, on voit aux Italiens [i.e. the Comédie-Italienne theatre] toutes les premières représentations de cette espèce de drames n'avoir pas l'ombre de succès, par cette raison que l'on n'entend pas encore les paroles des ariettes; *Le Roi et le fermier*, *Rose et Colas*, *Tom Jones* et tant d'autres sont tombés à leur première représentation.[13]

As the following sections will show, this issue of audience comprehension in the burgeoning genre was a vital one, and so the publication strategies of Sedaine and other librettists will be fully examined. (It is true that Sedaine's *Rose et Colas* almost failed, but Collé is incorrect when he implies that its libretto was not available to the first-night audience.)

The individual librettist's labour on an opera's behalf, documented by Collé, was a type of work which the latter as a well-patronised *homme de lettres* declined to undertake; it exemplifies the small-scale, personal level at which the cultural industry of *opéra-comique* operated, but also the degree to which those responsible for setting the cultural tone felt uncomfortable with the physicality of the new French type of *opéra-comique*, even some years after the freer style of the Monnet productions at the Fairs had ceased to exist. But then, Sedaine's allegiance before 1762 had been to Monnet's company, not the Comédie-Italienne; in a commentary to *Le Jardinier et son seigneur* in section (h) the characteristic flavour of the Fair style is probed further. Such factors help us to interpret Sedaine's prefaces. These were often limited in circulation to the earliest edition(s) of a piece, yet distributed, as we shall see, to perhaps two thousand theatre-goers and connoisseurs, people who would understand that the whole production had been blocked on stage and produced by Sedaine personally; some might have had access to a rehearsal. Because his art did not conform to expectation, Sedaine was necessarily vulnerable to criticism of several kinds: criticism of his literary authorship, of his work with actors and of his innovations in overall theatrical style and production. His prefaces surely need to be read as anticipations of all these elements.

---

12 *Journal et mémoires*, III, p. 156.

13 Ibid., p. 157.

But he had no lack of supporters, as for example the commentaries on his works in 1768 by the d'Orville brothers demonstrate.[14] And even they did not lavish such praise on Sedaine as did the Swiss theorist of *opéra-comique*, Laurent Garcin.

> La Capitale possède un homme d'un talent bien particulier dans ce genre de Drame. La postérité, non celle qui décerne la gloire à des cendres froides, mais celle qui s'élève continuellement sous nos yeux, le réclame déjà comme le Génie tutélaire de la Scène lyrique. Déjà il a des autels, puisqu'il reçoit des hommages. [...] Le Temps lui élève, quoique lentement, sur ce même Théâtre qu'il réhausse et qu'il annoblit, une Statue, qui est apperçue déjà par ceux devant qui la toile du préjugé est levée, et qui sçavent lire dans l'avenir.[15]

He goes so far as to refer to Sedaine as 'le Racine du Théâtre Italien' (i.e. of the reformed *opéra-comique*), giving reasons for his judgement. But then, the *Correspondance littéraire* dubbed him 'le *Corneille* de l'Opéra-Comique' (February 1777),[16] having already perceived him in 1764 as 'the creator' of the new lyric comedy.[17]

(c) Prefaces by other librettists

The important developments of the 1750s were certainly reflected in a number of *opéra-comique* prefaces by others, a few of which were extraordinarily combative and detailed. As will be explained, the first libretto listed below was not for a French work but belonged with one of the *intermezzi* acted by the Bambini troupe at the Paris Opéra during their extended stay.

---

14 [André-Guillaume Contant d'Orville], *Histoire de l'opéra bouffon* (2 vols, Amsterdam and Paris: Grangé, 1768; repr. Geneva, 1970). The book's *Avertissement* explains that its observations were the result of alternate visits by two brothers to the Paris theatre.

15 [Laurent Garcin], *Traité du Mélo-Drame, ou Réflexions sur la musique dramatique* (Paris: Vallat-la-Chapelle, 1772), p. 69. Garcin's and D'Orville's analyses are explored in my 'Continuing Polarities: Opera Theory and *Opéra-comique*', *French Opera 1730–1830* (Aldershot: Ashgate, 2000).

16 *Correspondance littéraire*, XI (February 1777), p. 427.

17 *Correspondance littéraire*, VI (15 September 1764), p. 71: 'M. Sedaine a créé cette comédie en musique qui a pris la place de l'ancien opéra comique français.' This occurs within an extended critique of Sedaine's work in the genre that seems to have been written by the same hand (probably Grimm's) as wrote the extended pieces on *Le Déserteur* in March–April 1769 and which testified to close personal acquaintanceship with the author. This 1764 essay echoes the published prefaces in several respects.

Table 1: *Opéra-comique* prefaces and essays 1750–64[18]

[1 Dec. 1752	unsigned	*La finta cameriera*	ARM]
3 Feb. 1752	Fleury et al.	*Le Retour favorable*	FSG
3 Feb. 1752	Fleury	*Les Amours de Nanterre* (revival)	FSG
27 July 1752	Fleury	*Le Miroir magique* (revival)	FSL
15 Sep. 1752	Fleury	*Le Rossignol*	FSL
12 July 1753	Fleury	*La Mort de Goret*	FSL
19 July 1753	Rochon de La Vallette	*La Coupe enchantée*	FSL
14 Aug. 1753	Parmentier	*Le Plaisir et l'innocence*	FSL
23 Mar. 1754	Laujon/Favart	*Zéphire et Fleurette*	CI
28 July 1755	Favart	*La Bohémienne*	CI
9 Sep. 1756	Quétant	*Les Amours grenadiers*	FSL
11 Sep. 1756	Favart	*Le Mariage par escalade*	FSL
26 July 1757	Duni	*Le Peintre amoureux de son modèle* (in score, not libretto)	FSL
7 Feb. 1759	La Ribadière	*Les Aveux indiscrets*	FSG
22 Aug. 1761	Quétant	*Le Maréchal ferrant* Title: 'De l'opéra-comique en général'	FSL
23 June 1762	Bibiena	*La Nouvelle Italie*	CI
8 July 1762	Poinsinet	*Sancho Pança*	CI
10 Feb. 1763	Poinsinet	*La Bagarre*	CI
14 June 1764	Framery	*Nanette et Lucas*	CI
20 Dec. 1764	Quétant	*Le Serrurier* Title: 'Essai sur l'opéra-comique'	CI

The majority provide basic information about the history of the work concerned, such as its adaptation from or updating of an earlier work. Certain prefaces, however, contain personal information, throwing the text into a politicised æsthetic arena presumably directed initially at the local circle of initiates referred to above. Even at the Opéra itself the anonymous translator of the Bouffons' version of *La finta cameriera* (originally given in 1737 with words by Federico and music by Latilla) felt constrained to give in a preface his embarrassed excuses: he has been given only four days to complete the work and exculpates himself from all responsibility attaching to the way in which the arias and recitatives were cut down, or even omitted entirely. 'Le Traducteur n'a aucune part dans cette réduction ni pour le fond, ni pour les

[18] Abbreviations: ARM: Académie Royale de Musique; FSG: Foire Saint-Germain; FSL: Foire Saint-Laurent; CI: Comédie-Italienne.

paroles.'[19] Back at the Opéra-Comique, Fleury in *Le Rossignol* describes in the preface how a rival *Rossignol* given at Rouen was investigated and found to have plagiarised particular couplets of which Fleury wants it known he is especially proud, because they were in a particular style (and sung to a beautiful melody by Paradis de Moncrif) recently developed in fact by Favart: 'Ce Couplet étant *fabriqué* dans le stile *doucereux* et *de Bergerie* qui s'est renouvellé de nos jours, & qui règne *souverainement* ...'.[20]

A far more acrid vendetta occurs in Rochon de La Vallette's *La Coupe enchantée*, which amounts to a *pièce à clef* explained in the preface, directed by its author against a former lover whose supposedly fickle behaviour has inspired this La Fontaine adaptation on the subject of infidelity. Thus the dedication: 'Epître à Madame D*** L****: Adorable Cloris / Que direz-vous de mon audace? / Quoi! vous offrir la Dédicace / D'un ouvrage de si bas prix / D'un Opéra comique?' The whole work is to be understood in the Parisian context both as illustrative of *mœurs* in general and as personal history.

> Comme cette Pièce est une peinture trop commune des ménages de Paris, j'ai cru y trouver quelque chose d'analogue avec le votre [the dedicatee's]; on y voit le Mathurin qui, selon le Portrait qu'il fait de sa femme, & les heureuses présomptions qui en résultent, semble vous peindre d'après nature ...[21]

In 1755 Favart's version of the intermezzo *La zingara* (*La Bohémienne*) contained a preface explaining that since the piece was more a translation than anything, the French words of its arias could not be taken as constituting plagiarism. But Contant d'Orville's *Histoire de l'opéra bouffon* implies that this preface, unexpectedly issued on the day of first performance, was part of a strategy by Favart to 'eclipse', as he puts it, Moustou's equally faithful version of *La zingara* that had appeared the year before, in July 1754.

> La *Bohémienne* ... fut rendue supérieurement par Madame *Favart* & Monsieur Rochard. La Pièce parut imprimée dès le premier jour, comme les paroles d'opéra, pour l'intelligence des airs; ce qui a depuis passé en usage, au grand plaisir de la critique, dont le sarcasme réfléchi porte plus sûrement ses coups. Le foible intérêt qu'on retire

---

19 *La finta cameriera, Intermezzo per musica* (Paris: Veuve Delormel, 1752), pp. [2]–[3].

20 Jacques Fleury, *Le Rossignol* (n.p., 1753), pp. [iii]–[iv]; the couplets in question, in scene III, used the Moncrif melody known under the *timbre* 'Quand vous entendrez le doux Zéphir'.

21 An ironic reference, since Mathurin alone of the villagers has a faithful wife: *La Coupe enchantée, opéra comique en un acte* (Paris: Duchesne, 1753), p. 4.

> d'une vente précipitée, ne peut compasser le danger où l'on s'expose.[22]

Favart's strategy of simultaneous publication carried precisely the same advantages and dangers later met with by Sedaine when he decided to adopt the same course.

The modest financial compensation remarked on here by d'Orville proved to be no deterrent to Favart: perhaps feeling the effects of 'le sarcasme réfléchi', Favart riposted with startling frankness in *Le Mariage par escalade* the next year, whose preface sought to counter apparent rumours that its author had contracted to work only for the Comédie-Italienne, and now received a regular *pension* from them. The preface also replied to unnamed critics who had objected to Favart's robust characterisation of English characters (in what was a *pièce d'occasion* on the capture of Minorca from the English at the beginning of what became the Seven Years' War). This defence of both personal and artistic *amour-propre* and principle was to become a hallmark of Sedaine's prefaces. As we shall see in several places in section (h), Favart and Sedaine maintained good personal relations.

The only preface to be penned by a composer was that by Egidio Duni in the score to his very first *opéra-comique* for Paris; it constitutes a surprisingly sharp attack on Rousseau both for denigrating the French language and for hypocrisy in using French in *Le Devin du village*.[23] In completely different vein, Framery's 1764 preface places on record the extent to which the Comédie-Italienne's artists had helped him revise and improve his work; his acknowledgement of individual singers would be echoed much later in two of Sedaine's last prefaces.

The early 1760s, doubtless stimulated by Sedaine's own early prefaces and the developing genre, saw a surge of more ambitious and longer prefaces. Antoine-François Quétant's five-page 'Essai sur l'opéra-comique', placed at the end of a libretto in 1765, shows the degree of material and theoretical expansion attained by librettos as instruments of debate.[24] In 1761 the same author's prefatory 'De l'opéra-comique en général' had extended to three pages constituting 'la défense d'un genre de poëme, que bien des personnes regardent comme frivole':[25] although 'smaller' than other genres, it follows the same rules and must be thought of as an 'ouvrage dramatique'. Jean Galli de Bibiena's preface to *La Nouvelle Italie* (1762) ran to five pages in such small

---

22 D'Orville, *Histoire de l'opéra bouffon*, I, pp. 66–7.

23 *Le Peintre amoureux de son modèle. Opéra comique de Mr Anseaume. Mise en musique par Mr Duny* (Paris: Chez l'auteur, n.d.).

24 Antoine-François Quétant, *Le Serrurier* (Paris: Duchesne, 1765), pp. 43–7.

25 Quétant, *Le Maréchal ferrant, Seconde Edition* (Paris: Claude Hérissant, 1761), pp. i–iv.

print that it permitted him to report in detail the objections raised against his libretto by the very actors now appearing in it, all in the attempt to attract public indulgence towards the piece, while not trying to deny that the libretto was a dual-language vehicle for the famous singer Mlle Piccinelli.[26]

Antoine-Henri Poinsinet avowed himself a disciple of Sedaine in 'Epître liminaire à Sedaine' in the form of verses heading the libretto *Sancho-Pança dans son isle* (1762), in which he both proposed that Molièresque comedy, not tragedy, was apt for the age, and reflected on the nature of the text–music relationship.[27] The same author's *La Bagarre* (1763) went to a further extreme in an extraordinary ten-page preface closely emulating Sedaine's beliefs and his combative mode. Like Sedaine, he discusses the difficulties of rehearsing complicated ensembles and retails anecdotes about contested premières encountered in *opéra-comique* (including mention of Sedaine's *On ne s'avise jamais de tout*) and the inability of actors to give sufficient attention in early performances to *jeu muet*. Poinsinet concluded with a strident attack on Establishment taste and on its main 'trumpet' of publicity, the *Mercure de France*, acting on behalf of the Paris Opéra at the expense of the new genre.

> Les Religieux défenseurs de l'ancien récitatif déclament contre nos Ariettes comiques, & le Mercure qui est le très-humble serviteur et la trompette de l'Opéra, ne manque pas d'informer les Provinces que tous les opéras-comiques qu'il appelle du nouveau genre sont détestables. Cela n'est-il pas fou, je dirai plus, n'est-il pas humiliant pour l'Académie Royale de Musique de souffrir que pour l'élever, on cherche aussi visiblement à détruire un genre qui lui est totalement opposé ...? Les grotesques Flamands ont-ils jamais fait tort aux chefs-d'œuvres d'Italie ...?[28]

Poinsinet's style here was never adopted by Sedaine (who went on to conquer the Opéra himself in *Aline, reine de Golconde*) and was hilariously mocked by Contant d'Orville, who concluded:

> Il est naturel qu'un père tendre aime ses enfans, quelques difformes qu'ils soient; mais cette amitié aveugle ne le met pas en droit d'exiger

---

[26] Anna Piccinelli had arrived from Italy the year before, and went on to join the Opéra.

[27] Sedaine had already challenged the relevance and importance of tragedy in his poem *Le Vaudeville* (1756): see the discussion in Mark Ledbury, 'Sedaine and the Question of Genre', pp. 19–20 above.

[28] Antoine-Henri Poinsinet, *La Bagarre, opera bouffon en un acte* (Paris: Duchesne, 1758 [*recte* 1763]), pp. 3–13 [13].

qu'on leur prodigue des caresses, ni qu'un peintre gracieux les choisisse pour modèle.[29]

(d) Bibliographical and other practicalities

The present study is based on the examination of all early editions of Sedaine's theatre texts with music in the British Library, and of almost all early copies in the following departments of the Bibliothèque Nationale de France: Musique, Opéra, Imprimés. Many early editions have been examined at the Bibliothèque de l'Arsenal. The search for prefaces extended to the United States, on the basis of *National Union Catalog*, involving twenty-one libraries, over half of which responded. Some 250 exemplars have been scrutinised, not counting these American copies. Reference is consistently made to Sonneck's catalogue of the Library of Congress collection.[30]

In order to locate libretto prefaces one often has to have recourse to the earliest edition(s) of a libretto, and in order to find these one has to be able to identify them as such. This is possible so long as one has access to certain independent pieces of information, and so long as one also takes due account of features attaching to the librettos themselves: collation of pages, their size, a careful note of the wording and disposition of title-pages. The details of precise copies used for preparation of the editions of Sedaine's prefaces below have been noted.

If a work was given at court, whether before or after a public première, it was subject to a separate edition, containing information particular to itself, such as names of performers and any specially written pieces of text. These were usually issued by the appointed printer, the Ballard family. Librettos for public performances were issued by one of the other *éditeurs*, such as Duchesne or Hérissant, who was Sedaine's main printer–bookseller for many years.[31] More work remains to be done on the business relationship between an author, the printer and the royal patron. A valuable letter from Sedaine to Favart in 1770, which is quoted in the commentary on *Thémire* in section (h) below, alludes to a lawsuit recently won by Sedaine allowing his usual *éditeur* to produce the court copy of this work.

---

29 D'Orville, *Histoire de l'opéra bouffon*, II, pp. 10–11. *La Bagarre*, as he notes, failed in the theatre.

30 Oscar George Theodore Sonneck, *Library of Congress. Catalogue of Opera Librettos Printed before 1800* (2 vols, Washington: Government Printing Office, 1914).

31 'Claude-Jean-Baptiste II Hérissant, fils de Claude-J.B. I, libraire à Paris depuis 1740 ... Il mourut en 1775. Son commerce fut repris par sa veuve ...'; he issued certain *opéras-comiques* by Monsigny. Anik Devriès and François Lesure, *Dictionnaire des éditeurs de musique français* (2 vols, Geneva: Minkoff, 1979), I, p. 80.

The use of the word 'edition' in such contexts is justified by its early uses. We find a precious chance reference to the word and to the duration of a certain print-run, as follows: in 1762 Favart's libretto for *Annette et Lubin* (a popular and important work) was referred to in *Mercure de France* for March 1762 (p. 200, note f): 'La première Edition, déjà presqu'épuisée, se trouve à Paris chez Duchesne'. The first night of the run had occurred only on 15 February, and the libretto's *approbation* is dated 12 February. Assuming that the *privilège* advertised by Duchesne had already been obtained, we can conjecture that the libretto was issued quickly, the print-run thereafter supplying only six weeks of demand. Further information on these processes is seen in a moment.

Additionally, but exceptionally, Sedaine might issue a later edition with a particular title-page indication showing its distinct status: *On ne s'avise jamais de tout* received a 'Seconde Edition augmentée', initially by Claude Hérissant, 1761; *Le Déserteur* received a 'Seconde Edition, revue par l'Auteur' by Claude Hérissant, 1770; *Félix ou l'Enfant trouvé* received a 'Nouvelle Edition, Corrigée et conforme à la Partition' by Broulhiet of Toulouse in 1782; and *Richard Cœur-de-Lion* received a 'Nouvelle édition, conforme à la partition gravée' by Les Libraires Associés, Paris, in 1786.[32] The differences between this last edition, which lacks a preface, and its predecessor (the first edition of the text, published earlier in same year by Brunet) are very instructive. They seem to show Sedaine in the act of refining the production details of his work, even after it had in this case been well polished between the première of 21 October 1784 and first publication by Brunet.[33] Most changes concern additions to the stage-directions: small but telling details that help to effect smoother transitions and increase the naturalism of the illusion. For example, there is the added direction given to the chorus during the overture: after 'plusieurs paysans ... en veste, [qui] portent leurs habits' is added 'et des havre-sacs vuides. Ils traversent le théâtre, & pour avoir le temps d'y chanter, ils ont l'air d'attendre des Camarades qui les suivent.' Very effective changes were made near the end of Act I, for originally Marguerite went into Williams's house without having heard Blondel play the Romance. In Act II Sedaine added to the king's reactions upon hearing the Romance: 'C'est Blondel! Ah grands Dieux! (*Il pose son visage sur ses mains.*)'

One should perhaps note that the *Bibliographie chronologique* of eighteenth-century imprints by Pierre M. Conlon has no occasion to list variant editions or impressions of this material and may not always describe a first

---

[32] *Aucassin et Nicolette*, which was issued in both four-act (1779) and three-act (1782) versions, is a special case.

[33] Publication by Brunet was held back while Sedaine wrote a fourth act, subsequently rejected. See Charlton, *Grétry*, and notes to the preface in section (h) below.

edition.[34] Datings become easier with the passage of time: once a court première had taken place, that place and date were recorded normally on all future title-pages, except those of editions for subsequent court performances. J. M. Quérard's *La France littéraire* does give variant editions and *éditeurs*, but no page-numbers.[35] As we shall see from consideration of print-runs below, a full bibliographical analysis of *opéra-comique* librettos will be an enormous future task.

A standard early libretto measures, untrimmed, c.13 or 13.5 cm across and c.21 cm down, octavo.[36] Later editions of Sedaine's and others' librettos tended to be issued in smaller octavo formats (typically 10 cm across and 17 cm down) and to be set in smaller print, occupying fewer pages, as well as losing any preface and *privilège* that had been present. However, court librettos were often larger than the more generous standard size and contained more pages, work for work, than the latter did because of often more generous typesetting and listing of the names of the singers and dancers, both solo and *corps*.

As was noted above from evidence in d'Orville and Collé, and is clear from the tenor of certain prefaces, Sedaine as author, and certainly not the theatre company concerned, was responsible for arranging the printing of a libretto. As with books, the normal process for dramatic literature was for the author to sell the manuscript at a price apparently 'calculated by the bookseller on the returns which he could expect from the first edition'.[37] Lough's study demonstrates such lump sums received (or expected) from the sale of several five-act plays, ranging between 960 *livres* in 1749 for a reprint edition to 3,600 *livres* for a new play. However, Rousseau apparently earned 500 *livres* from

---

34 For *On ne s'avise jamais de tout* Conlon's entry for a C. Hérissant (1761) edition indicates 48 pages of text and four of music, which seems to correspond (on account of this pagination) to the edition issued after the Versailles performance of 2 December that year, referred to on the title-page, whereas another 1761 edition by the same publisher whose title-page does not refer to the court performance must be regarded as anterior; it contains [iv] + 44 pages plus (in some exemplars) a further four of music (music pages were generally detachable and often separately paginated). Pierre M. Conlon, *Le Siècle des Lumières. Bibliographie chronologique* (Geneva: Droz, 1983 etc., in progress), XIII (for the years 1761–3), p. 127. This opera is admittedly one of the most tricky cases to solve, since it was popular and long-lived.

35 J. M. Quérard, *La France littéraire, ou Dictionnaire bibliographique* (Paris, 1838), IX, pp. 9–11.

36 Gatherings of four or eight pages, watermark at head of spine-fold. Criteria from Philip Gaskell, *A New Introduction to Bibliography* (Oxford: Clarendon, 1972), pp. 84–5.

37 John Lough, *Writer and Public in France from the Middle Ages to the Present Day* (Oxford: Clarendon Press, 1978), p. 201.

his bookseller for the libretto of *Le Devin du village*.[38] Clearly the differential reflected the far fewer words to be set up in type in a sung libretto.

In France nothing could be published or sold officially outside the legally defined systems which obtained more or less continuously between Louis XIV's time and the Revolution.[39] Four chief agents of power remained constant: the Chancellor (*Chancelier*) or Keeper of the Seals, whose overall permission (*permission de sceau*) was needed and with whom a manuscript of the work was deposited; the *lieutenant de police*, whose permission (the *permis*) was needed; the censor, working under the authority of the *lieutenant*, whose *approbation* was needed; and the Parisian guild (*communauté*) of printer–booksellers, a powerful cartel of interests founded in 1618. All official publications had to be registered with this guild in their chambers (*chambre syndicale*), according to a famous and wide-ranging law or *règlement* of 23 February 1723.[40] Alongside this structure ran the tradition of *privilèges*: a bookseller could request a *privilège* from the Chancellor giving him exclusive rights as publisher of a text for a fixed duration, often six years. Until Louis XVI's repeal of the laws on bookselling dated 30 August 1777 a *privilège* was understood to be renewable. After 1777 a text entered the public domain when a bookseller's *privilège* expired, after a minimum ten years. The same new rules also suppressed certain *chambres syndicales* and gave authors the right to apply for their own *privilège*, which would be perpetual.[41] Whether before or after 1777, booksellers were never obliged to obtain a *privilège*, only the necessary *permissions*.

The evidence of all these procedures is habitually found in librettos, and so we can deduce much about a complicated area of activity: the practical stages performed by Sedaine between finalising a manuscript libretto and taking delivery of the printed artefact. Collé was not exaggerating about 'tous les détails, qui sont immenses'. Deductions are possible owing to two factors: first, the official procedures were always certified somewhere with an exact date; second, many dated certifications were reproduced in librettos. The named censor's dated form of words and his *approbation*, the named *lieutenant de police*'s dated form of words and his permit, the dated registration with the

---

[38] Lough, *Writer and Public*, pp. 202–10. Three of his examples concern the bookseller Prault *fils*; but Duchesne (who was Sedaine's earlier bookseller) paid Mme de Graffigny 2000 *livres* for *Cénie* in 1750.

[39] Lough, *Writer and Public*, pp. 173ff; Raymond Birn, 'The Profits of Ideas: *privilèges en librairie* in Eighteenth-Century France', *Eighteenth-Century Studies*, IV/2 (1970–71), pp. 131–68.

[40] It is not appropriate to describe the many anomalies operating within and without this main framework, or the enormous trade in illicit and imported publications. These elements are not irrelevant to the world of librettos, but must be set aside for the moment.

[41] Birn, 'The Profits of Ideas', pp. 131–2. An author in these cases needed to reach a personal arrangement with a bookseller, if not undertake publication themselves.

bookseller's guild (*Communauté des Imprimeurs Libraires de Paris*) at their *chambre syndicale*, and the entire (usually two-page) text of a royal *privilège* with dates: the first two of these certifications always appear, the last two only sometimes appear. But we know that the printed libretto is reproducing the certification as it was entered upon the author's manuscript libretto, chiefly because one surviving manuscript libretto, not by Sedaine, shows these formulæ, signatures and dates duly in place.[42]

Before we turn to datings as such, a few supplementary remarks will help relate the official frameworks outlined above to the production of librettos in particular. Regarding censorship, librettos were in the care of one small part of a large machine, 'a growing army of censors – 73 in 1745, reaching 178 in 1789'.[43] For the years between *Blaise le savetier* and *On ne s'avise jamais de tout* (1759–61) two censors operated, Crébillon giving the *approbation* and either Bertin or Sartine the *permis*. From 1762 and *Le Roi et le fermier* to 1770 and *Thémire* (also 1771, *Le Mort marié*, spoken version) only one censor operated, giving both permissions in a single sentence. That censor was usually Marin, evidently the same *censeur de police* of that name who got into hot water over Favart's *Les Moissonneurs* (1768) when he departed from the approved wording.[44] From 1772 (*Le Faucon*) to 1787 (*Le Comte d'Albert*) the system reverted to two censors, and presumably remained in that form.

My own research regarding *privilèges* is still incomplete. The simple existence of a *privilège* is always signalled on a libretto's title-page; *opéras-comiques* without such protection simply advertised 'Avec Approbation et Permission', e.g. Sedaine's *Les Femmes vengées* or *L'Huitre et les plaideurs*. In some fortunate cases the surviving librettos appear complete with the text of the *privilège* generally reproduced at the end (they were officially supposed to be displayed here or at the head of the libretto). But the majority of protected librettos have lost the text of their *privilège*, or the wording refers the reader elsewhere, as for example 'Le Privilège & l'Enregistrement [i.e. at the *chambre syndicale*] se trouvent à la fin du recueil des Opera-Comiques' (*Le Diable à quatre*) or 'se trouvent au nouveau Théâtre de la Foire' (*Blaise le savetier*). Applications for *privilèges* were, to judge from their own wording, made

42 It is *Zélie et Lindor* by H. F. Pelletier, music by A. J. Rigade, first given on 12 November 1763, and housed with the large libretto collection in F-Pn (Mus) which I believe can be associated with the Comédie-Italienne company itself: ThB.2151 contains the autographs of Marin (the *approbation*) and Sartine (the permission to perform) on f.15v.

43 Lough, *Writer and Public*, p. 174.

44 Marin recommended it in personal terms and lost his *pension* of 2000 *livres*, at least temporarily. See *Correspondance littéraire*, VIII (15 March 1768), pp. 43–4 and report in Corinne Pré, 'Le Livret d'opéra-comique en France de 1741 à 1789', Doctorat ès Lettres, U. de Paris III, 1982, p. 779. For more information about Sartine, Marin and the business of permissions, see John Dunkley, 'Introduction' to Michel-Jean Sedaine, *Le Philosophe sans le sçavoir*, ed. John Dunkley (Runnymede Books: Egham, 1993), pp. 65–6.

through the office of the *Chancelier*, the same who under the terms of the document was mandated to receive a finally approved and adjusted libretto manuscript into his permanent care. (This archive was apparently destroyed during the Paris Commune.) The same office handled the overall process of permission, i.e. the Chancellor's *permission de sceau*, which was tacitly expressed in the libretto publication within the censorial *approbation* and *permis*. Thus the wording of Marin's *approbation* for *Thémire* shows that it was the *Chancelier*'s office which passed him the request (if not also the manuscript) in the first place.[45] After the changes of 1777 the Chancellor was allowed to award a *permission simple* as well as a *permission de sceau*.[46]

Claude Hérissant was granted three-year *privilèges* for *Thémire* and *Le Déserteur*, protecting himself against piracy and profit by others; for *Le Roi et le fermier* however he obtained a *privilège* that protected not just this text for six years, but also any subsequent new 'Pièces de Théâtre, & autres Ouvrages de M. Sedaine' within this period; thus *Rose et Colas* and *L'Anneau perdu et retrouvé* profited from this same *privilège*, and presumably also *Aline, reine de Golconde*, making an estimation of their detailed publication chronology easier for us (see below).

The most haphazardly placed indications of process concerned the registrations with the *chambre syndicale*; on one hand a police *permis* could be granted explicitly on condition the particular manuscript be registered, and a fee paid (the allowable period for this process was three months); on the other hand it often happens that registration passes without mention. The answer lies partly in the fact that there was no fixed order in which the processes occurred. Cases such as *Le Roi et le fermier* (see Table 3) indicate that the syndical registration could legitimately precede the censorship process. *Aucassin et Nicolette* illustrates another apparently anomalous question: the way that an original *permis* seemingly applied in advance to a rewritten version of a given *opéra-comique*. Whatever the official rules may have been, the original 1779 *permis* of this work and even its original date were retained for publication of the three-act version of 1782; '4' (acts) simply became '3'.

Let us finally turn to the issue of dating, a branch of bibliographical research for *opéra-comique* (maybe also for *tragédie-lyrique*) which is quite new. Collation of datings attaching to the rules of book-production will enable us to assess quite precisely the timetable of issue of a first-edition libretto, and thus its preface. In turn, this allows us to judge the intended impact of Sedaine's words within the public sphere, in sections (e) and (h) below, and the identity of Sedaine himself, considered as a published author. The importance

---

45 'APPROBATION. J'ai lû, par ordre de Monseigneur le Chancelier, *THÉMIRE, Pastorale*, & je crois qu'on peut en permettre l'impression. A PARIS, ce 20 Octobre 1770. MARIN.'

46 Birn, 'The Profits of Ideas', p. 151, n. 49.

of authors and relation of the book trade to the governance of *ancien-régime* France and its public sphere have been newly re-examined by researchers such as Roger Chartier, whose work provides a separate and parallel overview to the accounts following.[47]

We have seen that up to four different dates can potentially appear on a printed libretto in addition to the date(s) of first performance(s) and the year of publication, also habitually given on the title-page. They are: the date of the granting of a royal *privilège* if one had been applied for and allowed; the date on which the libretto was registered with the *chambre syndicale*; the date on which the censor issued his *approbation*; and the date on which the police representative issued a *permis* to publish and perform. We can use what information we have to judge the date by when Sedaine, or perhaps any similar author, submitted one or more manuscript text copies for the Chancellor's approval and to his bookseller for printing. Sometimes it was a last-minute affair, reserved until after the rehearsals had been going for some time and changes made. Using the example of *Le Roi et le fermier* we can gauge that if short of time, the author and *éditeur* could compress the whole business of printing into four or five days. The permission is dated (Friday) 19 November and the first night was (Monday) 22 November:

> J'ai lû, par ordre de Monseigneur le Chancelier, *Le Roi et le Fermier, Comédie*; & je crois qu'on peut en permettre l'impression. A Paris, ce 19 Novembre 1762. *MARIN*.

Obviously we do not know when Hérissant's men began setting up the text; but three days after the first night, on Thursday 25 November, Sedaine received his first printed copies, as demonstrated by the letter quoted in the commentary to this work within section (h) below. In planning to issue the preface of *Rose et Colas* (1764) on the first night, as its text states, Sedaine took care to have the *approbation* cleared further in advance: it was granted three weeks before the première. An interesting detail from printing history in general suggests that prefaces might well have been expected by the printer at a late stage:

> Books were normally imposed as a series of regular sheets of the chosen format, the preliminaries being printed last, perhaps (if they were not extensive) filling up the last sheet of text and then being detached so that they could be placed at the front.[48]

---

[47] Roger Chartier, *The Cultural Origins of the French Revolution*, trans. Lydia G. Cochrane (Durham, NC etc.: Duke University Press, 1991), especially chapter 2 ('The Public Sphere and Public Opinion') and chapter 3 ('The Way of Print'); Robert Darnton, *The Forbidden Best-Sellers of Pre-Revolutionary France* (London: HarperCollins, 1996).

[48] Gaskell, *New Introduction to Bibliography*, p. 108.

Yet even if all possible dates are present, analysis shows, as already noted, that there was no single order in which the official procedures were carried out. More than one manuscript copy of a libretto must have been available in most cases, simply to make the normal processes work. For example, in the case of *Thémire* one manuscript must have served for the Fontainebleau rehearsals and première on 20 October 1772 and a second for the censor Marin, who approved the text on the same day in Paris; the same copy probably served for Le Begue, who signed the *privilège* on 24 October. The Le Begue copy was duly registered for the *chambre syndicale* by the then Syndic, J. Hérissant, on 13 November.

Having outlined official publication procedures it remains to summarise, in chronological order, datings for Sedaine's unprefaced works with music, including unpublished works and incomplete entries.

Table 2: Works with music lacking any known preface

TITLE	PREMIÈRE	*APPROBATION/ PERMIS*	*PRIVILEGE/* SYNDICAL REG.
Le Diable à quatre	19 Aug. 1756 (FSL)	*Approbation* and *Permis* 1 Feb. 1757	*Privilège* granted to Duchesne
Les Troqueurs dupés	6 March 1760 (FSG)	unpublished	
On ne s'avise jamais de tout	14 Sep. 1761 (FSL)	*Approbation* 2 Sep. 1761; *Permis* 5 Sep. 1761	*Privilège* granted to Claude Hérissant (see TP of F-Pa, Rf.13.612) Registered: 11 Sept. 1761
Philémon et Baucis	1766 (Bagnolet)	unpublished[49]	

[49] Received as a text at the Académie Royale de Musique in 1782.

TITLE	PREMIÈRE	*APPROBATION/ PERMIS*	*PRIVILEGE/* SYNDICAL REG.
Le Faucon	2 Nov. 1771 (Fontainebleau) 9 Mar. 1772 (CI)	*Approbation* and *Permis* 18 March 1772	*Privilège* granted to Claude Hérissant
Le Mort marié (version with music)[50]	12 Feb. 1777 (CI)	unpublished	
Félix ou l'Enfant trouvé	10 Nov. 1777 (Fontainebleau); 24 Nov. 1777 (CI)	*Approbation* and *Permis* 19 Nov. 1777	No *privilège* granted
Aucassin et Nicolette (3-act version)	7 Jan. 1782 (CI)	*Approbation* and *Permis* 31 Dec. 1779	No *privilège* granted
Thalie	28 April 1783 (CI)	*Approbation* 14 April 1783; *Permis* 18 April 1783	No *privilège* granted
Alcine	1785–6: unperformed	unpublished	
Amphitrion	15 Mar. 1786 (Versailles); 15 July 1788 (ARM)	*Approbation* 11 July 1788	*Privilège* granted to De Lormel
L'Anneau perdu et retrouvé (newly set by Chardiny)	11 Sep. 1788 (CI)	unpublished	
Raoul Barbe-Bleue	2 Mar. 1789 (CI)	published 1791	(not applicable)
Pagamin de Monègue	received 1782/1785 (ARM); 29 Mar. 1792 (Th. Louvois)	unpublished	

[50] The spoken version has a short preface (Paris: Herissant, 1771).

Basile	17 Oct. 1792 (CI)	published 1792 but no copy known
La Blanche haquenée	22 May 1793 (OC)	unpublished
Robin et Marion	1795; unperformed	unpublished
L'Amoureux goutteux	date unknown; unperformed	unpublished

In the single case (*Guillaume Tell*) where a published libretto containing a preface by Sedaine is also known to survive in manuscript form, we unfortunately find no attached manuscript preface. There was a substantial delay in publishing this libretto, paralleled in Sedaine's career by the case of *Richard Cœur-de-Lion*, and the manuscript text attaches to earlier 1791/2 versions. The preface must have been prepared at the time when the definitive version (first staged on 30 September 1792) was published bearing the date 'An II': this marked the start of the Republican calendar, which commenced on 22 September 1793, shortly after the declaration of the Terror.[51]

Table 3: Works with music: dating of prefaces

SHORT TITLE	PRIVATE PREM.	PUBLIC PREM.	*APPROB./ PERMIS*	*PRIVILEGE/* REGN	PUBN DATE
Anacréon	1754	13/12/58			1760
Blaise	–	9/3/1759	24/6/1759 27/6/1759	Yes[52]	1759
L'Huitre	–	17/9/1759	10/7/1761 (*permis* only)	No; reg. 17/7/1761	1761

[51] Further information is found below at the end of section (h).

[52] Cf. F-Pn (Mus), Th.488: 'Le Privilège et l'Enregistrement se trouvent au nouveau Théâtre de la Foire.'

SHORT TITLE	PRIVATE PREM.	PUBLIC PREM.	*APPROB./ PERMIS*	*PRIVILEGE/* REGN	PUBN DATE
Le Jardinier	–	18/2/1761	3/5/1761 (both)	Yes; no reg. date	1761
Roi et fermier	–	22/11/62	19/11/62 (both)	9/6/1762 27/8/1762	1762
Rose et Colas	–	8/3/1764	15/2/1764 (both)	9/6/1762 27/8/1762	1764
L'Anneau	–	20/8/1764	22/8/1764 (both)	9/6/1762 27/8/1762	1764
Aline	–	15/4/66[53]	14/3/1766	?9/6/1762 ?27/8/1762	1766
Les Sabots	1768[54]	26/10/68	29/10/68 (both)	Yes	1768
Le Déserteur	–	6/3/1769	1/4/1769 (both)	10/5/1769 23/6/1769	1769
Thémire	Aug. 1770[55]	26/11/70	20/10/70 (both)	24/10/1770 13/11/1770	1770
Le Magnifique	–	4/3/1773	20/2/1773 21/2/1773	Yes	1773
Femmes vengées	c1767[56]	20/3/1775	5/2/1775 7/2/1775	No	1775

[53] Libretto TP gives 10 April, not 15 April, as first performance date.

[54] 'En 1768, pour une petite fête à Auteuil, chez M. Bertin, je fis la petite pièce des *Sabots*': 'Quelques réflexions', p. 510.

[55] 'J'ai fait, en 1770, la petite pastorale de *Thémire*, pour une fête à Auteuil, chez M. Bertin': 'Quelques réflexions', p. 511. The *Correspondance littéraire*, IX (1 Dec. 1770), p. 173, reports this as having taken place in August, and names M. Bertin 'le trésorier des parties casuelles'; his wife took the part of Thémire. Seen by the Duc d'Aumont, it was requested to be given at Fontainebleau, where the same source reports its failure on 20 October 1770.

[56] 'Quelques réflexions', p. 514, notes a prose version given for the Comte de Maillebois, eight years before the public première.

Aucassin (4)	30/12/79[57]	3/1/1780	31/12/79 (both)	No	1780
Richard	–	21/10/84	19/10/84 (both)	?	1786
Le Comte d'Albert	13/11/86[58]	8/2/1787	31/1/1787 5/2/1787	No	1787
Guillaume Tell	–	9/4/1791	–	(not applicable)	An II (1793-94)

Among other things, Tables 2 and 3 show that Sedaine was cautious and did not in his earliest works follow Favart's newer practice of publication in time for a first night: the dates above indicate that he could perhaps have issued *On ne s'avise jamais de tout* on 14 September. This work was in any case a turning-point, and is discussed in a moment. Sedaine therefore often risked the public's incomprehension of his words in the solo and ensemble numbers; indeed, he addresses this topic more than once in prefaces. Subsequently, in *Le Roi et le fermier* and *Rose et Colas*, he sets out to be read by his earliest audiences in a way that will entertain and woo them, deflecting shafts of criticism as well as he can by mixing various different topics with the principles of his music-dramatic theory. In 1769 Sedaine's great success *Le Déserteur* was (for reasons unknown) not prepared for publication at the first night: the author ruefully refers in its preface to various resulting difficulties of incomprehension in Act I.

The case of *Richard Cœur-de-Lion* is a parallel example inasmuch as Sedaine held back publication until well after the première, even though the *permis* had been granted in advance; publication was delayed until 1786, after the work had been tried out in an interim version.[59] The case, if exceptional, warns us that other works with early *permis* may not necessarily have been published in time for a public première. For example all librettos so far seen of *Le Magnifique* mention the court performance date of 26 March on the title-page (posterior to the public première) although the *permis* was obtained in February.[60]

57 Royal command, Versailles.

58 Royal command, Fontainebleau.

59 Later and posthumously published in 1822–3 in Lepeintre Desroches's *Suite du répertoire du Théâtre Français*; full details in the notes to the preface, below.

60 Indeed Ballard published a libretto for Versailles which is dated 19 March, and may constitute the earliest published edition. Perhaps unexpectedly, this does contain Sedaine's preface. More work remains to be done regarding the *privilège*, however. In principle the cycles of court performances warrant further research than I have given them. Court taste (as

It remains to mention the case of *On ne s'avise jamais de tout*, Sedaine's most important musical work, along with *Raoul Barbe-Bleue*, not to contain a preface. There are several reasons why it is worth explaining the case more fully, reasons connected with Sedaine's claim that this work was of itself instrumental in bringing about the closure of the still-unofficial Opéra-Comique company, operating seasonally at the Fairs, and its merger with the king's troupe, the Comédie-Italienne. What is not in dispute is that from 3 February 1762, the first day of the amalgamated companies, *On ne s'avise jamais de tout* was acted on seven successive nights, an achievement of the very greatest rarity. Although the many librettos examined carry no preface, the work's prefatory material in one particular edition amounts to a tacit preface whose meaning is elucidated in the 'Quelques réflexions'. The première at the Foire St Laurent (14 September 1761) was followed on 2 December by a Versailles performance using a substantially new cast, since the court felt awkward about employing the Fair company. The new cast was made up from three of the royal companies of which the identities were, unusually, appended to the actors' names, as follows:[61]

M. Tue	M. Caillot, de la Comédie Italienne
Lise	Mlle Villette, de la Comédie Italienne
Dorval	M. Rochard, de la Comédie Italienne
Margarita	Mlle Le Miere, de l'Académie Royale de Musique
Un Commissaire	M. Larivé, de l'Académie Royale de Musique
Un Porte-Faix	M. Gelin de l'Académie Royale de Musique
Une Revendeuse	M. Champville, de la Comédie-Italienne[62]
Un Clerc de Commissaire	M. Preville, de la Comédie Françoise.

'Quelques réflexions' comments in such a way as to suggest that these institutional affiliations were, to those in the know, enough to suggest not just the artistic nonsense of grafting Sedaine's style on to performers from different and alien theatre traditions, but also the cultural sclerosis that produced the attempt to begin with.

> Depuis les éloges donnés à *On ne s'avise jamais de tout*, on voulut le donner sur le théâtre de la cour; mais comment dégrader le théâtre

---

both Collé and Sedaine noted) was not the same as that of Paris, and the way of mounting a work differed because court officials tended to interfere with what would otherwise have been the author's responsibilities.

[61] Copies referred to: GB-Lbl 86.a.15 and 1608/5834; F-Pn Yth.13037/8.

[62] Role not present in the original Foire St-Laurent libretto. But cross-dressed roles were not uncommon at the Opéra-Comique.

> royal au point d'y recevoir des acteurs forains? Pour obvier à ce malheur, on s'avisa de faire jouer la pièce par les acteurs de la Comédie-Italienne, et l'opéra réussit. Je n'ai jamais rien vu, ni entendu de plus ridicule; malgré les répétitions sur le petit théâtre de la rue St-Nicaise, présidées par le maréchal de Richelieu, premier gentilhomme en exercice, et dirigées par moi; malgré tout l'art de ces messieurs, l'arrivée [Larivé], de Gelin, de Rochard, et toute l'attention du grand orchestre de l'Opéra, cela parut à la cour ce que cela était, détestable. Enfin, ce changement qui occupa le conseil jusqu'à en fatiguer le feu Roi, ce grand changement fut opéré en 1761 [=1762]. On fit entrer à la Comédie-Italienne les cinq acteurs qui jouaient dans *On ne s'avise jamais de tout*: les demoiselles Nacelle [Nessel] et Deschamps, et les sieurs Clairval, La Ruette, et Audinot. (pp. 506–7)

And in his rather later eulogy of Clairval in the preface to *Richard Cœur-de-Lion* Sedaine completes his picture:

> Il y a vingt-cinq ans qu'il a contribué au succès d'*On ne s'avise jamais de tout*, & ses talens naissans furent en partie la cause de l'union de ce nouveau genre de Comédie lyrique à celui dont s'occupoit le Théâtre Italien.

We have so far considered mainly the earliest editions of librettos. But librettos went on being sold. Valuable evidence concerning the quantities being bought and sold occurs in a letter from Sedaine to Favart dated 27 March 1781,[63] in the course of which he mentions that annually he can earn 500–600 *livres* from selling his own librettos from home at 20 *sols* each (instead of the 30 *sols* charged by booksellers). Since a *livre* comprised exactly 20 *sols* we therefore know that Sedaine privately sold up to 600 copies a year, ten or more librettos a week. The same letter also wagers that the booksellers are selling more copies than he does, implying annual numbers of well over a thousand. Such large numbers of continuing sales would profit from future analysis. They may be usefully compared with Collé's account of his *La Partie de chasse de Henri IV*, which specifies a first print-run of 2000 copies. This was in 1766, when his play had so far received only private performances. At such a rate, Collé says, the run would be exhausted in six to eight weeks. The hawkers had judged this public response to be level with enthusiasm for two recent popular plays by others, one of which was Belloy's *Le Siège de Calais* in 1765.[64]

---

[63] Antoine-Pierre-Charles Favart (ed.), *Mémoires et correspondance littéraires, dramatiques et anecdotiques de C. S. Favart* (3 vols, Paris: Léopold Collin, 1808), III, pp. 101–2.

[64] Collé, *Journal et mémoires*, III, p. 77. The estimate of selling out a first edition in six weeks matches the rate at which we saw that of Favart's *Annette et Lubin* sell out in practice in 1762.

(e) Prefaces and the public sphere

A recent historian has written of this period that 'the theatre represented for the French, to a greater degree probably than for any other nation, a unique focus of collective interest' such that 'The theatre impinged on the national life at every level, from the highest to the lowest, and those who steered the ship of state could not afford to neglect it.'[65] Any author of a dramatic text or a preface could expect to engage a wide range of persons, for whom collectively the historical moment was important in a new sense:

> As Keith Michael Baker has indicated, the concept of public opinion arose in discussions that took place around 1750, first in the controversy over the refusal of the sacraments to the Jansenists [which memorably fed into the *Querelle des Bouffons*][66] ... Powerless to forbid public debate, the monarchy itself was forced to enter into it to explain, persuade, and to seek to win approval and support. A new political culture thus took shape ...[67]

Central to these issues was the knowledge that printing and publishing were the key to forming and swaying public opinion. Chartier shows this through the figure of one who was from 1750 at the centre of both the administration and the bookselling regime:

> 'The age of print,' as Malesherbes wrote in his 1775 *Remonstrances*, had irremediably modified the conditions of the exercise of power. It had given the nation 'the taste for and the habit of self-instruction through reading'... By that token it had made discussion and criticism public.[68]

If then from the 1750s a bourgeois 'public' had come into being, its physical manifestation was concentrated in spaces such as theatres, where Sedaine's theatre texts reached a sensitised public consciousness. But it could be that his

---

[65] Frederick William John Hemmings, *Theatre and State in France, 1760–1905* (Cambridge: Cambridge University Press, 1994), p. 1.

[66] Elisabeth Ann Cook, 'The Operatic Ensemble in France 1763–1775', Ph.D. dissertation, U. of East Anglia, 1989, pp. 76–127.

[67] Chartier, *The Cultural Origins*, p. 30, citing Keith Michael Baker's essay 'Politics and Public Opinion under the Old Regime: Some Reflections' in Jack R. Censer and Jeremy D. Popkin (eds), *Press and Politics in Pre-Revolutionary France* (Berkeley: University of California Press, 1987), pp. 206–46.

[68] Chartier, *The Cultural Origins*, p. 44, citing Chrétien Guillaume de Malesherbes, 'Remonstrances relatives aux impôts, 6 Mai 1775', ed. Elisabeth Badinter in *Les 'Remonstrances' de Malesherbes, 1771–1775* (Paris: Union Générale d'Editions, 10/18, 1978), p. 273.

libretto prefaces managed to evade even the official sets of controls over publishing, and that his theatre public knew this. For we may, pending further research, question the assumption that a preface to a libretto was necessarily – if indeed at all – submitted to censorship; it was arguably an appendage, not an organic part of the work. After all, as one sees from Table 3 above, a libretto such as *Le Roi et le fermier* could be entered for a royal *privilège* five months before the first night. The final preface can only have been added later. Why not then simply assume that prefaces were always seen by the censors who signed their permission to print, even shortly before the first night? The case of *Aucassin et Nicolette* belies such certainties. Whereas its censors approved the manuscript libretto on the last day of December 1779, the wording of the end of the preface, and probably its wider content, show that it was written after 15 January 1780, the date of the third and last of the unsuccessful run of three performances of this version. As discussed in section (h), this libretto effectively became a polemic document rather than an adjunct to any performances.

John Lough has calculated that on average some 200,000 visits per year were made by the public which attended the Comédie-Italienne.[69] The clientèle was presumably economically more diverse than that of the Comédie-Française, where 'the public willing and able to support a new play was still small' at this time.[70] Something of the musical audience's social ambit is seen in the following English description in 1776, one which came to light relatively recently.

> The house [of the Comédie-Italienne] is long, narrow and badly lighted. The ornaments are in a poor style, very heavy and extremely old and tarnished. The lower part of the house has three divisions. [...] All round the house there are rows of lodges or boxes, I think four or five stories high, and in these, and especially in those that are nearest the stage, the ladies make a very brilliant figure. [...] But I see many ladies who dress in a very moderate and becoming manner, just as reasonable and modest ladies dress in England.[71]

Bentley does not say where he sat in the Hôtel de Bourgogne or whether he bought librettos for the works heard on 29 July when he was there (Grétry's *Silvain* followed by *La Bonne femme*, this last a recent parody of Gluck's *Alceste* as a pasticcio, with music by Rousseau, Monsigny, Grétry etc.). However, the novelist Laurence Sterne seems to have seen librettos being read there a few years before:

---

69 Lough, *Writer and Public*, p. 262.

70 Ibid., p. 263.

71 Peter France (ed.), *Thomas Bentley. Journal of a Visit to Paris, 1776* (Brighton: University of Sussex Library, 1977), pp. 37–8.

> There was nobody in the box I was let into but a kindly old French officer. [...] I strode over the two back rows of benches, and placed myself beside him.
>
> The old officer was reading attentively a small pamphlet, it might be the book of the opera, with a large pair of spectacles. As soon as I sat down, he took his spectacles off, and putting them into a shagreen case, returned them and the book into his pocket together.[72]

Librettos in general were certainly affordable to ticket-holders. For example, the various imprints collected in the six-volume *Recueil général des Opéra Bouffons* (1777) were all either 24 or 30 *sols* apiece, depending on the number of pages and the presence or otherwise of music. For comparison, admission to the parterre of the Comédie-Italienne, the cheapest area, cost 2 *livres* (40 *sols*).[73] We know that prefaces tended to be omitted from later editions. It was during earlier performances that Sedaine knew his words would be chiefly read in their true context, but he would also have known that the wider public made indirect use of libretto prefaces, for example in reports by journalists or documentary theatre chroniclers like Contant d'Orville.[74]

For his more proximate audiences, Sedaine engaged in a sometimes complex and witty game; his mind apparently wanders over various issues, as if to lower the reader's guard and engage him or her. He is self-deprecatory in *L'Huitre et les plaideurs*, admitting 'l'irrégularité de l'ouvrage'. In *Le Déserteur*, where at the end 'je crains de mettre des inutilités' and where he alludes to the preface itself as 'encore une de mes fautes', such language attracted indeed the attack mentioned earlier. It was made on the grounds of his unacceptable irony: 'vous ajoutez *les fautes de l'Auteur* ... est-il possible? c'est une modestie excessive ... une ironie que vous deviez nous épargner.'[75] *Rose et Colas* finds him full of *crainte* and *humilité*. In *Le Jardinier et son seigneur* 'Je demande pardon au Lecteur, de ces réflexions.'

Sedaine accumulated many ironic pretexts for bothering with prefaces at all. If in *Le Jardinier* he intends to use the preface as a reply to unjust criticism, in *Le Roi et le fermier* the opening effervesces in pure irony, as found again at the close of the preface to *Rose et Colas*. Irony also suffuses the *plaidoyer* for that to *Aucassin et Nicolette*, and similar sentiments open that to *Le Comte*

---

[72] Laurence Sterne, *A Sentimental Journey through France and Italy*, ed. Graham Petrie (Harmondsworth: Penguin Books, 1967), 'The Translation. Paris', p. 78.

[73] Two *livres* was basically equivalent to 1 shilling and 8 pence in English currency, and 24 *sols* was equivalent to a shilling. As the top price of a ticket elsewhere downstairs in the theatre was five *livres*, a libretto here would cost around a quarter of the ticket price.

[74] D'Orville's *Histoire de l'opéra bouffon* discusses and cites Sedaine's preface to *Le Jardinier et son seigneur* (I, p. 161) and paraphrases that to *Le Roi et le fermier* (I, pp. 251–3).

[75] [Anon.], *Remerci[e]ment du public à la préface du Déserteur* (n.p., n.d.), p. 5.

d'Albert, as if to challenge the reader not to dare read what he has to say. 'Le public ne les lit pas, ou s'en moque' is the brilliantly disingenuous attempt at alienation in *Le Roi et le fermier*. These tactics were probably the best tool suitable to an author who, like Sedaine, faced merciless mockery in public spaces to which he was not admitted, such as certain salons. The strength and sheer vulgarity of some of this mockery were later recorded by Grétry, reporting one such episode that took place at one of the abbé Morellet's monthly literary lunches.[76] The fact that Grétry was not writing this account for publication in his own lifetime, if at all, encourages belief in its veracity; and his reportedly spirited defence of Sedaine's art on the same occasion allows one to assume that he would not have left the librettist in complete ignorance of what kind of things were said.

Elsewhere Sedaine gives way, whether or not as an ironic technique, to feelings of acute defensiveness. This gives his prefaces a different quality from those of all others mentioned so far, except Poinsinet's. For *Le Jardinier et son seigneur* he conveys a tone of personal injury all through, rising to a shrill anecdote involving an unnamed ally at the close (storytelling is another Sedaine hallmark) who is given the task of rescuing the author imaginatively from accusations of immorality. By 1762 *Le Roi et le fermier* marks an advance: unnamed enemies ('quelques personnes indiscrètes ou mal intentionnées') have accused him of including 'des propos téméraires' ('reckless remarks') in the libretto, thus obliging him to print it as it supposedly existed originally, rather than as it has taken shape in performance.[77] 'La malignité' is evoked at the outset of *Rose et Colas*'s preface. Vivid descriptions in *Le Déserteur* evoke types of public malignity on a typical first night in Paris, where wit and worse replace true judgement. Poinsinet attested the same fever when his *Sancho Pança* suffered: 'le bruit des moucheurs qui n'étaient pas au ton de l'Orchestre couvrit facilement, dans certains endroits, la voix de nos Acteurs'; besides, 'Un Parterre toujours trop nombreux [est] par conséquent tumultueux.'[78] Sedaine's prefaces respond to this disorderly public atmosphere, as well as the viciousness of the salon.

By 1779, in *Aucassin et Nicolette*, Sedaine's enemies have become 'journalistes', and so he is more defiant, less ambiguous: ironically pointing out his self-confessed willingness to be compared to authors of the *grand*

---

[76] André Grétry, *Réflexions d'un solitaire*, ed. Lucien Solvay and Ernest Closson (4 vols, Brussels etc.: G. Van Oest, 1919–22), II, pp. 109–10. The jokes against Sedaine are attributed to d'Alembert and François Arnaud, who at least lowered his voice at the indecent phrases.

[77] See the commentary to that preface, below, and 'Quelques réflexions', p. 508: 'Il devait en première représentation être donné à la cour; mais les fausses interprétations données au titre et à quelques scènes, en empêchèrent.' Michel Noiray's analysis of this text and its surrounding sensitivities appears in Chapter 5.

[78] *La Bagarre*, 'Au Lecteur', pp. 10–11.

siècle, 'Je fais présent de cette note au premier journaliste qui voudra s'en servir.'[79] As with *Le Roi et le fermier*, the dramatic text of *Aucassin et Nicolette* was published in the form Sedaine originally wanted it, unblemished by the alterations of others.

The author is clearly aiming to instruct, even at the expense of pleasing. At one moment he admits this, in *Le Jardinier et son seigneur*: 'je suis assez vain, malgré mon ignorance, pour vouloir instruire mes contemporains'; at another he denies it: 'je n'ai point encore acquis par mes Ouvrages le droit de donner des leçons' (*Les Femmes vengées*). Elsewhere he risks patronising the first-night audience by implicitly calling them immature: they are (he says) as he once was, for 'depuis que j'ai acquis quelque connoissances théâtrales, j'écoute, & je me tais'. Perhaps he took this risk knowing that sections of the audience were genuine newcomers to this public arena. Having explained his technical endeavours in *Rose et Colas* he reminds his readers to follow the words in their libretto, not, however, in order to make up their own minds or think differently from him, but in order to give him their support.

The appeals to the audience's understanding, even *amour-propre*, are matched in the judgements Sedaine repeatedly invites of them regarding literary authorities: these remarks were also aimed at the invisible opinion-makers and defenders of the *status quo* who would finally destroy his attempt to reform spoken tragedy in *Maillard ou Paris sauvé* (see Chapter 1). He challenges *Aucassin*'s readers to compare him to Corneille in *Le Cid* (on the subject of affronts to fictional aristocrats) and to Sophocles, on the subject of morally irregular events. Greek theatre is again referred to as a model in *Le Déserteur*'s preface, and in that to *Rose et Colas* he suggests that modern lyric comedy has perhaps gone one better than the ancients. *Le Jardinier* closes with a reference to *Le Tartuffe*. *Le Magnifique*'s preface sketches the parallel treatment of the same subject-matter by Houdard de La Motte in his 1731 play of the same title; *Les Femmes vengées* almost offers a suggestion as to how to improve Racine's *Britannicus*, while *Le Comte d'Albert* hints at lessons learned from his *Andromaque*.

As he got older Sedaine ironised less, though he acknowledged his collaborators no less generously than before; his thanks extended now to Clairval in *Richard Cœur-de-Lion* and then to Mme Dugazon and her colleagues in *Le Comte d'Albert*. But all did not, in the event, end in a glow of approbation. The public sphere grew into the political tribunal, and Sedaine was vulnerable. Perhaps the greatest unsought threat arose from *Richard Cœur-de-Lion* and its stirring first-act solo by Blondel, 'O Richard, O mon roi', the avowal of fidelity to the incarcerated monarch.

---

79 An explanation of this defiance is offered by Mark Ledbury on p. 32.

> This became and remained the anthem of royalism throughout the Revolution, maintaining more consistent popularity than even the *Marseillaise*. The special meaning of the song came from its performance at a dinner given to welcome the Flanders Regiment to Versailles on 1 October 1789.[80]

Laura Mason's analysis documents the power and richness of this Sedaine–Grétry aria, which subsequently became the 'opposition' to *Ça ira*: these 'seemed able to represent political positions with great transparency and, in so doing, they acquired increasingly evocative associations', especially up to 1792.[81] One type of public pressure on Sedaine, now the suspected royalist, is exemplified in the open letter challenging his loyalty to the Revolution, and quoted in the commentary to *Guillaume Tell* in section (h) below. In another context Sedaine was forced to make textual changes to *Le Philosophe sans le savoir*.[82]

There is thus little doubt that Sedaine would have published the initial (1791) version of *Guillaume Tell* or else the definitive version (around September 1792) earlier than he eventually did, and thereby publicise his allegiance to liberty and fraternity. But, as explained later, he held back. When the text finally appeared it included, after the manner of the time, an optional 'Scène patriotique proposée', incorporating *La Marseillaise*. Its printed preface resists those who would suspect Sedaine of 'tenant à l'ancien régime',[83] on both the cultural and the political levels. Culturally, Sedaine 'proved' his credentials in an extended dedicatory poem to Antoine-Marin Lemierre, his late friend and the author of a very successful *Guillaume Tell* drama:

> Dans un tableau frappant, dans ton Poëme altier,
> Tu fis voir à la France un Peuple tout entier
> Qui se lève, aux accens de la Liberté fière ...

Politically, Sedaine accounted for the delayed publication of his text by impeccable reasoning: open reference to his leading role in the establishment of financial rewards for dramatic authors, matched by explicit reluctance to publish while the rapacity of provincial theatre directors remained unchecked.[84]

---

80 Laura Mason, *Singing the French Revolution. Popular Culture and Politics, 1787–1799* (Ithaca etc.: Cornell University Press, 1996), p. 46.

81 Ibid., pp. 54–5.

82 Paul d'Estrée, *Le Théâtre sous la Terreur (théâtre de la peur) 1793–1794* (Paris: Emil-Paul Frères, 1913), p. 122.

83 A phrase originating in 1790: Margaret Rayner, 'Sedaine's Dramatic Work', p. 27.

84 See section (h). Until 3 September 1793 Sedaine could not count on receiving any provincial performance dues for his work.

Once the law had been definitively changed on 3 September 1793, Sedaine, whose financial situation had progressively worsened, felt he could go ahead.[85]

(f) Categories of information contained

Sedaine's prefaces are remarkable in their very inconsistency: their diversity of size, tone and disposition of information. Single words or phrases can count for much. Often Sedaine is concerned to document the creative history of a theatre piece most frequently in lesser works such as *L'Anneau perdu et retrouvé*, which may be revisions of others' efforts. Little or nothing is said about inspirations for *Le Déserteur*, or the long route by which *Richard* attained definitive form. On the other hand Sedaine says a good deal about literary sources and why they attracted him to musical treatment, defining ways in which he has envisaged the musical interventions taking place. In *Le Comte d'Albert* he confesses that Grétry, not he, envisaged the possibility of operatic treatment for what had originally been a dramatic sketch for private performance. *Guillaume Tell* (see section (h)) appears to have been conceived as a prose tragedy mixed with musical episodes.

Sedaine frequently drew attention to the stage-directions he provided for actors, sympathetic to the plight of both trained singers who were less than fully skilled in effective acting, and of those living far away from his own wise counsels. It can be claimed, perhaps, that the nineteenth-century *livret de mise en scène* already existed in Sedaine's librettos in embryo, within the book of words, destined to encourage future performances outside Paris to reproduce exactly what the author/*metteur en scène* had personally ordained. And the prefaces are full of detail about stage performances: *Le Jardinier et son seigneur* had been given by the Paris players in Rouen; *Rose et Colas* describes the way ensembles went wrong, and the resonant disapproval on the part of 'les connoisseurs à tête froide et à oreille fine'. Close observation of singing-actors at work will be found in *Le Déserteur*'s preface, not least the skilful way in which, after a work had been run in, they maintained the dramatic impetus of a scene not simply in dialogue but also in the very different pacing of the musical sections. This preface mentions the same difficulties that Marmontel found in trying to find a manner of rehearsal which would avoid the ridicule that stray members of the public tended to voice when seeing a director in action (presumably this perceived incongruity stemmed from the actor-centred

[85] It continued to worsen. When Dufort visited him, seemingly in the winter of 1795–6 after a three-year absence, he found the family destitute. Jean-Nicolas Dufort, *Mémoires du comte Dufort de Cheverny*, ed. Robert de Crèvecœur (4th ed., 2 vols, Paris: Plon, 1909), II, p. 186.

traditions of stage production with which they were familiar).[86] The answer was a concealed director's box such as Jean Monnet constructed within his new theatre at the Foire St-Laurent in 1752, something also mentioned by Grétry in his posthumous memoirs.[87] But the implied purpose of the information was surely to promote good rehearsal conditions elsewhere. Such topics quickly spill over into discussions of reception. *Le Déserteur* is the richest source of this, but several other prefaces such as *Anacréon* discuss the subject, including the types of textual changes made both before and after first nights.

Not the least important category of prefatory information concerns Sedaine's attitude to the genre of *opéra-comique* itself. The preface to *Rose et Colas* is a revealing anatomy of the particular dynamics of the genre in performance, clearly something distinct from the way Sedaine felt that lyric tragedy worked in the 1760s. This understanding led to a restless search for new ways and means to quarry the genre, and encouraged Sedaine to avoid the generic cliché 'comédie mêlée d'ariettes', instead inventing generic phrases reflecting exactly which dynamics applied in a given case.[88] The same preface alludes to this cliché and the need for its avoidance. Sedaine's own labels are of course exactly reproduced in section (h) below, and repay full consideration; they silently complement the æsthetic nuances explored in the prefaces themselves.

While certain categories of information were perennial, such as sources, the *opéra-comique* prefaces became less occupied with the performative aspects of the genre and more with the individual flavour of the work: as he puts it in *Richard Cœur-de-Lion*, 'la texture de mon drame ... la physionomie du tems, du lieu et des personnages'. Authorial security regarding performance was matched by increasing insecurity about more far-reaching dramatic innovations. Unfortunately, the only preface for an all-sung Sedaine opera (*Aline, reine de Golconde*) is extremely bland by comparison, although there was no shortage of topics attaching to this particular subject that one wishes had been disussed.[89]

---

[86] Further notes on this subject are found in 'Rehearsal' within Stanley Sadie (ed.), *The New Grove Dictionary of Opera* (4 vols, London: Macmillan, 1992), III, p. 1269.

[87] Grétry, *Réflexions d'un solitaire*, II, chapter 29, p. 102.

[88] 'Ariettes' in this context originally meant any newly composed vocal music in an *opéra-comique*, even an ensemble, but it also carried various older resonances that Sedaine wished to avoid: these derived from its quite different meaning during the first half of the century, namely decorative, often triumphal arias in Italianate da capo form as used in lyric genres at the Opéra, whether *tragédie* or *opéra-ballet* or *pastorale héroïque*. The relaxed dramatic situations in which they habitually participated thus represented (ironically) the opposite dynamic function to that which Sedaine desired above all to promote for vocal music in *opéra-comique*.

[89] The opera's sources and genre are discussed by Manuel Couvreur in Chapter 4.

(g) The Sedaine 'agenda'

If Sedaine had wanted to write a theory of opera he would doubtless have done so; but he preferred to write more creatively. The prefaces transcribed below nevertheless contain sufficient fruits of meditation about opera to match the consistency and depth which we might expect from considering the works alone, or from the key extract quoted from *Le Vaudeville* at the outset. Grétry well understood that Sedaine's operatic genius lay in a willingness to make every aspect of theatre language function together, and yet achieve unity:

> Sedaine, qui avoit la tête des plus dramatique, étoit très peu musicien, ne sacrifiant rien à la musique, voilà pourquoi ses pièces ont de l'unité.[90]

The prefaces shed considerably more light on these words, especially regarding the way Sedaine conceived the role of music. His continual concern within the main dramatic text with providing acting-instructions, and his observations on actors in *Le Déserteur*'s preface, are merely symptoms of his belief in the necessity of an actor's identification with the role s/he serves, whether or not music be involved. Further, the sung portions must enable the drama to move forward, through both words and 'la situation théâtrale' (*Blaise le savetier*), seconded by the simultaneous arts of singing and gesturing, whilst appearing completely natural: 'des gestes faciles, des mouvemens arrondis, cette mollesse, cette aisance' (*Le Déserteur*). The ideal is to 'rendre la nature sans la forcer' (*Blaise le savetier*) and this must continue as well during any instrumental ritornellos (*Le Magnifique*). Unfortunately, those capable of musical as well as acting skills, and who also possess inborn taste, are rare: to make things worse, the very presence of music renders it harder to act with naturalness in comedy (*Le Jardinier et son seigneur*).

The most crucial statement regarding the standards by which Sedaine desired to be judged occurs in the same preface at the paragraph starting 'La sagesse du plan'. A translation may be useful:

> The wisdom of the dramatic scheme, the choice and presentation of characters, the *servetur ad imum* [observing things in their deepest sense], the creation of those situations most apt to put the soul of one's characters into play; that unteachable art which endows events with a natural sense of totality, tone and harmony, as well as with the chance occurrence; these are the points on which I should understand fair criticism, and by which a work of theatre must be judged; style follows after.

---

90 Grétry, *Réflexions d'un solitaire*, III, chapter 17, p. 97.

Literary quality is put in its place, and nowhere is music mentioned; yet numerous are Sedaine's thoughts elsewhere regarding musical function, whether on the level of the whole drama or on that of the individual solo. In a similar way, prefaces sometimes signal a particular dramatic experiment, yet these ambitions never in themselves concern music in their basic concept, except for *Richard Cœur-de-Lion*. *Le Comte d'Albert* announces the important, influential concept of embedding an old myth within a modern narrative by disguising its original characters (here La Fontaine's animals) and setting.[91] *Aucassin et Nicolette* was inspired morally by the notion of betrayal and injustice done to the son by the father, as well as æsthetically by the experiment of performing a medieval *fabliau* through reconceiving it as opera with spoken dialogue. *Les Femmes vengées* was provoked by the possibility of displaying three locations at the same time, clarified further through an engraving commissioned by the author to show the *mise en scène* (see Fig. 6, p. 162). Yet it may be argued that Sedaine's primary agenda surely did involve music; if musical inspiration for *Blaise le savetier* is only hinted at in its preface, the 'Quelques réflexions' seem to expose the author's real motivation:

> Si quelque chose m'excitait, ce serait le plaisir d'essayer de mettre toute une scène en musique, scène qui serait composée de plusieurs interlocuteurs mis en actions. (p. 504)

As far as *Richard Cœur-de-Lion* went, it was Grétry among others who pointed out that the 'public realised that the [Romance] was the pivot on which the whole piece turned'.[92] By the time Sedaine came to publish his preface this opera was already well known, even outside France, so Sedaine confined himself to thanking 'l'Auteur des deux couplets de Romance ... qui sont tirés de l'intéressant Fabliau qui m'en a donné l'idée',[93] that is, who gave him the fundamental inspiration for the libretto and determined the local colour of the literary and musical artefacts.

A careful reading of the prefaces throws valuable light on a subject difficult to construe today, namely the way that *opéra-comique* was perceived æsthetically in its own time. Moreover, some development of Sedaine's thinking is perhaps discernible here. In earlier prefaces he writes, as he did regarding *Blaise le savetier* in 'Quelques réflexions', most passionately about the imperatives of continuity in musical dramaturgy; the way music must be integrated ('enchaînés à la scène'; 'ne faisant qu'un' with the text) and in fact

---

91 This is the same process as led Wagner to embed the myth of Semele within *Lohengrin*, for example.

92 Grétry, *Mémoires*, I, p. 374: 'le public a senti que cet air étoit le pivot sur lequel tournoit toute la pièce', i.e. 'Une fièvre brûlante'.

93 Probably the Marquis de Paulmy, issuing his own version of the legend in the *Bibliothèque universelle des romans* (July 1776), pp. 163–94.

must promote qualities of *action, chaleur, mouvement, précision*. His defence of musical ensembles, made at a time of lively debate, was shrewdly logical: such means were arguably *more* natural, he says, at moments of surprise or general reaction, than were those of spoken drama, simply because music permitted natural simultaneity of expression denied to playwrights; the art lay in not prolonging the moment too far. All these observations (set out in the preface to *Rose et Colas*) stressed the duties to be laid upon music; but they led later to various longer-term considerations of perception, i.e. the way music, as opposed to text, was apprehended over the lifetime of a work. This was articulated by Sedaine through a parallel with the appreciation of verse in tragedy. Early audiences focus on the difficulties presented by an unfamiliar story, the unfamiliar placing of music, and various performance hazards. Later ones forget, so to speak, the text and focus on the music. These theories, found in the preamble to *Le Déserteur*, grew out of those in *L'Anneau perdu et retrouvé*, in which Sedaine says that text is comparable to invention and line in a painting, elements which only connoisseurs appreciate. Music, by contrast, is comparable to colour in painting, and is something which tends to dominate the æsthetic impact of the work for everybody. Consequently, Sedaine saw his task as one creatively foreseeing – even 'forehearing' – the whole impression, and in that sense requiring that his musicians be guided. Grétry agrees:

> Si Sedaine n'est pas le poëte qui soigne le plus les vers destinés au chant, les situations qu'il amène ... sont si impérieuses, qu'elles forcent le musicien à s'y attacher pour les rendre. [...] Il force donc le musicien à prendre des formes neuves pour rendre ses caractères originaux.[94]

Sedaine's better-known and later formulation in *Le Magnifique*, however, proposed that the libretto sets up the 'statue' of music with its necessary 'pedestal'; and the static, subservient nature of this metaphor apparently reveals a more compliant attitude to the musician's responsibilities. It virtually stresses the duties to be laid upon librettos, not scores. This is of course misleading. We need to recall that *opéra-comique* was not a static field of endeavour: by Grétry's heyday it was clear that Sedaine's drama-centred vision of *opéra-comique* had won majority support against both the proponents of *opera buffa* and the numerous advocates of *comédies à vaudevilles*. And in Grétry he enjoyed an exceptionally drama-oriented musical partner. My own view is that this preface pays Grétry a compliment more than it sets out an æsthetic stall.

To these notions should be added that of fidelity to a literary source, in the sense of aiming at an authentic transposition of a source's character into a

[94] Grétry, *Mémoires*, I, p. 254.

stage work employing music. This principle explains the grand sweep behind Sedaine's idea for *Guillaume Tell* and the music he somehow heard for it; blunt to the end, he publicly lamented Grétry's inadequacy in representing the echoing *ranz des vaches* across his Swiss valley.[95] At the close of Act II he envisaged a great storm entr'acte over the lake, 'un grand morceau de musique', and wishes the spectacle could have been given at the Paris Opéra, with mimed representations of Tell's escape by leaping onto a rock. Still developing, his imagined roles for music reached forward out of prose tragedy, *mélodrame* and *opéra-comique* and into the age of *grand opéra*.

(h) The Prefaces: edition and commentary

This section contains complete editions in chronological order of publication of all Sedaine's prefaces to stage works with music. These are gathered together for the first time. Since many libretto copies have been consulted in the course of preparation, certain variant readings have emerged. The editorial notes make it clear exactly which library copy or copies provide a main text, and which copies contain variant readings that are noted. However, because prefaces occurred in only the earliest edition or editions of a libretto, variant readings are far fewer than those for extant title-pages, for example.[96]

The library sigla used below are those adopted by the *Répertoire international des sources musicales*: GB-Lbl for the British Library, F-Pn for the Bibliothèque Nationale de France, qualified by (Mus) when the Music collections are referred to rather than the Département des Imprimés; F-Po for the Bibliothèque-Musée de l'Opéra; F-Pa for the Bibliothèque de l'Arsenal.

Since without integral bibliographical searches of all surviving exemplars one cannot be certain that any two copies of a given libretto will be identical, I have given a diplomatic transcription of the title-page essentials of the source libretto in each case. These are not complete transcriptions and omit publishers' addresses and notices of *approbation* and *privilège*, many of which will however be found in Chapter 11, 'A Sedaine Bibliography', within Section B. The existence of separable music pages at the ends of imprints has not been noted, since these were distinct publications, available optionally, and usually paginated separately; furthermore, their survival or disappearance today does not affect the current exercise. A word of caution is needed regarding front-

[95] Footnote to Act I, sc. I: 'Je l'avois indiqué ainsi au Musicien; mais cela n'est pas assez prononcé pour indiquer ce que je désirois faire sentir, qu'au lever de la toile on étoit dans une des vallées de la Suisse.'

[96] Readers wishing to verify the following transcriptions should check the collation of their copy against that described in respect of copies used for transcriptions below. Variant collations are the surest indication of a different edition.

matter: collations easily become problematic owing to haphazard binding and printing. A typical example is *Richard Cœur-de-Lion*.

Editorial principles have been to change no spellings or accents on title-pages, while in the main text I have regularised the word 'pièce' and a few other words sometimes spelled with an acute instead of a grave accent.

Source: GB-Lbl: 1065.d.27

TP: RECUEIL / DE / *POESIES* / DE M. SEDAINE. / SECONDE ÉDITION; / ... / A LONDRES, / *Et se trouve à Paris*, / chez DUCHESNE, ... / MDCCLX.

Collation: Two parts separately paginated. Part 2 p. 161: 'ANACRÉON, / *PASTORALE* / HÉROIQUE'

p. 163: AVERTISSEMENT.

§ Cette petite Pièce a été faite en 1754, pour la fête de M.L.B. & représentée la même année à sa maison de campagne. J'ai été confirmé dans l'idée que j'avois dès-lors, que les applaudissemens d'une Société, même choisie, ne font pas des cautions suffisantes de ceux du Public; j'ai donné quelques années après cette Pièce sur le Théâtre Italien. Elle n'a eu aucun succès. Je la fais imprimer; en partie pour donner à ce second Volume une grosseur suffisante. J'ai fait mettre en lettres italiques les Couplets, & même les Scenes que les Comé- [164] diens ont supprimés pour la facilité de la représentation. Je les ai remis pour l'intelligence de la Pièce, & pour la terminer comme j'avois crû qu'elle devoit l'être. §

Commentary

Anacréon was mentioned in 'Quelques réflexions' as follows: 'j'avais cependant donné aux Italiens, en 1758, une petite pièce intitulée *Anacréon*, que j'avais faite pour une fête d'amis donnée à Gerbelet, et dans laquelle Chassé faisait le rôle d'Anacréon. Elle n'eut aucun succès aux Italiens; mais elle avait rempli mon but, qui était de me soulager du paiement des entrées que mon peu de fortune me rendait pesant, et j'en profitai' (p. 503).

'M.L.B.' was presumably Jean Benjamin de La Borde (1734–94), the wealthy patron, writer and composer described in the same source as 'excellent artiste en musique et mon ami' (p. 508). He composed the score for *Les Bons amis*, later made by Sedaine into *L'Anneau perdu et retrouvé* (see below). Chassé was a celebrated bass at the Opéra, then near the end of his career, an 'excellent acteur' as the *Anecdotes dramatiques* noted.[97] *Anacréon* lasted for five public performances, 13–30 December 1758.

---

[97] Jean-Marie Clément, Joseph de La Porte, *Anecdotes dramatiques* (3 vols, Paris: Veuve Duchesne, 1775), III, p. 105; repr. Geneva, 1971, p. 329.

The second volume of Sedaine's *Recueil de poésies* is remarkable for the quantity of music-related texts it contains: the cantata *Éole* (set by one M. le Jay), *La Tentation de Saint Antoine*, the *cantatilles* entitled *Ariane* and *Acis et Galatée*, a 'rondeau' entitled *Léandre et Héro*, and many song texts intended for known melodies.

Source: F-Pn (Mus): Th.488[98]

TP: BLAISE / LE SAVETIER, / *OPERA-COMIQUE*, / SUIVI / DE LA NÔCE DE NICAISE, / Intermede mêlé de Chants & de Danses, / *Par Monsieur S. ...* / La Musique de M. PHILLIDOR. / *Représenté pour la première fois sur le Théâtre de / l'Opera-Comique de la Foire Saint Germain, / le 9 Mars 1759. / ...* / A PARIS, / Chez DUCHESNE... / MDCCLIX

Collation: pp. v + 6–46 [including *La Noce de Nicaise*]

p. [iii]:AVERTISSEMENT / DE L'AUTEUR.

§ Si quelqu'un me reproche l'attention avec laquelle j'ai écrit la Pantomime de cette farce, qu'il fasse réflexion que le grand défaut de la plûpart des Ariettes au Théâtre, est de se voir dénuées d'action, soit que ce défaut vienne des paroles & de la situation théâtrale, soit que l'Acteur seulement musicien, ne sçache point les revêtir des gestes, & du sentiment, vrais.

Cette petite Pièce annoblie par la musique de M. Phillidor sera (je l'espere) représentée en province; l'Acteur loin de tout conseil qui lui semble valable, en lisant la Pantomime, se trouvera aidé de l'avis de l'Auteur; il peut en partant de-là, fixer ses mouvements, étendre son jeu, & arriver à ce point si difficile de rendre la nature sans la forcer: peut-être pourra-t-il trouver mieux que ce que j'indique, mais s'il rencontre plus mal, les conseils qu'il a devant les yeux serviront de pièces au procès que lui fera l'Auditeur. §

Commentary

Sedaine obtained the censor's permission to print this text after a gap of three months following the first night. This was his last imprint with Duchesne before moving to Hérissant.

We saw in section (b) the comments on this work in 'Quelques réflexions', and the author's recruitment, so to speak, of Philidor, who was then starting his public composing career. Sedaine's *Le Diable à quatre* (1756) is sometimes attributed for its music to Philidor; but as Sonneck says, its music had consisted of popular airs: 'It is therefore a mistake if [he] is recorded as its

[98] The same TP wording with slight typographical differences is found in other copies bearing the same publication date and publisher name: GB-Lbl: 11735.d.2 for example. All exemplars spell the composer 'Phillidor'.

composer instead of as the arranger of the score.'[99] The 'Réflexions' bear out the deeper acquaintanceship of 1759, while the public testimony to Philidor is recorded in the preface to *Blaise*. Rarely again would Sedaine express such praise for his composers' work (and never for Grétry's), although his later disappointment at effective abandonment by Philidor found compensating expression in the warm remarks about Monsigny in *Le Roi et le fermier*'s preface.

Sources: GB-Lbl: 86.a.15; F-Pn (Mus): Th.B.3544

TP: L'HUITRE / ET / *LES PLAIDEURS*, / OU / LE TRIBUNAL DE LA CHICANE. / OPERA–COMIQUE, / *En un Acte, en Prose, mêlé de morceaux / de Musique & Vaudeville, représenté / sur le Théâtre de la Foire Saint-Laurent / en 1759 & 1761.* / Par M. SEDAINE. / La Musique de M. Philidor. / ... / A PARIS, / Chez Claude HERISSANT... / MDCCLXI

Collation: pp. [iv] + 1–34

p. [iii]: *AVERTISSEMENT* / DE L'AUTEUR.

§ Cette petite Pièce, ou plutôt cette farce a été représentée pour la première fois à la Foire Saint-Laurent de l'année 1760 [sic]; proposée, faite, mise en Musique, apprise & représentée en moins de dix-sept jours. Elle avoit tous les défauts d'un Ouvrage indigeste & précipité; cependant le reproche le plus unanime fut son peu de durée. C'est ce qui m'a excité à l'étendre en y joignant des Couplets, des Scènes & des morceaux de Musique qui couvrissent du moins l'irrégularité de l'Ouvrage. Et de fait, un Opéra-Comique qui n'est point composé de Scènes à tiroirs, & qui n'a ni amour, ni intrigue, ni mariage, ne peut guères tenir son succès que des charmes de la Musique, & du mérite de l'exécution. §

Commentary

'Quelques réflexions' explains that this work was written in response to the directors of the Foire, who needed something to end their summer season; it claims the even shorter time of fourteen days from inception to curtain-up, 'words and music'; the first night was 17 September.[100] The preface's mention of '1760' is an error for 1759 which was presumably caused by the fact that the text was not published until after 10 July 1761, when the libretto's *permis* was signed. However, the date 1761 may well betoken further Saint-Laurent performances at that time, as the title-page itself suggests. Sedaine's account in

---

99 Sonneck, *Library of Congress. Catalogue*, I, p. 376.

100 Sonneck's speculation in *Library of Congress. Catalogue*, p. 601, that the 1759 version lacked music, was thus incorrect.

that case would be incorrect: he says that 'Cet ouvrage finit la foire [1759], et on ne l'a pas donné depuis.' He continues:

> C'était cependant un intermède assez comique, à qui on ne reprochait que d'être trop court. M. Philidor, peut-être trop sévère, ne fut pas content de la musique, et ne la fit pas graver. Il n'en est resté qu'un duo parodié dans *Le Tonnelier*, dont la musique et les paroles ont été faites, dit-on, par M. Audinot.[101]

Sources: GB-Lbl: 86.a.15; F-Pn (Mus): ThB. 3612

TP: LE JARDINIER / ET / *SON SEIGNEUR*, / OPERA COMIQUE, / *En un Acte, en Prose, mêlé de morceaux / de Musique, représenté sur le Théâtre / de la Foire Saint-Germain le Mercredi / 18 Février 1761.* / Par M. SEDAINE. / La Musique de M. Philidor. / ... / A PARIS. / Chez CLAUDE HERISSANT... / MDCCLXI

Collation: pp. [1] [TP] – 48

pp. 3–7: *AVERTISSEMENT.*

§ Cette Pièce a été représentée avec quelque succès à Paris & depuis à Rouen, mais par les mêmes Acteurs de Paris. Si les Directeurs de Province vouloient la hazarder sur leur Théâtre, ils pourroient trouver quelques difficultés par le défaut de sujets; car je regarde comme très-rare de rencontrer dans un même Acteur un homme de goût qui sçache & exécute bien la Musique, & qui représente naturellement. La Musique est un Art qui rend plus difficiles les mouvemens de la Nature, sur-tout dans le Comique.

Pour faciliter la représentation de cette Pièce, qui exige trois Actrices & cinq Acteurs musiciens, j'ai mis à la fin deux Scènes en Prose, qui suppriment un Musicien & une Musicienne. Si, d'un côté, la Pièce perd quelques morceaux de Musique bien faits, d'un autre elle acquerra plus de rapidité, & ses comptes seront plutôt rendus.

Je me servirai de l'occasion de cet Avertissement pour répondre à quelques objections, à quelques critiques. La première est que ma Pièce est écrite d'un style bas & peu élevé. Voyez, m'a-t-on dit, cette Ariette.

> Mais, mais voyez l'insolence,
> L'impudence!
> Falloit-il pas les flatter?
> Et toi, tu mérites, sotte,
> Que dans l'instant *je te frotte*.

[101] 'Quelques réflexions', p. 505. The last sentence seemingly refers to the entry in Clément and La Porte's *Anecdotes dramatiques*, II, p. 235 (repr. p. 215), where the first version of this famous piece is referred to as 'Opéra-Comique en un acte, mêlé d'ariettes, attribué à Audinot, soit pour les paroles, soit pour la musique, à la Foire Saint-Laurent, 1761'.

[4] Au lieu de les écouter,
Tu devois les rebuter.
Tu sçais que sans la vertu
La beauté *n'est qu'un fétu.*
Tu sçais bien que sans l'honneur
Une fille est une horreur.
Quoi! tu quitterois ton père?
Tu laisserois-là ta mère?
Ta mère qui n'a que toi?
        Hé pourquoi?

Voyez, m'a-t-on dit, ces expressions: *que je te frotte*: *la beauté un fétu.* Peut-être mes censeurs ont-ils raison; mais j'ai cru avoir employé le style qui convenoit à l'être, aux mœurs, à la situation du personnage qui parle. Croit-on qu'il m'eût été difficile d'élever le ton, & de faire dire à cette mère irritée:

Mais voyez de quel front, avec quelle impudence
Ces femmes ont osé soutenir ma présence!
Il sembloit que mon cœur, trop prompt à s'irriter,
Devoit, foible & rempant, s'abaisser & flatter.
Moi, les flatter! O Ciel! Et toi qui dès l'enfance
Suças avec le lait l'honneur et l'innocence,
Comment, loin de frémir de ces affreux complots,
Osois-tu seulement écouter leurs propos?
Ma main, si je n'avois pour toi de l'indulgence,
Ma main devroit punir ta lâche complaisance.
Hélas! nos sentimens, tout ce que tu nous dois,
Ne t'inspiroient-ils pas? Je te l'ai dit cent fois,
L'éclat de la beauté, la fleur de la jeunesse,
[5] L'esprit, le bien, le rang n'est rien sans la sagesse.
Les regards, il est vrai, peuvent être déçus
Par ces habits que l'or & la soie ont tissus,
Par ce faste imposant, par le ton de ces femmes;
Mais si tu pénétrois dans le fond de leurs ames,
Sous ces dehors pompeux, sous ces brillans attraits,
Sous ce front si serein, si content, tu verrais
Les fruits, les tristes fruits des désordres extrêmes,
Les ennuis, les dégoûts, la honte d'elles-mêmes,
Le chagrin renaissant de voir qu'à chaque pas
On compte leurs défauts en montrant leurs appas,
Et que le cri public, qu'irrite leur audace,
Les arrache du sang où la Vertu nous place.
Et tu nous quitterois pour ces femmes? Grands Dieux!

Nous te verrions, ma fille, abandonner ces lieux,
Pour n'être qu'un objet d'opprobre & de misère?
Aux chagrins les plus vifs tu livrerois ton père?
Et tes yeux, occupés à séduire les cœurs,
Condamneroient les miens à pleurer tes erreurs?

Ces vers disent à peu-près la même chose que l'Ariette; & tout foibles, tout décousus, tout maniérés qu'ils sont, s'ils étoient dans la bouche de l'Actrice qui donne de la vie aux moindres expressions, ces Vers plairoient peut-être; & peut-être quelques-uns diroient: L'Auteur est un grand homme, car il fait de grands vers. Mais cette tirade emphatique auroit-elle rempli mon objet? La Musique, pour laquelle j'ai courbé les Scènes de cet Opera Comique, a des sentimens, a des branches trop étalées, trop ambitieuses, auroit-elle trouvé le moyen d'entrelacer ses fleurs? La marche constamment pesante de notre grand Vers Ale- [6] xandrin auroit-elle fourni au Musicien la mesure vive d'une femme animée de différens mouvemens qui se succedent en elle avec rapidité? Enfin, seroit-ce une Paysanne de Bagnolet qui parleroit?

La sagesse du plan, le choix & la tenuë des caracteres, le *servetur ad imum*,[102] la création des situations les plus propres à mettre en jeu l'ame des personnages; cet art qui ne s'apprend pas, cet art qui donne aux incidens l'ensemble, le ton, & les accords de la nature & du cas fortuit, voilà les points sur lesquels j'appréhendois une juste critique, & sur lesquels il faut juger un Ouvrage de Théâtre; le style vient ensuite. Je demande pardon au Lecteur, de ces réflexions; mais je suis assez vain, malgré mon ignorance, pour vouloir instruire mes contemporains.

On m'a fait un reproche qui m'a été plus sensible; celui d'avoir employé des Scènes indécentes. J'ai interrogé des femmes délicates & vertueuses, aucune n'en a fait la remarque. J'aurois été bien loin de mes motifs; moi qui, même à l'Opéra Comique, ai cherché à laisser dans l'esprit des Auditeurs des idées de morale et d'instruction; moi qui dans deux Pièces, *Le Diable à quatre & Blaise le savetier*, Pièces qui prêtoient à l'équivoque & à un certain genre de plaisanterie, n'ai rien hazardé qui ne pût être écouté.

Qui voudra juger sans prévention *Le Jardinier et son seigneur*, verra que je ne peux avoir manqué mon but; mais que mon dessein n'étoit pas de faire ma cour aux vices. D'où viennent donc les reproches qui sont venus jusqu'à moi? Un de [7] mes amis, qui n'a nulle pudeur lorsqu'il prend ma défense, m'a dit, que de même qu'au Tartuffe les impies seuls avoient crié à l'impiété, il n'y avoit à ma Pièce que les indécens qui eussent crié à l'indécence, & que les filles seules & leurs champions avoient élevé la voix, trop honteux pour la baisser. Je souhaite que mon ami ait raison; mais il oublie quelle Pièce c'est que le Tartuffe, pour oser lui comparer quelque chose. §

---

102 That is, 'observing things in their deepest sense'.

Commentary

Some of the most useful insights of all in 'Quelques réflexions' occur in connection with *Le Jardinier et son seigneur*.

> Cet ouvrage eut sur le théâtre de la foire un succès qu'il n'a jamais eu et ne peut avoir sur le théâtre Italien; la dignité des actrices ne leur permettant pas de jouer comme il le faut les rôles des deux demoiselles qui y sont en scène. A l'Opéra-Comique, la demoiselle Arnoud [Arnoult] me demanda dans quel genre je désirais qu'elle jouât ce rôle? Comme chez vous, Mademoiselle. – Oh! me dit-elle, je suis au fait, et elle le joua bien. – C'est un grand malheur pour un spectacle lorsque les acteurs voient leur personne au lieu de voir leur rôle. (pp. 505–6)

From this one can more easily interpret the moral objections alluded to in the work's preface. And the evidence of difference in performance styles between the two companies referred to is as rare as it is vital. Mlle Arnoud (who took the part of the actress Victoire) was actually a recent soloist at the Opéra-Comique, playing at the Foire Saint-Laurent from 1759 to 1761: she was not taken over into the Comédie-Italienne at the fusion of companies early in the next year.[103] Moreover Sedaine's closing observation above teaches us an unsuspected nuance about his philosophy of acting, as well as his rehearsal methods themselves.

The preface's thoughtful tenor is not necessarily related to its delayed publication, for the equally thoughtful preface to *Rose et Colas* came out on the first night. For whatever reason, *Le Jardinier*'s libretto did not appear until perhaps three months after the first night, the *permis* being dated 3 May, well after the winter fair of Saint-Germain ended; presumably it was issued in time for the Saint-Laurent season.

The splendid engraving found in one or two early copies of the libretto was by Gabriel de Saint-Aubin, dated 1761, and engraved by Augustin de Saint-Aubin (see Fig. 12, opposite). The quotation beneath ('Parbleu, Jacques, soufle donc'), taken from scene XVII, is part of the *Ariette en Duo* between Le Harangueur and Le Soufleur, where the phrase occurs three times in Philidor's setting, as against only once in the libretto.[104] As an image it is an exceedingly valuable clue to the naturalism of approach referred to all through this preface

[103] Main roles played: La Justice in Sedaine's *L'Huitre et les plaideurs* (1759); Lisette in Harny de Guerville's *Les Nouveaux calotins* (1760); Georget in the same author's *Georget et Georgette* (1761), set by C. G. Alexandre; and La Tante de Julie in Favart's *Le Bal bourgeois* (1761).

[104] *Le Jardinier et son seigneur, opera bouffon en un acte* (Paris: De La Chevardière, n.d.), pp. 49–50. The Harangueur is here called Maître Thomas, the Soufleur Maître Jacques.

Fig. 12: Augustin de Saint-Aubin, after Gabriel de Saint-Aubin, frontispiece to *Le Jardinier et son seigneur*. Engraving, 1761. Photo: © Bibliothèque Nationale de France, Paris.

by Sedaine, and in his various references here and elsewhere to the actor's art. That is, even if it cannot be read like a photograph its extreme naturalism of style counts as part of its authoritativeness. As Martine de Rougemont has observed in Chapter 7, Saint-Aubin was closely allied to Sedaine. Space does not permit a study of all the actors and attitudes portrayed, but mention is required of the Seigneur's role, taken by Clairval (Jean-Baptiste Guignard, 1735–95), the greatest male *opéra-comique* exponent of the later *ancien régime*. Clairval would often subsequently work with Sedaine, up to his finest hour as Blondel in *Richard Cœur-de-Lion*, afterwards receiving the author's acknowledgement in the preface to that work.[105] Mlle Arnoud as Victoire and the obscure Mlle Groslier as Rosalie are seen on the left at the back: these were the roles which provoked moral objection and whose acting Sedaine says could never be recreated properly at the Comédie-Italienne. Maître Simon, the title-role, is the bald figure cringeing at the extreme right. The actor was the celebrated Nicolas-Médard Audinot (1732–1801), author of (and actor in) *Le Tonnelier*, and later the founder of the Théâtre de l'Ambigu-Comique. Considering that 'Audinot était grand et robuste' ('robuste' in later years, no doubt),[106] we can clearly appreciate the way his body-language on stage has been suggested, whether or not in reality managed by the actor's art, to make him appear as abject as possible.

Sedaine's preface, like the engraving, resembles a manifesto for a theatrical language: not coarse, but sometimes taken from the diction of the people; not afraid to mix characters of high and low estate; and demanding a special fluidity of ensemble performance. He would develop these themes in the preface to his next work.

Sources: F-Pn (Mus): ThB.893; F-Po: Liv.18.1920; GB-Lbl: 86.a.16; also 11741.aaa.39 (5). These have the same collation but the first's typesetting is very slightly different, and I have consequently often preferred ThB.893, since its preface text is slightly freer of typographical errors than the others.

TP: LE ROI / *ET* / LE FERMIER. / *COMEDIE* / EN TROIS ACTES; / Mêlée de morceaux de Musique. / *Représentée pour la première fois par les Comédiens / Italiens ordinaires du Roi, le Lundi / 22 Novembre 1762.* / Par M. SEDAINE. / *La Musique de M. de M.**** / ... / A PARIS, / Chez CLAUDE HERISSANT... / MDCCLXII. /

[105] Clairval had established himself at the Opéra-Comique since 1759 but not worked before with Sedaine.

[106] Citation without precise source made in Emile Campardon, *Les Comédiens du Roi de la troupe italienne* (Paris: Berger-Levrault, 1880; repr. Geneva, 1970), p. 7. See also 'Audinot' by Michel Noiray in *The New Grove Dictionary of Opera* (London: Macmillan, 1992).

Collation: pp. [vi] + [1] – 72 (*Privilège du Roi* on 71–2)
pp. [iii] – [iv]: *AVERTISSEMENT* / DE L'AUTEUR.

§ L'Auteur d'une Pièce croit qu'on a les yeux sur lui comme il les a sur lui-même, voilà l'origine de la plûpart des Avertissemens. Le Public ne les lit pas, ou s'en moque. Cependant ils préparent l'Histoire d'une Pièce, & les Almanachs s'en enrichissent: n'y verrois-je que cela, j'en mettrois un à la tête de celle-ci.

Jamais bon ou mauvais Ouvrage n'a eu tant de peine que celui-ci à paroître au Théâtre: il avoit en lui-même sa première difficulté; il falloit que je trouvasse un grand Artiste, un Musicien habile qui voulût bien avoir un peu de confiance en moi, enfin un ami qui voulût bien risquer un genre nouveau en musique; & quelque rares que soient les Poëtes en ce nouveau genre, les Musiciens le sont encore plus.

Cette Pièce est tirée du Théâtre Anglois, ou plutôt d'une ancienne Histoire qui n'a guères pour elle que la Tradition. Charles-quint ou Henri IV (dit la Tradition) s'égara la nuit dans une forêt, au retour d'une chasse: il entra chez un Bucheron; & là il vit peut-être pour la première fois ce qu'est un homme vis-à-vis d'un autre homme dépouillé par son ignorance du profond respect qu'il doit avoir pour son Roi.

Jamais Scène au Théâtre n'a ouvert à tout Poëte une plus vaste carrière, un moyen plus simple pour faire entendre des vérités utiles sans [iv] manquer à la vénération profonde dont il doit être pénétré.

Entraîné par la Scène, & par le lieu où elle se passe, & par l'Original Anglois qui m'a beaucoup servi; j'avois fait dire à mon Fermier des vérités de toutes les Cours, & de tous les temps: mais quelques personnes animées de ce zèle que j'aurois eu peut-être moi-même à leur place, ont crû voir des duretés; ils ont fait changer cette Scène, & elle est représentée telle qu'elle a été changée.

Cependant comme j'ai sujet de craindre que quelques personnes indiscrètes ou mal intentionnées ne prennent de là occasion de m'accuser d'avoir voulu mettre sur le Théâtre des propos téméraires, propos qui me rendroient coupable à mes propres yeux dès l'instant qu'ils le paroîtroient, je désire que cette Scène soit sous les yeux du Public telle que je l'avois faite, j'espère qu'on n'y verra que ce qu'un Fermier Anglois irrité contre un Courtisan injuste auroit pu dire en pareille circonstance: je me fiois à l'illusion du Théâtre, à l'intérêt de la Scène. Que de Vers & que de maximes seroient des horreurs, si on les détachoit du cadre pour lequel ils sont faits!

J'ai, suivant ma coutûme, fait mettre dans l'impression le jeu des Acteurs. Les Acteurs de Province sont loin de tout conseil, & peuvent en avoir besoin. §

Commentary

The challenge to his unnamed effective censors (who enforced textual changes seemingly before rehearsals began) was set out here by Sedaine in a preface which was, as we may assume from his letter to Favart, dated 25 November 1762, ready in printed form only three days after the first night:

> Je vous envoie, monsieur, les premiers exemplaires qui m'ont été remis de ma pièce; il y en a un pour madame.[107]

This timing agrees fully with other facts concerning the libretto, as in Table 3 above. The force of Sedaine's challenge was increased by the evident fact that the text as officially approved had been passed by the censor, Marin, signing his approval on 19 November, this coming after long preparation: the *privilège* was agreed for Hérissant on 9 June. Although any *privilège* laid down that the manuscript of the protected work, duly corrected in accordance with any changes imposed by the *approbation*, be deposited with the *Chancelier*, there was nevertheless an official mechanism for permitting the unchanged printing of a text that had needed softening for stage performance, involving 'une permission tacite' which was duly registered.[108] This would have presumably taken time to organise, however, and accounts perhaps for the gap between syndical registration on 27 August and Marin's *approbation* many weeks later. As final support for the date of 25 November we note that the verbal fanfare opening the preface to *Rose et Colas* (below) seems to suggest that this work had primacy in being issued for the first night itself.

Sedaine's profitability for Hérissant is seen in the terms of the new *privilège* of 9 June 1762: granted for a duration of six years, it covered not just this libretto but '*Le Roi & le Fermier, Pièces de Théâtre; & autres Ouvrages de M. Sedaine*', an advance blanket protection of the kind which, up to the Revolution, inevitably provoked provincial booksellers into pirate editions.

'Quelques réflexions' (p. 508) notes that the première of *Le Roi et le fermier* was due to have been given at court: adversaries and their 'fausses interprétations' prevented this. Michel Noiray's study earlier in this book has identified the particular sensitivities involved, and the scenes most probably altered in performance. One of the production crises merely implied at the opening of the work's preface was caused by the death of Mlle Nessel, who

---

[107] Favart (ed.), *Mémoires ... de C. S. Favart* (n. 63 above), III, p. 93. We should note however that the dates of letters in this collection are sometimes provably incorrect.

[108] The register survives at F-Pn: MSS f.fr. 21981-2 and 21989; for details and also Collé's evidence regarding *permissions tacites* see Dunkley, 'Introduction' to *Le Philosophe sans le sçavoir* (n. 44 above), p. 66 n. 1; Lough, *Writer and Public*, pp. 180, 192; Birn, 'Profits of Ideas', p. 149.

had started to learn the role of Jenny. She had earlier taken solo roles in three Monsigny *opéras-comiques*, and other works.[109]

Sedaine's praise for Monsigny testifies to what he probably felt was his ideal partnership with a composer, a 'grand Artiste', friend, and (unlike Philidor) someone who was willing to 'take risks'. 'Quelques réflexions' speaks it all more plainly:

> Philidor, après avoir gardé cet ouvrage très-longtemps, me l'avait rendu, en me disant qu'il le croyait infaisible. Il y a tout lieu de croire que quelqu'un l'avait dissuadé de le mettre en musique. Je priai M. Monsigny de le tenter; il n'hésita pas, et fit la musique telle qu'elle est, et en très-peu de temps. (p. 507)

The fuller story of Sedaine's first admiration for Monsigny's art in 1761 is told as the result of a late interview with the composer: it arose from hearing the duet between the Cadi and the Teinturier in Monsigny's *Le Cadi dupé*.[110] Philidor still subsequently worked on occasion with Sedaine; *Les Femmes vengées* (1775) seems to have been given directly to him, but 'Quelques réflexions' does not make it clear whether Philidor had set it originally around 1767 when the text was apparently first cast in prose, or only when it was made into verse (pp. 513–14). Around 1776–7 Philidor was given *Protogène*: 'mais il ne le fera pas plus qu'il n'a fait *Le Roi et le fermier*' (p. 515) was Sedaine's accurate comment.

Sources: GB-Lbl: 86.a.17; F-Pa: Rf.13.586(2)

TP: ROSE ET COLAS, / *COMEDIE* / EN UN ACTE, / PROSE ET MUSIQUE. / *Représentée, pour la première fois, par les Comédiens / Italiens ordinaires du Roi, le 8 Mars 1769* [sic]. / ... / A PARIS, / Chez CLAUDE HERISSANT ... / MDCCLXIV.

Collation: pp. [viii] + [1] – 62 (*privilège* on [vi] – [vii])

pp. [iii] – [v]: L'AUTEUR AU LECTEUR.

§ Je fais imprimer cette Pièce avant qu'elle soit représentée, & je la fais distribuer le propre jour de la représentation. Si la malignité daignoit jetter les yeux sur cet Ouvrage, elle pourroit taxer l'Auteur du Poëme d'un amour propre très-indiscret.

---

109 Roles of Lise in *Le maître en droit*, 1760; Zelmire in *Le Cadi dupé*, 1761; and Lise in *On ne s'avise jamais de tout*. The part of Jenny was taken over by Mlle La Ruette.

110 'Sedaine ... fut tellement émerveillé du duo ['Je veux former de nouveaux nœuds', sc. VIII] entre le Cadi et le Teinturier, qu'il s'écria: *Voilà mon homme*; et il ne put dormir, qu'il n'eût fait la connaissance de Monsigny.' Alexandre Choron, François Fayolle, *Dictionnaire historique des musiciens* (2 vols, Paris: Valade, 1810–11), II, pp. 61–2. My thanks are due to Michel Noiray for this reference.

Je suis bien éloigné de toute prévention; & si j'agis ainsi, c'est bien plutôt par crainte & par humilité.

Ce petit genre, (je ne dis pas de Pièces à Ariettes, comme on le nomme pour le faire ressembler à tout,) ce petit genre a l'ambition de joindre la flûte d'Euterpe au masque de Thalie, tel que les Grecs l'ont unie au sceptre de Melpomène. Ses efforts tendent à introduire la vraie Comédie, ne faisant qu'un avec les morceaux de musique nécessairement enchaînés à la scène, & vicieux dès que le concours heureux de l'harmonie ne donne pas à l'action, de là chaleur, du mouvement & de la précision, sur-tout dans ces momens rapides sur lesquels la Tragédie & la Comédie ne peuvent & n'osent appuyer. J'en vais citer un exemple; je dois rougir de le choisir dans un de mes Ouvrages: mais comme il est plus présent à mon esprit, & que même l'honneur en revient au Musicien, je l'emploie, & le voici.

C'est l'instant où, dans *Le Roi et le fermier*, le Roi est reconnu. Les complimens affectueux des Courtisans, les interrogations du Roi, la crainte [iv] de Richard d'avoir manqué de respect, la surprise mêlée de joie dans Jenny, respectueuse dans la mère, naïve dans la petite fille, étonnement simple dans les Gardes; tout ce concours de passions & d'affections n'eût été qu'un dans la nature, & rendu dans le même instant. La Tragédie ou la Comédie eût été forcée de le prolonger, de faire parler les Acteurs l'un après l'autre, & d'affoiblir la situation pour la rendre nettement avec noblesse ou décence: & la musique, en les faisant parler ensemble, a le droit de fixer le tableau, & de le tenir plus long-temps sous les yeux. Mais quel goût ne faut-il pas dans le Musicien, pour ne pas abuser de son art, & finir à propos! Tel est ce petit genre. Il emploie à la fois, ensemble, en même temps, trente à trente-cinq exécutans, & peut en employer d'avantage. La Tragédie, la Comédie la plus compliquée n'a jamais dans sa marche plus de deux ou trois interlocuteurs. Que l'un manque, c'est l'affaire du Souffleur de le remettre. Mais ici, dans un *quinque*, *sexto*, *septuor*, quelque excellens que soient les Acteurs et l'Orchestre, le moindre hazard, la moindre partie discordante à une première représentation, fait fraper du pied les connoisseurs à tête froide & à oreille fine: ceux qui se trouvent à leurs côtés, & qui ouvrent de grands yeux pour mieux écouter, ne manquent pas d'imiter les connoisseurs, & de marquer même un dépit plus décidé en proportion de l'ignorance. Les Acteurs chanteurs se déconcertent, le bruit augmente, le morceau de musique va de mal en pis; & si l'on ose redonner la Pièce, ce n'est qu'à la troisième représentation, [v] lorsque les roues sont bien engrainées, lorsque sous la lime d'usage, les ressorts ont perdu leur dureté, lorsque les trente-cinq exécutans ont acquis cette aisance, cette mollesse, qui fait oublier à l'Auditeur la fatigue de l'exécution, & lui permet de s'abandonner à un plaisir sans mêlange. Ce n'est qu'alors que la Pièce acquiert cette rondeur, ce gracieux, cet ensemble qui la fait goûter.

A l'une des Pièces dont j'ai fait le Poëme, un Acteur, par une inadvertance bien excusable, commença un *duo* dans un autre ton que l'Orchestre. Les Connoisseurs se récrièrent avec justice; leurs échos renchérirent, & jamais on n'a eu la hardiesse d'essayer une seconde fois si ce *duo* bien exécuté seroit bon ou mauvais.

C'est donc pour désirer donner à l'Auditeur toute la facilité de suivre la musique sur les paroles, & pour me servir de tout l'appui qu'elle leur donne, que j'ai anticipé l'instant de l'impression.

Si cette Pièce réussit, voilà, dira le Lecteur, bien des phrases inutiles pour peu de chose. Eh! que dira-t-il donc, si elle ne réussit pas? §

Commentary

This preface is one of the key texts for our understanding of the operatic ensemble in the eighteenth century, not least regarding performance practice and reception.

The *approbation* with *permis* was obtained three weeks before the first night of *Rose et Colas*, and the *privilège* was covered by Hérissant's six-year protection of Sedaine's theatre works issued in 1762.[111] This was seemingly the first Sedaine libretto with a preface to be available for sale at the première; a mere five years later, in *Le Déserteur*, the author would refer to this practice as his own norm. Yet the hazards of appreciation referred to in the *Rose et Colas* preface were certainly not deflected by this strategy: 'Quelques réflexions' asserts that the work was not understood and welcomed ('goûté') until its seventh performance; it thereafter held the boards. This pattern of delayed appreciation was to become, for Sedaine's supporters, evidence of the originality of his work. But his detractors were vocal in their condemnation of dramatically functional ensembles. Elisabeth Cook has shown the extent of controversy provoked by those in *Le Roi et le fermier*, not least as contained in reviews published in *Mercure de France* and *L'Avant-coureur*; the latter urged 'le poëte & le musicien' to cut half the duet between Betsy and Richard, the whole of the trio of women opening Act III (which it thought would never be correctly performed) and two-thirds of the quartet ending Act II. Moreover, this was all expressed in quite confrontational language.[112]

Sources: GB-Lbl: 86.a.16; F-Pn (Mus): ThB.243

TP: L'ANNEAU PERDU[113] / ET RETROUVÉ, / *OPERA COMIQUE* / EN DEUX ACTES; / Mêlée de morceaux de Musique. / Par M. SEDAINE. / *La Musique de M. B.* *** / *Représenté pour la première fois par les Comédiens / Italiens ordinaires du Roi, le Lundi /*

[111] Valid between 9 June 1762 and 9 June 1768.

[112] Cook, *Duet and Ensemble*, p. 273.

[113] Apostrophe missing in ThB.243 but present in ThB.4300, a parallel imprint lacking the *privilège* and corresponding pages.

20 Août 1764. / ... / A PARIS, / Chez CLAUDE HERISSANT... / MDCCLXIV
Collation: pp. vi + [1] – 56 (*privilège* on 55–6)
pp. [iii] – iv: *AVERTISSEMENT* / DE L'AUTEUR.

§ Le 5 Mars 1761 on a donné à l'Opéra Comique de la Foire S. Germain, une Pièce intitulée: *Les Bons compères, ou les bons amis*; qui, comme dit le Dictionnaire des Théâtres, n'eut pas de succès. L'Auteur de la Musique qui m'honore de son amitié, me pria de vouloir y faire des changemens, je les fis du jour au lendemain. Je retranchai des Scènes, & j'en fis des neuves pour joindre les Scènes divisées; mais tous mes efforts ne purent retarder la chute de la Pièce: la Musique cependant avoit fait plaisir, & sur-tout une des Ariettes. Séduit par elle, je me mis en tête de mettre cette Pièce en état d'être rejouée.

Cette sorte de travail donne beaucoup de peine & promet peu d'honneur; cependant je le commençai, mais de même qu'un Architecte (on peut me permettre cette comparaison) je jettai à terre toutes les parties de l'édifice, l'une après l'autre, & il s'est trouvé à la fin que j'avois fait une maison neuve: cela a obligé le Musicien de faire toute Musique nouvelle, à l'exception d'un morceau qui, par le plus grand hazard, s'est rencontré ajusté sur mes paroles, & de cette Ariette en question que j'avois parodiée. Mais le Musicien a exigé de moi que je laissasse les anciennes paroles; & de fait elles sont plus conformes [iv] à la Musique qui avoit été faite pour elles. Je les ai donc conservées, du consentement du propriétaire de l'ancienne Pièce.

Dans la première Pièce il n'y avoit que cinq Personnages, & l'intrigue étoit double. Les deux amis étoient fiancés, & l'un d'eux cherchoit à se venger sur la Maîtresse de son Compere de l'entreprise faite sur la sienne. Dans celle-ci l'intrigue est simple, & j'ai douze Acteurs; le plan, la marche, les mœurs & les caractères sont différens. Je consens cependant, si elle ne réussit pas, qu'on dise qu'elle est de moi toute entière; & si elle réussit, que je suis fort heureux d'avoir travaillé d'après les idées d'un autre.

Dans ces sortes d'Ouvrages, l'invention & le dessein sont comptés pour peu de chose; ils sont éteints par l'éclat du coloris: & ces deux premières parties, qui ne frappent que les Connoisseurs, cèdent les honneurs à la Musique, qui sçait se faire admirer, & de ceux qui s'y connoissent, & de ceux qui ne s'y connoissent pas.

J'oubliois de dire que dans l'une des Ariettes j'ai employé deux Vers de La Fontaine, & que Shakespere, par les Scènes qui terminent ses *Commeres de Windsor*, m'a donné l'idée de celles qui finissent ma Pièce. §

Commentary

The now-lost text of the original *Les Bons compères ou les Bons amis* (Foire Saint-Germain, 5 March 1761),[114] music by La Borde, remains anonymous; further light on the failure of the final work (five performances between 20 August and 2 September 1764) is shed by 'Quelques réflexions', which complains about La Borde's failure to rehearse the singers: evidently he had asked another musician to act as substitute, and the latter crossed Sedaine's path.

> Elle [*L'Anneau perdu et retrouvé*] me donna d'autant plus de peine, que le compositeur de musique occupé ailleurs, ne suivit pas avec soin les acteurs et les répétitions, et me laissa dans le sot embarras d'une querelle avec un musicien qui prétendait avoir des droits sur cet ouvrage. Je le retirai, et il n'a pas paru depuis. Cependant, il y a une situation assez neuve, du mouvement et de la gaîté. (pp. 508–9)

The libretto's *privilège* and even registration went back to 1762, so with the issuing of the *approbation* on 22 August Sedaine could well have issued the libretto soon after the first night. Significantly later, Sedaine allowed Louis Armand Chardiny to make a new musical setting, which did not survive beyond its first night on 11 September 1788, and is lost. From its press review we know that Sedaine made further additions and cuts to his text for Chardiny, whose music was given only a mixed reception.[115]

---

[114] Details from Clarence D. Brenner, *A Bibliographical List of Plays in the French Language, 1700–1789* (Berkeley and Los Angeles: University of California Press, 1947; repr. New York, 1979), p. 15, item 11014 (listed as by Sedaine) and the review mentioned in the following footnote.

[115] Unsigned article in *Affiches, annonces et avis divers* (12 September 1788), pp. 2566–7. This gives accurate details about the work's history since 1761.

Sources: First version: F-Pn (Mus): ThB.4441; Pa: R°.1280; second version (see below): GB-Lbl: 86.a.18

TP (first version): ALINE, / REINE DE GOLCONDE, / *BALLET-HÉROÏQUE*, / En trois Actes, / REPRÉSENTÉ, POUR LA PREMIÈRE FOIS, / PAR L'ACADÉMIE – ROYALE / *DE MUSIQUE*, / Le Jeudi 10 Avril 1766. / PRIX XXX. SOLS. / [device] / *AUX DÉPENS DE L'ACADÉMIE*. / A PARIS, Chés DE LORMEL ... / MDCCLXVI.

Collation: pp. [1] + [52]

p. 8: [Préface]

§ Le joli Conte d'*Aline* m'a paru si répandu dans le Public, & si digne de l'être, que je n'ai point hésité de le mettre au Théâtre. Le sujet est si connu, qu'il pourroit se pâsser de Programme; en effet, qui ne sait pas que *St Phar*, Gentilhomme Français, à peine adolescent, rencontra l'innocente *Aline* dans un Vallon, au lever de l'Aurore.

Se voir, s'aimer, se le dire, ne fut pour ce joli Couple que l'affaire d'un instant. *St Phar*, forcé de quitter sa Bergere, lui donna un Anneau d'or, qu'il pria de conserver toute sa vie.

Quelques années après, par un de ces événemens qui n'a pas besoin de preuve, *Aline* devint Reine de Golconde. Le cœur toujours occupé de son premier amour, elle fit arranger dans son Parc un lieu semblable à celui où elle avoit connu *St Phar*.

Par un événement, peut-être aussi singulier, *St Phar* quitte la France, pâsse dans les Indes, & est nommé Ambassadeur vers la Reine de Golconde: il en est reconnu (Ier. Acte), elle se présente à lui habillée en Bergère (IIe Acte), & ils s'aiment comme le premier jour (IIIe Acte).

L'Histoire ne dit pas que *St Phar* monta sur le Thrône de Golconde; mais *Aline* a sans doute fait pour *St Phar*, ce qu'Angélique a fait pour Médor. §

TP (second version): LA REINE / DE GOLCONDE, / *OPÉRA* / EN TROIS ACTES; / *Représenté à Paris en* 1766, *repris en* 1767, / *donné à Versailles devant SA MAJESTÉ*, / *le* 16 *Mai* 1771 *& le Samedi suivant*, *&* / *redonné à Paris en* 1772. / La Musique est de M. MONSIGNY.[116]

Collation: pp. [77] – 122.

pp. 79–81: *AVERTISSEMENT*.

---

[116] No other publication details follow; this is part of a Sedaine collected edition in 4 volumes entitled *Œuvres dramatiques de M. Sedaine* (Paris: Veuve Duchesne, 1776), involving a mixture of old plates and newer title-pages, with some older and some newer pagination. Obviously there may well be other copies consonant with the present one which bear 1772 publication details, such as that noted in Sonneck, *Library of Congress. Catalogue*, I, p. 67 (Paris: De Lormel, 1772), pp. 59, which however has a different TP again. F-Po: Liv.18.29 (Ballard, 1782) and other copies share the second version of the preface.

§ Le sujet d'ALINE, Reine de Golconde, est si connu, qu'il pourroit se passer de Programme; en effet, qui ne sait pas que SAINT PHAR, Gentilhomme François, à peine adolescent, rencontra l'innocente ALINE dans un vallon, au lever de l'aurore?

[Continues as for the above first version, starting at the second paragraph, with minor differences of spelling, grammar and typography.]

Commentary

A letter from Sedaine to Favart dated 8 April 1766 helps confirm the continuing advance preparation of librettos. The *permis* for that of *Aline* had been signed on 14 March. A copy of the newly printed libretto was enclosed and sent to Favart with Sedaine's letter, the terms of which also confirm that the première of the opera had not yet occurred.[117]

The date of first performance mentioned on the TP of the first version, above, is not correct: the work's première was on 15 April, the delay owing to the indisposition of one singer.[118] That part of 'Quelques réflexions' which bears on the above preface(s) concerns the work's source and dramaturgy. Sedaine's idea was to realign the boundaries of genre at the Opéra:

> J'étais cependant satisfait d'avoir fait un poëme qui remplissait tout le spectacle avec deux acteurs seulement, et les personnages étant Français, sans baguette, sans féerie, nulle magie, point de combats, ni dieux, ni diables; et, cependant, il fit plaisir. Depuis 1766, il a été repris plusieurs fois, et joué à la cour pour des fêtes de mariage. (p. 510)

The generic novelty of the work is itself reflected in the alteration of its genre denomination, seen through the two versions of the title-page reproduced above. For more details about genre and source, the former a notorious *conte* by the chevalier de Boufflers (1761), Manuel Couvreur's essay, Chapter 4 in the present book, may be consulted.

Sources: GB-Lbl: 86.a.17; F-Po: Liv.18. 1959

TP: LES SABOTS, / *OPERA COMIQUE* / EN UN ACTE, / Mêlé d'Ariettes. / Par Mrs C.... & SEDAINE. / *Représenté pour la première fois par les Comédiens / Italiens ordinaires du Roi, le Mercredi / 26*

[117] 'Voici, mon cher maître en Apollon, ma timide Aline qui va chercher près de vous de quoi se rassurer sur le jugement qu'en doit porter le public...': Favart (ed.), *Mémoires ... de C.S. Favart*, III, p. 97.

[118] Date of 15 April, and circumstances, kindly verified by Michel Noiray.

Octobre 1768. / ... / A PARIS, / Chez CLAUDE HERISSANT ... / MDCCLXVIII
Collation: pp. [iv] + [1] – 33
p. [iii]: AVERTISSEMENT.

§ Un Homme de Lettres avoit jetté rapidement sur le papier quelques Scènes, pour disposer en Opera Comique une Chanson assez connue, dont le refrain est que *Colin donne à propos & son pain & ses sabots.* L'Auteur, forcé de rester en province, ne put mettre la dernière main à cet Ouvrage, & travailler de concert avec le Musicien. Il le remit entre les mains de M. Duni, pour en faire ce qu'il plairoit. Invité par quelques circonstances à finir cet Ouvrage, il me pria de m'en charger, il me dit ses motifs: ils m'encouragèrent, & j'y travaillai avec plaisir. Mais chacun a sa façon de voir; & je n'ai conservé que la première Ariette, quelques parties du plan, & quelques phrases dans les détails. Peut-être cela étoit-il mieux, avant qu'il passât sous ma plume: mais le Musicien a approuvé mes changemens, & il s'en est servi. §

Commentary

It is clear, taking into account 'Quelques réflexions', that the rewriting that Duni and Sedaine undertook was done before the private first performance:

> En 1768, pour une petite fête à Auteuil, chez M. Bertin, je fis la petite pièce des *Sabots*. Duny en a fait la musique, laquelle est bien analogue au genre. Ce petit ouvrage avait été ébauché par M. Cazotte, auteur de *Richardet*; mais je n'ai conservé de son ouvrage que l'idée et la première ariette. (pp. 510–11)

The detailed and amusing account of Duni's artistic seduction of Sedaine, in *Correspondance littéraire*, explains how these came to collaborate for the first time: Duni attained it through first getting Sedaine to supervise the rebuilding of a certain staircase at his home.[119] The same source reproduces the whole song-text taken by Cazotte as his starting-point. *Les Sabots* was a success that prompted a second collaboration with Duni in *Thémire* (see below). It remains

[119] *Correspondance littéraire*, VIII (1 November 1768), p. 197. The account is full of praise for Sedaine's skill, and correctly predicted the work's prolonged presence in the theatre.

to be discovered whether this work was covered by an extension of the 1762 *privilège* issued for *Le Roi et le fermier* and subsequent works, which otherwise ran out in June 1768.

Sources: (1769 public version):[120] F-Pn: Yf.11610; Pa: Rf.13.684; (1770 edition): GB-Lbl: 86.a.17; (1771 edition): Pn (Mus): ThB.2059C.
TP (1769 public version): LE DESERTEUR / *DRAME* / EN TROIS ACTES, / EN PROSE MÊLÉE DE MUSIQUE. / Par M. SEDAINE. / La MUSIQUE par M *** / *Représentée, pour la première fois, par les Comédiens / Italiens ordinaires du Roi, le Lundi 6 Mars 1769. / ...* / A PARIS, / Chez CLAUDE HERISSANT ... / MDCCLXIX

TP (1770 edition): LE DESERTEUR / *DRAME* / EN TROIS ACTES, / EN PROSE, MÊLÉ DE MUSIQUE. / Par M. SEDAINE. / La MUSIQUE par M +++ / *Représenté à PARIS, pour la première fois, par les / Comédiens Italiens ordinaires du Roi, le Lundi 6 / Mars 1769. / Et à FONTAINEBLEAU, le 8 Octobre 1769, en / présence de Sa Majesté. /* Seconde Edition, revue par l'Auteur. / ... / A PARIS, / Chez CLAUDE HERISSANT ... / MDCCLXX

TP (1771 edition): broadly as for 1770 edition except for publisher's details: Pellet & Fils, A Paris, et se vendent à Geneve, 1771.
Collation (1769 public version): pp. [x] + 82; (1770 edition): pp. viii + [1] – 84; (1771 edition): pp. vii + 8–68.

The prefaces between 1769 and 1770 were changed significantly only in respect of the final sentence; between 1770 and 1771 an awkwardly fitting phrase ending the third paragraph was removed (see below).

[120] The Court 1769 version for Fontainebleau, 11 October, contains no preface (Pierre-Robert-Christophe Ballard, 1769), pp. [vi] + 82. It is found at F-Pa: Ra3.236.

pp. [iii] – viii:[121] *PREFACE.*

§ Lorsque j'ai donné *Blaise le savetier*, Opéra Comique, après la première représentation, un homme de robe vint me dire: Votre Pièce m'a plû, la musique en est bonne: mais l'intrigue porte à faux, il s'agit de l'exécution des meubles de Blaise, & l'Huissier n'est pas en règle: par l'Ordonnance de 1667, il doit être assisté de deux témoins, il n'y en a qu'un, ainsi la saisie est nulle.

Par quelque raison semblable, je ne doute pas qu'on n'ait trouvé des nullités dans l'affaire de mon *Déserteur*; j'ai cependant lû ma Pièce à des connoisseurs en cette partie: après avoir eu la bonté de l'écouter, ils m'ont assuré que mon Soldat étoit dans le cas d'être condamné.

Il est vrai que j'aurois dû, suivant ma coutume, faire débiter l'Ouvrage le jour même de la représentation, j'avois même cette fois-ci une raison très-forte.[122] J'ai placé des parties d'exposition dans un *Quinqué* dont les paroles sont per- [iv] dues, sur-tout les premiers jours; les Gardes disent: *Suivons ses pas, voyons, voyons ce qu'il va faire, voyons s'il court vers la frontière.*[123] Cela n'a pas été entendu, & ne pouvoit pas l'être.

Le jour d'une première représentation, une grande partie du public n'a que de l'esprit, il n'a point d'entrailles, il se roidit contre le plaisir qu'on veut lui donner, ce n'est (pour ainsi dire) qu'à son corps défendant qu'il veut bien en prendre; ajoutez l'ambition de deviner le dénouement, de prévenir la critique, de précipiter son jugement avant celui des autres. Je me souviens que dans ma jeunesse j'aurois été bien fâché que mes voisins m'eussent enlevé un bon mot. Hélas, je n'en voulois ni à l'Auteur ni à l'Ouvrage, c'étoit seulement pour prouver à ceux qui m'entouroient, que j'avois plus d'esprit qu'eux. Depuis que j'ai acquis quelques connoissances théâtrales, j'écoute, & je me tais, peut-être encore par amour propre, de crainte de voir démenti aux représentations sui- [v] vantes le sentiment que j'aurois avancé, peut-être aussi par d'autres motifs.

Dans ce genre d'Ouvrage, qui peut acquérir de l'importance en se rapprochant du Théâtre des Grecs,[124] que de choses peuvent nuire le jour d'une première représentation, sur-tout lorsque le dialogue est serré! Et je crois nécessaire qu'il le soit. Un mot passé, répété, transposé, substitué à un autre; une phrase simple débitée du ton d'une maxime, une replique oubliée (ce qui

---

[121] 1769 and 1770 editions only. 1771 edition ends on p. vii.

[122] See Table 3 above: permission to publish the libretto was dated 1 April 1769, a month later.

[123] Here the 1769 and 1770 editions included the phrase, no longer distinguished by italicisation, 'c'est annoncer l'entr'acte', which was probably incorrectly printed from a deleted portion of Sedaine's manuscript. Pellet's edition was of course illicit.

[124] [*Note by Sedaine*:] Il paroit qu'ils ne mettoient en musique que les Chœurs & l'instant de la Scène qui y paroissoit propre.

jette du louche sur toute une scène), une entrée retardée, ou précipitée, les mouvemens trop vifs, ou trop lents dans les airs.

L'Acteur, quelque talent qu'il ait, ne peut encore avoir acquis ce qu'il ne peut obtenir que d'un long usage, des gestes faciles, des mouvemens arrondis, cette mollesse, cette aisance qu'il n'a pas, tant qu'il y songe, & l'à propos continuel d'une situation que le chant embarrasse jusqu'à ce qu'il l'embellisse, enfin les fautes même de l'Auteur.

[vi] A l'une des représentations de ma Pièce, j'ai fait une partie de ces remarques, autant que les distractions données par mes voisins pouvoient me le permettre, & l'un d'eux ne m'a point gâté par ses éloges; d'instant en instant il s'écrioit: Ah! que c'est gauche! ah! que c'est mauvais! ah! que c'est bête!

Dans nos Salles de Spectacle l'Auteur ne sçait où se mettre pour observer son Ouvrage, pour le juger tranquillement, sainement, & d'après ses observations se prescrire à lui-même les corrections indispensables: s'il s'expose aux regards du public, il ne peut manquer d'y paroître ridicule. Mais, dira-t-on, ses amis lui reportent ce qu'il doit faire, Ses amis! L'un blâme ce que l'autre approuve, un troisième vient lui dire qu'il faut absolument qu'il change telle ou telle phrase; & la phrase citée n'est pas dans la Pièce.

Un Directeur de l'Opéra Comique, homme intelligent, en faisant construire une salle au fauxbourg saint Laurent, [vii] avoit eu l'attention de faire pratiquer sous l'Amphithéâtre une lorgnette d'où les regards passoient sur les têtes du Parterre; là il écrivoit lui-même sous la dictée de l'Auteur les réflexions, les observations, les critiques; & dès le jour même l'Ouvrage prenoit une nouvelle forme, & même assez rapidement pour faire douter si les fautes y avoient été.

Une de celles qui m'ont été reprochées dans la Pièce du *Déserteur*, est d'avoir placé des morceaux de musique dans les instans où l'intérêt a de la chaleur, & ils l'éteignent: je ne l'ai pas fait sans y avoir réfléchi.

Dans ce genre d'Ouvrage, l'intérêt doit soutenir la musique pendant les premières représentations, dût-elle y nuire; mais lorsqu'ensuite la Pièce est sçue, lorsqu'on peut l'entendre sans l'inquiétude de ce qui doit arriver, la musique fait écouter le Poëme sans dégoût, cinquante représentations dans la même année, avantage que n'ont pas des Ouvrages de littérature beaucoup plus [viii] estimables; ainsi j'attends, pour me rendre sur cet article, que la Pièce ait tout son ensemble.

La faute sur laquelle j'ai plus de peine à me justifier, est cette grace apportée par cette jeune fille. Que signifie (m'a-t-on dit) ce papier qu'elle a dans son sein? Le paquet donné au Grand Prévôt a dû renfermer sa grace, puisqu'elle est notifiée avant que Louise arrive dans la place publique: cela est vrai; mais voilà comme j'ai conçu ma fable.

Louise a demandé de porter cette grace, on ne s'en est fié ni à son zèle ni à sa personne: cependant pour calmer ses inquiétudes, on lui a donné un papier par lequel il est dit qu'Alexis a sa grace; & elle croit que ce papier est nécessaire. Eh, que ne le disiez-vous? Hé, qui pourroit tout dire? J'oublie souvent les choses les plus nécessaires, tant je crains de mettre des inutilités. Pourquoi donc avez-vous fait cette Préface? Vous avez raison, mais c'est encore une de mes fautes.[125] §

Commentary

Le Déserteur's *approbation* was granted on 1 April 1769, its *privilège* on 10 May, and the syndical registration was finally recorded on 10 June. The corresponding fact that this libretto and its preface must have been published over two months after the work's première may relate simply to Hérissant's desire for a *privilège*, otherwise to the process of polishing the text. The preface itself probably echoes actual experience before and after the first night; perhaps its description of first-night audiences was a reminiscence. Sedaine had been looking forward anxiously to this, his first musical *drame*, for years. 'Quelques réflexions' mentions 'four years of impatience', and the *Correspondance littéraire* noted:

> M. Sedaine avait [*Le Déserteur*] dans son porte-feuille depuis environ trois ans, et ... la négligence de son musicien avait frustré l'attente du public jusqu'à ce moment. Depuis que M. Monsigny a aspiré à une place de maître-d'hôtel de M. le duc d'Orléans et qu'il l'a obtenue, il a paru négliger son métier de compositeur ... A force de persécutions on a enfin arraché ce *Déserteur* des mains du musicien.[126]

Sedaine was clearly stung by the anonymous sixteen-page *Remerciment du public à la préface du Déserteur*, published illicitly and without title-page, which attacked his preface and libretto with equal gusto. The preface was mocked for its 'charitables instructions', its arrogance in lecturing the public; for its odd turns of phrase, its familiar tone concerning members of the aristocracy, its generalisations in treating the public as a 'vraie machine, qu'un grand génie doit remuer à son gré'; and finally for its unacceptably disingenous appeal to the public to overlook 'les fautes de l'Auteur'. This is castigated as 'une modestie excessive'. One of the broadside's jokes was at Sedaine's supposed prediction of fifty or more performances of his new piece, i.e. in the third paragraph from the end. 'Quelques réflexions' retorts:

---

[125] This main text gives the 1770 version of the final sentence. The 1769 and the 1771 editions have the following: 'Vous avez raison, mais il est si aisé de ne la pas dire.' The satirical broadside *Remerci[e]ment du public à la préface du Déserteur* (found in F-Pa: Rf.13.684) seized on the wording reproduced in the 1770 text.

[126] *Correspondance littéraire*, VIII (15 March 1769), pp. 307–8; 'Quelques réflexions', p. 512.

> Il y a peu d'ouvrage dont on ait dit autant de mal, et qui, depuis neuf ans, se soit soutenu avec autant d'avantage ... Le public a voulu à toute force que j'aie fait imprimer dans la préface de cette pièce qu'elle aurait certainement cinquante représentations, dans la même année: assertion que je n'ai jamais écrite. (p. 512)

Actually, Sedaine's words (which form part of his developing theory of *opéra-comique*, briefly sketched in section (g) above) are a tribute not to himself but to Monsigny.

The sixth paragraph of the preface describes the special skills required in the *opéra-comique* performer. They surely applied to Joseph Caillot (1733–1816), the first Alexis in *Le Déserteur*, and known as an exceptional actor–singer. His retirement in 1772 caused 'Quelques reflexions', to note 'un tort irréparable' done to the opera: in the preface to *Le Magnifique* (below) lies similar evidence of the way Sedaine's own production style ideally needed to be preserved by the original actors, but in practice could quickly become lost.

Sources: (Court première): F-Po: Liv.18.648; (public première): GB-Lbl: 86.a.18; F-Pn (Mus): ThB.1265.
TP (Court première): THEMIRE, / *PASTORALE*, / EN UN ACTE, / REPRÉSENTÉ, DEVANT SA MAJESTÉ, / A FONTAINEBLEAU, / *Le Samedi 20 Octobre 1770.* / [device] / DE L'IMPRIMERIE / DE PIERRE-ROBERT-CHRISTOPHE BALLARD ... / MDCCLXX

TP (public première): THEMIRE, / *PASTORALE*, / EN UN ACTE, / DÉDIÉE A MADAME B**, / *PAR M. SEDAINE*, / LA MUSIQUE DE M. DUNY: / *Représentée, pour la première fois, devant* / *Sa Majesté, à Fontainebleau, le Samedi* / *20 Octobre 1770*; / *Et, à Paris, pour la première fois, par les* / *Comédiens Italiens Ordinaires du Roi*, / *le Lundi 26 Novembre 1770.* / ... / *A PARIS*, / Chez CLAUDE HERISSANT. ... / MDCCLXX
Collations: (Court première): pp. [ii] + 44; (public première): pp. [viii] + [1] – 46 (*Approbation* and *Privilege* on [45–6]) .
p. [vii]: AVERTISSEMENT.

§ Cette Pastorale est tirée d'une Eglogue de Fontenelle; je l'ai même terminée par le dernier vers:[127]

Je m'expose à l'amour, & n'aimez pas Doris.

---

127 The main text follows the public première version throughout. The court version of the first sentence is as follows: 'Ce petit Ouvrage est tiré d'une Eglogue de Fontenelle: je l'ai même terminé par le dernier vers.' Three small typographical and orthographical differences occur in the remainder of the court text.

On peut me reprocher que mon dénouement a quelque ressemblance avec celui de *La Princesse d'Elide*; mais (je ne sçais) il me semble que cet amour, que cette jalousie qui se dévelope avec naïveté, conviennent bien autant à une Bergère qu'à une Princesse: d'ailleurs l'Eglogue m'a entraîné à finir ainsi. §

Commentary

A letter from Sedaine to Favart dated 26 October 1770 was sent just after the court première of *Thémire*, with the new libretto:

> J'ai l'honneur de vous envoyer ma pastorale, et vous verrez que je justifie en ma personne ce que j'ai dit des pastorales dans le Jardinier et le Bon Seigneur.[128]

Favart must have been sent the Ballard libretto since the public one, which cites 26 November as the first night, cannot yet have been contemplated. But Sedaine was clearly in a position to issue the public's version text in time for its first night: the *approbation* was signed on 20 October and the *privilège* was issued on 24 October, protecting it for three years.

La Princesse d'Elide (1728) was a *ballet-héroïque* by Simon-Joseph Pellegrin, music by Alexandre de Villeneuve. The *Correspondance littéraire* detailed Sedaine's source as the ninth eclogue in a collection of poetry entitled *Ismène* by Bernard Le Bovier de Fontenelle; it also placed blame for the work's failure squarely at the hands of Duni.

> ... c'est un singulier homme que ce Sedaine. Il a quitté Philidor avant qu'il fût ce qu'il est devenu; il a fait réussir Monsigny, malgré toute la pauvreté de son style; il prend Duni quand il est vieux; quand Grétry sera mort, il voudra travailler avec lui, et je crains que ce ne soit bientôt.[129]

'Quelques réflexions' acknowledges the possibility of weakness in this score, Duni's last, and explains the reason why, some time later, Sedaine felt able to approach Grétry: Monsigny, his preferred composer, retained two unset Sedaine librettos in his possession (pp. 511–13).

---

[128] Favart (ed.), *Mémoires ... de C. S. Favart*, III, p. 100. It continues with information requiring further research: 'J'ai gagné mon procès sur l'impression de cet ouvrage; elle a été faite par mon imprimeur: je pourrai en payer la dépense, mais celui qui corrige le premier un abus doit les [sic] supporter, et je ne m'en plaindrai pas.'

[129] *Correspondance littéraire*, IX (1 Dec. 1770), p. 174. The work was withdrawn after four performances. For the surviving music, see Kent M. Smith, 'Egidio Duni and the Development of the Opéra-Comique from 1753 to 1770', Ph.D. dissertation, Cornell U., 1980, p. 300.

Sources:[130] (public première): GB-Lbl: 86.a.18; F-Po: Liv.18.1983; (Court première): F-Pn (Mus): ThB.1649A; Pn: Yf.11617

TP (public première): LE MAGNIFIQUE, / *COMÉDIE* / EN TROIS ACTES, / EN PROSE, ET EN VERS / MIS EN MUSIQUE, / *Terminée par un Divertissement.* / PAR M. SEDAINE. / La Musique est de M. GRETY. [sic] / *Représenté à Paris, pour la première fois, par les / Comédiens Italiens ordinaires du Roi, / le Lundi* 4 *Mars* 1773. / *Et à Versailles en présence de SA MAJESTÉ, / le 26 Mars* 1773. / ... Chez CLAUDE HERISSANT ... / MDCCLXIII

TP (Court première): LE MAGNIFIQUE, / *COMÉDIE* / EN TROIS ACTES, / EN PROSE ET EN VERS; / MIS EN MUSIQUE, / *Terminée par un Divertissement.* / *Représentée devant SA MAJESTÉ,* / *à Versailles, le 19 Mars 1773.* / [device] / DE L'IMPRIMERIE / DE PIERRE-ROBERT-CHRISTOPHE BALLARD ... / MDCCLXXIII

Collation (public première): pp. [viii] + [1] – 71; (Court première): pp. [viii] + [1] – 71.

pp. [v] – vii: *AVERTISSEMENT.*

§ En 1731, Houdart de la Mothe, de l'Académie Françoise, a fait représenter *Le Magnifique*, Pièce en deux actes & en prose; elle est tirée du conte de La Fontaine, qui le même titre, & elle est restée au Théâtre François.

Ce n'est point pour joûter contre cet Auteur que j'ai traité le même sujet; je n'ai ni l'esprit, ni l'élocution de Monsieur de la Mothe: mais ce conte m'a paru propre au genre de l'Opéra Comique; il promettoit des situations sur lesquelles la Musique pût s'arrêter, & j'ai cherché à en profiter.

Je l'avouerai à ma honte, je ne connoissois de cet Ecrivain célèbre qu'*Inès de Castro*, Tragédie très-intéressante, & ses Fables qui ont bien de l'esprit; je n'avois ni lû, ni vû représenter *Le Magnifique* lorsque j'ai composé celui-ci, & ce fut un [vi] bonheur pour moi, n'ayant fait aucun effort pour éviter l'intrigue qu'il a choisie: mon imagination n'a point été obsédée de ses idées, & nous ne nous sommes rencontrés que dans les scènes inévitables.[131]

Son Aldobrandin est dupé par tout ce qui l'entoure, le mien au contraire a trompé tout le monde par une fausse probité. Les situations (à l'exception de celle donnée par le conte), l'exposition, le nœud, le dénouëment, les caractères même sont différens; il me reste à apprendre si j'ai été aussi heureux que mon prédécesseur.

---

[130] It will be seen from the TP transcriptions that two different court dates are recorded. At present we know the accuracy of neither date; nor which libretto was issued first.

[131] This apparent unfamiliarity with Houdar de La Motte's work helps in dating the conception of *Le Magnifique*: Mark Ledbury notes that at the time of writing *Maillard ou Paris sauvé* (1769–70) Sedaine knew La Motte's *Œdipe*, as the preface to that work's printed version indicates.

Si cet Ouvrage réussit, je dois encore être bien modeste: le Musicien enlève, & mérite toujours la plus grande partie des éloges. Il faut quelque réflexion pour s'appercevoir du soin avec lequel l'Auteur du Drame écarte les moyens de paroître aux dépens de son Associé, comme il se replie, comme il s'efface, combien enfin il a fait de sacrifices pour n'être que le piédestal de [vii] la Statue qu'il lui éleve. Il est besoin, il est vrai, que le piédestal soit solide, & je n'ose m'en flater.

J'ai mis avec une sorte d'affectation le jeu du Théâtre, & la Pantomime[132] qui occupe la scène pendant les ritournelles (toujours trop longues pour tout Auditeur qui n'est pas Musicien); mais je n'ai eu cette attention que pour l'utilité des Acteurs qui sont loin des premiers conseils donnés par les Auteurs. §

Commentary

Sedaine's account above of text–music functions was discussed above in (g); these developing views probably also relate to the fact that *Le Magnifique* was his first work with Grétry, whose meteoric career had begun with his first Paris production, *Le Huron* (1768), text by Marmontel.

> ... les Monsignistes sont fâchés que Sedaine ait travaillé avec un autre musicien que Monsigny et ... les Marmontélistes sont fâchés que Grétry ait travaillé avec un autre poète que Marmontel. Ces deux cabales se sont réunies pour crier à tort et à travers.[133]

As if to anticipate the intrinsic attention which Grétry's more Italianate style would attract by comparison with the less florid style of Monsigny, Sedaine's preface emphasises the librettist's role in general rather than the particulars of, say, ensembles: to precompose a work, as it were, envisioning the best roles for music. Thus one can better understand his chagrin, expressed in 'Quelques réflexions', at the vitiation of a grand design, before as well as after the première:

> Dès les premières représentations, la faible santé de M. La Ruette [in the role of Aldobrandin] en a fait supprimer le divertissement de la fin, nécessaire cependant au dénouement, et au complément du caractère du *Magnifique*. Dès la cinquième représentation, presque tous les rôles ont été doublés, ce qui enlève toute la tradition des répétitions. (p. 513)

---

[132] 'Pantomine' in the present sources; 'Pantomime' in the Hérissant edition of 1773, pp. 56, here p. 4.

[133] *Correspondance littéraire*, X (March 1773), p. 210. 'Quelques réflexions', p. 513, confirms that Sedaine offered his text directly to Grétry.

Rehearsal work went for little once leading actors started using understudies. Since Clairval acted the part of Octave (the Magnifique) this was a serious matter. Cast-lists in librettos, unfortunately for us, never reproduce the understudies' names.

Antoine Houdard de La Motte's *Le Magnifique*, a two-act *comédie* in prose with *divertissement*, was first seen at the Théâtre-Français on 30 November 1731. When revived at Fontainebleau in November 1753 it was given a prologue and three *intermèdes*, perhaps after the style of the *intermezzi* then being given at the Opéra by the Bambini troupe.[134]

Sources: GB-Lbl: 86.a.18; F-Pn (Mus): ThB.3261 (lacks frontispiece)

TP: LES FEMMES / VENGÉES, / *OPÉRA-COMIQUE*, / EN UN ACTE ET EN VERS; / *PAR M. SEDAINE.* / LA MUSIQUE DE M. PHILIDOR. / *Représenté, pour la première fois, le Lundi 20 Mars, / par les Comédiens Italiens ordinaires du Roi. / ... / A PARIS*, / Chez MUSIER fils... / MDCCLXXV

Collation: pp. [iv] + [1] – [77]. Whole-page engraving opposite TP. Music on 69–74; 'Errata' on [75]

p. [iii]: *AVERTISSEMENT.*

§ J'ai hasardé cet Opéra-Comique, pour essayer l'effet que pourroient produire sur le Théâtre, trois Scènes à la fois, en trois lieux différens. Je crois, cependant, qu'elles ne sont admissibles, qu'en observant l'unité d'action; c'est-à-dire, en donnant aux Personnages, occupés dans les parties latérales, l'application à la Scène qui remplit le milieu du Théâtre.

La Tragédie même pourroit peut-être, employer ce moyen avec succès. Je n'ai jamais vu la Scène entre Junie & Britannicus, sans penser que, si Néron, caché pour les Personnages, étoit présent à nos yeux, il n'auroit pas sur le visage un seul mouvement qui ne fît éprouver (à moi Spectateur) un sentiment confus & profond d'inquiétude, de terreur & de pitié.[135]

Je pourrois étendre cette observation sur le concours de plusieurs Scènes ensemble, mais je n'ai point encore acquis par mes Ouvrages le droit de donner des leçons.

J'ai fait mettre une Gravure [see Fig. 6, p. 162] qui représente la situation de la Scène. Cet Ouvrage pourroit être porté en Province par la Musique, & j'ai voulu donner aux Entrepreneurs de Spectacles l'intelligence de la distribution des trois Scènes. §

---

134 Brenner, *A Bibliographical List*, p. 85, item 7819.

135 Racine, *Britannicus* (1669), Act V, sc. I, in which Britannicus is warned of the threat posed by the character of Néron: the latter has him poisoned immediately afterwards.

Commentary

No *privilège* was sought by Musier for this work; with the *approbation* and *permis* obtained by 21 February, we can assume early or first-night sale of the libretto. In the 56-page Musier editions dated 1775 and after, the work acquired the subtitle *Les Feintes infidélités.*[136] Perhaps this addition was connected with the prudery noted in 'Quelques réflexions', stemming from knowledge of the rather joyful female infidelities in La Fontaine's source tale:

> La pudeur de nos dames s'effaroucha d'abord de voir représenter un sujet tiré des *Rémois*, et ne virent la pièce qu'à travers le conte. Elles paraissent cependant s'être réconciliées avec cet ouvrage, et le regardent jouer sans le secours de l'éventail. (p. 513)

Source: F-Pn (Mus): ThB.4204

TP: AUCASSIN / ET / NICOLETTE, / OU / *LES MŒURS* / DU BON VIEUX TEMS, / COMÉDIE / EN QUATRE ACTES ET EN VERS, / Dont une partie est mise en Musique; / *Représentée, pour la première fois, devant / LEURS MAJESTÉS à Versailles, le 30 / Décembre 1779, par les Comédiens Italiens / Ordinaires du Roi, & à Paris, le 3 Janvier / 1780.* / .... / A PARIS, / Chez la Veuve BALLARD & Fils ... / MDCCLXXX

Collation: pp. [xii] + [1] – 86

pp. [iii] – x [*recte* xi]: *PRÉFACE*

§ Il est peu de Préfaces qui ne prouvent l'importance qu'un Auteur met à son ouvrage; mais que l'homme de Lettres qui n'en met aucune à ses productions, se leve & m'accuse. Ceci posé, je commence.

J'ai travesti le fabliau d'Aucassin en Opéra Comique pour obéir au désir de M. de la Curne de Sainte Palaye, cet Académicien, ce vieillard respectable, qui, dans le cours d'une longue vie, a fait peu de pas qui n'aient eu pour motif d'augmenter les trésors de notre Littérature.

C'est pour faire connoître celle du douze & du treizième siècle, qu'il fit imprimer le [iv] fabliau d'Aucassin & Nicolette, *en mettant* (comme le dit son Avertissement) *dans un françois intelligible, le texte original qui n'auroit pû être entendu que d'un petit nombre de personnes.*

Je n'ai fait, ainsi que M. de Sainte Palaye, aucun changement dans les mœurs & dans les caractères de ce fabliau; mais j'ai ménagé, autant qu'il m'a été possible, notre dédaigneuse délicatesse, qui, malgré toute mon attention, a fait voir encore quelque mécontentement.

---

136 Sonneck, *Library of Congress. Catalogue*, I, p. 490.

On m'a reproché le manque de parole du Comte de Garins à son fils; je n'entrerai pas dans une discussion; je n'examinerai pas si un père doit être fidèle à sa promesse, lorsque son exécution peut conduire son fils à une action qui le déshonore. Je me contenterai de répondre; je n'ai fait que suivre le fabliau. Que seroit-ce donc, si j'avois mis dans mon Drame toute la dureté des scènes qui se passent entre le père & le fils. En voici l'extrait.

[v] "De quoi me parlez-vous, mon père, dit Aucassin (c'étoit le nom de l'enfant), que Dieu ne m'accorde jamais rien de ce que je lui demande, si l'on me voit armer chevalier, monter à cheval, & me mêler dans aucun tournoi, ni combat, où je fasse sentir la vigueur de mes bras aux chevaliers, & où j'éprouve la force des leurs, avant que vous m'ayez donné Nicolette, ma douce amie, que tant j'aime: cher fils, dit le père, cela ne se peut, laissez-là cette chétive créature, &c."

Aucassin de retour du combat, dit: "Mon père, voici votre ennemi qui vous a tant fait de maux & de tourmens depuis dix ans que dure cette guerre, sans que personne en ait pu venir à bout."

"Beau fils, dit le père, ce sont là de ces tours de jeunesse qui conviennent à votre âge, sans songer d'avantage à vos folles amours. N'allez-vous pas encore me prê- [vi] cher, mon père, dit Aucassin, songez plutôt à me tenir la parole que vous m'avez donnée. Quelle parole, beau fils? Quoi! mon père, l'auriez-vous déjà oubliée? Par mon chef, l'oubliera qui voudra, pour moi je ne la veux pas oublier; mais je l'ai fort à cœur. Comment? ne m'avez-vous pas promis, quand je pris les armes & quand j'allai au combat, que si Dieu me ramenoit sain & sauf, vous me laisseriez voir ma douce amie que j'aime tant, tant voir que je pourrois lui dire deux ou trois paroles, & la baiser une fois, ainsi me l'avez-vous promis, & je veux que vous la teniez.

"Dieu me punisse, dit le père, si j'en fais rien, & si elle étoit ici, je la brûlerois dans un feu, & vous même auriez tout à craindre de moi. Est-ce là tout? dit Aucassin, oui, par Dieu, oui, fait le père; certe, répond Aucassin, je suis faché de voir mentir un homme de votre âge. Puis s'adressant au Comte de [vii] Valence, n'êtes-vous pas mon prisonnier? lui dit-il; oui certe, fait le Comte; donnez-moi donc votre main, dit Aucassin; très-volontiers, fait le Comte, en mettant sa main dans celle d'Aucassin qui exige sa foi d'accomplir tout ce qu'il lui dira de faire. Jurez-moi, dit Aucassin, que toutes les fois qu'il vous prendra envie, ou que vous ferez en pouvoir de faire honte, ou dommage à mon père, soit en sa personne, soit en ses biens, vous ne vous y épargnerez pas. Cessez de vous mocquer de moi, Sire, dit-il, imposez-moi telle rançon qu'il vous plaira, vous ne sçauriez me demander, or, argent, chevaux, palefroi; fourure de vair ou de gris, chiens, ou oiseau que je ne vous les donne. Comment, fait Aucassin, ne vous reconnoissez-vous donc pas pour mon prisonnier? Je l'avoue, fait le Comte Bongars! Dieu me damne, fait Aucassin, vous me donnerez votre foi, ou je vous [viii] fais sauter la cervelle. Je vous jurerai par Dieu tout ce qu'il vous plaira, répond-il, & lui en donne sa parole.

Aucassin alors le fait monter sur un cheval, en monte un autre, & le conduit en lieu de sureté."

Voilà les mœurs que j'ai voulu peindre, voilà les faits que j'ai voulu représenter; si le fond de l'ouvrage étoit de mon invention, on auroit droit de me dire: pourquoi cela n'est-il pas autrement? Mais a-t-on jamais reproché à un Auteur Dramatique d'avoir fait Œdipe incestueux, ou Oreste parricide? Peut-être m'accusera-t-on d'avoir mal choisi mon sujet; mais j'ai dit la raison qui me l'a fait entreprendre: j'ai cru que la foi faussée, la parole manquée à Aucassin, seroient en partie le foyer de l'intérêt que je desirois qu'il excitât.

La vue d'une injustice nous attache fortement à celui qui la supporte, surtout s'il en est profondément affecté, & si l'offenseur se croît sûr de l'impunité.

[ix] A la première représentation du *Cid*, le soufflet donné sur la scène au vénérable Don Diègue doit avoir porté dans l'âme des spectateurs une terrible indignation; les vieillards ont dû croire avoir reçu le soufflet, & les jeunes gens l'ordre de le venger: aux représentations suivantes, le sentiment de l'outrage doit avoir été mitigé par la certitude de la vengeance que le fils doit en tirer.[137]

Ainsi je pense qu'un Auteur, ne doit adopter qu'avec beaucoup de circonspection les changemens que les mouvemens du Public semblent lui prescrire aux premières représentations de son ouvrage, l'auditeur ne sachant point encore ce qui va suivre, l'impression qu'il reçoit est quelquefois si forte, qu'il peut en être trop affecté, & sa bruyante émotion peut avoir les accens d'une réprobation générale qui n'a plus lieu aux autres représentations.

J'avois pris la précaution de faire annon- [x] cer & afficher les mœurs du bon vieux tems; cela ne m'a pas réussi, l'auditeur n'a pas voulu se transporter au douzième siècle; c'est avec peine qu'il a supporté un Souverain qui se livre à la gaité d'un repas, qui croît à la magie, un Vicomte qui ne sait pas lire, &c. On m'a fait même changer ce vers:

> "Vien, mon fils, vien passer la nuit près de ton père."

Cependant la coutume étoit alors de coucher dans la même chambre, & quelquefois dans le même lit, je me garderai bien de dire la raison qui m'a été alleguée, pour me forcer à ce changement; ce seroit calomnier le Parterre.

J'ai laissé dans cette édition bien des choses que j'ai supprimées aux représentations, je les ai laissées, parce qu'elles me paroissent nécessaires. Les Directeurs des Comédies de province auront recours à la partition gravée pour sçavoir ce qui a été retranché aux représentations qui ont suivi les premières.

[x=xi] Nota. Vous remarquerez que dans cette Préface, l'Auteur met sur la même ligne un misérable Opéra Comique, & les grandes Tragédies d'Oreste &

---

[137] Pierre Corneille, *Le Cid* (1636–7), Act I, sc. III, in which Don Diègue is struck by Le Comte (Don Gomes).

d'Œdipe, il compare le Cid à Aucassin; ainsi il se compare à Corneille. (Je fais présent de cette note au premier Journaliste qui voudra s'en servir.) §

Commentary

Only three public performances of *Aucassin et Nicolette* in its initial four-act incarnation were given. The above preface was printed neither in the Court libretto for 30 December 1779 (Ballard et Fils, 1780), nor in the three-act librettos of 1782 and later; no *privilège* was sought by Veuve Ballard for the work. Although the official permissions to publish the libretto both came through on the last day of 1779, one sees from the words ending the preface that this libretto and its preface were, in effect, directed into a Parisian void: the imprint was the mere record of an unsuccessful run, a justification after the event, an archival text that reinstated changes imposed in production, and an expression of hope that provincial theatres might take it up.[138] All this may help to explain the extraordinarily combative tone of the final 'note', issued in the bitterness of defeat. Among the problems noted by contemporaries, aside from the archaisms, were Sedaine's poetic shortcomings and the yet greater ones evinced by the actor-singers, especially Menier as Garins, comte de Beaucaire.[139]

More fortunately, the revised version – seen on 7 January 1782 – was quite successful.

Sources: F-Pn: Yf.11302; Pa: Rf.13.585(6)

TP: RICHARD, / CŒUR DE LION, / COMÉDIE EN TROIS ACTES, / EN PROSE ET EN VERS, MIS EN MUSIQUE. / *Représentée, pour la première fois, à Paris, / par les Comédiens Italiens ordinaires du / Roi, le* 21 *Octobre* 1784; *& à Fontaine- / bleau, devant leurs Majestés, le* 25 *Octobre* / 1785. / ... / A PARIS, / Chez BRUNET. ... / MDCCLXXXVI
Collation: pp. [viii] + 67[140]
pp. [v] – vii: [Préface]

§ Je ne peux m'empêcher de faire précéder ce Drame par un mot de Préface; il est de mon devoir de remercier l'Auteur des deux couplets de Romance que j'ai employés dans cette Pièce, & qui sont tirés de l'intéressant Fabliau qui

---

[138] Publication delays might also have been caused by the need to obtain *permission tacite* to reproduce the original text: see commentary and notes to *Le Roi et le fermier*, above.

[139] 'Un des principaux rôles et des plus difficiles en même temps, celui du vieux comte de Beaucaire, a été indignement défiguré par le sieur Menier': *Correspondance littéraire*, XII (Jan. 1780), p. 364. Mme Dugazon was a success as Nicolette, however.

[140] The TP and its verso are unpaginated and the numbering sequence omits pp. iii and iv.

m'en a donné l'idée; je ne me suis permis que d'y changer une expression. Je n'aurois pu composer une complainte plus favorable à la texture de mon Drame; elle a (si j'ose le dire) la physionomie du tems, du lieu et des personnages que je mets en scene, & le chant qu'elle a inspiré au Musicien paroît être du même siècle.

J'avois manqué mon dénouement; en donnant à mon Gouverneur une importance qui divisoit l'intérêt, & qui me faisoit [vi] négliger une des grandes regles du Théâtre: *Ad eventum festina*, cours à l'événement.

Tous ceux qui me parloient de ma Pièce & de ses défauts me conseilloient de la terminer en faisant donner un assaut à la forteresse où est renfermé Richard; mais j'avois la plus grande répugnance à employer ce moyen, il me paroissoit trop connu, trop commun; je n'y avois pas assez réfléchi; la situation de Blondel & de Richard le rend, en quelque façon, neuf, par la nécessité de finir ainsi; eh! quels charmes nouveaux ne donneroient pas à des mouvemens déjà connus la musique de M. Grétry, & le jeu plein de graces, de finesse & de sensibilité de l'aimable Blondel? Ce que je lui dois d'éloges n'ôte rien à ceux qui sont bien dûs aux Acteurs qui ont concouru avec lui à la perfection de la représentation; mais il a tant de droits à ma reconnoissance.

Il y a vingt-cinq ans qu'il a contribué au [vii] succès d'*On ne s'avise jamais de tout*, & ses talens naissans furent en partie la cause de l'union de ce nouveau genre de Comédie lyrique à celui dont s'occupoit le Théâtre Italien. §

Commentary

Sedaine's new printer–bookseller Thomas Brunet started business in 1777 and had close connections with the Comédie-Italienne.[141] The 'Nouvelle édition, conforme à la partition gravée' (Paris: Les Libraires Associés, 1786), discussed in section (d) above, contains no preface. By the time that *Richard* was published, it had been performed initially in three acts; then in a four-act version; and finally in the familiar version.[142] The above preface, uniquely, takes its place in a sequence of documents forming a semi-public discourse about the way the opera should be ended: Sedaine himself contributed a letter to the *Journal de Paris* following the unsuccessful four-act version. There is one surviving source for this fourth act, which indeed shows that Sedaine

[141] Devriès and Lesure, *Dictionnaire des éditeurs*, I, p. 43. Brunet had published the 1782 version of *Aucassin et Nicolette*: see 'A Sedaine Bibliography', Chapter 11, p. 291, entry for Bibliothèque Municipale de Nantes.

[142] The original three-act ending contained no siege, and had 34 performances over the space of a year. The four-act version, with added music, received a court performance and one public performance, on 22 December 1785. The definitive version was first seen on 29 December 1785.

developed the character of the castle governor, Florestan.[143] Although the preface declares Sedaine's objection to the final siege on grounds of being 'trop commun', that is, a physical action familiar from both popular theatre and pantomime, as well as action-ballets at the Opéra, he was conscious of approaching popular theatre in conceiving *Guillaume Tell* (see below). The reference to 'charmes nouveaux' of Grétry's music somehow justifying the familiar style of action is in part ironic, since in the general rush to stage the definitive version, Grétry re-used an orchestral march from *Les Mariages samnites* (1776).

Sources: F-Po: Liv.18.169; Pa: Rf.13.585(7); Pn: Yf.11629[144]

TP: LE COMTE / D'ALBERT, / DRAME, / EN DEUX ACTES, / EN PROSE ET EN VERS, / MIS EN MUSIQUE. / *Représenté à Fontainebleau, le 13 Novembre* 1786, / *& à Paris, le 8 Février* 1787, *par les Comédiens / Italiens ordinaires du Roi.* / Les Paroles, par M. SEDAINE; la Musique, par / M. GRÉTRY. / [device] / A PARIS, / Chez BRUNET. ... / MDCCLXXXVII

Collation: pp. [vi] + [1] – 83.

pp. iii–v: AVERTISSEMENT.

§ C'est presque toujours l'importance qu'un Auteur met, ou desire qu'on mette à son Ouvrage, qui lui fait hasarder un Avertissement, & je n'ai guere d'autres raisons[145] à donner pour faire excuser celui-ci.

Il y a quinze à seize ans qu'on me fit demander quelques scenes de Comédie, où il n'y eût point d'amour, & que de jeunes personnes du plus haut rang pussent jouer dans l'intérieur de leur appartement. Flatté de la demande, après y avoir acquiescé, je pensai que je ferois bien de me servir de ce moyen, pour faire sentir à des enfans l'application que l'on peut faire des Fables de La Fontaine aux actions de la vie civile, & leur apprendre à *retransporter* des animaux aux hommes, ce qui avoit été transporté des hommes aux animaux.

Je choisis la Fable du Lion & du Rat, & sa morale, qui dit qu'on a souvent besoin d'un plus petit que soi, me parut présenter une instruction nécessaire aux augustes enfans qui devoient s'en occuper.

[iv] Un homme de la lie du peuple, qui, par reconnoissance, tire de prison un homme très-puissant, étoit le Rat qui délivre le Lion.

---

143 Pierre-Marie-Michel Lepeintre Desroches (ed.), *Suite du répertoire du Théâtre Français avec un choix des pièces de plusieurs autres théâtres* (81 vols, Paris: Vve Dabo, 1822–3), LVIII, p. 63; (repr. Geneva, 1970), XX, p. 451.

144 Pn: Yf.11629 was published by Emmanuel Flon (Paris, 1787) with [ii] + 63 pages; no TP transcription was made, but two preface readings were preferred and are noted (plus three minor orthographical readings, not noted).

145 Brunet edition: 'd'autre raison'.

A la fin de mes scenes, amenées très-rapidement, esquissées & annoncées comme proverbe, on devoit donner à deviner à la respectable assemblée, quelle étoit la Fable de La Fontaine, déguisée sous l'action de mes personnages.

Mon ouvrage fait, je donnai copie de mon manuscrit à l'homme de considération, qui s'étoit chargé de me demander ce travail; j'ai depuis ignoré si cela avoit rempli son objet, personne ne m'en parla plus, & je n'en parlai à personne.

Le manuscrit qui m'étoit resté entre les mains, fut lu par M. Grétry, qui trouva dans la scène de la prison assez de motifs pour intéresser & pour exercer ses talens; j'ai joint des scenes à celles qui étoient faites, j'ai cherché à les préparer; mais l'empreinte de proverbe est restée à cet Ouvrage, & il se sentira toujours de sa première destination.

J'ai ajouté un troisième Acte, dont j'ai cru faire excuser l'irrégularité, en l'intitulant 'suite', j'ai pensé qu'alors on me pardonneroit de transporter à quinze jours & à soixante [v] lieues de distance le tems & le lieu de la scene: ce n'est pas que j'approuve cette liberté, qui dispense un Auteur de deux parties difficiles de l'art du Théâtre, de l'exposition primitive de son sujet, de la création des personnages, & le conduit souvent à ne faire qu'un Ouvrage dégénéré.

Je suis persuadé qu'il y a peu de Fables de La Fontaine qui ne puissent[146] être le germe d'une production dramatique; mais au lieu que la Fable indique hautement son point de morale, il conviendroit que l'action théâtrale forçât l'Auditeur à faire lui-même la réflexion dont le Poëte a le désir de le pénétrer.

Nous sommes bien autrement frappés de celle que nous imaginons, que celle qui nous est sentencieusement articulée. Le *Qui te l'a dit?* d'Hermione à Oreste m'auroit à jamais garanti de la séduction & des fureurs de l'amour, si la nature m'avoit condamné à en être tyrannisé.[147]

Je ne peux finir cet Avertissement, sans payer à Madame Dugazon le tribut d'éloges & de reconnoissance que nous lui devons (M. Grétry & moi) ainsi qu'aux Acteurs, qui ont partagé avec elle les dangers & le succès de la représentation. §

Commentary

Le Comte d'Albert was Sedaine's first *drame* for music since *Le Déserteur*, but he avoids mention of its contemporary and realistic subject-matter, and a supposedly factual source noted at the time: the escape from prison in 1721 by

[146] Brunet edition: 'puisse'.

[147] Racine, *Andromaque* (1667), Act V, sc. III, in which Hermione questions Oreste concerning the death of Pyrrhus, which she has previously demanded.

a Flemish Comte Albert after imprisonment for duelling.[148] The unusually wide range of emotion and action in the drama must have caused the acting and production difficulties alluded to in the final paragraph of the preface; although it was not liked at court, the work succeeded in Paris.[149] Respect for the dramatic unities caused Sedaine to publish a separate title-page and cast-list for the concluding act within the libretto ('Suite du Comte d'Albert, opéra-comique en un acte, en prose et en vers, mis en musique. Composé ... par les mêmes auteurs'): there was no question of it being 'Act III' even though the third act is essential for the resolution of the story. Both this aspect and the inspired transmutation of the La Fontaine fable (using historical characters!) can be regarded as significant events in the development of opera.

The implications for Sedaine's dramatic style of the observation in the preface's penultimate paragraph have been discussed by John Dunkley.[150]

Sources: F-Po: Liv.18.2194; Pa: Rf.13.773

TP: GUILLAUME TELL, / DRAME EN TROIS ACTES, / EN PROSE ET EN VERS; / PAR LE CITOYEN SEDAINE, / Musique du Citoyen GRETRY. / Représenté, au mois de Mars 1791, sur le ci-devant Théâtre / Italien. / *PRIX, 30 sols.* / A PARIS, / Chez MARADAN... / SECONDE ANNÉE DE LA RÉPUBLIQUE FRANÇOISE.

Collation: pp. [viii] + 42[151]

p. [v]: AVERTISSEMENT.

§ J'avois, en 1790, fait le drame de *Guillaume Tell* pour être accompagné de musique, ce genre ayant pris une faveur singulière.

J'avois le plus grand desir qu'il fût représenté sur les grands théâtres des départemens, tels que ceux de Bordeaux, de Lyon, de Toulon, &c., et qu'il eût le bonheur d'y alimenter le feu sacré du patriotisme; mais mille circonstances s'y sont opposées, et l'une des plus fortes est celle qu'a brisée le décret rendu par la Convention nationale, par lequel les Auteurs dramatiques ont été mis en possession de leurs propriétés, et dont vouloit les priver l'avidité de quelques directeurs des grands théâtres de plusieurs départmens. Il est cependant aussi nécessaire d'étendre l'empire des pièces utiles à la cause commune, que de condamner au silence celles qui peuvent y nuire.

---

148 *Correspondance littéraire*, XV (Mar. 1787), p. 9.

149 Sedaine's exasperation at the November failure is described in Jullien, *L'Opéra secret* (see n. 8), pp. 51–3.

150 Dunkley, 'Introduction' to *Le Philosophe sans le sçavoir*, p. 56.

151 The front matter is largely unpaginated, and contains (immediately after the Avertissement) a dedicatory 52-line poem headed 'HOMMAGE / AUX MANES DE LEMIERE, / Auteur de la Tragédie de GUILLAUME TELL, / *Par SEDAINE, Qui, vingt ans après lui, a / traité le même sujet.*'

Il viendra un temps, sans doute, où les anciens ouvrages qu'on ne peut voir jouer sans se prêter à des allusions indiscrètes et peut-être dangereuses, ne feront pas plus d'effet sur les imaginations françaises, que n'en fait sur celle de notre âge viril l'aspect des joujous ou des pédantesques férules qui ont amusé ou affligé notre enfance.

Oui, le temps viendra, où lorsque l'on mettra sous nos yeux le tableau des anciens abus et de l'ancienne servitude, nous saisirons avec plaisir cet instant, pour nous applaudir d'avoir brisé des fers dont nulle puissance humaine ne peut plus à présent nous accabler. §

Commentary

It is a mark of long-delayed publication that the title-page of *Guillaume Tell* records a false première date (it was actually 9 April 1791). The quite recent reappearance of a part-autograph libretto for an earlier version of the work than that published shows Sedaine's own datings of 16 November 1790 for Act I and 22 November for Act II. The undated third act is in another hand.[152] The 1791 press reviews demonstrate that this early version was duly staged.[153] Although the printed libretto was dated 'An II', i.e. after 22 September 1793, and the ink annotation on a surviving exemplar ('17 9bre 1793') suggests a plausible enough appearance date,[154] the pattern of Parisian performances suggests rather that a penultimate version marked the run of six performances in March 1792[155] and that the definitive version appeared on 30 September 1792 with the first of a long and regular series of performances. One or more performances of *Guillaume Tell* occurred in each of the next sixteen months except three.[156]

Sedaine's late decision to publish was perhaps affected by pressures such as those demonstrated by the open letter to the *Journal des spectacles* of 14 August 1793, urging him to publish *Maillard, ou Paris sauvé* and thereby

---

152 F-Pn (MSS): N.a.fr. 17358; announcement and description in *Nouvelles acquisitions latines et françaises du Département des Manuscrits pendant les années 1977–1982* (Paris: Bibliothèque Nationale, 1985).

153 *Affiches, annonces et avis divers*, supplément (11 April 1791), pp. 1353–5; *Chronique de Paris* (11 April 1791), pp. 402f. I thank Monique Abud for permission to make use of her newspaper discoveries and transcriptions, noted here and below, and to use various pieces of information drawn from her research on this manuscript.

154 F-Pn (Mus): ThB. 4287.

155 André Tissier, *Les Spectacles à Paris pendant la Révolution. Répertoire analytique, chronologique et bibliographique* (Geneva: Droz, 1992), p. 79, notes 'nouv. dénouement' for *Guillaume Tell* on 10 March 1792, the first of these six (no source indicated). There were then no performances between March 1792 and 30 September 1792.

156 Information gathered from F-Po, the MS *Registres* of the Comédie-Italienne (Opéra-Comique).

'prove that his sentiments have always been pure, and that he has always loved liberty and equality'.[157] But Sedaine's real reasons for delay were financial and moral, as he himself makes public in his *Avertissement*. Since the start of the Revolution he had been involved in Beaumarchais's Bureau de Législation Dramatique (founded in 1777 in order to establish proper financial rewards for authors), chairing some meetings. On 13 and 19 January 1791 new theatre laws finally established such rewards for all dramatists, yet provincial theatre directors often refused to comply with their obligations.[158] Indeed, they caused a reverse in progress through a law of 30 August 1792 which suppressed these obligations. Only on 3 September 1793 were dramatic authors' rights finally asserted legally and maintained. Sedaine's preface refers to this 1792 setback ('[la circonstance] qu'a brisée le décret rendu ... par lequel les Auteurs dramatiques ont été mis en possession de leurs propriétés') and thus we can be sure that *Guillaume Tell* was published only after 3 September 1793 so as to benefit from provincial performance rights. (Unfortunately, its author's financial hopes were not to be realised in the immediate short term.)[159]

A likely reason why Sedaine originally chose his subject was the stage revival of Antoine-Marin Lemierre's verse tragedy *Guillaume Tell* (1766) on 1 August 1790, shortly after the Fête de la Fédération.[160] The published libretto expresses Sedaine's debt as follows: 'Hommage aux mannes de Lemiere, Auteur de la tragédie de GUILLAUME TELL, Par *SEDAINE*, qui, vingt ans après lui, a traité le même sujet'. A 52-line poem follows, concluding 'IL ÉTOIT MON AMI.'

The first sentence of Sedaine's preface has recently been construed by Emilio Sala as meaning that Sedaine originally intended *Guillaume Tell* as a *mélodrame*; Sala lists twelve works using this generic designation between 1779 and January 1790, and explains the complex point of evolution that the

157 Christiern Kretzicoff, 'Aux auteurs du journal', letter dated 'Paris, le 11 août', *Journal des spectacles*, no. 44 (14 August 1793). Quotations from this are reproduced under the name 'Christian' Kretzicoff in d'Estrée, *Le Théâtre sous la Terreur*, p. 123, where Grétry's involvement is wrongly implied.

158 Between Easter 1791 and Easter 1792 only 8,868 *livres* were collected in the whole of the French provinces. Marie-Claire Le Moigne-Mussat, 'L'activité des théâtres lyriques en province, 1794–1796' in Jean-Rémy Julien and Jean Mongrédien (eds), *Le Tambour et la harpe. Œuvres, pratiques et manifestations musicales sous la Révolution 1788–1800* (Paris: Du May, 1991), pp. 57–79 [58]. On Sedaine's roles, see Jacques Boncompain, 'Dalayrac, Fortune d'une Œuvre. Du droit d'auteur aux droits d'auteur' in Françoise Karro-Pélisson (ed.), *Nicolas Dalayrac, musicien murétain, homme des lumières* (Muret: Société Nicolas Dalayrac, 1991), pp. 53–63.

159 Only seven provincial theatres mounted *Guillaume Tell* between 1794 and 1796, in a total of only twenty-one performances. There were a further two in Brussels and two in Liège. Le Moigne-Mussat, 'L'activité des théâtres lyriques', pp. 72–3, 78.

160 My thanks to Monique Abud for this suggestion. Lemierre gave the speech for Sedaine on the occasion of his reception at the Académie Française in 1786.

genre had reached by the latter point.[161] However, the dated manuscripts of Acts I and II (16 and 22 November 1790) show that the characters originally sang operatically, rather than simply declaimed, and also reveal the presence of a chorus.[162] Thus Sedaine did not mean *Guillaume Tell* to be what was taken then, or is taken now, to be a *mélodrame*. But the manuscript's generic label 'Drame Tragique en prose, et en Vers mis en musique' marks an interesting difference from the published version, the great significance of which is explained by the story of Sedaine's unperformed prose tragedy *Maillard*.[163] This manuscript genre designation suggests that Sedaine initially conceived a type of spoken *tragedy* interleaved by, or alternating with, musical episodes; this discovery consequently signals a final stage in his lifelong search for innovative types of music theatre, as well as a partial resolution of the *Maillard* débâcle.

161 Emilio Sala, 'Mélodrame. Définitions et métamorphoses d'un genre quasi-opératique', *Revue de musicologie*, LXXXIV/2 (1998), pp. 235–46; idem, *L'opera senza canto. Il mélo romantico e l'invenzione della colonna sonora* (Venice: Marsilio, 1995), p. 41.

162 F-Pn: N.a.f. 17358. 39 folios, 240 x 190 mm. Ex-libris A.-G. Du Plessis.

163 Recounted on pp. 28–32 above.

PART IV

Sources

Chapter 10

An Iconography of Sedaine and his Works

Mark Ledbury

This iconography lists images in two categories:

1. portraits of Sedaine and his family;
2. eighteenth-century images related to Sedaine's literary and dramatic output, organised alphabetically.

It was compiled with much help from David Charlton and Nicole Wild. As Martine de Rougemont remarks in Chapter 7, where the majority of our figures will be found reproduced, much work remains to be done on illustrations of eighteenth-century French theatre, and the following list, although complete to the best of my knowledge, will inevitably be supplemented in the course of time. Short-title references to articles and books (other than those used throughout this book) are elucidated in the list of bibliographical sources found at the end of the chapter.

1. Portraits of Sedaine and his family

by Jacques-Louis David

1. *Portrait of Michel-Jean Sedaine* (before 1772). Oil on canvas, formerly de Brisay collection, whereabouts unknown. Last traced in Hudnut Sale, American Art Associates New York, December 1933, no. 65. Reproduced in Schnapper (ed.), *Jacques-Louis David*, p. 561, fig. 158. See de Rougemont, p. 154; Ledbury, 'Greuze and Sedaine', p. 462. Engraved by Levesque in 1772. (See below.)
2. *Portrait of Madame Sedaine*. Oil on canvas, formerly de Brisay collection, whereabouts unknown. Reproduced in Schnapper (ed.), *Jacques-Louis David*, p. 561, fig. 159; Ledbury, 'Greuze and Sedaine', fig. 74.
3. *Portrait of Henri Sedaine* (Sedaine's son). Presented for sale (but not sold) at auction, Etude Couturier-De Nicolay, Paris 1995 [Fig. 13].

Fig. 13: Jacques-Louis David, portrait of Henri Sedaine.
Oil on canvas, c.1774–5. Private collection. Photo: Etude Couturier-De Nicolay, Paris.

4. *Portrait de Jeanne-Suzanne Sedaine* (Sedaine's elder daughter). Black chalk and plumbago on black chalk background. Musée du Louvre, Département des Arts Graphiques, inv. RF4607 [Fig. 14].
5. Portrait de Madame (Suzanne-Charlotte) Sedaine. c.1783–4. Pen and ink. Sold at auction by Etude Briest, Paris, 24 March 1997 (Lot 101a).

by Gabriel de Saint-Aubin

1. *Portrait présumé de Sedaine* (c.1753). Sold at auction Audap, Godeau, Solanet, Sale 11 March 1987, no. 199 [Fig. 2].
2. *Portrait de Sedaine*. Sanguine on paper, on reverse of a letter from the Marquis de Marigny to Sedaine, March 1771, in Archives de l'Institut, Carton B22 (réserve), Dossier 1771, pièce 15. Signed and dated 'G. de St Aubin, 1er Avril 1771' [Fig. 3].

Fig. 14: Jacques-Louis David, portrait of Jeanne-Suzanne Sedaine. Black chalk and plumbago, 1783. Paris, Musée du Louvre, Département des Arts Graphiques. Photo: © RMN–Michèle Bellot.

3. *Portrait de Sedaine.* Cited by Dacier, *Gabriel de Saint-Aubin*, II, no. 240. Sale: Paris, 3–7 April 1866, no. 349.

by Augustin Pajou

1. Bust of Michel-Jean Sedaine (1775). Terracotta. H. 485 W. 460 D. 225 mm. Victoria and Albert Museum, London (inv a27-1959). Exhibited in the

exhibition *Augustin Pajou, sculpteur du roi* (Paris and New York, 1997–8), no. 99 [Fig. 5].

2. Bust of Madame Sedaine (1781). Terracotta. Boston Museum of Fine Arts (inv. 65, 2220). Exhibited in *Augustin Pajou, sculpteur du roi* (Paris and New York, 1997–8), no. 103.

by other artists

ENGRAVINGS AND LITHOGRAPHIC DERIVATIVES

1. *Michel-Jean Sedaine. Secrétaire perpetuel de l'Académie Royale d'Architecture. Né à Paris* [Fig. 4]. Pierre-Charles Levesque, after Jacques-Louis David. Undated, but published in 1772. For comment on its publication, see *Année littéraire*, VI (1772), p. 261: 'J.-L. David pinx. P. Car. Levesque sculp. A Paris, Chez Bligny, Cour du manege aux Thuilleries'. Source: F-Pn (Est), Series N (Sedaine).
2. *M.-J. Sedaine, né à Paris en 1719, Mort en 1797.* Galerie Universelle, Publiée par Blaisot, Place Vendôme, no. 24. Lith. de Ducarme (no. 339). This is an early nineteenth-century lithograph after a relatively young image of Sedaine. Source: F-Pn (Est), Series N (Sedaine) folio 10.
3. *Sedaine, d'après le tableau peint par M. David.* Inscribed: 'H Gravedon.....Lith. de Demanne' [possibly Joseph-Arnold Demmannez (1826–1902)].
   ¾ facing left, like the original painting, but not the Levesque engraving. Source: F-Pn (Est), Series N (Sedaine), folio 11.
4. *Sedaine composant son Opéra de Rose et Colas*. Clearly of nineteenth-century origin, this print shows Sedaine with mason's tools, writing, inspired by a couple representing Rose et Colas. It is surrounded by an ornate border inscribed with the titles of Sedaine's most famous works. It is reproduced in Ledbury, 'Greuze and Sedaine', Fig. 1, p. 390. Source: F-Pn (Est), Series N3.
5. *Sedaine*. Inscribed 'Méhu del ... couché fils dir. ... villerey fils sc...'. Source: Archives de l'Institut, dossier *Sedaine*. Méhu is unidentified, possibly Mehus or Meus; Louis-François Couché (1782–1849); Auguste or Nicolas Scholastique Villerey (*b.*1801).

OTHER MEDIA

Roger Portalis, *Dessinateurs d'illustration*, p. 126, has a reference to a portrait drawn by Charles Nicholas Cochin in 1777: 'Portrait de Sedaine, dessin de forme ovale, aux deux crayons, signé et daté 1777'. I have not been able to locate this drawing.

A bust of Sedaine by E. Gatteux (1843) which featured in the Salon of 1844 is cited by Rey in *La Vieillesse de Sedaine*, p. 67, as in the 'galerie' of the Théâtre Français.

Bronze statue of Sedaine by Léon Lecointe (1882), originally sited in the Square d'Anvers, Paris, forming part of a series of eight eighteenth-century writers (including Condorcet, Rousseau, Voltaire, Diderot). Destroyed in 1942. Photograph in Pougin, *Monsigny*, p. 131.

Portraits by other artists of other members of the Sedaine family

1. Guèret (l'ainée): *Portrait de la Citoyenne Sedaine l'ainée* (Jeanne-Suzanne).
2. Guèret (la jeune): *Portrait de la Citoyenne Sedaine la Jeune* (Agathe): Salon of 1793, nos 474, 475. Now lost. See Rey, 'Sedaine à Saint-Prix', p. 127. See also the portrait of Mme de Brisay (Agathe Sedaine), published opposite the title-page of Rey, *La Vieillesse de Sedaine*.

Doubtful or disputed portraits of Michel-Jean Sedaine

1. Jean Baptiste Siméon Chardin(?): *Portrait de Sedaine ou Le Petit tailleur de pierres*(?) [Fig. 1]. On this portrait see Martine de Rougemont, p. 151.
2. Jean Honoré Fragonard: *Sedaine.* See de Rougemont, p. 158. Reproduced in Cécile Giteau (ed.), *Les plus beaux manuscrits du théâtre français* (Paris: BNF/Robert Laffont, 1996), p. 163.
3. Miniature of Michel-Jean Sedaine, reproduced in Auguste Rey, 'Le mariage de Sedaine', *Revue de l'histoire de Versailles et de Seine-et-Oise*, XI (1910), pp. 5–15, unpaginated, and described as 'd'après une miniature conservée dans sa famille'.

2. Images related to literary and dramatic works

These are arranged alphabetically by title of work, and comprise only material created in Sedaine's lifetime.

Aline, reine de Golconde

Gabriel de Saint-Aubin: Sketch representing a scene from *Aline, reine de Golconde*. Made during a performance in March 1767, and inscribed 'Mlle Baumesnil, reine de Golconde Mars 1767'. Dacier, *Gabriel de Saint-Aubin*, II, no. 741.

F-Po: Unattributed costume drawing of Sophie Arnould as Aline. Pougin, *Monsigny*, p. 109.

F-Pn: Engraving by Gravelot after a design by B. Dandridge, showing Larrivée as St-Phar, posing against a detail of the stage-set showing a wall, an urn and foliage, 'B. Dandridge Pinx. H. Gravelot Sculp.' Pougin, *Monsigny*, p. 107.

Two probably apocryphal costume illustrations are discussed by Manuel Couvreur in Chapter 4, pp. 92–3.

Blaise le savetier

US-NYp, Spencer Coll: Grangeret, C. L. Desrais [illustrators]; J. V. Dupin, Thérèse Martinet [etchers]. Published: A Paris: Chez Martinet [1762?]. Six prints: etching; 24 × 17 cm [Fig. 7].

F-Pcarn: Five etchings for *Blaise le savetier* from this Martinet set (inv. G11095–99).

Le Déserteur

US-NYp, Spencer Coll: A. J. Duclos [illustrator]; C. L. Lingée, A. B. Duhamel, A. J. Duclos, Patas, Nicolas Ponce, Jme. Prévost [etchers]. Published: A Paris: Chez Martinet, 1770. Six prints: etching; 24 x 17 cm.

There is one example of an illustrated edition of *Le Déserteur*, produced outside France, utilising these engravings: *De Déserteur. / Zangspel / Naar Het Fransch Gevolgd. / Door / Bartholomeus Ruloffs / Te Amsterdam, by / Jan Helders ... / 1782. / Met previlegie.* F-Pa: Rondel Rf 13, 696.

F-Pcarn: Four etchings designed by Quéverdo, etched by Duhamel, Chatelain, and Dambrun for *Le Déserteur* (inv. G 18103-6) [Fig. 11]. These are from a different set from those for the Martinet enterprise. They all bear the same dedication: 'A M. Le Marquis de Guerchiville / ancien capitaine de la cavalerie'. Cohen (p. 947) notes that four original encre de chine drawings for these illustrations, signed and dated 1770, were sold at the Portalis sale in 1878.

Musée du Louvre, Cabinet des Dessins: two ink and wash drawings for one of the etchings portraying Bertrand and Montauciel in the Martinet set, by A. J. Duclos: inv. RF 36047 and RF 36048.

F-B, Collection Pierre-Adrien Pâris: one large-scale sketch design for décor no. 238, inscribed 'Le Déserteur, Fontainebleau 1785' (showing entrance to the king's camp).

F-Po: Two gouache paintings by Moreau, inspired by events within the opera. The first shows Alexis at the end of Act I escaping from soldiers gathered on a bridge over a river. The second shows Louise rescuing Alexis from the firing-squad.

F-Pn (Est): Jean-Baptiste Meunier, scene as performed at the Théâtre de Richelieu, 1790. Reproduced in Guibert and Thomas, *Le Théâtre et la dramaturgie*.

Le Faucon

US-NYpm: Gabriel de Saint-Aubin: Sketch for a scene from *Le Faucon*. Dacier, *Gabriel de Saint-Aubin*, II, no. 151. Pen and brown ink, with watercolour and gouache, inscribed 'Fait pour Monsieur Sedaine en mars 1771'. Dacier notes another inscription on the bottom right, 'peinte en mars 1772'. It is reproduced in Carlson et al., *Prints and Drawings by Gabriel de Saint-Aubin*, no. 51, p. 101.

Les Femmes vengées

Frontispiece for the *livret* edition (Paris: Musier, 1775), drawn by Charles-Nicholas Cochin and engraved by Lingée. This illustration has been discussed by de Rougemont, p. 162, where it appears as Fig. 6.

Le Jardinier et son seigneur

US-NYp, Spencer Coll: A. J. Duclos [illustrator]; F. N. Martinet, J. V. Dupin [etchers]. Published: A Paris: Chez Martinet, [1761?]. Set of six prints: etching; 24 × 17 cm. Three etchings from this set for *Le Jardinier et son seigneur* are in F-Pcarn (inv G 11101-3).

Frontispiece for the *livret* edition (Paris: Hérissant, 1761) drawn by Gabriel de Saint-Aubin and engraved by Augustin de Saint-Aubin. See de Rougemont, p. 163 and Charlton, p. 240 and Fig. 12. The sketch (pen and black ink, brush with grey wash over graphite) and the engraving are catalogued and described by Dacier, *Gabriel de Saint-Aubin*, II, nos 899 and 899a. The sketch was catalogued and reproduced in Carlson et al., *Prints and Drawings by Gabriel de Saint-Aubin*, no. 44 and p. 90 (in 1975, it was the property of Rosenberg and Stiebel, Inc., New York).

Le Magnifique

Gabriel de Saint-Aubin: Sketch from *Le Magnifique*. Dacier, *Gabriel de Saint-Aubin*, II, no. 778. This sketch represents Act II, sc. II of the work, and shows Aldobrandin in a cape and a plumed hat drawing Octave seated and leaning toward Clémentine. Underneath the sketch in Augustin de Saint-Aubin's writing is the inscription 'Croquis du Magnifique'.

Bowes Museum, Barnard Castle, UK: a painting by an unidentified painter of a scene which corresponds in precise detail to Act II, sc. XI of *Le Magnifique* (inv. 301).

On ne s'avise jamais de tout

US-NYp, Spencer Collection: Devere, F. N. Martinet, Jme. Prévost, Thérèse Martinet [etchers]; F. M. I. Quéverdo, F. N. Martinet [illustrators]. Published: A Paris: Chez Martinet, 1771. Six prints: etching; 24 × 17 cm.

F-CH: Gabriel de Saint-Aubin made a sketch for an illustration for the final scene, which is sketched into a copy of the *Recueil de poésies* in the Musée Condé. See below, and see also Dacier, 'Le "Sedaine" du Musée Condé'; de Rougemont, pp. 165–6.

Dacier, *Gabriel de Saint-Aubin*, II, no. 918, lists another version of this drawing, in pencil, ink and gouache, 12 × 7.5 cm, and also an aquaforte after this drawing, no. 918a, claiming that it was being prepared for engraving for an illustration, which was never finally made. These are illustrated in Emile Dacier, *L'Œuvre gravé de Gabriel de Saint-Aubin. Notice historique et catalogue raisonné* (Paris: Imprimerie Nationale, 1914), I, no. 24, plate 22. Dacier describes four states of this aquaforte, two of which are in F-Pn (Est), cat. ef37a (first state) and e7 (third state).

Le Vacher de Charnois (ed.), *Costumes et annales*, IV (1788), plate 6: Costume of M. Tue.

Engraved portrait (unattributed) of Clairval as Dorval, reproduced in Pougin, *Monsigny*, p. 49 (owned by Pougin).

Raimond V, Comte de Toulouse

F-Pcf H9–H6: A precious set of costume drawings for minor characters in *Raimond V* is currently held in the archives of the Comédie-Française. We know from references in Grimm's correspondence with Catherine II that

Sedaine and Grimm had researched medieval costume in the King's Library, and that C.-N. Cochin drew the costumes. See Letter of Grimm to Catherine II, 15 February 1779, in Friedrich Melchior von Grimm, *Lettres à l'Impératrice Catherine II, publiées par Jacques Grot* (2nd ed. St Petersburg: Académie des Sciences, 1885), pp. 34–6.

Raoul Barbe-Bleue

Le Vacher de Charnois (ed.), *Costumes et annales,* V, issue 9 [1789]: Costumes of Raoul and Isaure (colour plate opposite p. 75): see also the commentary on pp. 75–7. Reproduced in Charlton, *Grétry*, p. 292.

Recueil de poésies

Sedaine's *Recueil de poésies* (2 vols in 1, Paris: Duchesne, 1760) contains a frontispiece designed by Gabriel de Saint-Aubin. On the sketches and aquafortes for this frontispiece, see Dacier, *Gabriel de Saint-Aubin*, II, nos 919 ('étude pour le frontispice: le profil de Sedaine, tourné vers le gauche, dans un medaillon, entouré de petits génies portant des objets allégoriques') and 920 (pp. 170–2). Two states of the aquaforte are extant, both are in F-Pn (Est), E37a, and the second state is the frontispiece which was published.

F-CH: For a discussion of the other remarkable sketches in the copy of the *Recueil de poésies* in the Musée Condé, see Dacier, *Gabriel de Saint-Aubin*, II, pp. 205–7, and idem, 'Le "Sedaine" du Musée Condé'. The developed frontispiece to the Condé *Recueil de poésies* is reproduced in Ledbury, 'Greuze and Sedaine', Fig. 71, p. 460.

Richard Cœur-de-Lion

F-Pn (Est): A suite of three illustrations for *Richard Cœur-de-Lion*, engraved by Claude Bornet, is to be found in the series AA3 (Bornet, Claude). Like the Martinet engravings, these are self-standing illustrations, and not included in a *livret*. Two are reproduced in Charlton, *Grétry*. See comment on them in *Année littéraire* (1786), VII, pp. 285–6.

F-B, Collection Pierre-Adrien Pâris, volume 5 (*Cinquième volume contenant les théâtres*): Four sketches for décors for *Richard Cœur-de-Lion*: no. 316: 'Fond du dernier acte de Richard Cœur de Lion' (showing medieval castle with its ramparts); no. 317: 'cote de la première acte de Richard Cœur de Lion'; no. 336: backdrop for *Richard Cœur-de-Lion* (including castle, turret, bridge); no. 337: another view of an entrance to the castle (moat, drawbridge, fortification).

Le Vacher de Charnois (ed.), *Costumes et annales,* I (1786), issue 11 (8 July 1786): illustration of Clairval as Blondel.

F-Pa, Rondel: Various scenes from the Album Ziesenis. See Guibert and Thomas, *Le Théâtre et la dramaturgie*.

Le Roi et le fermier

US-NYp, Spencer collection: F. M. I. Quéverdo [illustrator]; L. Auvray, C. Frussotte [etchers]. Published [Paris: F. N. Martinet, 1763?]. Set of six prints: etching; 24 × 17 cm.

F-Pn (Est): Pierre Alexandre Wille (fils): Pencil drawing dated 1767 of a scene presumed to be from Act III of *Le Roi et le fermier* [Fig. 9].

F-Po: [Attributed to both P. A. Wille and to Gabriel-Jacques de Saint-Aubin]: Ink, wash, black chalk: drawing closely related to the above image, dated 1772. See de Rougemont, p. 166 and Fig. 10.

F-Pn: unattributed, unknown medium, after a drawing by Gravelot: oblong horizontal format, showing Act III, the king seated and still booted. Pougin, *Monsigny*, p. 88.

Rose et Colas

US-NYp, Spencer collection: Marie Quéverdo, F. M. I. Quéverdo [illustrators]; Thérèse Martinet [etcher]. Published: A Paris: Chez Martinet, [1764?]: set of six prints: etching; 24 × 17 cm.

F-Pn: Engraving by Simonet after a gouache by P. A. Baudouin, undated. Rustic interior with Colas having entered by the skylight and Rose still half-concealed. 'Rose et Colas Gravé d'après le Tableau Original Peint à gouache par P. A. Baudouin, appartenant à Mr Prault. Baudouin pinx. Simonet sculp^t'. Pougin, *Monsigny*, p. 101.

Le Vacher de Charnois (ed.), *Costumes et annales*, III, part 2, p. 9, illustration of Clairval as Colas.

Les Sabots

US-NYp, Spencer collection: A. J. Duclos [illustrator]; Jean Massard, Nicolas Ponce, Thérèse Martinet, J. J. A. Le Veau, A. J. Duclos, F. G. [etchers]. Published: [Paris]: Chez Martinet, 1770–71. Six prints: etching; 24 × 17 cm.

F-Po: Portalis, *Dessinateurs d'illustration*, p. 699, has a reference to illustrative drawings for *Les Sabots* by Lavreince. An engraving after one drawing by Lavreince, engraved by Jacques Couché, is now in F-Po, Collection André Mayer.

Toronto, Art Gallery of Ontario: François Boucher, *Les Sabots* (1768). Oil on canvas, (64 × 53.7 cm) [Fig. 8]. Boucher had long and close associations with the Opéra-Comique, but this is the only image known to me directly inspired by a scene in one of Sedaine's dramas. See Richard Rand (ed.), *Intimate Encounters. Love and Domesticity in Eighteenth-Century France* (Princeton: Princeton University Press, 1997), pp. 116–18, no. 14.

La Tentation de Saint-Antoine

La Tentation de Saint-Antoine was issued as a separate, illustrated edition, full details of which can be found in Cohen, *Guide de l'amateur des livres*, pp. 948–9. A copy of this edition can be found in GB-Lbl: 11474.e.18.

The Spencer Collection engravings by the Martinet enterprise

The full title of this collection is *Illustrations des opéras-comiques et comédies du XVIIIème siècle (1762–1773)*. A rare complete set is in US-NYp. Catalogued as: 'Spencer Collection French 1762 92-92'. This set was once owned by Victorien Sardou, and is cited in Cohen, *Guide de l'amateur des livres*. It is a collection of 21 series of six prints each, as published by F. N. Martinet to accompany contemporary musical comedies, operettas, etc. Eight proof states to four prints by A. J. Duclos are laid in. Each series has a caption title on first print; imprint (varies slightly) usually on first print: A Paris: Chez Martinet. Foliated in ms. 1–126. The complete list of works illustrated is:

Rose et Colas — Tom Jones — Zémire et Azor — Lucile — Les Moisson[n]eurs — Le Maréchal — On ne s'avise jamais de tout — An[n]ette et Lubin — Les Jardiniers — Les Sabots — Le Bucheron — Les Deux chasseurs et la laitière — Le Huron — Le Tonnelier — Le Jardinier et son seigneur — Blaise le savetier — Les Deux avares — Le Roi et le fermier — L'Amoureux de quinze ans — Le Déserteur — Isabelle et Gertrude.

Further details can be obtained from the 800-volume *Dictionary Catalog of the Research Libraries of the New York Public Library* (New York: G. K. Hall, 1911–72), and its internet version, CATNYP (at http.catnyp.nypl.org).

A drawing by Sedaine

A drawing by Sedaine himself is signalled by Rey, *La Vieillesse de Sedaine*, pp. 71–2, as being located in the Bibliothèque Municipale de Versailles, under the call no. Vatel no 491. According to Rey, the drawing is a copy of a work by J.-B. Lemoine, and is inscribed with the Latin inscription 'Ludovico Russeau, Johannes-Michael Sedaine amicissimus amicissimo hoc opusculum offerre felicitate fruitus est' and the verse:

> Ce dessein [*sic*] chef d'œuvre nouveau
> Serait en son genre un modèle
> Si l'adresse de mon pinceau
> Eût suivi l'ardeur de mon zèle.

Bibliographical sources

Bouchot, Henri, *Catalogue des dessins relatifs à l'histoire du théâtre conservés au Département des Estampes de la Bibliothèque Nationale* (Paris: Bouillon, 1896).

Carlson, Victor, Ellen D'Oench, Richard S. Field (eds), *Prints and Drawings by Gabriel de Saint-Aubin 1724–1780* (exhibition catalogue) (Baltimore: Museum of Art, and Middletown: Davison Art Center, Wesleyan University, 1975).

Cohen, Henri, *Guide de l'amateur de livres à gravures du XVIIIe siècle. Sixième édition revue, corrigée et considérablement augmentée par Seymour de Ricci* (Paris: Roquette, 1912).

Dacier, Emile, *Gabriel de Saint-Aubin* (2 vols, Paris and Brussels: G. Van Oest, 1929–31). Volume II contains a *Catalogue raisonné* of Saint-Aubin's work.

Dacier, Emile, 'Le "Sedaine" du Musée Condé, ou Gabriel de Saint-Aubin poète', *Revue de l'art ancien et moderne*, XXXVIII (June 1920), pp. 5–18; XXXIX (July–August 1920), pp. 93–104.

Guibert, Noëlle, and Michèle Thomas, *Le Théâtre et la dramaturgie des Lumières. Images de l'album Ziesenis* (Arceuil: Anathèse, 1999).

Le Vacher de Charnois, Jean-Charles, *Costumes et annales des grands théâtres de Paris* (7[?] vols, Paris: Janinet, 1786–9). A periodical begun in April 1786, by Hilliard d'Auberteuil, and continued by Le Vacher de Charnois until November 1789, with 48 parts for each of the first three years and 32 for the fourth. Illustrations: portraits, coloured plates of stage actors in celebrated parts; engraved music and words.

Portalis, Roger, *Les Dessinateurs d'illustration au dix-huitième siècle* (2 parts in 1, Paris: Morgand et Fatout, 1877).

Pougin, Arthur, *Monsigny et son temps* (Paris: Fischbacher, 1908).

Rey, Auguste, 'Sedaine à Saint-Prix', ***Revue de l'histoire de Versailles et de Seine-et-Oise***, V (1904), pp. 277–92; VI (1905), pp. 25–46 and 128–44.

Rey, Auguste, *Notes sur mon village. La Vieillesse de Sedaine* (Paris: Champion, 1906).

Schnapper, Antoine, and Arlette Serullaz (eds), *Jacques-Louis David 1748–1825* (exhibition catalogue, Paris, Louvre and Versailles, Château, 1989–90) (Paris: Réunion des Musées Nationaux, 1989).

Tchemerzine, Avenir, ***Bibliographie d'éditions originales et rares d'auteurs français des XVe, XVIe et XVIIIe siècles*** (10 vols, Paris: M. Plee, 1927–34).

Chapter 11

A Sedaine Bibliography: Archival, Biographical and Bibliographical Sources for his Life and Work

David Charlton, Mark Ledbury

This bibliography is designed as a basic research tool for further study of Sedaine and his work. We are grateful to Margaret Rayner, whose unpublished M.A. dissertation was of inestimable value in the creation of this bibliography, especially in the section concerning editions of Sedaine's work. Short-title references are made to the following: Joseph-Marie Quérard, *La France littéraire, ou Dictionnaire bibliographique des savants, historiens et gens de lettres de la France: ainsi que des littérateurs étrangers qui ont écrit en français, plus particulièrement pendant les XVIIIe et XIXe siècles* (12 vols, Paris: Firmin Didot, 1827–64, repr., 12 vols, Paris, 1964); and Werner Krauss and Martin Fontius, *Französische Drücke des 18. Jahrhunderts in den Bibliotheken der Deutschen Demokratischen Republik* (2 vols, Berlin: Akademie-Verlag, 1970). It is organised into the following sections:

- A. Archival material relating to Sedaine:
  - i. Sources in Paris;
  - ii. Sources outside Paris;
  - iii. Sources outside France.
- B. Single editions of Sedaine's dramatic works in chronological order of first publication.
- C. Collected editions of Sedaine's dramatic works.
- D
  - i. Other published works by Sedaine in chronological order of publication;
  - ii. Works published by others in which Sedaine had an involvement;
  - iii. Autobiographical writings.
- E. Critical and biographical writings:
  - i. Biographical sources;
  - ii. Biographical studies;
  - iii. Studies of Sedaine's career;
  - iv. Memoirs, correspondence and theoretical works written before 1830;
  - v. Books and articles published after 1830.
- F. Sources concerning the production and performance of Sedaine's dramas.
- G. Bibliographical aids to the study of Sedaine.

Section A: Archival material relating to Sedaine

i. SOURCES IN PARIS

Archives Nationales, Paris

(Maison du Roi)

O^1 614 (253) Sedaine–Amelot.
O^1 614, O^1 620–621 Correspondence of the directors of the Opéra.
O^1 621 (3, 1783) Correspondence between Sedaine and the Opéra concerning *Philémon et Baucis*
O^1 621 (1771), 120, 121 Correspondence between Papillon de La Ferté and Rebel, and including 'Observations sur la Reine de Golconde. Ballet héroïque'.
O^1 621 (1783), nos 78, 138 *Philémon et Baucis.*
O^1 629 Letter of 17 July 1788, from Dauvergne, on changes to *Amphitrion.*
O^1 636 Accounts for performances of *Amphitrion.*
O^1 843 a–b (papers relating to the Société des Auteurs et Compositeurs Dramatiques).
O^1 845 (2) Documents relating to Sedaine's *entrées* at the Comédie-Française.
O^1 1073 Correspondence of the Académie Royale d'Architecture.
O^1 1673 (1775, 68, 74) On Sedaine's lodgings, 1775, nos 68 and 74.
O^1 1931 Correspondence of the Académie Royale d'Architecture.
O^1 1932 Correspondence of the Académie Royale d'Architecture.
O^1 1933 Correspondence of the Académie Royale d'Architecture.
O^1 1911– O^1 1917 Correspondence of the Académie Royale d'Architecture.
O^1 3064 Report on cost of scenery for a private performance of *Les Sabots* at Trianon.
O^3 281 *Philémon et Baucis*, manuscript of Sedaine's libretto.

Minutier Central

Etude LIV 949 (21 March 1774) 'Partage des Successions des M et Mdme Sedaine'.
Etude LIV 949 (29 January 1774).
Etude LIV 949 (18 February 1774).
Etude LIV 921 (16th March 1767).
Etude XXI R. 684 (4 Pluvoise an XIII).
Etude XXI R.706.

Other series

Series AA 66 (97, 98, 99) Assorted letters.
Modern Series A.J.13/1102 Sedaine and Favières, *L'Espièglerie de garnison* [1791].

Châtelet Records

Y. 15, 623, Y. 15, 792 Records of complaints brought by and against Sedaine in his role as foreman.
Y. 413 Gift of Madame Lecomte's house in Rue de la Roquette, dated 16 March 1767. (For transcriptions of all these documents, see Emile Campardon, *Les Comédiens du Roi de la troupe italienne* (2 vols, Paris: Berger-Levrault, 1880, repr. Geneva, 1970), II, pp. 137–40).

Bibliothèque Nationale de France

N.a.f. 17358 Part-autograph manuscript of *Guillaume Tell*: 'Guillaume Tell/Drame tragique/en Prose et en Vers mis en musique/en trois actes/Premier Acte/ le 16 9bre 1790.

Bibliothèque de l'Arsenal

Ms 6874 (no. 136) 'Le Commissionnaire de Saint-Lazare' (poem, 1793).

Ms 13,519 (1 and 2) Letters from Sedaine.

Ms 13,959 (2) Letter from Sedaine (re: *Maillard*).

Ms 14, 021 (15) Letter from Sedaine (re: *Thémire*).

Bibliothèque de l'Arsenal, Collection Rondel

Rondel Ms 727: anon. (Sedaine), *Hinkelmann ou Les journalistes*. (For a commentary, see Ledbury, 'Greuze and Sedaine', appendix 2.)

Bibliothèque-Musée de l'Opéra

Ms rés. 2140 (1/2) Libretto and orchestral score of *Robin et Marion* (Sedaine and Monsigny autographs, dated 1795).

Ms rés. (Carton 2073) L.A.S Suzanne Sedaine (Letters from Sedaine's daughter, mostly to René Guilbert de Pixérécourt. They contain useful information and indicate how some of Sedaine's effects may have been dispersed.)

Ms Mus. 1017 Fragment of the orchestral score of *Pagamin de Monègue* (Sc. I–VIII), music by Monsigny and Désaugiers [before 1785].

Ms Rés. A.215 (a): *Ernelinde* orchestral score.

Recueils de Ballets vols XI and XIX.

Bibliothèque de l'Institut

MS 2717 (Dossier 7) Assorted documents relating to Sedaine (including accounts for play receipts due to Sedaine during the Revolutionary period).

Archives de l'Académie Française

Dossier Sedaine: Especially two rough letters, dated 'I Vendémiaire, an 4' concerning a play called *L'Espièglerie de garnison*. Name of recipient illegible (see above, Archives Nationales, other series).

Archives de l'Institut

Pièces annexes to the *Procès-verbaux* of the Académie Royale d'Architecture (see Henri Lemonnier's edition of the *Procès-Verbaux*, below, Section E.iv). This archive contains a great deal of correspondence between Sedaine and the court concerning his activities as secretary of the architectural academy. Some material is duplicated in the *Maison du Roi* files of the Archives Nationales. Especially important are the Dossiers: B3, B4, B5, B7, B21, B22, B22 Rés.

Important single items:

B22 Rés: Portrait by Gabriel de Saint-Aubin of Sedaine on the back of a letter (*pièce* 15, Marigny–Sedaine, 1 April 1771).

Carton B3 'Papiers rélatifs à l'élection de M. Blondel'.

Carton B8 *pièce* 1 (autograph) 'Réflexions sur la grande galerie': Sedaine's fascinating intervention in the ongoing debate about the best way of lighting the Gallery of the Louvre.

Carton B7, *dossier* S.D. (undated documents), *pièce* 1. Sheet marked 'Théâtre de Corneille de Voltaire'. A discussion of theatrical architecture, starting from an analysis of Voltaire's views on Corneille's *Cinna*. Although not in Sedaine's usual hand, there are corrections recognisable as autograph.

Carton B4, *dossier* 1776 'Réflexions sur les expressions de bon ou mauvais goût appliqués aux arts. Lues a l'académie Royale d'architecture par M. Sedaine, le 10 Décembre 1776'. An interesting discussion of the differences between *goût* and *genre*, in which Sedaine, significantly, defends some Gothic architecture against accusations of bad taste. This manuscript was first cited and discussed in Jacques Guillerme, 'Über einige Wandlungen des Wahren in der Architektur', *Daidalos. Architectural Journal Berlin*, VIII (1983), pp. 38–47. It is discussed towards the end of Chapter 1 of the present book.

Archives de la Comédie-Française
Dossier Sedaine
Containing Sedaine's correspondence with the *Comédie* on diverse subjects. Letters on *Maillard*, also receipts for plays and letters concerning his family after his death. Another folder contains details of autographs sold at auction. Some of the letters contained in the *Dossier Sedaine* were published in *Revue Retrospective*, VIII (1836), pp. 151–6.
MS 248 Manuscript of *Le Philosophe sans le savoir* in the hand of the *souffleur* to the Comédie-Française. (See editions by Dunkley, 1993, and Oliver, 1913, within Section B, below.)
MS 368 Manuscript of *Raimond V, comte de Toulouse*.
See Rey (1906, within Section E.ii, below) and Ledbury, 'Greuze and Sedaine'.

Musée du Louvre. Centre de Documentation
Dossier Sedaine contains useful photocopies of notarial records.

Archives de la Société des Auteurs et Compositeurs Dramatiques
Records of provincial theatre performance payments, 1794–.

ii. SOURCES OUTSIDE PARIS

Blois, Bibliothèque Municipale
Ms 98–9 Anon. (Jean-Nicolas Dufort de Cheverny) 'Notice sur la vie de Sedaine'. See the text of this manuscript in Ledbury, 'Greuze and Sedaine', Appendix 1.

Besançon, Bibliothèque Municipale
Ms 1442 (354) Sedaine–David, 1 August 1780.
Ms 1442 (355) Sedaine–Suard, 8 May 1789. Re: *Maillard* and *Raimond V*.

Nantes, Bibliothèque Municipale
Labouchère MS 674 (242) Contract with Brunet to sell rights to publish *Aucassin et Nicolette*.

Rouen, Bibliothèque Municipale
Collection DuPutel Cartons V, VI (784); Collection De Blosseville, no. 1760. Letters.

iii. SOURCES OUTSIDE FRANCE

Brussels, Bibliothèque Royale Albert I
Mus. ms. 341c: Grétry's autograph working score of *Bazile, ou A trompeur, trompeur et demi*, last four items (sung text only).

Liège, Musée Grétry
[no shelf-mark]: Grétry's autograph working score of *Bazile, ou A trompeur, trompeur et demi*, first nine items (sung text only), 77 ff. See M. Elizabeth C. Bartlet, 'Grétry and the Revolution' in Philippe Vendrix (ed.), *Grétry et l'Europe de l'opéra-comique* (see Section E.v, below), pp. 47–110.

Stockholm, Royal Library

Ms Vu 60 Manuscript (dating from 1775) of *Maillard ou Paris sauvé*. (This manuscript is discussed at length in Lennart Breitholz, *Le Théâtre historique en France jusqu'à la Révolution*: see Section E.v, below.)

Section B: Single editions of Sedaine's dramatic works in chronological order of first publication

We have listed all editions of the spoken and musical dramas published in Sedaine's lifetime, and important editions thereafter. We have given a library reference number for an example of each edition.

L'Impromptu de Thalie ou la Lunette de vérité

L'Impromptu de Thalie ou la lunette de vérité (Comedy in one act).
Published in *Pièces fugitives* (1752), pp. 151–201.
Republished in *Recueil de poésies* (1760), II, pp. 111–60.

Le Diable à quatre ou la Double métamorphose

Le Diable à quatre ou la double métamorphose (opéra-comique, en trois actes. par M S ... A Paris, Chez Duchesne, Libraire, Rue St Jacques, au dessous de la fontaine St Benoît, au temple du goût, M.DCC.LVII. Avec Approbation et privilège du Roi.
8vo, 90pp. GB-Ob: Douce 13 653.

A La Haye, Chez Pierre Gosse, Libraire, MDCCLVII.
4o, 44pp. F-Pa, Rondel: Rf. 15, 172.

A La Haye, Chez Jean Neaulme. MDCC.LVII.
4o, 56pp. F-Pn: 8o Yth 5105.

Seconde édition. Vienne en Autriche, dans l'Imprimerie de Ghelen. MDCCLIX.
8vo, 74pp. F-Pa, Rondel: Rf.15, 172.

A Amsterdam, Chez la veuve de J. F. Jolly, Libraire sur le Rockin près de la bourse MDCCLX.
8vo, 88pp. F-Pn: 8o Yth 5106.

A Paris, Chez Duchesne, Libraire, rue St Jacques, au-dessous de la Fontaine St Benoît, au Temple du Goût. MDCC.LXX.
8vo, 60pp. GB-Lbl: 11735.b.2, vol. 2.

n.p., n.d: in *Œuvres dramatiques* (Paris: Duchesne, 1776) and *Œuvres dramatiques* (Paris: Brunet, 1800).

Paris, Chez Louis, Md de Musique, Rue du Roule à la Croix d'Or no 290. n.d. 8vo, 78pp.

Le Diable à quatre, ou la femme acariâtre
Musique nouvelle de M. Solié ... Paris, Chez Barba, Libraire, Palais Royal, derrière le Théâtre Français, no. 51. [1809]
8vo, 67 pp. Some adaptions made in the libretto by Creuzé de Lesser.
GB-Lbl: 11738.c.27, vol. 2.

Nouvelle édition, conforme à la représentation. A Paris, Chez Barba, Libraire, au Palais Royal, derrière le Théâtre Français, no. 51; Hubert, Libraire, au Palais Royal, galerie de bois, côté du Jardin, no. 222 [1817]
4o, 68pp. F-Pa, Rondel: Rf.13, 597.

Le Diable à Quatre Vaudeville-Féerie en 3 actes, imité de Sedaine. Par MM Jaime et Michel Delaporte ... Paris, Marchant, Editeur, Boulevart St Martin 12, Bruxelles, Tarride, Libraire, Passage de la Comédie. n.d. 4o, 28pp. F-Pn: Yth 1207.

Blaise le savetier

Blaise le savetier opéra-comique, suivi de la *Nôce de Nicaise*, Intermède mêlé de Chants et de Danses; par Monsieur S. ... La Musique de M. Philidor. Représenté pour la première fois sur le Théâtre de l'Opéra-Comique de la Foire Saint Germain, le 9 Mars 1759. Le prix est de 24 sols sans Musique. Les Ariettes se vendent séparément 24 sols. A Paris, Chez Duchesne, MDCC.LIX. Avec Approbation et Privilège du Roi.
8vo, 46pp. F-Pn: Yth 2056.

Paris, Chez N.B Duchesne ... M.DCC.LIX.
4o, 31pp. F-Pa, Rondel: Rf. 13, 599.

Représenté à Versailles devant Leurs Majesté [sic] le Mercredi 17 Mars 1762, par les Comédiens Italiens Ordinaires du Roi. A Paris, de l'Imprimerie de Ballard, seul Imprimeur du Roi pour la Musique, et Noteur de la Chapelle de Sa Majesté. M.DCC.LXII. Par exprès commandement de Sa Majesté.
8vo, 32pp. F-Pa, Rondel: Ra3–213.

A Liège, Chez F. J. Desoer, Marchand Libraire et Imprimeur, sous la Tour Saint-Lambert. n.d.
8vo, 52pp. F-Pn: Yf 5938.

A Paris, Chez la Veuve Duchesne ... M.DCC.LXVIII.
4o, 32pp. F-Pa, Rondel: Rf. 13, 600.

A Paris, Chez Duchesne, MDCC.LXXI.
8vo, 29pp. GB-Lbl: 11735.b.2.

n.p., n.d. In volume I of Sedaine's *Œuvres dramatiques* (Paris: Veuve Duchesne, 1776) and *Œuvres dramatiques* (Paris: Brunet, 1800).

Quérard, *La France littéraire* (IX, p. 9) cites an edition published in The Hague in 1760, and another published in Besançon in 1765. P. L. Jacob [i.e. P. Lacroix], *Bibliothèque dramatique de Monsieur de Soleinne. Catalogue redigé par P. L. Jacob* (6 vols, Paris: Administration de l''Alliance des Arts', 1843–5), III, no. 3196, mentions an edition by Veuve Duchesne, 1769.

Anacréon

Anacréon. Pastorale Héroique.

Published in *Recueil de poésies de M. S****, (1760), II, pp. 161–216.

Le Jardinier et son seigneur

Le Jardinier et son seigneur (opéra comique, En un Acte, en Prose, mêlé de morceaux de Musique, représenté sur le Théâtre de la Foire Saint-Germain le Mercredi 18 Février 1761. Par M. Sedaine. La musique de M. Philidor. La musique des ariettes s'y trouve imprimée. A Paris. Chez Claude Hérissant, libraire-imprimeur, Rue Neuve-Notre Dame aux trois vertus. M.DCC.LXI Avec approbation et privilège du Roi.
4o, [viii] + 48pp. F-Pn: 8o Yth 9316.

A Paris, Chez Claude Hérissant ... MDCCLXII.
8vo, 32pp. F-Pn: 8o Yth 9317.

A Avignon, Chez Louis Chambeau, Imprimeur Libraire, près les RR.PP. Jésuites. MDCCLXII.
4o, 27pp. F-Pa, Rondel: Rf. 13, 605.

A Avignon, Chez Jacques Garrigan imprimeur-libraire, Place St Didier, MDCCLXV.
4o, 27pp. F-Pa, Rondel: Rf. 13, 606.

A Paris, par la Compagnie des Libraires. MDCC.LXIX.
4o, 35pp. F-Pa, Rondel: Rf. 13, 607.

A Paris, Chez La Veuve Duchesne, Rue St Jacques, au temple du goût. MDCC.LXX.
4o, 35pp. F-Pa, Rondel: Rf. 13, 608.

A Paris, Chez Claude Hérissant ... MDCCLXXI.
8vo, 45pp. GB-Lbl: 11735.b.2 (vol. 6).
A Paris, Chez Claude Hérissant ... MDCCLXXXV.
8vo, 38pp. F-Pa, Rondel: Rf. 13, 609.
An edition published in Besançon in 1765 is mentioned by Quérard, *La France littéraire*, IX, p. 10. Krauss and Fontius, *Französische Drücke* (p. 469) cite an edition issued at Paris and Dunquerque: Boubers, 1762, in the Landesbibliothek, Halle.

L'Huître et les plaideurs
L'Huître et les plaideurs, ou le tribunal de la chicane Opéra-comique En un Acte, en Prose, mêlé de morceaux de Musique & Vaudeville, représenté sur le Théâtre de la Foire Saint-Laurent en 1759 & 1761. Par M. Sedaine. La Musique de M. Philidor. La Musique, Les Ariettes et le Vaudeville s'y trouvent gravés. A Paris, Chez Claude Hérissant, Imprimeur-Libraire, rue Neuve Notre Dame, aux trois vertus. MDCCLXI. Avec Approbation et Permission.
4o, [iv] + 34pp. F-Pn: 8o Yth 8787.
A Paris, Chez Claude Hérissant ... MDCC.LXVII.
4o, 28pp. F-Pa, Rondel: Rf. 13, 603.

On ne s'avise jamais de tout
On ne s'avise jamais de tout. Opéra-comique en un acte en prose, Mêlé de morceaux de Musique; Représenté sur le théâtre de la Foire S. Laurent, le Lundi 14 Septembre 1761. Par M. Sedaine. La Musique de M. de M*** Le Prix est de 24 sols avec les Ariettes et Vaudevilles gravés à la fin. A Paris, Chez Claude Hérissant, Imprimeur-libraire, rue Neuve Notre-Dame, aux trois vertus. MDCC.LXI. Avec Approbation et Permission.
4o, [iv] + 44pp. F-Pn: Yth 13035.
A Paris, Chez Claude Hérissant ... MDCC.LXI.
8vo, 48pp. F-Pn: Yth 13032.
A Paris, Chez Claude Hérissant ... MDCC.LXI. Avec Approbation et Privilège du Roi.
8vo, 55pp. F-Pa, Rondel: Rf. 13, 612.
Représenté à Versailles devant LEURS MAJESTÉS le Mercredi 2 Décembre 1761 ... Seconde Edition augmentée ... A Paris, Chez Claude Hérissant ... aux trois vertus. MDCCLXI.
4o, [iv] +48pp. F-Pn: 8o Yth. 13034.
A Paris, Chez Claude Hérissant ... aux trois vertus ... MDCCLXII.
4o, 38pp. F-Pa: Rondel Rf. 13, 613.
Représenté devant LEURS MAJESTÉS à Fontainebleau le Mercredi 3 Novembre 1762, par les comédiens Italiens Ordinaires du Roi. De l'Imprimerie de Christophe Ballard ... MDCCLXII. Par exprès Commandement de Sa Majesté.
8vo, [iv] + 56pp. F-Pn: 8o Yth 13039.
Seconde Edition. Vienne en Autriche, Dans L'Imprimerie de Ghelen. 1762.
56pp. F-Po: Liv. 18. 2445.
3e Edition Augmentée. A Avignon, Chez Louis Chambeau ... M.DCC.LXIV.
35pp. F-Pn: Z. Rothschild 5184.
Paris, Chez Claude Hérissant ... MDCC.LXV.
12o, 48pp. F-Pn: 8o Yth 13040.
A Avignon, Chez Louis Chambeau ... M.DCC.LXV.
32pp. F-Po: Liv. 18. 2346.
A Paris, Chez Claude Hérissant ... M. DCC.LXVII.
39pp. F-Po: Liv. 18. 1951.

Représenté devant sa Majesté, à Fontainebleau, le 14 novembre 1770. De l'imprimerie de P. Robert-Christophe Ballard ... MDCCLXX.
8o, 46pp. F-Pn: Yf 7955.
Nouvelle Edition. A Paris, Chez Didot l'aîné ... M.DCC.LXXIII.
32pp. F-Po: Liv. 18. 1985.
A Paris, Chez Claude Hérissant ... A la croix d'or. MDCCLXXV.
8vo, 46pp. GB-Lbl: 11735.b.2.
Paris, ed.Gustave Legoux, 1910.
8vo, 16pp. GB-Lbl: F.690.x.[3].

Le Roi et le fermier

Le Roi et le fermier, comédie en trois actes; Mêlé de morceaux de Musique. Représentée pour la première fois par les Comédiens Italiens ordinaires du Roi, le Lundi 22 Novembre 1762. Par M. Sedaine. La Musique de M. de M***. Le prix est de 24 sols. Les Airs detachés 36 sols: ils se vendent séparément. A Paris, Chez Claude Hérissant ... MDCCLXII. Avec Approbation et Privilège du Roi. La Partition générale se trouvera Chez le même Libraire et Chez les Marchands de Musique.
4o, [viii] + 72pp. GB-Lbl: 11741.aaa.39 [5].
A Paris, Chez Claude Hérissant ... MDCCLXIII.
8vo, 52pp. F-Pa, Rondel: Rf. 13, 617.
A Paris, Chez Claude Hérissant ... MDCCLXIV.
4o, 52pp. F-Pa, Rondel: Rf. 13, 618.
A Bruxelles, Chez Pierre Paupie MDCCLXV.
4o, 52pp. GB-Ob: Douce, 13, 653.
A Dresde, Chez Georg Conrad Walter, 1766.
78pp. F-Pn (Mus): ThB. 839(a).
A Paris, Chez la Veuve Duchesne ... MDCCLXX. Avec Approbation et Privilège du Roi.
8vo, 55pp. GB-Lbl: 11735.b.2.
A Paris, Chez Claude Hérissant ... MDCCLXXIV.
4o, 44pp. F-Pa, Rondel: Rf. 13, 619.
Nouvelle édition. A Paris, Chez N. B. Duchesne ... MDCCLXXVI.
4o, 36pp. F-Pa, Rondel: Rf. 13, 620.
A Paris, Chez la Veuve Duchesne ... MDCCLXXIX.
8vo, 56pp. F-Pa, Rondel: Rf. 13, 622.
A Paris, Chez Fages, au magasin de pièces de théâtre, boulevard St Martin, no. 29, vis-à-vis le théâtre des Jeunes Artistes. 1807.
4o, 36pp. F-Pa, Rondel: Ro 1770.
A Paris, Chez Fages ... vis à vis la rue de Lancry. 1809.
4o, 32pp. F-Pa, Rondel: Rf. 13, 624.
A. Tchemerzine, *Bibliographie d'éditions originales et rares* (see Section G below), X, p. 299, mentions a 1770 edition by Claude Hérissant.

L'Ouvrage du Cœur

L'Ouvrage du Cœur, Par un François, Représenté au mois de juin 1763. Le prix est de 12 sols. A Paris, Chez Claude Herissant ... M.DCC.LXIII. Avec Approbation et Permission.

This work, performed at Nicolet's theatre in Paris (and in Rouen, according to Brenner, *A Bibliographical List*), in June 1763 to mark the end of the hostilities now known as the Seven

Years' War, is anonymous. On the back page of the edition cited above it is not listed among Sedaine's works, but attributed to M. M***, together with *Le Bûcheron ou les Trois souhaits*. This information is repeated on the 1764 Hérissant edition of *L'Anneau perdu et retrouvé*, on the 1764 Hérissant edition of *Rose et Colas* and on the 1766 Hérissant edition of *Le Philosophe sans le savoir*. This, and the terms of the Hérissant *privilège*, would seem to indicate that Sedaine was not the work's author. However, on the 1768 Hérissant edition of *Les Sabots* we find *Le Bûcheron* attributed to Guichard and *L'Ouvrage du cœur* listed among the plays of Sedaine. (Listed too is *L'Isle sonnante*, on which see Charlton, pp. 200ff, above.) The attribution of *L'Ouvrage du cœur* (but not *L'Isle sonnante*) to Sedaine is repeated in *Le Déserteur* (Hérissant, 1769); *Thémire* (Hérissant, 1770); *Le Mort marié* (Hérissant, 1771); *Le Faucon* (Hérissant, 1772) and *Le Magnifique* (Hérissant, 1773). As Hérissant enjoyed a privileged(!) relationship to Sedaine in these years, it is odd for the author not to have corrected a misattribution, which is an argument for accepting the text as Sedaine's. Moreover, the work is included in the 1776 Duchesne *Œuvres dramatiques*, III, the 1800 Brunet *Œuvres dramatiques*, I, and the undated Duchesne *Théâtre de Sedaine*, II.

One might speculate that Sedaine preferred anonymity, but on seeing his work (minor though it was) attributed to another, ensured that the publisher corrected the lists. However, this would not explain why Sedaine never made mention of the work in any correspondence or other writing. Modern scholarship has attributed the work to Sedaine. (See Brenner, *A Bibliographical List*, p. 125, no. 11033, and Rayner, 'Sedaine's Dramatic Work', p. 253.)

The text itself is in fact more of a prologue to a ballet than a self-standing drama, is set in the theatre itself and concerns a poet, who, distracted by drink and women, has difficulty writing a eulogy of Louis XV upon the peace in time for a performance. Its ironies and its *chansons* have something of Sedaine about them, but from its slender text it is impossible to attribute or positively deattribute the text. If we are to accept the attribution, however, we must ask several questions: why did the by now highly successful Sedaine write an anonymous short prologue for a marginal theatre? And why keep a veil of anonymity until four years later? It is perhaps possible that Sedaine, then associated with the Philosophes, did not want to give any hostages to fortune or find his ironic *éloge* mistaken as unpatriotic at a time of defeat.

The attribution to Sedaine must remain doubtful until firmer documentary evidence becomes available.

Rose et Colas

Rose et Colas, comédie en un acte, prose et musique. Représentée, pour la première fois, par les Comédiens Italiens ordinaires du Roi, le 8 Mars 1769 [sic for 1764]. Le prix est de 24 sols. A Paris, Chez Claude Hérissant ... MDCCLXIV. Avec Approbation et Privilège du Roi. On trouve Chez le même libraire les Airs détachés. 21 16s. On grave la partition.
4o, [viii] + 62pp. F-Pn: 86.a.17.

A Besançon, Chez Fantet, Libraire, plus haut que la place St Pierre. MDCCLXIV. Avec Permission.
4o, 44pp. GB-Lbl: 11741.a.49.

A La Haye, Chez Pierre Marteau. MDCCLXIV.
4o, 59pp. F-Pa, Rondel: Rf. 13, 629.

A Paris, Chez Claude Hérissant ... MDCCLXV.
4o, 40pp. F-Pa, Rondel: Rf. 13, 630.

A Paris, et se vendent [sic] à Genève, Chez P. Pellet et fils, MDCCLXVI.
12o, 52pp. F-Pa, Rondel: Rf. 13, 631.

A Copenhague, Chez Philibert, 1767.
(Ballenstadt, Stadtbibliothek) See Krauss and Fontius, *Französische Drücke*.

A Paris, Chez Duchesne, Libraire, Rue St Jacques, au Temple du Goût. MDCCLXVII.
4o, 39pp. F-Pa, Rondel: Rf. 13, 632.

A Paris, Chez Cailleau, rue St Jacques, au dessus de la rue des Mathurins, à St André. MDCCLXIX. Avec Approbation et Privilège du Roi.
4o, 39pp. F-Pa, Rondel: Rf. 13, 633.

A Paris, Chez la Veuve Duchesne ... MDCCLXX. Avec Approbation et Privilège du Roi.
8vo, 52pp. GB-Lbl: 11735.b.2.

A Paris, Chez la Veuve Duschesne ... M.DCC.LXXIX.
8vo, 43pp. F-Pa, Rondel: Rf. 13, 634.

Quérard (IX, p. 11) and Tchemerzine (X, p. 301: see Section G below) mention an edition by Ballard, Paris, 1769.

L'Anneau perdu et retrouvé

L'Anneau perdu et retrouvé, opéra comique en deux actes; Mêlée [sic] de morceaux de Musique. Par M. Sedaine. La Musique de M.B *** Représenté pour la première fois par les Comédiens Italiens ordinaires du Roi, le Lundi 20 Août 1764. Le prix est de 24 sols. A Paris, Chez Claude Hérissant ... MDCC.LXIV. Avec Approbation et Privilège du Roi. Les airs détachés 36 sols: et la partition 12 liv.
[viii] + 56pp. F-Pa, Rondel: Rf. 13, 640.

A Bruxelles, Chez J. J. Boucherie, Imprimeur-Libraire, rue de l'Hôpital. MDCC.LXIV. Avec Approbation et Privilège.
[vi] + 46pp. F-Pa, Rondel: Rf. 13, 642.

Le Philosophe sans le savoir

There follows a list of known editions before 1797 and major editions thereafter. For more detailed lists readers should consult the bibliography of the Variorum Critical Edition by T. E. Oliver (1913, described below) and John Dunkley's edition (1993, described below, pp. 72–8), against which this list has been cross-referenced. For nineteenth-century editions, see both Oliver and Rayner, 'Sedaine's Dramatic Work', pp. 257–8.

Le Philosophe sans le savoir Comédie en prose et en cinq actes représentée par les Comédiens François ordinaires du Roi le 2 Novembre [sic for Décembre] 1765. Par M. Sedaine. Le prix est de trente sols. A Paris, Chez Claude Hérissant, libraire-imprimeur, rue Neuve Notre-Dame, à la Croix d'Or ... MDCC.LXVI. Avec Approbation et Privilège du Roi.
4o, [iv] + 95 + 16pp. F-Pn: Yth 14125. [Dunkley A]

Le Philosophe sans le sçavoir, Comédie en cinq actes et en proses [sic], représentée par les Comédiens Françoises ordinaires du Roi le 2 décembre 1765. Seconde édition ... A Paris, Chez Claude Hérissant ... MDCCLXVI ...
Avec Approbation et Privilège du Roi.
8vo, [iv] + 119 + 18. F-Pn: 8o Yth 14126. [Dunkley B]

See Dunkley, pp. 74–5, for variations on the Hérissant 1766 edition, which he labels C (F-Pn: Z Rothschild 5186) and D (F-Psg: Z 8o 1329 inv. 3568).

Le Philosophe sans le savoir, Représentée par les comédiens François de la cour sur le nouveau Théâtre de S. A. E de Saxe, à Dresde. 1766. Avec Approbation de la cour. Chez George Conrad Walter, Libraire de la cour.
8vo, 116pp. F-Pa, Rondel: Rf. 13, 645.

Le Philosophe sans le savoir ou le gentilhomme commerçant A Amsterdam et à la Haye Chez Constapel et Le Febure, libraires MDCCLXVI.
8vo, 72pp. (See Oliver, 1913, p. 24.)

Le Philosophe sans le savoir A Genève, Chez Louis Caille au bas du collège, MDCCLXVI. Avec permission. 8vo, 104pp. (Oliver, pp. 25–6.)

Oliver, pp. 26–7, mentions a Paris Hérissant 1767 edition. Dunkley has an edition [E] that corresponds to this (though dated 1768) which he regards as probably a counterfeit edition.

A Paris. Par la Compagnie des libraires. MDCCLXIX. Avec Approbation et Permission. [Dunkley F]

Nouvelle édition. A Avignon, Chez Louis Chambeau, Imprimeur-Libraire, près le collège. M.DCC.LXXII.

4o, 53pp. F-Pa, Rondel: Rf. 13, 646. [Dunkley G]

A Paris, Chez Hérissant ... M.DCC.LXXIV. Avec Approbation et Privilège du Roi. [Dunkley H] Probably a counterfeit edition.

Nouvelle édition. A Paris, Chez Delalain, rue et à côté de la Comédie Française. M.DCC.LXXVII.

47pp. F-Phvp: 613 125, no. 2. [Dunkley I]

Nouvelle édition. A Paris, Chez Didot, l'aîné, imprimeur et libraire, rue Pavée. M.DCC. LX. XVIII.

4o, 55pp. F-Pa, Rondel: Rf. 13, 647.

A Londres, Chez T. Hookham, Libraire, dans Bond Street, au Coin de Bruton Street. M.DCC.LXXXV.

8vo, [ii] + 94pp. GB-Lbl: 85.i.12.

Publiée pour la première fois d'après le manuscrit de la Comédie-Française, avec une préface par George d'Heylli. (Paris: Librairie des Bibliophiles, 1880).

4o, [ii] + xxiv + 102pp. GB-Lbl: 11736.b.11.

Ed. Martin Gisi (Berlin: Weidmannsche Buchhandlung, 1883).

8vo, 90pp. F-Pa, Rondel: Rf. 13, 654.

Variorum Critical Edition by Thomas Edward Oliver, University of Illinois Bulletin (The University Studies), IV, no. 3 (March 1913).

8vo, 175pp. GB-Lbl: 11735.h.23.

Ed. T. E. Oliver (New York: Oxford University Press, 1914).

8vo, xlvii + 159pp.

Ed. Félix Gaiffe (Paris: Hatier (Les classiques pour tous), n.d.).

16o, 64pp.

Ed. Graham Rodmell (Durham: University of Durham, 1987).

Ed. Robert Garapon (Paris: Société des Textes Françaises Modernes, 1990).

Ed. John Dunkley (Egham: Runnymede Books, 1993).

Aline, reine de Golconde

Aline, reine de Golconde, Ballet-Héroïque, En Trois Actes, representé, pour la première fois, par l'Académie Royale de Musique, le Jeudi 10 Avril 1766. Prix XXX sols. Aux dépens de l'Académie. A Paris, Chés De Lormel, Imprimeur de ladite Académie, rue du Foin, à l'image Sainte Geneviève. On trouvera des Livres de Paroles à la Salle de l'Opéra. M.DCC.LXVI. Avec Approbation et Privilège du Roi.

4o, 52pp. F-Pn: Yf 673.

Représenté, à Versailles, devant Sa Majesté, le Jeudi 16 Mai 1771. De L'Imprimerie de Pierre-Robert-Christophe Ballard ... M.DCC.LXXI ...

8vo, [x] + 59pp. F-Pa, Rondel: Rf. 13, 586 (10).

A Paris, Chez de Lormel ... M.DCC.LXXII.

4o, 30 pp. F-Pa, Rondel: Rf. 13, 662.

A Paris, ches de Lormel ... MDCC.LXXII.

4o, 59pp. F-Pa, Rondel: Ro 1281. This copy includes ms. stage directions.

A Paris, Chez Musier fils, Libraire, quai des Augustins, au coin de la rue Gît le Cœur; et à Pacques, rue du Foin-Saint-Jacques, vis-à-vis la Chambre Syndicale des Libraires. M.DCC.LXXV.
8vo, pp. 76–122. GB-Lbl: 86.a.18 [5].

A Paris, et se vend à Marseille, Chez Sube et Laporte, Libraires à la Canebière au Parnasse François. M.DCC.LXXVII.
4o, 29pp. F-Pa, Rondel: Rf. 13, 663.

Représenté pour la première fois a Vienne, pour le Benéfice de M. de Dupont ...Vienne 1780.
8vo, 44pp. F-Pa, Rondel: Rf. 13, 664.

Représenté, A Versailles, devant Leurs Majestés, le 23 Mai 1782. De L'Imprimerie de P.R.C Ballard, seul Imprimeur du Roi pour la Musique de la Chambre, Menus-Plaisirs, et grande Chapelle de sa Majesté; Imprimeur de Monseigneur Comte et Madame Comtesse d'Artois. M.DCC.LXXXII. Par Exprès Commandement de Sa Majesté.
8vo, [x] + 56pp. F-Pn: Yth 15242.

Nouvelle édition ... de l'Imprimerie de P. De Lormel ... M.DCC.LXXXII.
4o, 28pp. F-Pa, Rondel: Rf. 13,666.

A Paris, Chez Didot l'aîné, Imprimeur et Libraire, Rue Pavée. M.DCC.LXXXII.
4o, 27pp. F-Pa, Rondel: Rf. 13, 665.

La Gageure imprévue

La Gageure imprévue Comédie, en prose, et en un acte, représentée pour la première fois à Paris, par les Comédiens François ordinaires du Roi, le Vendredi 27 Mai 1768. Par M. Sedaine. Le prix est de trente sols brochée. A Paris, Chez Claude Hérissant ... M.DCC.LXVIII. Avec Approbation et Permission.
4o, [iv] + 82pp. F-Pa, Rondel: Rf. 13, 668.

A Paris (n.p.), M.DCC.LXVIII.
4o, 38pp. F-Pa, Rondel: Rf. 13, 669.

A Paris, Chez Cailleau, Rue St Jacques, au dessus de la Rue des Mathurins, à S. André. M.DCC.LXX. Avec Approbation et Permission.
4o, 40pp. F-Pa, Rondel: Rf. 13, 670.

A Paris, Chez la Veuve Duchesne, Rue St Jacques, au Temple du Goût. M.DCC.LXX. Avec Approbation et Permission.
8vo, 36pp. F-Pm: 54, 661.

A Paris, Chez la Veuve Duchesne ... M.DCC.LXXIII ...
4o, 44pp. F-Pa, Rondel: Rf. 13, 671.

Nouvelle édition. A Paris, Chez Delalain ... M.DCC.LXXVIII.
4o, 32pp. F-Pn: Yf 11176.

A Paris, Chez la veuve Duchesne ...1778.
8vo, 40pp. F-Pa, Rondel: Rf. 13, 672.

Nouvelle Edition. A Paris, Chez Ruault, Libraire, rue de la Harpe. M.DCC.LXXVIII.
4o, 40pp. F-Pa, Rondel: Rf. 13, 673.

A Paris, Chez l'Auteur, au Louvre, à l'Académie d'Architecture; ou Chez Prault, Imprimeur du Roi, quai de Gêvres. M.DCC.LXXIX. Avec Approbation et Privilège du Roi.
8vo, [iv] + 82pp. F-Pn: 8o Yf 465 [4].
This copy contains some ms. stage directions, as does F-Pa, Rondel: Rf. 13, 675.

A Paris, Chez l'Auteur, au Louvre, à l'Académie d'Architecture; ou Chez Prault, Imprimeur du Roi, Quai des Augustins, à l'immortalité. 1788.
8vo, [iv] + 84pp. F-Pn: 8o Yth 7750.

A Paris, Chez les libraires qui vendent les nouveautés. MDCCXCII.
4o, 56pp. GB-Lbl: 1479.c.4 [6].

For editions published in the nineteenth century, see Rayner, 'Sedaine's Dramatic Work', pp. 262–4.

The following modern editions should also be mentioned:
Ed. Félix Gaiffe (Paris: Hatier, Les Classiques pour tous, n.d.).
Ed. Robert Niklaus (Exeter: Exeter French Texts, 1970). This text is also available in electronic format, at http://www.exeter.ac.uk/french/textes/gageure

Les Sabots

Les Sabots, opéra comique en un acte, Mêlé d'Ariettes. Par Mrs C ... & Sedaine. Représenté pour la première fois par les Comédiens Italiens ordinaires du Roi, le Mercredi 26 Octobre 1768. Le prix est de vingt-quatre sols broché. A Paris, Chez Claude Hérissant, M.DCC.LXVIII. Avec Approbation et Privilège du Roi.
4o, [iv] + 33pp. F-Pn: 8o Yth 15976.
A Paris, Chez Claude Hérissant ... MDCC.LXVIII.
4o, 30pp. F-Pa, Rondel: Rf. 13, 681.
A Paris, Chez Claude Hérissant, M.DCC.LXIX.
4o, 22pp. F-Pa, Rondel: Rf. 13, 682.
Représenté, devant Sa Majesté, à Fontainebleau, le 10 Octobre 1770. De L'Imprimerie de P. Robert-Christophe Ballard ... [1770].
8vo, 32pp. F-Pn: Yf 7950.
A Paris, Chez Claude Hérissant ... M.DCC. LXXVII.
8vo, 24pp. GB-Lbl: 11735.b.2, vol. I.
A Paris, Chez Claude Hérissant ... [undated]
4o, 27pp. F-Pa, Rondel: Rf. 13, 683.

Le Déserteur

Le Déserteur, drame en trois actes, en prose mêlée de musique. Par M. Sedaine. La musique par M ***. Représentée [sic] pour la première fois, par les Comédiens Italiens ordinaires du Roi, le Lundi 6 Mars 1769. Le prix est de 24 sols. A Paris, Chez Claude Hérissant, M.DCC.LXIX. Avec Approbation et Privilège du Roi. On trouve Chez le même libraire les airs détachés. La Partition paroîtra à la fin du mois d'Avril.
4o, [x] +82 pp. F-Pa, Rondel: Rf. 13, 684.
Représenté devant Sa Majesté, à Fontainebleau, le 11 Octobre 1769. De l'Imprimerie de Pierre-Robert-Christophe Ballard ... M.DCC.LXIX.
4o, [vi] + 82pp. F-Pa, Rondel: Ra 3, 236.
A Paris, Chez la veuve Duchèsne, M.DCC.LXIX.
4o, 43pp. F-Pn: 8o Yth 4708.
Seconde Edition, revue par l'Auteur. A Paris, Chez Claude Hérissant ... M.DCC.LXX.
[viii] + 84pp. GB-Lbl: 11741.aaa.39 [4].
A Paris, Chez Claude Hérissant ... M.DCC.LXX.
4o, 60pp. F-Pn: Yf 11284.
A Hérissant edition of 1770 with 47 pages is at F-Pn: Z Rothschild 4167.
Pellet et Fils, A Paris, et se vendent à Genève, 1771. 68pp.
F-Pn (Mus): ThB.2059 (c).
Nouvelle Edition … A Paris, Chez la Veuve Duchesne, M.DCC.LXXIII.
8o, 59pp. GB-Lbl: 1609/5962.
Nouvelle édition. A Paris, Chez N.B Duchesne, Libraire ... M.DCC.LXXIV. Avec Approbation et Permission.
4o, 44pp. F-Pa, Rondel: Rf. 13, 686.

A Paris, Chez Claude Hérissant ... M.DCC.LXXIV.
8vo, 62pp. F-Pa, Rondel: Ro 1784.
Naples, De L'Imprimerie de Jean Gravier. MDCCLXXVII Avec Approbation et Privilege.
[ii] + 71pp. F-Pn: 8o Yth 4712.
Nouvelle Edition ... A Toulouse, Chez Broulhiet, Libraire, rue Saint-Rome, au coin de la rue Dumai. M.DCC.LXXXII. Avec Approbation et Permission.
46 pp. F-Po: Liv. 18.208. *ter.*
A Paris, Chez Claude Hérissant ... M.DCC.LXXXIII.
8vo, 56pp. F-Pa, Rondel: Rf. 13, 687.
A Paris, Chez Brunet, Libraire, Place de la Comédie Italienne. M.DCC. LXXXVI.
4o, 63pp. F-Pa, Rondel: Rf. 13, 688.

Thémire

Thémire, Pastorale, en un acte, dédiée à Madame B**, par M. Sedaine, la musique de M. Duny: Représentée, pour la première fois, devant Sa Majesté, à Fontainebleau, le Samedi 20 Octobre 1770; Et, à Paris, pour la première fois, par les Comédiens Italiens Ordinaires du Roi, le Lundi 26 Novembre 1770 ... A Paris, Chez Claude Hérissant ... MDCCLXX. Avec Approbation et Privilège du Roi.
4o, [iv] + 44pp. GB-Lbl: 86.a.18 [2].
Représenté, devant Sa Majesté, à Fontainebleau, Le Samedi 20 Octobre 1770. De L'Imprimerie de Pierre-Robert-Christophe Ballard ... M.DCC.LXX.
4o, [iv] + 44pp. F-Pn: Yi 7749.
A Paris, Chez Claude Hérissant ... M.DCC. LXXI ...
4o, 24pp. F-Pa, Rondel: Rf. 13, 700. (Title-page dates the première at the Comédie-Italienne to 'Octobre', not 'Novembre'.)

Le Mort marié

Le Mort Marié, comédie en deux actes en prose. Par M. Sedaine. Le prix est de trente sols brochée. A Paris, Chez Claude Hérissant ... M.DCC.LXXI. Avec Approbation et Privilège du Roi.
4o, [iv] + 61pp. GB-Lbl: 86.a.18 [1].
A Paris, Chez les Libraires Associés. MDCC.LXXIV.
8vo, 35pp. F-Pa, Rondel: Rf. 13, 702.
Nouvelle édition. A Paris, Chez Delalain, rue et à côté de la Comédie Françoise. M. DCC.LXXV. Avec Approbation et Privilège du Roi.
4o, 24pp. F-Pa, Rondel: Rf 13, 704.
A Paris, Chez les Libraires Associés. MDCC.LXXVI.
4o, 32pp. F-Pa, Rondel: Rf 13, 705.

Le Faucon

Le Faucon, Opéra-comique, en un acte, en prose mêlée d'ariettes. Représenté devant Sa Majesté, à Fontainebleau, le Samedi 2 Novembre 1771. De l'Imprimerie de Pierre-Robert-Christophe Ballard ... MDCC.LXXI. Par exprès commandement de Sa Majesté.
[iv] + 57pp. F-Pn: Yf 11294.
Représenté devant Sa Majesté, A Fontainebleau, le 2 Novembre 1771. Et à Paris, par les Comédiens Italiens ordinaires du Roi, le 19 Mars 1772 ... A Paris, Chez Claude Hérissant ... MDCC.LXXII. Avec Approbation et Privilege du Roi.
4o, [iv] + 60pp. F-Pn: 8o Yth 6539.
A Paris, Chez Claude Hérissant ... M.DCC.LXXII.
8vo, 32pp. GB-Lbl: 11735.b.2, Vol. VII.

A Bruxelles, Chez J. Vanden Berghen, Imprimeur-Libraire rue de la Magdelaine. M.DCC.LXXII. Avec Privilège de Sa Majesté.
8vo, 38pp. F-Pa, Rondel: Rf. 13, 710.
Nouvelle édition. A Avignon, Chez Louis Chambeau ... pres le collège ... MDCC. LXXIII.
4o, 27pp. F-Pa, Rondel: Rf. 13, 711.

Fête à l'occasion du mariage de Monseigneur le Comte d'Artois, avec Marie-Thérèse, Princesse du Savoie

Fête à l'occasion du Mariage de Monseigneur le Comte d'Artois, avec Marie-Thérèse, Princesse du Savoie. Exécuté à Saint Cyr, en leur présence, par les Démoiselles de la Royale Maison de Saint-Louis. [Hérissant] M.DCC.LXXII.
8vo, 22pp. GB-Lbl: F.881 [1].

Le Magnifique

Le Magnifique, Comédie en trois actes, en prose, et en vers mis en musique, Terminée par un Divertissement. Par M. Sedaine. La Musique est de M. Grety [sic]. Représenté pour la première fois, par les Comédiens Italiens ordinaires du Roi, le Lundi 4 Mars 1773. Et à Versailles en présence de Sa Majesté, le 26 Mars 1773. Le prix est de trente sols. A Paris, Chez Claude Hérissant ... M.DCC.LXIII [Sic for LXXIII] Avec Approbation et Privilège du Roi.
4o, [viii] + 71pp. F-Pa: Rondel Rf. 13, 585 (5).
A Paris, Chez Claude Hérissant ... M.DCC.LXXIII.
4o, 48pp. F-Pa, Rondel: Rf. 13, 715 (with 'Grety' corrected to 'Gretry').
A Paris, Chez Claude Hérissant ... M.DCC.LXXIII.
4o, 52pp. F-Pa, Rondel: Rf. 13, 713.
A Paris, Chez Claude Hérissant...MDCCLXXIII
4o, 56pp. F-Pa, Rondel: Rf. 13, 712.
Représentée devant Sa Majesté, à Versailles, le 19 Mars 1773. De L'Imprimerie de Pierre-Robert-Christophe Ballard ... M.DCC.LXXIII.
4o, [viii] + 71pp. F-Pn: Yf 11617.
A Paris, Chez la Veuve Duchesne ... M.DCC.LXXIV. Avec Approbation et Permission.
4o, 50pp. F-Pa, Rondel: Rf. 13, 716.
A Paris, Chez Claude Hérissant ... MDCC.LXXXII.
8vo, 56pp. F-Pa, Rondel: Rf. 13,717.
Représentée à Parme devant leurs Altesses Royales dans le Carnaval 1788. Chez son Excellence Mr Le Comte de Flavigny Ministre Plénipot. de France. A Parme, de L'Impriméric Royale. n.d.
8vo, 67pp. F-Pn: 8o Yth 10610.

Les Femmes vengées

Les Femmes vengées, Opéra-comique, en un acte et en vers; Par M. Sedaine. La musique de M. Philidor. Représenté, pour la première fois, le Lundi 20 Mars, par les Comédiens Italiens ordinaires du Roi. Se vend 30 sols broché. A Paris, Chez Musier fils, Libraire ... M.DCC.LXXV.
8vo, [iv] + 74pp. F-Pn: 8o Yth 6866.
A Paris, Chez Musier fils ... M.DCC.LXXV.
4o, 43pp. F-Pa, Rondel: Rf. 13, 724.
A Paris, Chez Musier fils ... M.DCC.LXXV.
4o, 48pp. F-Pa, Rondel: Rf. 13, 722.

A Paris, Chez Musier fils ... MDCCLXXV.
4o, 56pp. GB-Lbl: 11735.b.2, vol. IX.
Nouvelle édition. A Paris, Chez N.B Duchesne ... M.DCC.LXXVI.
4o, 40pp. F-Pa, Rondel: Rf. 13, 725.
A Avignon, Chez les Frères Bonnet, Imprimeurs, Libraires, vis à vis le puits des boeufs. M.DCC.LXXVI.
4o, 42pp. F-Pa, Rondel: Rf. 13, 726.
Nouvelle édition ... A Paris, Chez Delalain ... M.DCC. LXXXVII.
4o, 40pp. F-Pa, Rondel: Rf. 13, 727.

Félix ou l'Enfant trouvé

Félix ou l'Enfant trouvé, Comédie en trois actes; En Prose & en Vers mis en Musique. Représentée devant Leurs Majestés à Fontainebleau, en Novembre, 1777. De L'Imprimerie de P.Robert-Christophe Ballard ... MDCC.LXXVII. Par exprès Commandement de Sa Majesté.
8vo, [iv] + 83pp. F-Pn: Yf 11298.
Représentée devant Leurs Majestés à Fontainebleau le 10 Novembre, & par les Comédiens Italiens ordinaires du Roi, le 24 Novembre 1777. Le prix est de 30 sols avec la musique. A Paris, Chez la Veuve Ballard & Fils ... M.DCC.LXXVII.
8vo, [iv] + 90pp. F-Pn: 8o Yth 6752.
A Paris, Chez Didot l'aîné, Imprimeur-Libraire, Rue Pavée ... M.DCC.LXXX1. Avec Approbation et Permission.
4o, 59pp. F-Pa, Rondel: Rf. 13, 730.
Nouvelle édition, Corrigée et conforme à la partition. A Paris, Chez Brunet, Libraire rue Mauconseil ... M.DCC.LXXXII. Avec Approbation et Permission.
4o, 40pp. F-Pa, Rondel: Rf. 13, 731.
Félix ou l'Enfant trouvé, Comédie en trois actes, prose et ariettes. Représentée aux Italiens, le 24 Novembre 1781. Nouvelle édition, Corrigée et conforme à la partition. A Toulouse, Chez Broulhiet, Libraire ... M.DCC.LXXXII. Avec Approbation et Permission.
4o, 54pp. F-Pa, Rondel: Rf. 13, 732.
A Paris, Chez Brunet, Libraire ... M.DCC.LXXXVI.
4o, 59pp. F-Pa, Rondel: Rf. 13, 733.
A Paris, Chez les Libraires Associés, rue de la Comédie. M.DCC.LXXXVI.
4o, 40pp. (The example of this edition cited here is incomplete.) F-Pa, Rondel: Rf. 13, 734.
A Paris, et se trouve a Bruxelles, Chez J. L. Deboubers, Imprimeur-Libraire. 1793.
4o, 48pp. F-Pa, Rondel: Rf. 13, 735.
A Avignon, Chez Offray aîné, imprimeur-libraire, place St.Didier. Undated.
[iii] + 60pp. F-Pn: Yth 6758.

Aucassin et Nicolette

Aucassin et Nicolette ou les moeurs du bon vieux tems, comédie en quatre actes, en vers, mêlée d'ariettes. Représentée devant Leurs Majestés, à Versailles le 30 Décembre 1779. De l'Imprimerie de P. R. C Ballard, seul Imprimeur de la Musique du Roi ... [1780]. Par Exprès Commandement de Sa Majesté.
8vo, [iv] + 84pp. F-Pn: Yth 1422.
Comédie en quatre actes et en vers, Dont une partie est est mise en Musique. Représentée, pour la première fois, devant Leurs Majestés à Versailles, le Décembre 1779, par les Comédiens Italiens Ordinaires du Roi, & à Paris, le 3 Janvier 1780 ... A Paris, Chez la Veuve Ballard & Fils ... M.DCC.LXXX. Avec Approbation & Permission.
8vo, [xii] + 86pp. F-Pn: Yf 11624.

Comédie remise en trois actes ... reprise le 7 Janvier 1782. A Paris, Chez Brunet, Libraire, rue Mauconseil, à côté de la Comédie Italienne. M.DCC.LXXXII.
4o, 44pp. F-Pa, Rondel: Rf. 13, 739.
A Paris, Chez Delalain, 1782.
36pp. F-Pn (Mus): Th. 340 (b).
A Paris, Chez Brunet ... M.DCC.LXXXII.
8vo, 64pp. GB-Lbl: 1345.e.1.
(There is a fragment of an English translation of act II, sc. II bound in to this copy.)
A Paris, Chez Brunet ... M.DCCC.LXXXIV.
48pp. F-Po: Liv. 18. 2055.
Comédie, en quatre actes ... A Paris, Chez Didôt l'aîné, Imprimeur et Libraire, Rue Pavée. M.DCC.LXXXIX.
4o, 46pp. F-Pa, Rondel: Rf. 13, 740.

Thalie au Nouveau Théâtre
Thalie au Nouveau Théâtre, prologue, En Prose, En Vers, Ariettes & Vaudevilles. La musique est de M. Grétry. Prix 1 liv. 4 sols. A Paris, Chez Brunet, Libraire ... M.DCC.LXXXIII.
8vo, 30pp. F-Pn: Yf 11626.

Amphitrion
Amphitrion, opéra en trois actes, représenté devant Leurs Majestés, à Versailles, le 15 Mars 1786. De L'Imprimerie de P. R. C. Ballard ... M.DCC.LXXXVI.
8vo, [vi] + 76pp. GB-Lbl: 640.g.11 [6].

Représenté devant Leurs Majestés, à Versailles, le 15 Mars 1786. Et pour la première fois à Paris, sur le théâtre de P. de Lormel, Imprimeur de Ladite Académie ... M.DCC.LXXXVIII. Avec Approbation et Privilège du Roi.
4o, vi + 69pp. F-Pa, Rondel: Ro 1, 351.
n.p., n.d., but with ms. annotations, provenance the Académie Royale de Musique.
76pp. F-Pn (Mus): Rés. Th. B. 11.

Richard Cœur-de-Lion
Richard Cœur de Lion, Comédie en trois actes, en prose et en vers, mis en musique. Représentée, pour la première fois, à Paris, par les Comédiens Italiens ordinaires du Roi, le 21 Octobre 1784; & à Fontainebleau, devant leurs Majestés, le 25 Octobre 1785. Prix, 1 liv. 10 sols. A Paris, Chez Brunet, Libraire ... M.DCC.LXXXVI.
8vo, [viii] + 67 pp. F-Pn: Yf 11302.
A Paris, Chez Brunet ... M.DCC.LXXXVI.
4o, 48pp. F-Pa, Rondel: Rf. 13, 743.
Nouvelle édition. A Paris. Chez Didot l'aîné, Imprimeur & Libraire Ruë Pavée. M.D.CC.LXXXVI.
4o, 33pp. F-Pn (Mus): Th.B. 857.
Nouvelle édition, conforme à la partition gravée. A Paris, Chez les Libraires associés. M.DCC. LXXXVI.
4o, 48pp. F-Pa, Rondel: Rf. 13, 744.
A Paris, Chez Vente, Libraire des Menus-Plaisirs du Roi ... M.DCC.LXXXVIII.
4o, 32pp. F-Pa, Rondel: Rf. 13, 745.
A Amsterdam, Chez César Noël Guerin, Libraire. MDCCLXXXIX.
8vo, 50pp. F-Pa, Rondel: Rf. 13, 746.

Ed. Félix Gaiffe (Paris: Hatier, 1924).
8vo, 46pp. F-Pa, Rondel: Rf. 13, 756.

Le Comte d'Albert

Le Comte d'Albert drame, en deux actes, en prose et en vers, mis en musique. Représenté à Fontainebleau, le 13 Novembre 1786, à Paris, le 8 Février 1787, par les Comédiens Italiens ordinaires du Roi. Les Paroles, par M. Sedaine; La Musique, par M. Grétry. A Paris, Chez Brunet, Libraire ... M.DCC.LXXXVII.
8vo, [vi] + 83pp. F-Pn (Mus): Th. 737. (Copy contains a pencil cartoon on rear endpaper of a man with a pipe, possibly M. Narbonne in the character of Froment in the *Suite du Comte d'Albert*, 'opéra-comique en un acte, en prose et en vers, mis en musique', which forms the third and final part.)

A Paris, et se trouve à Bruxelles, Chez Emmanuel Flon, Imprimeur-Libraire, rue des Fripiers, M.DCC.LXXXVII.
4o, [iv] + 63pp. F-Pn: Yf 11629.

An edition by Bornet, 1787, 40pp. is at F-Pn: Z. Rothschild 5164.

A Toulouse, au Magasin général des Pièces de Théâtre, Chez J. B. Broulhiet, Libraire. M.DCC.LXXXVII.
4o, 27 + 27pp. F-Pa, Rondel: Rf. 13, 763.

A Paris, Chez Brunet, Libraire ... 1788.
48pp. F-Pn (Mus): Th. 738.

An edition 'Chez Louis' undated, 83pp. is at F-Po: Liv. 18. 2127.

Maillard ou Paris sauvé

Maillard ou Paris sauvé, Tragédie en cinq actes en prose. (Sujet tiré de l'histoire de France, année 1358). Par M. Sedaine, de l'Académie Françoise. *Tragicus plerumque dolet sermone pedestri* (Horace). Prix trente sols broché. A Paris, Chez Prault, Imprimeur du Roi ... Ou Chez l'Auteur, au Louvre. 1788.
8vo, [xvi] + 147pp. F-Pn: Yth 10646. This copy has a manuscript dedication by Sedaine to Grimm inscribed on the inside flyleaf.

Raoul Barbe-Bleue

Raoul Barbe Bleue, Comédie en trois actes et en prose, représentée, pour la première fois, par les Comédiens Italiens ordinaires du Roi, le lundi 2 mars 1789. Paroles de M. Sedaine. Musique de M. Grétry. A Avignon, Chez Jacques Garrigan, Imprimeur-Libraire, Place St-Didier. 1791.
4o, 32pp. F-Pa, Rondel: Rf. 13, 769.
(Another copy of this edition, also in F-Pa, Rondel: Rf. 13, 770, has manuscript changes made for a revolutionary performance of this work.)

A Bruxelles, Chez Loiseau, Imprimeur-Libraire. 1791.
4o, 39pp. F-Pa, Rondel: Rf. 13, 767. Both this copy and F-Pa, Rondel: Rf.767 have ms. corrections.

A Amsterdam, Chez Gabriel Dufour, Libraire. MDCCXCI.
4o, 40pp. F-Pa, Rondel: Rf. 13, 766.

Comédie en Prose & en 3 Actes, mêlée d'Ariettes ... A Amsterdam, Chez Gabriel Dufour ... M.DCC.XCI.
8vo, 48pp. F-Pn: 8o Yth 15144.

A Avignon, Chez les Frères Bonnet ....1791.
32pp. F-Pn (Mus): Th.B. 785 (A).

A Avignon, Chez Alphonse Berenguier, Imprimeur Libraire, Place du Change. An VI.
4o, 28pp. F-Pa, Rondel: Rf. 13, 771.

Guillaume Tell

Guillaume Tell, Drame en trois actes, en prose et en vers; par le Citoyen Sedaine, Musique du Citoyen Grétry. Représenté, au mois de Mars [sic] 1791, sur le ci-devant Théâtre Italien. Prix, 30 sols. A Paris, Chez Maradan, Libraire ... Seconde Année de la République Françoise.
8vo, [viii] + 42pp. GB-Lbl: F. 435 [6].

Section C: Collected editions of Sedaine's dramatic works

Œuvres dramatiques de M. Sedaine A Paris, Chez la Veuve Duchesne ... MDCC.LXXVI. Avec Approbation et Privilège.
4 vols of dramatic texts, put together from previously issued editions, sometimes furnished with new title-pages.
GB-Lbl: 86.a.15.

Œuvres dramatiques de M. Sedaine A Paris, Chez Brunet ... MDCCC. An VIII.
Collection of earlier editions, in 5 vols.
F-Pa, Rondel: Rf. 13, 587.

Théâtre de Sedaine A Paris, Chez Duchesne ... (undated).
A collection of earlier editions in 6 vols, but distinguished by consistent presence of music, including, in vol. II, the main source for Francesco Bianchi's music to *Le Mort marié.* (1777).
F-Pn: Yf 11591–11632.

Œuvres choisies de Sedaine A Paris, de l'Imprimerie et de la fonderie stéreotypes de P. Didot, l'aîné, et de Firmin Didot. 1813. Edited and with introduction by L.-S. Auger.
F-Pa, Rondel: Rf. 13, 588.

Œuvres choisies de Sédaine Paris, L. Hachette et cie. 1860.
Reprinted 1865, 1869, 1876, 1888, 1906.

Théâtre de Sedaine Publié avec notice et notes de Georges d'Heylli. Paris, Imprimerie Génerale, 1877.

Théâtre de Sedaine. Avec une introduction par M. Louis Moland. Paris, Garnier Frères. Undated.

Section D.i: Other published works by Sedaine in chronological order of publication

Epître à mon habit. Issued anonymously. No place or date of publication given, and the first page is dated 'Ce premier Mars 1751'.

[ii] + 3pp. F-Pn: Ye 33090. This poem was subsequently reissued in both the volumes of poetry below.

*Pièces fugitives de Monsieur S****
12o, x + 211 + [1]p. n.p. [The Hague and Paris: Durand?] MDCC.LII .
F-Pn: Ye 9526. Available as microfiche.

Le Vaudeville, Poème didactique, en quatre chants ... Issued anonymously. N.p., M.D.CC.LVI.
8vo, viii + 64pp.
F-Pn: Ye 7253. This poem was subsequently reissued in the *Recueil de poésies.*

Recueil de poésies de M. Sedaine, Seconde édition; revue et augmentée des pièces faites depuis la première, et de plusieurs airs notés. A Londres, et se trouve à Paris, Chez Duchesne, Libraire ... MDCCLX.
12o [viii] + 216 + 220pp.
GB-Lbl: 1065.d.27. The two parts of this work are bound together, but the parts are paginated separately, as if they were separate volumes.

Troisième édition, revue et corrigée. A Londres, et se trouve à Paris, Chez L'Auteur au Louvre. Pissot, Libraire, rue du Hurepoix. Durand, Libraire, Rue Gallande. M.DCC.LXXX.
12o, [viii] + 232 +119pp.
F-Pn: Ye 21669.

Bagatelle, ou description anacréontique d'une maison de campagne dans une des fauxbourgs d'Abbeville Par M. Sedaine ... A Amsterdam, et à Abbeville, Chez la veuve de Verité, Libraire. MDCC.LXX.
18pp. F-Pn: Ye 10026.

Romance par M. Sedaine.
Published in *Correspondance littéraire*, XI (April 1776), pp. 243–4.

Proverbe par M. Sedaine.
Published in *Correspondance littéraire*, XI (September 1777), pp. 517–26.

La Tentation de Saint Antoine (this was first published in the *Recueil de poésies*)
Ornée de figures et de musique. A Londres. M.DCC.LXXXI.
10pp + 8pp of music.
GB-Lbl: 11474.e.18. (Anonymous).

GB-Lbl has other editions from 1782 and 1795: P.C. 30.a.15 (1); P.C. 23.a.15 (3); P.C. 30.d.9 (2). Other editions are mentioned by Tchemerzine, *Bibliographie d'éditions originales et rares* (see Section G), X, p. 310 and by Jacques-Charles Brunet, *Manuel du libraire et de l'amateur de livres* (5th ed., 8 vols, Paris: Didot, 1860–80)(Supplement, II).

Discours prononcés dans l'Académie Françoise, le Jeudi XXVII Avril M.DCC.LXXXVI, à la réception de M. Sedaine. A Paris, Chez Demonneville ... M.DCC.LXXXVI.
4o, 29pp. Sedaine's speech, pp. 3–16; Lemierre's speech, pp. 17–19.
F-Pn: Z. 5053 [162].

Discours prononcés dans l'Académie Françoise, le Mercredi XIV Mai M.DCC.LXXXVIII, à la réception de M. Florian. Paris, Chez Demonneville, Imprimeur-Libraire de l'Académie Françoise ... M.DCC.LXXXVIII.
4o, 30pp. Florian's speech, pp. 1–20; Sedaine's speech, pp. 21–30.
F-Pn: X 4826 [37].

Discours renfermant l'avis de M. Sedaine, lu au Comité d'instruction publique, le 23 Décembre 1791.
GB-Lbl: 936.f.10 (7).

Pétition adressée à l'Assemblée Nationale ... 1791.
GB-Lbl: F. 566 (4).

Lycée des Arts. Le Commissionaire de Saint-Lazare Imprimé aux frais du lycée, au profit du C. Cange.
4pp. Page 4 gives the author as 'Le citoyen J. M. Sedaine, la 1e Sansculotide de l'an 2e de la République, une et indivisible'. A Paris, de L'Imprimérie de la Feuille du Cultivateur et du Lycée des Arts.
GB-Lbl: 936.f.7 [32]. See also manuscript copy, F-Pa, in Section A (above).

Les Dangers de la Solitude Romance de Sédaine [sic] ... A Paris, Chez F. Bruguière ... A Lyon, Chez Arnaud, Editeur..(no date of publication) 4pp.
F-Pa, Rondel: Rf. 13, 776.

Section D.ii: Works published by others in which Sedaine had an involvement

Tom Jones (A. H. H. Poinsinet, set by Philidor) first given at the Comédie-Italienne on 27 February 1765, total of seven performances. Revised by Sedaine, 30 January 1766.

Ernelinde (Poinsinet, set by Philidor) first performed at the Opéra, 24 November 1767. Revised by Sedaine after death of Poinsinet, and given at Versailles, 11 December 1773. For details of editions of the four main versions, see Julian Rushton, 'Introduction' to the facsimile of the 1769 edition (French Opera in the 17th and 18th Centuries, LVI)(Stuyvesant, N.Y.: Pendragon, 1992).

L'Ile sonnante (Collé, set by Monsigny) was corrected and revised by Sedaine before its first performance at the Comédie-Italienne, 4 January 1768.
See Collé, *Journal et mémoires*, III, pp. 178–82, and Charlton, p. 200, above.

Section D.iii: Autobiographical writings

'Quelques réflexions inédites de Sedaine sur l'opéra-comique' in René Charles Guilbert de Pixérécourt, *Théâtre choisi* (4 vols, Paris and Nancy: Chez l'auteur, 1841–3), vol. IV, pp. 501–16.

Section E: Critical and biographical writings

This cannot be an absolutely exhaustive list, but it aims to give the most important works of biographical and critical literature published on Sedaine. Works are ordered alphabetically by author within each section.

E.i: Biographical sources

Auger, Louis-Sébastien, 'Notice sur la vie et les ouvrages de Sedaine' in *Œuvres choisies de Sedaine* (3 vols, Paris: P. Didot, 1813), I, pp. vi–viii.

Bouilly, Jean-Nicolas, *Mes récapitulations* (3 vols, Paris: L. Janet, 1836–7). These rather unreliable memoirs contain, in vol. II, pp. 13–35, a bizarre description of Sedaine and his working methods. Fascinating, but almost certainly fictional!

Ducis, Jean-François, *Notice sur la vie de Sedaine* in *Œuvres* (3 vols, Paris: A. Nepveu, 1826), III, pp. 455–60.

Dufort de Cheverny, Jean-Nicolas, *Mémoires du comte Dufort de Cheverny*, ed. Robert de Crèvecœur (4th ed., 2 vols, Paris: Plon, 1909).

Dufort de Cheverny, Jean-Nicolas, 'Notice sur la vie de Sedaine', published in Ledbury, 'Greuze and Sedaine', pp. 357–69.

Jal, Auguste, *Dictionnaire critique de biographie et d'histoire* (Paris: H. Plon, 1877), pp. 1116–17.
His entry on Sedaine, although substantial and important, was interrogated and found wanting in several respects by Rey, in 'Le Mariage de Sedaine' and *La Vieillesse de Sedaine* (see below, E.ii).

Lepeintre-Desroches, Pierre-Marie-Michel, 'Notice sur Sedaine' in *Suite du Répertoire du Théâtre Français* (81 vols, Paris: Veuve Dabo, 1822–3), LVII, pp. 51–9.

Pipelet, Constance-Marie (née de Théis, later Princesse de Salm-Dyck), *Eloge historique de M. J. Sedaine ... Lu par l'auteur à la 54e séance publique du Lycée des arts, le 30 Messidor an V* (Paris: Desenne, 1797).

Vandeul, Marie-Angélique de [née Diderot], 'Notice historique sur Sedaine' in *Correspondance littéraire*, XVI (1797), pp. 234–46.

There are more or less substantial and important entries on Sedaine in various dictionaries of biography published in the course of the nineteenth century. The best single source for these is now the microfiche collection *Archives biographiques françaises* (London and Munich: Saur, 1993), fiche 949, images 267–310. The information contained in these entries varies in reliability and usefulness.

E.ii: Biographical studies

Guieysse-Frère, Emile, *Sedaine. Ses protecteurs et ses amis* (Paris: Flammarion, 1907). The most well-known and most notorious of Sedaine biographies, to be used with great caution, as its sources remain mysterious.

Mont-Louis, Renée de, *Michel Sedaine, sa vie, anecdotes* (Limoges: E. Ardant, 1879 etc.). Reprinted as *Michel Sedaine. Histoire anecdotique d'un maçon Académicien* (Limoges: Ardant, 1894). Anecdotal and unreliable.

Rey, Auguste, 'Sedaine à Saint Prix', *Revue de l'histoire de Versailles et de Seine-et-Oise*, V (1904), pp. 277–92; VI (1905), pp. 25–46 and 128–44.

Rey, Auguste, *Notes sur mon village. La Vieillesse de Sedaine* (Paris: H. Champion, 1906).

Rey, Auguste, 'Le Mariage de Sedaine', *Revue de l'histoire de Versailles et de Seine-et-Oise*, XI (1910), pp. 5–15. Rey's work constitutes the best documented biographical study of Sedaine's life and work after 1767.

Vigny, Alfred de, 'De Mlle Sedaine et de la propriété littéraire' in *Journal d'un poète* (Paris: E. Fasquelle, 1904), pp. 349–407.

E.iii: Studies of Sedaine's career

Gisi, Martin, *Sedaine, sein Leben und seine Werke* (Berlin: Weidmann, 1883).

Günther, Ladislas, *L'Œuvre dramatique de Sedaine* (Paris: Larose, 1908).

Ledbury, Mark, 'Greuze, Sedaine and Hybrid Genre in Late Eighteenth-Century France', D.Phil. dissertation, U. of Sussex, 1996.

Arnoldson, Louise Parkinson, *Sedaine et les musiciens de son temps* (Paris: L'Entente Linotypiste, 1934).

Rayner, Margaret, 'The Social and Literary Aspects of Sedaine's Dramatic Work', M.A. dissertation, Westfield College, U. of London, 1960.

Waterhouse, Francis Asbury, 'Sedaine as Librettist', Ph.D. dissertation, Harvard U., 1918.

E.iv: Memoirs, correspondence and theoretical works written before 1830

Anon., *Etat actuel de la musique du Roi et des trois spectacles de Paris* (11 vols, Paris: Vente, 1759–77).

Anon., *Journal des spectacles représentés devant Sa Majesté* (Paris: Pierre-Robert-Christophe Ballard, 1764–73).

Bachaumont, Louis Petit de [and continuers], *Mémoires secrets pour servir à l'histoire de la république des lettres en France depuis 1762 jusqu'à nos jours* (36 vols, London: J. Adamson, 1777–89).

Beaumarchais, Pierre-Augustin Caron de, *Correspondance*, ed. Brian M. Morton and Donald C. Spinelli (4 vols, Paris: Nizet, 1969–78).

Catherine II, Empress of Russia, *Lettres à Grimm, publiées sous les auspices de la Société Impériale d'Histoire Russe*, ed. J. K. Grot (St Petersburg: Académie des Sciences, 1878).

Collé, Charles, *Journal et mémoires sur les hommes de lettres, les ouvrages dramatiques et les événements les plus mémorables du règne de Louis XV (1748–1772)*, ed. Honoré Bonhomme (3 vols, Paris: Didot, 1868, repr. Geneva, 1967).

Collé, Charles, *Journal historique inédit pour les années 1761 et 1762*, ed. Adolphe Van Bever (Paris: Mercure de France, 1911).

Collé, Charles, *Correspondance inédite*, ed. Honoré Bonhomme (Paris: Plon, 1864).

Correspondance littéraire, philosophique et critique par Grimm, Diderot, Raynal, Meister, etc., ed. Maurice Tourneux (16 vols, Paris: Garnier frères, 1877–82). This journal (though read by only a select band of subscribers) contains perhaps the most informative and significant corpus of contemporary criticism of Sedaine.

Deffand, Marie Anne, Marquise du, *Lettres de la Marquise du Deffand à Horace Walpole (1766–80)*, ed. Paget Toynbee (3 vols, London: Methuen, 1912).

Deffand, Marie Anne, Marquise du, *Correspondance inédite de Mme du Deffand précédée d'une notice par le Marquis de Sainte-Aulaire*, ed. V. Saint-Aulaire (2 vols, Paris: Michel Lévy frères, 1859).

Desboulmiers [Jean-Auguste Jullien], *Histoire du théâtre de l'Opéra-comique* (2 vols, Paris: Lacombe, 1769).

Desboulmiers [Jean-Auguste Julien], *Histoire anecdotique et raisonnée du Théâtre Italien depuis son rétablissement en France, jusqu'à l'année 1769* (7 vols, Paris: Lacombe, 1769, repr. 2 vols, Geneva, 1968).

Diderot, Denis, *Correspondance complète*, ed. George Roth (16 vols, Paris: Editions de Minuit, 1955–70).

Dixmerie, Bricaire de La, *Les Deux âges du goût et du génie français, sous Louis XIV et sous Louis XV* (Paris and The Hague: Lacombe, 1769).

Dixmerie, Bricaire de La, *Lettres sur l'état présent de nos spectacles* (Paris and Amsterdam: Duchesne, 1765).

Ducis, Jean-François, *Lettres de Jean-François Ducis*, ed. Paul Albert (Paris: G. Jousset, 1879).

Favart, Charles-Simon, *Mémoires et correspondance littéraires, dramatiques et anecdotiques de C.S. Favart*, ed. Antoine-Pierre-Charles Favart (3 vols, Paris: Léopold Collin, 1808).

Fréron, Elie-Catherine, *L'Année littéraire, ou Suite des lettres sur quelques écrits de ce temps* (Amsterdam and Paris: Lambert, 1754–75) (see also the index by Dante Lénardon, Geneva: Slatkine, 1979)

Genlis, Stéphanie-Félicité Du Crest, Comtesse de, *Mémoires* (10 vols, Paris: Ladvocat, 1828).

Grétry, André-Ernest-Modeste, *Mémoires, ou Essais sur la musique* (3 vols, Paris: Imprimerie de la République, An V [1796–7]; repr. New York, 1971).

Grétry, André-Ernest-Modeste, *Réflexions d'un solitaire*, ed. Lucien Solvay and Ernest Closson (4 vols, Brussels and Paris: Van Oest, 1919–22: repr. New York, 1978).

Grimm, Friedrich Melchior von, *Lettres de Grimm à l'Impératrice Catherine II*, ed. J. K. Grot (2nd ed., St Petersburg: Académie des Sciences, 1885).

Journal encyclopédique, 1756–93 (repr. Geneva, 1968).

La Harpe, Jean-François de, *Correspondance littéraire* (6 vols, Paris: Migneret, 1801–7, repr. Geneva, 1968).

La Harpe, Jean-François de, *Lycée, ou Cours de littérature ancienne et moderne* (3 vols, Paris: Didot, 1840).

[La Porte, Joseph de, et al.] (eds), *Les Spectacles de Paris ou suite du calendrier historique et chronologique des théâtres* (Paris: Duchesne, 1752–1815).

La Porte, Joseph de and Nicolas de Chamfort, *Dictionnaire dramatique* (Paris: Lacombe, 1776, repr. Geneva, 1967).

Lemonnier, Henry (ed.), *Procès-verbaux de l'Académie Royale d'Architecture (1671–1793)* (10 vols, Paris, 1911–29), esp. vols VI–X, which contain a record of all the administrative proceedings of the Academy while Sedaine was secretary.

Léris, Antoine de, *Dictionnaire portatif des théâtres* (Paris: Joubert, 1754, 2nd ed. 1763).

Le Vacher de Charnois, Jean-Charles (ed.), *Journal des théâtres, ou le Nouveau spectateur* (4 vols, Paris: Esprit, 1777–8).

Marmontel, Jean-François, *Eléments de littérature* (3 vols, Paris: Didot, 1846). [Originally published as vols V–X of *Œuvres complettes de M. Marmontel* (17 vols, Paris: Née de La Rochelle, 1787).

Origny, Antoine-Jean-Baptiste Abraham d', *Annales du Théâtre Italien, depuis son origine jusqu'à ce jour* (3 vols, Paris: Veuve Duchesne, 1788, repr. Geneva, 1970).

Orville, André-Guillaume Contant d', *Histoire de l'opéra bouffon* (2 vols, Amsterdam and Paris: Grangé, 1768, repr. Geneva, 1970)

Palissot de Montenoy, Charles, *Mémoires pour servir à l'histoire de notre littérature* (2 vols, Paris: Gérard, 1803).

Voltaire [François-Marie Arouet], *Correspondence and Related Documents*, ed. Théodore Besterman (51 vols, Geneva: Institut et Musée Voltaire; Oxford, Voltaire Foundation, 1968–77).

E.v: Books and articles published after 1830

Breitholtz, Lennart, *Le Théâtre historique en France jusqu'à la Révolution* (Uppsala Universitets Årsskrift, Band II, no. 12) (Uppsala: Lundequist; Wiesbaden: Harrassowitz, 1952).

Brown, Bruce Alan (ed.), *Le Diable a quatre, ou la Double métamorphose: opéra-comique in drei Akten von Michel-Jean Sedaine und Pierre Baurans* in Christoph Willibald Gluck, *Sämtliche Werke*, XIV (Kassel: Bärenreiter, 1992).

Brunetière, Ferdinand, *Les Epoques du théâtre français (1636–1850)* (Paris: Hachette, 1909), pp. 299–303. Brief, but important and influential rehabilitation of Sedaine.

Charlton, David, *Grétry and the Growth of Opéra-comique* (Cambridge: Cambridge University Press, 1986).

Charlton, David, '"L'Art Dramatico-Musical": An Essay' in Nigel Fortune (ed.), *Music and theatre. Essays in Honour of Winton Dean* (Cambridge: Cambridge University Press, 1987), pp. 229–63.

Cook, Elisabeth, *Duet and Ensemble in the Early Opéra-comique* (New York etc.: Garland, 1995).

Cucuel, George, *Les Créateurs de l'opéra-comique français* (Paris: Félix Alcan, 1914).

Cucuel, George, 'Le Moyen Age dans les opéras-comiques du XVIIIe siècle', *Revue du dix-huitième siècle*, II (1914), pp. 56–71.

Curzon, Henri de, 'Actualités bibliographiques: M. J. Sedaine 1719–1797', *Le Bibliographe moderne*, II (1898), pp. 63–8.

Curzon, Henri de, 'Autour de l'ancien opéra: un opéra inédit de Sedaine et Monsigny', *Revue internationale de musique* (August 1898), pp. 545–51.

Curzon, Henri de, 'Histoire et mésaventures d'un opéra inédit: *Philémon et Baucis* de Sedaine et Monsigny', *Bulletin de la Société de l'Histoire du Théâtre* (1910), pp. 18–39.

Dacier, Emile, 'Le "Sedaine" du Musée Condé, ou Gabriel de Saint-Aubin poète', *Revue de l'art ancien et moderne*, XXXVIII (June 1920), pp. 5–18; XXXIX (July–Aug. 1920), pp. 93–104.

Dunkley, John, '"Natural" Dialogue in Sedaine's *Le Philosophe sans le savoir*' in John Dunkley and Bill Kirton (eds), *Voices in the Air: French Dramatists and the Resources of Language* (Glasgow: University of Glasgow Press, 1992), pp. 71–85.

Faguet, Emile, *Propos de théâtre* (5 vols, Paris: Société Française d'Imprimerie et de Librairie, 1903–10), V, pp. 171–6.

Frantz, Pierre, 'Noble sans le savoir (ambiguità di una dramma borghese)', *Quaderno di teatro* (March 1981), pp. 155–62.

Frantz, Pierre, 'Sedaine' in Jean-Pierre de Beaumarchais, Daniel Couty and Alain Rey (eds), *Dictionnaire des littératures de langue française* (3 vols, Paris: Bordas, 1987), III, pp. 2316–18. The most important recent summary of Sedaine's place in the canon of French literature.

Gaiffe, Félix, *Le Drame en France au XVIII*e *siècle* (Paris: Armand Colin, 1910, repr. 1971).

Guibert-Sledziewski, Elisabeth, 'Le Spectacle bourgeois des antagonismes des classes: *Le Philosophe sans le savoir* de Sedaine', *Dix-huitième siècle*, VII (1975), pp. 259–74.

Hallays-Dabot, Victor, *Histoire de la censure théâtrale en France* (Paris: Dentu, 1862). Rather brief, but contains useful information on the censorship of *Maillard* and *Raimond V.*

Heartz, Daniel, 'The Beginnings of the Operatic Romance: Rousseau, Sedaine and Monsigny', *Eighteenth-Century Studies*, XV/2 (Winter 1981–2), pp. 149–78.

Kant, Theodore, *Die Sprache in Sedaine's 'Recueil de poésies'* (Hamburg: Lütke & Wolff, 1901).

Larroumet, Gustave, 'Sedaine' in *Revue des Cours et Conférences*, IX/1 (1890–1), pp. 11–21.

Mason, Haydn, '*Le Philosophe sans le savoir* de Sedaine: an aristocratic *drame bourgeois*?', *French Studies*, XXX (1976), pp. 405–18.

Maude, Emile, 'Les Deux Sedaine', *Le Censeur* (2 February 1907), pp. 152–5.

Morel, Jean, 'Le Théâtre français: le XVIIIe siècle' in Guy Dumur (ed.), *Histoire des spectacles. Sous la direction de Guy Dumur* (Paris: Gallimard, Encyclopédie de la Pléïade, 1965) pp. 766–88.

Paissa, Paola, 'Il Linguaggio Teatrale di M. J. Sedaine: spettacolo e parole' in Giorgio De Piaggi (ed.), *Temi e tecniche dal medioevo ai nostri giorni* (Quaderni del Dipartimento di lingue e letterature straniere moderne, I) (Abano Terme: Piovan, 1987), pp. 87–115.

Pougin, Arthur, *Monsigny et son temps* (Paris: Fischbacher, 1908). This text is rare but important, and contains on p. 48 an unfamiliar version of some lines from Sedaine's 'Quelques réflexions', which among other things cites the date of Monnet's visit to Sedaine as 1751, not 1756.

Pré, Corinne, 'Le Livret d'opéra-comique en France de 1741 à 1789', thèse de Doctorat ès Lettres, U. de Paris III, 1982. A substantial and important study of *opéra-comique*, in which Sedaine's work is discussed at length.

Regnier [François-Joseph Philoclès], 'Sedaine' in *Souvenirs et études de théâtre* (3rd ed., Paris: Ollendorff, 1887), pp. 327–49.

Schneider, Herbert (ed.), *Timbre und Vaudeville. Zur Geschichte und Problematik einer populären Gattung im 17. und 18. Jahrhundert* (Hildesheim: Georg Olms, 1999).

Schneider, Herbert and Nicole Wild (eds), *Die Opéra-comique und ihr Einfluß auf das europäische Musiktheater im 19. Jahrhundert* (Hildesheim: Georg Olms, 1997).

Smith, Kent Maynard, 'Egidio Duni and the Development of the *Opéra-comique* from 1753 to 1770', Ph.D. dissertation, Cornell U., 1980.

Vendrix, Philippe (ed.), *L'Opéra-comique en France au XVIII*e *siècle* (Liège: Mardaga, 1992).

Vendrix, Philippe (ed.), *Grétry et l'Europe de l'opéra-comique* (Liège: Mardaga, 1992).

Vercruysse, Jérome, 'Grimm correcteur de Sedaine: une lettre inédite sur *Maillard*' in *Du baroque aux lumières; essais en honneur de Jean Varloot* (Limoges, 1983), pp. 162–6.

Vitu, Auguste, 'La maison de Sedaine', *La Revue de l'art dramatique*, I (1886), pp. 257–64.

Wade, Ira Owen, 'The title of Sedaine's *Le Philosophe sans le savoir*', *Proceedings of the Modern Language Association of America*, XLIII/4 (December 1928), pp. 1026–38.

Section F: Sources concerning the production and performance of Sedaine's dramas

Bourges, Ernest, *Quelques notes sur le théâtre de la Cour à Fontainebleau 1747–1787* (Paris: E. Lechevalier, 1892). Contains brief but illuminating notes on performances of Sedaine's work at Fontainebleau.

Brenner, Clarence D., *The Théâtre Italien. Its Repertory, 1716–1793* (University of California Publications in Modern Philology, LXIII) (Berkeley and Los Angeles: University of California Press, 1961).

Brenner, Clarence D., *A Bibliographical List of Plays in the French Language, 1700–1789* (Berkeley and Los Angeles: University of California Press, 1947).

Lancaster, Henry Carrington, *The Comédie-Française 1701–1774, Plays, Actors, Spectators, Finances* (Transactions of the American Philosophical Society. New series vol. XLI, pt 4) (Philadelphia: American Philosophical Society, 1951).

Joannidès, A., *La Comédie-Française de 1680 à 1900. Dictionnaire général des pièces et des auteurs* (Paris: Plon-Nourrit, 1901).

Jullien, Adolphe, *La Comédie à la cour de Louis XVI* (Paris: Baur, 1875). Gives some data on court performances of Sedaine's plays.

Kennedy, Emmet, Marie-Laurence Netter, James P. McGregor and Mark Olsen, *Theatre, Opera and Audiences in Revolutionary Paris. Analysis and Repertory* (Westport, Conn.: Greenwood Press, 1996).

Tissier, André, *Les Spectacles à Paris pendant la Révolution. Répertoire analytique, chronologique et bibliographique* (Geneva: Droz, 1992).

Section G: Bibliographical aids to the study of Sedaine

Cioranescu, Alexandre, *Bibliographie de la littérature française du XVIIIe siècle* (Paris: Editions du CNRS, 1968), esp. pp. 4653–7. Now slightly dated, and not always completely reliable, but still useful.

Cohen, Henri, *Guide de l'amateur de livres à gravures du XVIIIe siècle* (6th ed., rev. Seymour de Ricci, Paris: A. Rouquette, 1912, repr. Breuil-en-Vexin, 1973). The information on Sedaine in this volume is supplemented by 'An Iconography of Sedaine', Chapter 10 above.

Lacroix, Paul, *Bibliothèque dramatique de M. de Soleinne* (6 vols, Paris: Administration de l''Alliance des arts', 1843–5) contains valuable information about then extant editions of Sedaine's plays.

Rondel, Auguste, *Catalogue analytique sommaire de la collection théâtrale Rondel* (Paris: Berger-Levrault, 1932). The full Rondel catalogues, which remain in manuscript, have now been transferred to microfiche. The Rondel collection represents perhaps the richest and most complete collection of Sedaine's work anywhere in the world.

Rougemont, Martine de, *La Vie théâtrale en France au XVIIIe siècle* (Paris and Geneva: Champion-Slatkine, 1988). A very useful critical bibliography of literature on eighteenth-century French theatre (to 1988).

Tchemerzine, Avenir, *Bibliographie d'éditions originales et rares d'auteurs français des XVe, XVIe, XVIIe et XVIIIe siècles,* (10 vols, Paris: M. Plee, 1927–34), especially X, pp. 290–317.

Vendrix, Philippe (ed.), *L'Opéra-comique en France au XVIIIe siècle* (Liège: Mardaga, 1992), contains useful and comprehensive guides to *opéra-comique* in theory and practice.

INDEX